D1170923

KNOWLEDGE OF ILLNESS IN A SEPIK SOCIETY

A Study of the Gnau, New Guinea

LONDON SCHOOL OF ECONOMICS
MONOGRAPHS ON SOCIAL ANTHROPOLOGY

Managing Editor: Peter Loizos

The Monographs on Social Anthropology were established in 1940 and aim to publish results of modern anthropological research of primary interest to specialists.

The continuation of the series was made possible by a grant in aid from the Wenner-Gren Foundation for Anthropological Research, and more recently by a further grant from the Governors of the London School of Economics and Political Science. Income from sales is returned to a revolving fund to assist further publications.

The Monographs are under the direction of an Editorial Board associated with the Department of Anthropology of the London School of Economics and Political Science.

LONDON SCHOOL OF ECONOMICS
MONOGRAPHS ON SOCIAL ANTHROPOLOGY
No. 52

KNOWLEDGE OF ILLNESS IN A SEPIK SOCIETY

A study of the Gnau, New Guinea

BY
GILBERT LEWIS

UNIVERSITY OF LONDON
THE ATHLONE PRESS
NEW JERSEY: HUMANITIES PRESS INC.
1975

Published by
THE ATHLONE PRESS
UNIVERSITY OF LONDON
at 4 Gower Street London WCI
Distributed by Tiptree Book Services Ltd
Tiptree, Essex

USA and Canada
Humanities Press Inc.
New Jersey

UK SBN 0 485 19552 6
USA SBN 0-391-00389-5

Printed in Great Britain by
T. & A. CONSTABLE LTD
EDINBURGH

ACKNOWLEDGMENTS

The fieldwork on which this study is based continued from December 1967 to November 1969. The Social Science Research Council made a generous grant to Anthony Forge, supervisor of the research, which enabled me to work in the Sepik and my wife and son to join me there from May 1968 onwards. Throughout this period as Research Officer of the London School of Economics and Political Science and until April 1971, the Council supported my studies with a generosity for which I am very grateful. I have also to thank the Medical Research Council for a Junior Research Fellowship from October 1965 to October 1967 that allowed me to begin learning social anthropology at the London School of Economics.

Anthony Forge had the burden of making my project practicable and possible, but none of the delights of the field trip. I owe him very great debts for his teaching while I was a student, and for his valuable advice and genial criticism during my research.

I thank all those in New Guinea who gave me and my family hospitality and assistance; the staff of the Christian Missions in Many Lands at Anguganak, particularly John and Agnes Sturt; Austin and Rita Roach; David and Helen Graham; Dr Lyn Wark and Don McGregor at Lumi; and Fr Tim Elliott, O.F.M. of the Catholic Mission at Ningil. The Public Health Department of the Territory, through the good offices of Dr Risto Gobius at Wewak, was kind enough to provide the medical supplies I used during my study.

I wish to make particular acknowledgment of the warm welcome we were given by Dr John Sturt and his family. It will be clear that I have benefited greatly from the way he has combined devoted service to the people in this part of New Guinea with lively sustained research on their illnesses. He has been most generous to me with his knowledge and assistance.

My greatest debt is to the people of Rauit village who received my family and me with curiosity and hopes in which I was bound to disappoint them. Yet they accepted us as we turned out to be, cared for us and gave us friendship. I received great help in my work especially from Purkiten, Tuawei, Kantyi and Maka,

Tawo, Selaukei, Maluna and Dameku. Dauwaras was among the first to assist me. He was doughty and good-natured – his illness tragic. The gentle laughing Wankyi, eldest daughter of Kantyi and Maka, helped us as a family there with perhaps greater kindness and understanding than anyone else: we have learnt that she died suddenly some months after our departure.

I am very grateful to my wife for her support; without her resourceful assistance in the field, and her help all through the research, my study would have been both much poorer and far harder.

G. L.

CONTENTS

PLATES

MAP

FIGURES

TABLES

Introduction

The subject of this book is a limited one. It deals with the occurrence, recognition and explanation of illness in a small-scale society. The misfortune of illness is bound to be part of life in any society. Its occurrence and the responses of people to it have often provided anthropologists with revealing information about the nature of religious belief, morality and social obligation in the different societies they have studied. Health is a basic value. The prevention and treatment of illness bear directly on survival as a matter both of individual and of social concern. Every culture must offer guidance to its members on how to avoid illness or be rid of it; such guidance is necessary for the preservation and continuity of the society. The placing of illness and its causal explanation in relation to other cultural themes opens one crucial and illuminating perspective on the society's view of its world. I have therefore sought to present the full range of such explanations available in one society, rather than to concentrate only upon certain aspects.

In part the reason for this lies in the dual training I have had in anthropology and medicine. For this equipped me to define the occurrence of actual illness on external grounds and to observe the relations between the nature of the illness, its explanation and management. Suffering and disability vary according to the kind of illness; the tendencies to natural healing, remission or exacerbation, may affect the outcome independently of any treatment offered. Such factors might be expected to play a part in the particular social recognition given sickness. I have tried to investigate these relations because of this expectation and my fitness to do so. For obvious reasons, few anthropologists are in the same position and their study of illness has been selective; they have described mainly the explanation and management of illnesses which illuminated other themes in the centre of the social frame of their inquiry. Illness that provoked no concern or failed to find an explanation, was unlikely to come within the scope of their analyses. On the other hand, the very fact of no explanation, or of neglect, might be a distinctive cultural feature in handling illness in a society, and significant for an understanding of its cosmology, and the value set on health, or social attitudes towards status or role. The external standpoint of modern medicine thus enabled me to define a field of misfortune and then to see the differential social pressures and concerns which acted to select certain of these events for more marked attention. In his careful study of the social setting of a large number of established cases of Cewa sorcery, Marwick (1965, 1967) observed that ideally the 'universe' from which certain people were chosen to be accused of sorcery should be defined. This would also apply to the universe of possible appropriate events from which presumably only some are selected to act as evidence of the effects of sorcery. The frequency or inevitability with which events are taken as such evidence would provide an index of the level of concern with sorcery in that society.

From this methodological standpoint, the external definition of a particular field of medical misfortune might make it possible to show up the relative levels of concern with different kinds of cause. For example, I often heard talk of sorcery and my questions on this topic, my asking for examples from past case histories, all contributed to an impression that sorcery was prominent as a cause of illness. Yet in fact little illness is explained in this way. I have chosen therefore in this book to look at the pertinence of belief. I present in some detail the evidence on which my views are based and the methods by which I reached them. As the causes of illness do not belong within a sharply demarcated or restricted domain but ramify into many aspects of life in the society I studied, I have necessarily been led to describe these. These aspects contribute to a partial ethnographic account of the people. The social structure of these people differs in certain respects from that of their nearest ethnographically described Sepik neighbours, and indeed it differs from that of most mainland New Guinea people in respect of their genealogical knowledge.

I begin with a brief account of this structure; its full bearing on the diagnosis of illness will not emerge until the final part of the book in which I analyse the factors entering into the choice of explanation. Their environment and its relation to the incidence and prevalence of disease and the patterns of their illness are presented from an external standpoint so that the reader may grasp the nature of the burden of illness they face. The total body of recorded illness is analysed and used, after discussion of their views on its causes, to examine the application of these views in practice. Although I have attempted the analysis of the whole cognitive field of illness for the reasons stated, I have not dealt with treatment and the question of their response to modern medicine in this book. The limitations of space preclude an adequate analysis of these. I also regret that I have not been able to present a full account of their knowledge and concepts about the person, the normal human body and its functioning. A statement of Gnau anatomy and a thesaurus relevant to the description of illness has been published in *Oceania* 1974.

The book is intended then to make a contribution to the anthropological study of illness and it is directed towards the cognitive aspects involved in diagnosis and explanation; from the point of view of method, I have tried to show a way to analyse some features of pertinence or the level of concern with certain beliefs; and finally the book contains some ethnographic information about one people living in the Lumi Sub-district of the Sepik area from which little ethnographic report has previously emerged.

The people I studied lived on the forested south side of the Torricelli mountains. From the villages placed on ridges at between 1500 and 2000 feet above sea level, the hills decline southwards towards the plain of the Sepik river a few days' walk away. The village Rauit, in which I lived, is in the East Au census division of the Lumi Sub-district, West Sepik District. Its people speak a language called Gnau by convention from its word for 'no', which is spoken also in De'aiwusel (Bogasip) and Mandubil (Maiambel). In broad terms, the culture of the people living along the Torricelli range appears to an outsider uniform. The villages are compact and small. The people's diet is sago supplemented by yams, taro, bananas and a variety of greens. People in the villages which lie last among the southern foothills of the mountain range, such as the one where I lived, are able to hunt for pig, cassowary and small mammals to the south in extensive tracts of uninhabited bush. Although their culture appears superficially uniform, there are differences of detail almost from village to village.

Before the Australian Administration was established, relationships between members of neighbouring villages included fighting; intermarriage[1] and consequent exchanges; individual friendship between two men of hostile villages shown in rare and secret bush meetings; visits to other villages when peace existed between them – this applied only to immediately surrounding villages and the peaceable relationship varied over time, the visits were short and occurred when one village held a big ceremony; sporadic trade also took place; longer stays were rarely made by young men who wished to participate in initiation rites or who wished to avoid a marriage not to their liking.

The coming of Europeans and the establishment of Australian Administrative control led to the following changes. Recruiters were active near to the area of my study by 1937 although they did not visit the village where I worked until after the War had ended. The first village men left for indentured labour about 1938. Since then, most men have left at some time to work for two years, usually on plantations producing copra – a few men have been three times. No women have left the immediate area as have the men. Those men who first left as labourers returned able to speak Pidgin English: two of them were appointed at Aitape *luluai* and *tultul* for their home village; they were given hats. There were not until about 1955 many who could speak Pidgin in the village. At present in Rauit, eight of ninety-six adult men are still unable to speak Pidgin English, but all youths as well as some of the senior men can speak it fluently even though they have not left the village. Women over 30 years old, with a few exceptions, do not speak Pidgin except for some limited sentences needed to sell food and buy things at a mission store. Among the women under 30 years old, there is variation and most can speak some Pidgin although they are usually reluctant to do so and it is difficult to be sure how fluent and comprehensive their command of it is.

The Japanese invasion of New Guinea and the consequent fighting between 1943 and 1945 only just came within the villagers' ken; some village men who had left as labourers, remained absent too long; occasionally a monstrous and terrifying thing flew over the villages; they heard the explosions of a few bombs which were dropped near villages to the north of them. No Japanese or Allied soldiers came to their immediate

[1] A small proportion, less than a fifth, of the total number of marriages in a given village.

area although they heard rumours of some to the north. Soon after the War ended the labourers with their tales returned. A patrol post was established at Lumi in 1949. The first Administrative patrol to the villages of Rauit and Mandubil was made then but control and census of the villages was not effected until 1952, after an armed confrontation at Rauit between Administrative Officers and a large party of Rauit men. Warfare in the area was stopped but visits between, for example, Rauit and Mandubil people formerly hostile did not begin until after about 1955. Since then men and women have gone visiting without fear of attack and the range of visiting now reaches to neighbouring villages within a radius of about five or ten miles while occasional excursions are made to the Administrative centres at Lumi and Nuku. The possible range of hunting and gardening has been extended by peace.

Administration was by annual patrol and census, with appointed *luluai* and *tultuls* until 1967. Disputes and offences were administratively dealt with on these annual patrols and a few (about ten in Rauit) of these were taken for settlement to Lumi. A Franciscan mission and aidpost was opened in about 1951 at Yemnu but missionary activities in the area I worked in did not begin until late 1958 when a Franciscan mission was opened at Ningil and the Evangelical mission of the Christian Missions in Many Lands, called Anguganak Mission, was opened near the village of Yankok. Both missions made airstrips, opened trade stores and schools and at Anguganak, a hospital run by a missionary doctor. The Franciscan mission priest visited the Gnau-speaking villages once every one to three months from then on. A native Catholic catechist from somewhere in the Lumi Sub-district was settled in each village from about 1960 onwards. The villagers provided food and labour for money at the mission stations although they were more distant, less regular, suppliers than the villages immediately surrounding the stations. Evangelical teaching by the C.M.M.L. in Rauit began in about 1965 and consisted of visits once every month or two. A few boys have attended school at Ningil or Anguganak, none regularly. During my stay no child of Rauit was attending school at these or Government centres; except for four boys who began some regular schooling in the last half-year I was there.

In addition to annual census and the settling of disputes,

Administrative Officers collected taxes from 1957 onwards, they explained Administrative decisions which affected villagers directly, supervised general village layout, sanitation, road upkeep and sought to introduce and encourage rice and coffee growing. An Agricultural Officer was placed at Lumi later on. One Rauit man in 1966 left for six months' training in rice, peanut and coffee growing at Bainyik and Lumi. Rice is now grown on a small scale for cash by more than half the men in Rauit, less than half in Mandubil; it must be carried down to Yankok for sale. As well as making changes in local methods for the disposal of the dead and of excreta, in the water supply, in house construction and lay out, the Administration carried out a programme for the eradication of yaws and some inspections of health: patrol officers were able to order people to present themselves for treatment at aidposts or at Anguganak Hospital. From 1959 onwards, villagers in this area have at times attended the hospital for treatment. The C.M.M.L. Mission has organized an infant welfare service in which a trained nurse visits each village about monthly: this was begun in December 1963 for Rauit. In October 1967 the first elections for Local Government Councillors were held in the area. As the villages took part in the Lumi Local Government Council, the *luluai* and *tultul* system was abolished. The collection of taxes became the job of the L.G.C. as did their spending. Villages were combined in groups of two or three to elect a councillor and committee man. In the village I studied, the Councillor fell out of a coconut tree soon after election and for the first nine months of his office did not attend the monthly meetings of the L.G.C.; in consequence the workings of the L.G.C. remained vague to people in the two villages he represented. He later attended and during my stay there was a general though confused development in the knowledge of villagers about the council's organization and powers to decide about tax, the limits on bridewealth and about certain local projects and the councillor's role in settling disputes. In 1964 and 1968, the villagers voted in the elections to membership of the House of Assembly. Few men had much idea of where or what the House of Assembly was; some men knew the name of their member; most of those who voted did not know what the result was.

I have outlined these changes to indicate that experience of plantation work, Administrative control and instruction, missionary activity and teaching and participation in a Local Government Council have made the villagers aware of a wider world and in this respect men more so than women. They have extended the range of their social relations and have to a limited extent, through the Administration and the L.G.C., become involved in a larger society than before.

I

Social Structure

The forms of society in New Guinea so vary that I must begin by an account of the main features of Gnau social structure. Few assumptions would be valid for any New Guinea society and these couched only in most general terms. The Gnau differ from most New Guinean people by maintaining long genealogies which follow a strict patrilineal pattern. They live in the Sepik hills far distant from the Highland peoples. Differences of ecology and subsistence economy would reduce the mutual relevance of a detailed comparison, for example, of the stress given to agnation by peoples of these two regions. I cannot compare the Gnau with their near neighbours; there is almost no ethnographic information published on other peoples in the Lumi Sub-district where the Gnau live. In the wider context of both Sepik districts, we have detailed report of various groups lying to the east of that which I studied. Although the distances measured in miles on the map, and the numbers of people, might not be called great, in some respects the cultures are diverse. One striking instance of this diversity is language for, within a radius of ten miles of Rauit, there are 42 villages whose people speak ten different languages. Most of the previously described Sepik peoples belong to a different language phylum from that to which Gnau belongs (Laycock 1968): but Mountain Arapesh appears to be in it. Moieties, a tambaran cult, totemic alignments, competitive exchange partnerships, and the big-man leader complex, are all features commonly described of Sepik social organization which do not occur among the Gnau. For these reasons, the structure of Gnau society cannot be indicated briefly by reference to a more general well-known pattern. But as the chief subject of this study is sickness, I have not attempted to provide a full account and discussion of Gnau social organization here. The account given is limited to a brief descriptive summary of the chief features of Gnau society.

The political units are small, for each village acts almost as an autonomous unit. The village is easy to demarcate with its clustering of houses on the ridgetop, surrounded below by garden land and forest; for most of the year people belonging to the village sleep there. Settlement is nucleated not dispersed over a tract of land, although at times people may stay for a few days at their garden houses. If an area is marked off to contain the Gnau-speaking villages and those with which they have direct social relations (i.e. from 142° 09′ to 142° 21′ East in longitude, and from 3° 32′ to 3° 45′ South in latitude, an area of 210 square miles), there are 23 villages whose average population size is 260 people[1] with a standard deviation of ± 110. The village where I lived, Rauit, was large for the area: it had 373 people (1 November 1969). The size of villages in this area clearly varies greatly (the smallest contained 111 people, the largest 500). The terrain is rugged and forested, the direct map distances between neighbouring villages vary between one and five and a half miles. There is no obvious relation between the distance set apart and the size of two villages. In the more densely settled Lumi Local and Somoro census districts 15 miles to the north-west, the average villages sizes are smaller and less variable. The Gnau area I deal with is not densely settled; the average density of population in it is 28 people per square mile.

I shall first describe the ways in which the Gnau class their social units and then deal with the functional significance of these units. In brief there are two principles of classification. One is that of locality – which identifies people by where they now live or alternatively by where their ancestors lived. The other is that of patrilineal descent. The differences and similarities between social units defined by one or other of the principles will first be investigated.

The place where someone now lives provides a simple clear way of identifying some of his ties. The place referred to may be his village which is the named unit identifying the largest collection of people by locality. Names for assemblies of villages are not found except where people now refer to the Administrative Sub-district, the Local Government Council, or the census district names which they have recently learnt. I do not think that indicating a group of villages by the name of the language they speak

[1] Calculation based on population figures from census data supplied by the Sub-district Office, Lumi, for the years 1955–65.

is a native practice. The village is compact, but it is made up of named subdivisions of ground; in effect the larger component parts of a village are the hamlets which may also be further subdivided by distinctive names for the ground. The boundaries of ground are defined and the smallest named subdivisions may be less than 200 square yards.

Village	*Hamlet*	*Hamlet subdivided*
Rauit	Wimalu	Wulpakasel Wimalu Basilasel
	Pakuag	Pakuag Mambilgat
	Dagetasa	
	Watalu	Malpetem or Watalu Gabagi Taki
	Animbil	Gagaori Gepagdel Lai'ingindel Basdel
	Bi'ip	Bi'ip Niyisa

The word *wiget* could apply to any of these divisions and in a general sense *wiget* means a place of settlement as opposed to bush or forest – *tuwi*. Someone is ascribed to a place according to the context of discussion; so between people of different villages he is said to be of Rauit and within the village he is ascribed to his hamlet. If, and more rarely, they wish to distinguish within the hamlet, he is placed by his attachment to a part of the hamlet ground. All these usages refer to current place of residence. People change their classification if they move from one hamlet to another or change village. The hamlet ground subdivisions are known to villagers but not usually by outsiders. Distinctions of culture – of attire, weaponry, food habits, language, marriage and exchange practices – correlate with this system of classification rather than with the classifications by the past which may cross linguistic and cultural boundaries.

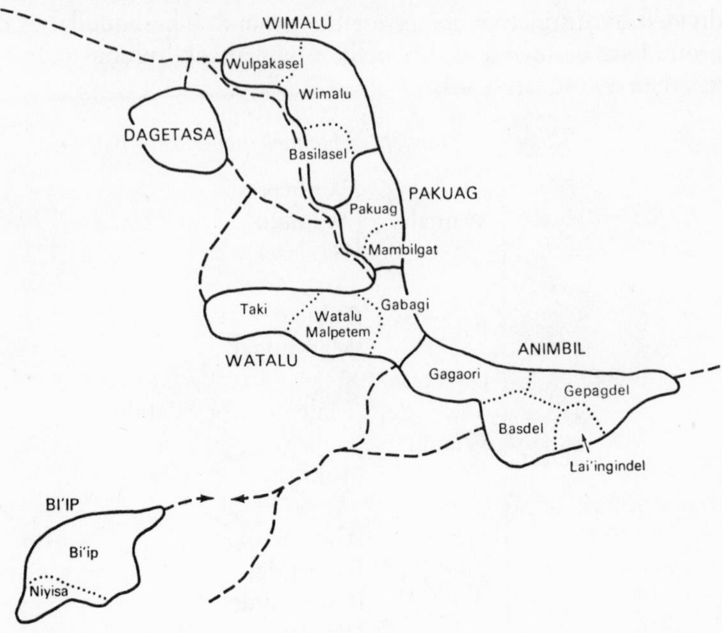

PAST LOCALITY

Besides these current ascriptions anyone in Rauit can align himself by the name of one or more ancient village site. In the case of this village, four of the many remembered ancient sites can serve to class all its members into one of four mutually exclusive categories – the ancient names are Wimalu, Wuninangiwut, Saikel and Nembu. A group of people may say '*dap Saikel*' – we are Saikel. I wish to show below that classification by these four ancient villages resembles in some respects a classification by clan name such as is found in many unilineal societies. Although the alignment is explicitly by village name, the people of a number of particular genealogies are associated and between them terms of brotherhood apply; they also jointly observe a rule of exogamy. But unlike clans elsewhere, people so associated may state when they distinguish their links with people of other villages, that another ancient village gives them their name. And even within the Rauit alignments people may be further differentiated by links to other ancient sites than the four I first mentioned, as well as by genealogy. Thus ancient village names are used as a basis of association and differentiation. The ground where the ancient village stood retains its name; many of these sites are now forest-covered hills, enduring places of reference.

GENEALOGICAL NARRATIVES

If one asks a Gnau man to tell the story of his origins, or his ancestry, if willing, he will recount a long narrative containing both the names of ancestors and the places where they lived. These are interwoven in a detailed and vivid account of the origins and vicissitudes of the line of men who lead down to the narrator. He may be constrained by the ethnographer only to list the members of his pedigree but spontaneous accounts are far more discursive and revealing than that. Most, though not all, begin with a mythological event or a catastrophe after which men fled from some place in fear or confusion. The myths, except for one, do not explain the creation of men, but put the most remote ancestor among other men who at that time were together and then dispersed. What happened afterwards, the places at which they settled, the associations with other people that they formed, their fortunes in war and so on, are told as history, understandable in the light of common experience, not myth.

The collections of people traced out by known agnatic links are small. Larger collections are formed by reference to ancient sites. Although reference is by site name, they assume the common agnatic descent of those in the assembly. If, instead of a site name, the identification were by the names of ancestors or totemic animals, we might not shy at calling these larger collections 'clans'. Within them, members of equivalent generations use terms of brotherhood and seniority to each other. The phrases *dap mamibutebandel* (we men of one ancestor) or *lil bulpeg ebam* (they the semen indeed), which affirm why they share the site name ascription, imply common ancestry. The right to claim classification by a particular site name is determined by birth and is transmitted agnatically, so site name classifications are bounded.

The unusual feature is the varying salience of one site or another as people consider interrelationships inside and outside the village.

It is this which makes it difficult to see the larger collections named by ancient village site as similar to clans. If we compare the sites salient in association and differentiation, we see that differentiation within Saikel, Wuninangiwut and Nembu is based on sites anterior to the site of association which comprehends them all, while for Wimalu the reverse is the case. Imputed common ancestry would seem consistent with the pattern of Wimalu but not with that of the three other sites, in which any common ancestor is lost perhaps in the obscurity of Delubaten[1] or the first Wuninangiwut.

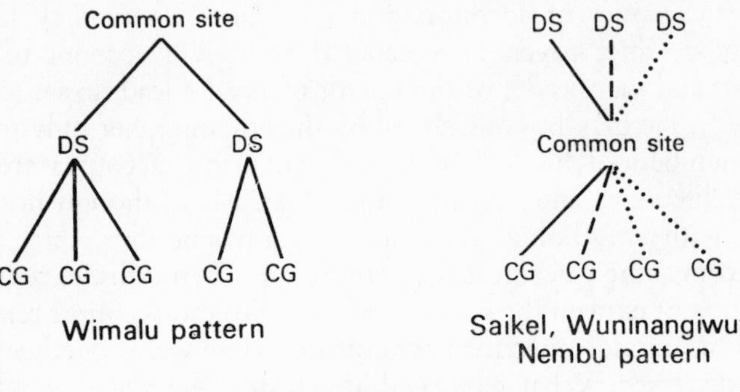

Fig. 1. Sites salient in association and differentiation

The site relevant to classification in one village may have no significance at another, yet people in both villages share a common distinguishing site of reference, ascribed brotherhood and the possibility of finding a position in the classificatory scheme of either village. If we call Wimalu a clan at Rauit, its members are also clan members of clans otherwise named at different villages, such as the village of Libuat where a different language is spoken. The sites which provide the primary orientations within a village are usually ones which can be claimed by many of the genealogies making up the village. Where only a few men, or a single genealogy can claim connection to an ancient site, it is unlikely to be used as their primary classification if there is an alternative. One

[1] Delubaten is the hill near Rauit where, according to one myth, men were created and dispersed.

genealogy, classed Saikel at Rauit, has an anterior tie with Maiyi-Wolgam, one of Mandubil's primary sites of orientation, the source of a major myth and a chain of ties to Womil, Sabig Sebap – but these possibilities of reference are abandoned at Rauit in favour of orientation within the large collection formed by Saikel.

What this amounts to is that within each village, there are a number of mutually exclusive units resembling clans whose members are conceived to be related as agnatic brothers. In relations between villages, brotherhood may be shared as in a clan, but the differentiating orientations split up the intravillage

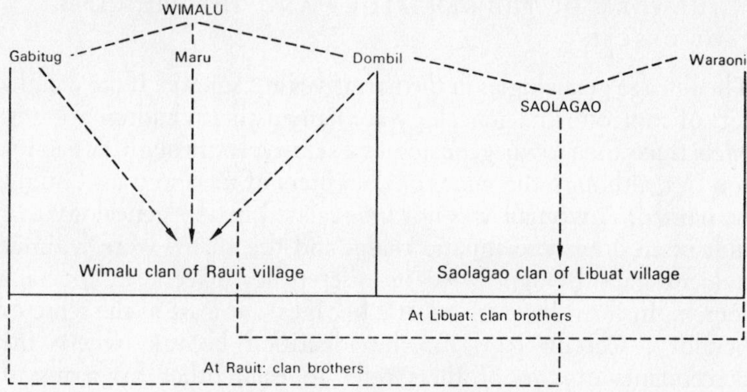

Fig. 2. The ascription of brotherhood

clans. If we show this by Figure 2, it is clear that some ascriptions of brotherhood were achieved by residence and that, though a putative common ancestry may be assumed for intravillage purposes, the intervillage associations overlap and contradict an assumed over-arching common ancestry. Intervillage associations form an overlapping network. Three of the four Rauit 'clans' associate by a common site of residence subsequent to their differentiating sites. The Wimalu pyramid in Figure 2 is unusual, the Saolagao form is usual. The intravillage unit has clear boundaries but is not necessarily extensible beyond the village. In some cases, as for example with Saikel, the associating site reference is the same in different villages and in this case the name appears to identify an intervillage clan.

The achievement or assumption of agnation through common

residence has been widely reported in New Guinea, what is remarkable here is that they also maintain long genealogies and traditions of settlement which expose their diverse origins. Agnation is not achieved or altered in the recent generations; indeed in contrast to what has been reported from the Highlands of New Guinea, the people of this area seem to maintain strict agnatic accuracy over many generations, manipulating or achieving changes only in the remote past which precedes genealogical reckoning by the fiction that common residence implies common agnatic origin.

THE FORM OF THE GENEALOGY AND THE PRINCIPLE OF DESCENT

The lineage genealogies in the narratives are agnatic. If the daughters of someone in a genealogy are named their children are not. Men trace their own genealogies exclusively through father-to-son ties, although the wives or daughters of men so traced might be named. A woman was not intercalated in any genealogy as a link in an otherwise agnatic chain, and the chains were without evident gaps by ignorance or discrepancy except in four instances. In form they are agnatic lineages – at least in the sense of heraldry. Certain gaps can be identified because where the descendants of two brothers refer to each other by terms of generational equivalence, it is possible to count back and find a discrepancy in the number of generations between the two fraternal ancestors and their respective coeval descendants. Such discrepancy could be due to lapses in memory or past manipulation of fictive genealogical ties. I have no evidence to suggest that genealogies were recast for reasons of politics or inheritance. Inheritors of defunct lineages seem now to regard it as their duty to tell the anthropologist the separate and extinct genealogy from which they inherit. On certain grounds a number of lineages may be put together as brother lineages but there is no attempt to specify a genealogical point at which they had a common ancestor: people do not speculate on how brother lineages might have been genealogically grafted together. The emphasis is rather on the discrete and particular history of a consecutive line of men. My eventual estimates of the form of their lineage genealogies are based on the most exhaustive and consistent version I was able to obtain. The lineage genealogies of Rauit villagers now alive are summarized in Table 1 and Figure 3:[1] they include the lineage genealogies based on Rauit but none of those belonging to women who married into Rauit from elsewhere.

From this account of the form and consistency of their classifications of people, we see that ideally common descent and common residence are related; a present shared locality should be the result of a common origin in the past. The narratives show that the ideal is not held to and they reveal traditions about the

Table 1. Depth and span of Rauit lineage genealogies

Number of lineages	20
Total number of recorded members by birth	1198
Range of genealogical depth	5–15 generations
Average genealogical depth	9 generations
Range of total recorded Rauit* membership by birth in a single lineage	12–165 members
Average number of recorded members in a single lineage	60 members
Range of living members per lineage	2–60 members
Median number of living members per lineage	15 members
Average number of living members per lineage	17 members

* The largest lineage genealogy is one with members in many villages, whose fully accounted membership is about 520.

migrations and dispersal of clans, and of lineages, whose ostensibly consecutive links are traced over many generations. Attachment to a present place defines collections of people by clear topographical boundaries. Ties to ancient sites are modelled on a recognition of patrilineal descent, brotherhood and seniority found in their kinship system. Where consecutive genealogical links are known, the boundaries of a unit are clearly established by the agnatic descent rule. Within this unit all members of each generation are classified as siblings and siblings of the same sex differentiate their relative seniority. Seniority among true siblings of the same sex is determined by birth order, and this relative order is transmitted to their descendants: thus within the genealogical unit, in every generation there exists a hierarchy of seniority

[1] I have not included here the full description and analysis of their genealogical knowledge which I hope to publish elsewhere. The relevance of genealogy for ritual access to spirits is discussed further in Chapter 4.

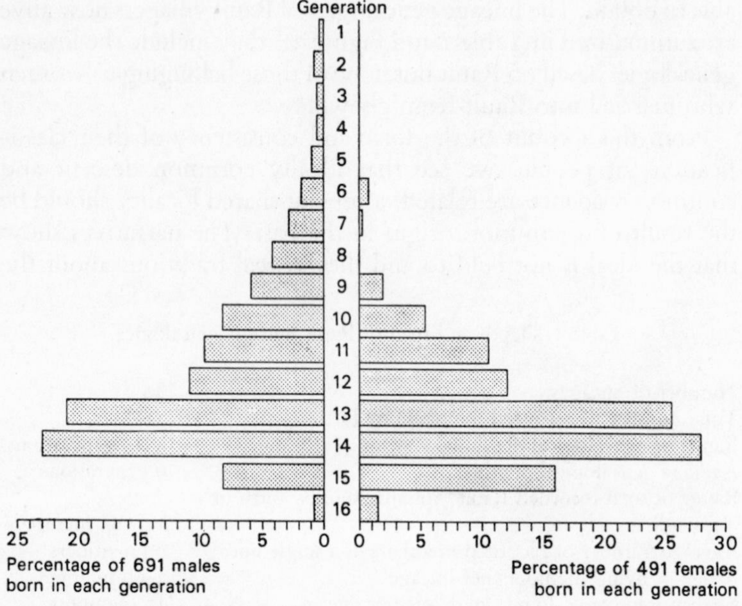

Fig. 3. Percentage distribution by generation of all males and all females whose births are recorded in the lineage genealogies of Rauit

among coevals transmitted lineally. As a system, it may be drawn in the form of Figure 4 where relative seniority is read horizontally for any generational level from left to right (A). From the point of view of an individual within the system, relative seniority

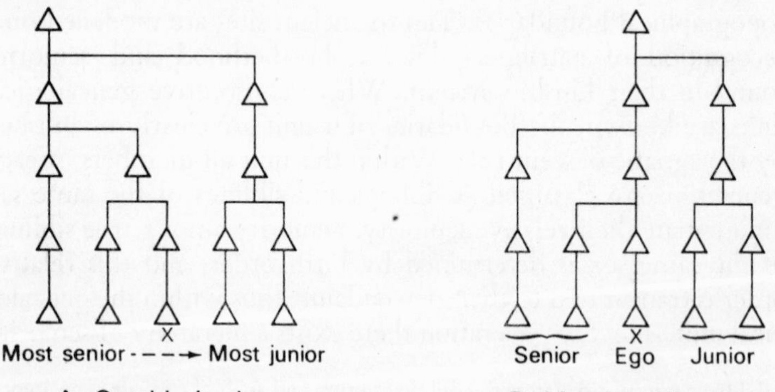

Fig. 4. Seniority among coevals

is divided by the axis of his lineal descent (B). The classification by past ancient site in some respects resembles clan classification but by changing the site of reference at different villages, people can find positions in various differently bounded 'clan' units, and seen from outside as the system of a number of villages, these classifications overlap.

ORGANIZATION AND FUNCTIONS OF THE PRESENT VILLAGE UNITS

The compact village with its subdivisions constitutes a clearly isolated collection of people who spend nearly all their lives together, except where women by marriage change their villages. But only about a fifth of marriages take place between villages. The people of a village are able to supply all their traditional subsistence requirements by their own production and by hunting in the extensive forests which lie to the south. Stone adze heads and shell valuables were acquired by sporadic trade. Apart from this, a village could in theory have been entirely self-sufficient given the one proviso that marriages could take place within it and so enable it to reproduce its population.

The arguments familiarly used to explain village size, siting, compactness and isolation in New Guinea have combined factors of competition for resources, population size and warfare. In the Gnau case, if one begins with the finding that villages are compact, the amount of suitable garden land conveniently close by would put a gross upper limit to the increased population one village can support. As the overall population density is small, a far greater dispersed population could presumably exploit the large amount of available but unused land. The stated reason for compact residence with large numbers and the siting of villages on ridge-tops was safety from attack. Fighting formerly was chiefly between single, not combined, villages (or by parts of villages against parts of other villages), and some danger of attack was rarely if ever absent until Administrative control was established. Now peace prevails, families stay in houses at their distant gardens to work there for a week or more: before they did not dare to. Read's summary of the political structure of Highlands New Guinea society would apply well enough to the area in which the Gnau live.

> The macroscopic view is of a region with many contiguously situated culturally identical communities. The communities have no political unit; no concept of common territorial inclusiveness. Government is distributed laterally amongst them; all are of the same structural type, are autonomous and are opposed to others by a complex system of cleavages. Each is subdivided into smaller social units which have closer bonds *inter se* than any of them have with units of the same order which surround them. (Read 1954, p. 35)

The overt difficulty is defining the unit to call the given society. The area of effective social life is small, congruent in most cases with the range of kinship and affinal ties. Members of cultural linguistic groups seldom have any conception of common identity and each such group furthermore comprises a multiplicity of socially distinct autonomous communities. In the discussion of the Gnau structure I take the former pattern of fighting, ambush and danger of attack as a given, then try to use it to explain aspects of their social structure.

I cannot answer very satisfactorily the question of why they fought and attached such prestige to fighting. They did not greatly need to fight to acquire land for there is plenty of it. They lacked formal legal institutions and depended more directly on physical force and the support of numbers to defend themselves in dispute or competition for the things they wanted. Security and strength were thus correlated and fighting ability therefore valued. But on top of this, success in fighting gave prestige. Intervillage fighting was pursued as a means to prestige, and maintained in a series of more or less balanced murders between villages. The virtual lack of ceremonial exchanges between villages as a non-violent way to rise in general renown left fighting success as the prime way to become famed, or notorious. Within a man's own group he was admired for being feared by the people of other groups: his prowess in some degree gave them security. To the extent that men generally are ambitious to be admired, fighting which was exciting, fierce and tragic, gave an outlet for competitive and ambitious striving which otherwise could not be found except in hunting wild pig and cassowary, where similar daring and ability were required, or in the staging of magnificent ritual – but this gave prestige less clearly to the individual than to the group. In the discussion therefore I have assumed the former value given to fighting.

The security of numbers may have a further effect on village composition. If for any reason some members must leave, they are likely to prefer to join another established village rather than to try to begin a new village alone, unless of course there were a lot of them leaving together. Similarly a village might welcome an addition to its strength but only within bounds dictated by its resources and current size. With time and the shifts of demographic fortune we would expect that some or many villages had become composed of small groups of people with diverse origins. Security is not the only motive for migrants to settle in an established village. Most of their chief material resources are immovable – land, sago and coconut palms, other trees providing food – so moves are hazardous and impoverishing if they are made to new sites which have not been prepared in advance.

The compact form and size of Gnau settlement has the obvious practical effect that the people of a village know each other well, they have daily contact, they see and hear each other, eat together and walk the same paths. They produce their own food, implements and weapons and so they could be independent of other places. If the villages then are discrete, compact and bounded, and can also be economically self-sufficient, we must find the basis for association of village inhabitants in both their theory and practice. The physical solidarity, or closeness, of village life may both foster dispute and mischief and make its containment and resolution urgent. Associations based on unilineal descent or on affinal links do not either of themselves assure social harmony. Social solidarity, corporateness or integration are relative not absolute concepts: they may be measured in terms of strength and persistence. If village harmony may be gauged from intravillage killings (variables of control and sanction make comparisons complex), the finding that over a quarter of all the homicides experienced by Rauit villagers were effected by other Rauit villagers would suggest that the solidarity of villagers was at least not consistently maintained. On the other hand, there has been little migration into or out of Rauit in the last five generations: one Rauit man went to Mandubil; one man came to Rauit from Nembugil; and one came from Mandubil. In this sense the village lineage constitution has been stable. Temporary changes of hamlet or village residence by men are also rare except for brief visits.

Ideally Gnau agnation determines the alignment of all men

linked in the male line to one male ancestor and the alignment cannot be changed; it applies both to past and future. In each generation there is an unalterable overall order from most senior to most junior brother, which is consistently determined through all generations from the first; the seniority placings of the children of one brother relative to the children of another are consequent upon the relative seniority of those two brothers. All male descendants of the same generation are 'brothers' and each is either *gemin* (senior brother) or *subin* (junior brother) to any other. The enduring inheritance of a descent unit is land and ritual knowledge, and these belong in common to all those who share the descent. The land which any one of them uses belongs to all; the user is only he who stays upon it at that time and grows things there. The inheritance of senior brother does not differ from that of junior brother, although trees, palms, temporary things which grow upon the land are individually inherited. Brothers should live together – the assumption of residential solidarity occurs in their equation of past ancient residence and brotherhood; in their ascriptions of brotherhood to those who now live together; in the traditional pattern of one man's house to each hamlet, where ancestors of a descent unit were said to be localized; and in the accounts of the motives of those who moved and settled together in genealogical narratives. But if the descent ideal takes for granted the unity and solidarity of a group of men and orders its members by the overall and enduring genealogical frame, it must be reconciled with the facts of demographic fortune, migration and dispersal.

The inheritance and ownership of land and ritual are not conceived in terms of division and separation. Other things like trees and sago palms are not movable; and if brothers would separate they can take with them only ritual and valuables, the fruits, seeds, shoots or tubers which will in time provide them with food. Thus split or fission must involve an unequal and, for some, impoverishing division of their goods, loss of planted trees and palms and land, and the loss of the security which attaches to a large united group. It is not surprising that almost every split or dispersal of a descent group is accounted for in genealogical narrative by cataclysm, disease, dispute, death and sorcery.

The agnatic descent rule and its associated jural values provide a basis, an ideal basis, for association at a place. With exogamy, marriages must be made outside the descent group, and unless people of differing descent live together at one village, they must go outside the village to find spouses. The way Gnau-speakers phrase the marriage orientations of their clan-like groups is in fact consonant with a hypothetical scheme of villages constituted by single descent groups; they say that *geminsubin* (senior junior brother = descent group) of that place have *munganulma* (husband wife = affinal group) at those places; the places they mention are ancient village sites, usually the sites which give their names to 'clans'.

Intervillage hostility creates problems for achieving and preserving affinal and matrilateral relationships where they occur between villages which fight. If there were no dangers of attack, there would be little problem to visiting between villages, to maintaining relationships between families linked through marriage. But the presence of fighting, the danger of attack, was a condition for the form of their village, which we took as given in this argument. Dual or conflicting sympathies are to be expected in a wife who is elsewhere a daughter and a sister, if fighting may occur between the two groups of her attachment.

Earlier I considered why it was likely that over time villages became composed of people of diverse origin; that small numbers of people detaching and attaching were more to be expected than large block movement of people. Villages are not, we find, made from a single descent unit, nor are hamlets. Despite their deep genealogies, few descent isolates with internally consecutive agnatic links would be large enough to form even a hamlet of usual size. Such descent isolates may join together and maintain that they are brothers, that the reason for their solidarity is an implied common ancestor. As we saw, in fact they do this but often pay no attention to the common ancestor or his name and instead they take an ancient site as their distinctive name and the remembered ground of their unity: but the unity is even so conceived as of descent. These associations cannot therefore solve the problems of intermarriage because the rule of exogamy applies where descent is shared.

However, if villages are not exclusively assembled by shared descent but may be composed of disparate descent units, marriages may be made close at hand; there is then no necessary loss of contact between a wife and her parents or brothers. The woman –

wife and mother in one group, sister in another – unites in her person the interests of diverse groups. As the interests of the husband's and the brother's descent groups in each marriage are made mandatory and ramify widely, and as these interests are sequential and enduring even over generations, so separate descent elements can be bound together. If marriages are made more exclusively within the village, the village's component elements become more close knit by duties and shared interests, and the village as an overall unit is relatively more isolated by its economic and reproductive self-sufficiency.

The ideals of shared descent require fraternal friendship even where residence is not shared. Descent is given a moral loading: friendship is right, murder abhorred. These values are assumed, expected as natural, part of the ordering of the world, controlled by the given or natural sanctions of identified taboo rather than beset by human laws and to be achieved or controlled by human effort, by force, by threat, or by sorcery. Descent is agnatic and women move at marriage to the home of their husband. A woman will have ties to both the family of her birth and to the family in which she bears children, although the relative strength of these attachments may vary during her married life. The relations between the two groups pivoted about the woman are not necessarily friendly. Their relationships might be more or less formally ruled; they might be competitive and hostile, or co-operative and friendly, or intermediate between these poles; but villagers cannot easily be continually prepared for or suspicious of attack and mischief from each other. If the groups pivoted about a woman live in the same village, overtly hostile relationships between them are less feasible than when they live distantly in separate villages. On the other hand, a shared, friendly and equal interest in the woman must, at least in the matter of her fertility and children, compromise the dominance of an agnatic principle of descent.

A clearly ruled but unequal recognition of rights and duties towards the woman and her children is what we would expect where agnatic descent rules and affinal proximity must coexist. Unless these relationships are unequal, complementary, and subject to formal ordering, there will be competition for the allegiance of the woman and her children and compromise of the principle of agnatic descent. Since the husband, by the rule of residence, has the woman to live in his hamlet and the child grows up with him, the obligations towards the group from which she came must be compellingly sanctioned if good relationships are to continue after her death, possibly even from the time she first comes. As we shall see the negative compulsion to recognize these obligations lies in the beliefs about magical techniques which are available to a wife's brother and his descendants, by which a sister's child may be killed and against which there is no protection except fair fulfilment of matrilateral duty. More positively there are the beliefs of how a mother's brother may influence the growth and health of his sister's child and the ritual duties by which he benefits the child. I suggest that we can best interpret some aspects of Gnau social structure as results of the emphasis they put on relationships set up by marriage; the effect of intravillage marriage in isolating the village as an independent community may be set in contrast to the recognition of ties of common descent outside the village. The isolating stress on the village is reflected in the contributions to exchange obligations. If an outside girl comes in marriage to a village where she also shares descent with some people then they will take part in the duties towards her which they share with her brothers in her natal village: otherwise the exchange obligations of shared descent do not extend beyond the limits of the village.

Through long genealogies and traditions of common descent, differentiated units within the village preserve social ties beyond the village and so also retain options to live at other places. The limited employment of these descent ties occasionally occurred in time past when aid was given to agnates of other villages when they fought. If dispersal from a village had to take place because the population had outgrown its resources or because of internal strife, an individual's crime or sin, or because of external dangers, then the limiting size to which another village could grow imposed restrictions on its acceptance of large numbers of refugees; while for a smaller village, the security of added numbers impelled it to seek or welcome immigrants. These pressures would lead to the splitting off of small numbers, not a division into halves creating two small exposed communities; and similarly the taking on of small numbers, over time, would lead to villages of mixed and various sources, if we assume that it was always best to live in as large a village as possible, given the garden resources and their availability. The other factor, besides the danger in small numbers, which makes it difficult to separate from a community and found a new one, is that some necessary foods, like coconuts and sago, take a long time to grow, and other crops take months too; so separation to live at a new site can only occur without great hardship where the move is to a chosen place prepared and planted against the move. This explains why sometimes descent lines of many different origins occur together. They must find some basis for association: in fact they take an ancient place name, but treat it as though it meant shared descent. Given the isolating emphasis on village and hamlet, and the actual effectiveness of physical proximity in producing co-operation and solidarity, such associations, which we may suppose are sometimes based on fictions, can in fact work. But descent ties beyond the village are not supported, or were not, by regular contact, exchange, communal rites or shrines, yet they were important as offering possible alternatives, possible bases for refuge in misfortune, and friendship, a welcoming host in time of peace. Formerly the individual friendship between pairs of men in enemy villages continued despite hostilities, but face-to-face meetings were rare. The right ground on which to base ties outside one's own village was genealogical; the separate charters of origin lead backwards through a series of unshared ancestors to a certain shared pair of brothers, mutually recognised, who were together at a certain site; or who shared in the same downfall and dispersal.

MARRIAGE

In the given view a marriage affects relationships between two agnatic lines for a few generations. Those involved by these relationships are shown in Figure 5: A and B apply vertically and represent two agnatic lines. The numbers 1 to 5 are for the sequence of generations in which members of these two lines are in some way affected by a marriage marked * made in generation 2. The marriage in generation 5 is the ideal and preferred marriage which has been determined by the generation 2 marriage. Members of A and B in generations 3 and 4 should not intermarry and may still be taking part in the exchange relationships consequent on the marriage in generation 2. These relationships are terminated by people of generation 4 when the man of B 3 dies. But the men of generation 4 should ideally set again in motion the sequence of relationships between A and B by betrothing their children of generation 5.

The preferred marriage (FFMBSSD) thus requires, if it is to be followed, genealogical recall over 5 or 6 generations to cover the different orientations of parent, self and child. These are in fact the generations in which we find genealogical detail, the thick base of the pyramid in Figure 3 above. The marriage rule reflects the prolonged relationships set up by one marriage which end with the death of the child of that marriage, possibly requiring

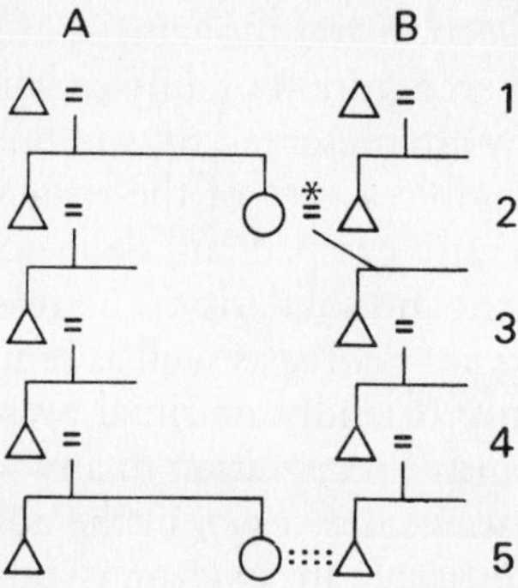

Fig. 5. Schema of relations set up by marriage

exchanges by the inheritors of that child, i.e. between the children of cross cousins: they terminate the exchanges consequent on the first marriage and then it is their children who may by preference enter upon similar relationships again. Thus the man of B4 may be involved in duties of exchange, giving to groups of other agnatic kin from whom came (1) his FFW, (2) his M, (3) his W, and possibly (4) his SW; conversely he may receive gifts from different sets of kin to whom he or his forebears gave (1) a FFZ, (2) a FZ, (3) a Z, (4) a D. Multiply these ties by the numbers of siblings in each generation, by his duty to help and share in his agnates' duties and rights, and one will see rightly that the ties of marriage establish a dense, long-term and many-stranded web of obligation and interest between people of the bounded patrilineal units I have described.

Instituted exchange relationships are characteristic of New Guinea. They usually belong to one of two main classes: (1)

balanced or competitive exchanges in which people strive to maintain their status or outdo each other and so acquire added prestige; or (2) unbalanced, asymmetric exchanges, commonly determined by affinal or matrilateral ties, the exchanges then being part of the obligations entailed by the relationships, and confirming or expressing recognition of them. Almost all Gnau effort in exchange is put into the asymmetric category set by affinal and matrilateral relationships – the exchanges continue for more than one generation, the exchanges made at the time of marriage being only the first of a long series. Formal exchange institutions present to the observer a tangible expression of structural principles which he can see in the collection and movement of material objects: he can study the shared recognition of duty to help gather the objects together, whom they are presented to, and how after this they are shared out. This tangible aspect of the structure of relationships can often be more easily grasped and delineated, than statements about value, sentiment and solidarity. The relationships also carry such qualities in varying degree as well as requiring other expression in duties of daily, friendly or ritual assistance. But the tendency to give substantive recognition to any social tie is a marked feature of Gnau relationships. Even in the absence of a marriage tie, people may institute an exchange relationship which is closely modelled on the pattern of affinal and matrilateral exchanges. The clearest example is the optional exchange system which may be entered into by the families of two sisters after each has married, or between a married woman and her father's married sister. Or a woman's husband may choose to preserve a tie to the family of his wife's MB by exchanging with them, although such exchanges are not required of a ZD to her MB after her marriage. Or a man may choose to exchange with the brother of a girl his parents wanted him to marry and betrothed him to in infancy, but whom he did not in fact marry because she died, or she grew up before him and married elsewhere.

Asymmetric exchange is a useful index, showing the degree of interweaving of relationships between groups of kin. As I mentioned before, the isolation and solidarity of the village as a unit can also be gauged from the differential recognition of the exchange obligations of shared descent if the shared descent crosses village boundaries.

On the other hand, balanced or competitive exchange has little place in Gnau society in contrast to the descriptions of most other New Guinea societies. I have mentioned competition and balance in homicide, and the boasting or prestige which went with it. If two villages wished to make peace they could, if a balance of killings had been reached, end their enduring enmity by a ceremony in which each village as a unit matched the other in exchange of shell valuables, compensating the equal tally of their killings. In asymmetric exchange shell valuables, and nowadays money, are given almost exclusively by one side only of the exchange relationship. A description of the formal pattern of asymmetric exchange now follows in which, for clarity of exposition, I deal with the transfer of rights and money, neglecting the other things given.

EXCHANGE AND THE TRANSFER OF RIGHTS IN WOMEN AND THEIR CHILDREN

The exchanges which are occasioned by a single marriage and its development through resulting children show the interests of two groups – the groups are in essence two agnatic groups but I will consider below the enlarged circle of those involved when I show the amounts of contribution to the different payments of money and their distribution. These interests are spread over a four-generation period. Although I did not find informants who analysed in explicit terms the rights which were transferred by the payments of money, some deductions about the transfer of these rights seem reasonable. Rights over a girl past puberty are held by her father and brothers. These, in respect of her domestic and sexual services, are provisionally transferred to her husband when they accept bridewealth for her. By a parental agreement in her childhood shown in exchanges of food, or by transfer of a part of the bridewealth, the father of her prospective husband may establish a prior claim on her. The transfer of the full bridewealth gives to the family of the bridegroom the right to ask for her to come to their hamlet and fulfil her domestic and sexual services forthwith. But the decision that the bride is ready is usually left to her mother who shows this by inviting the bridegroom to eat food she has cooked.

The acceptance or rejection of the match is shown by the girl's willingness to move to her husband's hamlet. The boy's acceptance of the match is shown by his eating of food the bride has cooked.

Until the marriage has produced a child, it is on trial and the bridewealth is fully recoverable if the wife should desert. When a child has been born, the bridewealth is distributed and the husband has established and exclusive rights to his wife's domestic and sexual services. Compensation for his wife's adultery is paid to him. Yet a residual interest in the wife remains with the group to whom she was born. This is severed at her death by a final payment. Her dead spirit remains exclusively with the group of her husband's agnates. Throughout her life, her natal agnates have residual responsibility for her welfare, support and defence. She has claims to their support and food if she temporarily deserts her husband because of ill-treatment. She inherits no land or trees, only one coconut palm in their hamlet which reverts to them at her death. In the lifetime of her father, he may grant her and her husband use of plots of his land. At his death the use of these plots reverts to her brothers. Her father or her brothers may plant useful trees or sago palms on their land for the use of her children; these trees remain to her children until their death when they revert to the agnatic descendants of her brothers.

The payment for a first child is distributed together with that of the bridewealth. The payment establishes the legitimacy of the children and the transfer of rights over them. The MB however retains residual rights in the children which are recognized at the first eating of meat and yams, and at puberty, and at the death of the first son of the marriage. In each instance, a payment is made once to the mother's brother's agnatic group and covers the transfer of rights in respect of all the children resulting from the marriage. If the marriage only produces daughters, the payment at puberty is the final payment due to the MB.[1] A man who has had no children is called *gipi'in* (literally, nothing man) and so too is a man who has had seven daughters but no surviving sons. A girl may still find refuge with her MB when her parents seek to give her in marriage against her wishes.

Each sister's son, however, makes further presentations to his matrilateral relatives on return from plantation labour (formerly

[1] The girl's husband occasionally chooses to make exchanges with her matrilateral relatives.

seclusion in Tambin rites and the assumption of male head-dress) at the birth of his first child, and at its puberty. These repay the interests of his matrilateral relatives in his own individual welfare for they have no influence or rights over his children (i.e. the sister's son's children). The payment at death of the first ZS severs the rights held by the original wife's agnates over her children. The spirits of the ZS remain with their own agnates.

It is worth mentioning a variation of the paradigmatic form: sons and daughters are not necessarily balanced and in consequence there is some informal sorting out of responsibilities so that each is provided for. In contrast to the nearby Au-speaking villages where a girl and her husband give to the brother who precedes the girl in birth order, a Gnau sister gives her prestations to her eldest brother. The eldest brother is nominally responsible to his younger brothers for their fair share in her bridewealth, and if his father is dead he must find them wives.

If there are many brothers, and/or either many sisters or many sister's sons, there is an informal pairing off of responsibilities so that the pairs contribute relatively more to each other: a particular MB looks after one particular ZS, bleeds his penis for him, provides him with more shillings for his bridewealth, receives more of his plantation earnings; is father to the son who as MBS exchanges with ZS: in brief that brother and his descendants are closely linked to that sister and her children, but not exclusively.

If there are no appropriate brothers, other agnatic kin, or kin suitable by clan group, assume the duties. If a man dies without sons, those who inherit his land may assume his avuncular rights and duties and also kin terms appropriate for him. (I noted one instance only of this which took the inheritor terminologically two generations backwards.)

People also acquire rights to bridewealth and other payments or obligations, because they have shared in the upbringing of the girl, or because at her birth her mother threatened to kill her, and they took the child, cut the umbilical cord and washed it, thereby promising to take some responsibility for the child.

OPTIONAL EXCHANGE SYSTEM BETWEEN WOMEN

I have not so far described the optional exchange system which is patterned in similar fashion to that of the affinal/matrilateral system, but takes place between married women. It is similarly patterned in the sense that one side gives meat and other exchange foods (to be discussed later), while the other side gives money and different exchange foods. The meat-giving, money-receiving side is similar to the MB side of the 'male' exchange system; the women who do this are either married senior sisters or married father's sisters. The other side, which gives money and receives meat, is the side of a married junior sister or a married brother's daughter. Participation in these exchanges obviously requires the co-operative interest of husbands. In the case of true sisters the exchanges are usually maintained. In general, men say they preserve these relationships, which follow from their wives' kinship if their exchange partners will be close to them; that is, either close in a geographical sense of being hamlet co-resident but not lineage co-agnate; or socially close in the sense of being village co-clan-agnate but not hamlet co-resident. The exchange relationships are limited usually to the annual exchanges, except at the payment for the delivery of a woman's first child when her elder sister or father's sister receives a part of this payment. The exchanges emphasize the shared kinship of the two women and their children, who will use cross-sex and senior/junior same-sex sibling terms towards each other and observe certain food restrictions. The children of two sisters may carry on these relationships after their marriage too.

AMOUNTS OF PAYMENT

I have indicated below the rates of payment prevailing in 1968–9. As each year the rates tend to increase, it is difficult to compare particular kinds of payment because people frequently decide to add to the later payments so that some recompense is made for the lower rates that previously held. This is especially marked where exchange marriages have been made and one sister went in marriage for what now seems a low bridewealth. Her brother who marries after her may pay more than she received, in which case the sister's husband balances the difference by making a proportionately greater payment for the delivery of their first child.

I have therefore indicated by percentage of payment what relative part was contributed to or received from the different payments by different kin or co-residents. The amounts given are at the currently accepted rate, but all are variable – the bridewealth (and plantation money of £15)[1] least so.

Bridewealth	£25 (already by 1969 some gave up to £35)
Delivery of first child	£10–£15
The child's first eating of meat	£5
Puberty of the first child	£25
Return from plantation of the son	£15
Death of the wife	£5–£25
Death of her first son	£10

Contribution

To Bridewealth:

Groom's lineage agnates (F, FB, FBS, eB)	65–90%
Groom's clan agnates	5–30%[2]
Groom's hamlet co-residents (non-agnate)	0–30%
Groom's matrilateral relatives MB, MBS)	5–10%

For delivery of the first child, and for puberty of this child:

Father's lineage agnates	60–90%
Father's clan agnates	10–30%
Father's co-residents	0–30%

Distribution

Of Bridewealth:

Wife's natal lineage agnates	60–80%
Wife's natal clan agnates	20–30%
Wife's natal hamlet co-residents	0–30%

[1] I have listed the amounts in pounds (£): £1 should be taken to refer to Australian $2.00.

[2] Clan agnates not resident in the same hamlet rarely contribute more than 5%.

For delivery of first child:

Wife's natal lineage agnates	60–80%
Wife's natal clan agnates	15–20%
Wife's natal hamlet co-residents	0–20%
Wife's eZ or WFZ	0–10%
Husband's MB and MBS	5–15%
Wife's and Husband's co-initiates	0–8%

For first child's puberty:

Mother's natal lineage agnates	60–90%
Mother's natal clan agnates	10–20%
Mother's natal hamlet co-residents	0–20%
FMB and FMBS	0–5%

I did not obtain adequate comparable data on death payments: of the three I have recorded, one was exceptional as £40 was paid by a very wealthy family; another was restricted in distribution to the true agnates as the dead woman had married within her natal hamlet. There was conspicuous lag in meeting death payment obligations and some death payments were unpaid more than two years after death.

The exchanges described above for marriage and the main stages of family development are large in scale and demand resources beyond those of a single nuclear family. In these exchanges besides money (or formerly shell valuables), game and vegetable foods are given. The kinds of food given by either side of the exchange relationship are formally set and different. Each year, quite apart from the large-scale duties already described, families involved in such asymmetric exchange relationships must recognize this relationship by exchanging meat and vegetable food according to the same rules of what must appropriately be given. The scale of these annual exchanges is much smaller and the obligations can be met by the work of a nuclear family; indeed in these annual exchanges we see individual nuclear families as effective units more clearly than in most other activities.

The objects to be given in the exchanges are set by the relationship. In giving them, both larger and smaller groups of people show their interest in maintaining the relationships correctly. Sometimes they can or must choose to whom from among people appropriately related they will link themselves in the smaller exchanges. Choices may be determined by the need to adjust to demographic changes. They may honour their obligations more or less satisfactorily. The exchanges for stages in the development of the family are large in scale calling for co-operative effort by

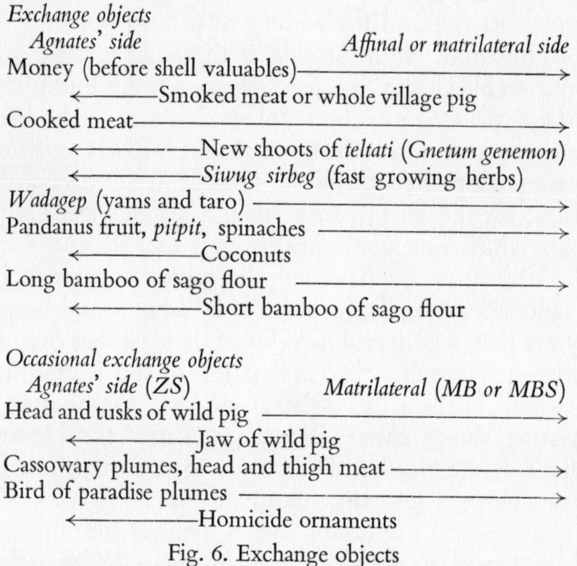

Fig. 6. Exchange objects

the descent and often the hamlet groups involved, and they reflect a group responsibility and interest. *Mingep* (shell valuables) and money stand out among the objects of exchange because the amounts given may be settled only after demands and bargaining. The other objects are accepted as they come and, to express dissatisfaction with their quantity or quality directly, someone must take the drastic step of rejecting or throwing away what has been presented – drastic because such action could sever good relations for some time.

SOME COGNITIVE ASPECTS OF DUTY, SANCTION AND RITUAL IN AGNATIC AND MATRILATERAL RELATIONSHIPS

In youth and manhood, a man learns spells and ritual from his agnates but not from his matrilateral relatives; he inherits from his agnates and not from his matrilateral relatives: but he benefits from ritual made by his mother's brothers to make him grow well–as they say: 'they work things so that he may stand up well'. Chief of these are rites of puberty and entry into adulthood when the mother's brother (*wauwi*) must bleed himself from the penis and provide this blood both for smearing on the sister's child (*mauwin* or *mauwi*) and for adding to a food portion (*wa'agep*) eaten by the child. He must also, if the child is male (*mauwin*), be the one to bleed him first from the penis. Although why men bleed their penises can be explained more elaborately, the ordinarily given reason is the same as that for MB's gifts of meat; for the rites which first allow the toddler to eat meat and certain vegetables; for the rites to strengthen a youth's *wuna'at*, or vital centre, in which hot stones are pressed to and scar the surface over the centre; in all these acts the *wauwi* appeals to his own agnatic ancestors to make his sister's child grow and be well.

They say that youths and men bleed their penises first, to make themselves grow well – the explanation of this is that blood can become 'bad' in the sense of 'stale' or 'dry', or become impure from wrong things eaten. Bleeding purifies the blood to the betterment of the bleeder. The phrase to refer to penis bleeding which can be used in general company is 'he washes or bathes' (*nega*). The second important theory behind bleeding is something like that of an exchange transfusion – for after the youth or girl has been smeared with blood and betel juice, he or she is given penile blood to eat which is mixed with specially cooked meat and coconut. The girls – women generally – do not know this. The blood should be, but is not always, penile blood of a mother's brother. This blood and the blood smeared externally, is to make the young person grow well; the blood eaten is said to fill the skin and replace blood lost and bad blood. I will expand the picture further: when a boy is taken to the stream or river for his first bleeding at puberty, younger boys, mainly those of his hamlet, go too and many men; after the boy is bled many of the men bleed themselves and smear the small boys, and these small boys are also given a little of the meat with blood intended for the boy at puberty. Thus small boys see penis bleeding done, and receive blood to make them grow, years before the time of their own puberty. Though spoken of as 'filling up' or changing the blood, it is not necessary for them to lose some first.

The rules on eating human blood are these: (1) not your own blood in any form (you must not lick a cut finger), nor anything that you have killed with an arrow for your own blood is said to enter your kill invisibly with the arrow; (2) not the blood of your father, your genitor, for his blood is in you and to eat it is as though you ate your own blood; (3) not that of any man you call junior to you, typically that of a younger brother or a son. These are the prohibitions which any Gnau man states. They require some further elucidation. The Gnau distinguish seniority between siblings; they have rules, strictly observed, on eating game, the sequence of drinking, use of proper names, instruction in certain forms of magic, and other things, which depend on precedence of birth. (Those concerning eating and drinking apply to true siblings, brothers and sisters irrespective of sex, but apart from these the rules apply between classificatory 'brothers' but not between 'brothers' and 'sisters' in the classificatory sense.) The rules forbid to the senior brother the same things from his junior brother as are forbidden to a man of the father's generation who is a classificatory father from anyone he calls son: i.e. elder B to younger B is as F to S. The theory by which they explain this is that a man in begetting a child provides it with some blood, although they do not make it clear how, any more than we do in our folk theory of consanguinity. At maturity, in early manhood, a man is become whole (*nemblin*) and has his blood entire (*gungi nembli*). After his first child, each successive one is relatively less the product of his 'whole blood', and each child is spoken of as *gungi nemblisa* – entirish blood – relative to those who follow him, who are products of part of what was left after he was born. I remark on the detail of this statement because they say it is in theory permissible for an elder sibling brother to smear his penile blood on a younger one but certainly not the reverse, despite the rule that the begetting father's blood is forbidden. (A father's younger brother's blood is also permissible.) If one relates the prohibitions on the father's blood simply to a concept of identical substance, something the same as your own blood, it cannot be reconciled with the possibility of having an elder brother's blood smeared on, for he too must share in that identity with the parent. If one follows the stress they give to precedence and the idea of a diminishing stock of blood, one can rationalize the permission to have an elder brother's blood which was never part of that which your father might have given you, while that which remains to him after your birth is stuff which, were it used in the begetting of another child, would necessarily belong to your younger sibling. The rules of seniority are recognized within one generation and they also establish enduring positions of seniority as between the male lines of all men of common descent within each subsequent generation, that is between all classificatory brothers. They behave towards elder brothers in some ways as they behave towards men of the ascending generation. They often speak of blood given or smeared on as stuff given by grown men to the immature so that they may grow to maturity as their seniors, big men, have. Elder brothers are allied in a sense with the preceding generation and in fact a father's elder brother has the same kinship term as a grandfather, a younger brother's son the same term as a grandson.

I have dealt with the negative side to rules about eating blood; the positive side is that the blood should come from your mother's brother, and replace some of the blood which you were born with. This is one of the chief duties of a mother's brother to benefit his sister's children. However, the theory of *gungi nembli*, the whole blood successively diminished, is a theory of consanguinity and it also applies to the blood contribution of the mother, so that her children where they have different fathers, are also unambiguously senior and junior according to the order in which she bore them. The mother's brother's gift of blood pre-eminently is to benefit the child's growth, just as his gifts of meat are also reason for him to claim that he has grown his sister's child to a fine maturity. Further than this, the particular mother's brother who gave a youth his blood to eat has established a tie of substance such that he cannot eat what that sister's son has shot, for the blood of the shooter which has entered the kill is partly his own, though his sister's son is obliged to give certain things he shoots to him. The differential nature of the two ties, matrilateral temporary and patrilineal enduring, is well indicated by this answer to my question 'Can a son never eat his father's blood?', 'Yes he eats his father's bones; but his mother's brother's blood', for men keep some of their dead father's bones to scrape and eat them in certain rites, and so that their father's spirit will stay near watching over them.

The blood of men has occupied much space: what of women's

blood? Bridewealth is given to the bride's relatives and kept intact and undistributed by them when with little ceremony she comes to live at her husband's hamlet as his wife. But the rites following the birth of her first child are in contrast complex, festive and public – at one point in them, her husband bleeds himself and gives her his own blood hidden in a betel quid. When these rites are done he may go into her house, and see his child. His wife's relatives may then distribute the bridewealth they have kept intact. Although the purpose they give to explain this ceremony is benefit to the newborn child and to allow the father to enter his wife's house, the rites take place even if the child is still-born; and for subsequent children they do not bleed. It is possible to see the transfer of blood, the wife unaware eating her husband's blood, as an act establishing a tie of blood between them, an incorporation.

I referred earlier to the need to sanction and define obligations if good relationships are to be ensured between the groups linked through marriage, and particularly after the death of the wife, when her children live among their agnates. A variety of ritual sanctions are controlled by the MB and his descendants: some of these are thought to be lethal. The sanctions are like curses in which the MB can call upon his ancestors to strike down a sister's child who fails to fulfil his obligations; some methods also employ special magical techniques. The MB carves a mark or image of his ZS on a great tree growing on his land, curses it, then cuts it down; or he stops up something his sister's son has touched or left in a natural hole or fissure of his land. There are also magical means to cause a sister's child to be still-born or die in infancy. These are severe potential sanctions for relationships which are usually assumed to be, and are, friendly and dependable, particularly that between an actual MB and his sister's child. The MB is indulgent and helpful to his sister's child; the sister's child almost always turns to him if forced by agnates to do something against his will, especially if pressed into a displeasing marriage, or chided beyond endurance.

SUMMARY

The main points I have sought to bring out are: (1) the isolation of the village as a social unit; (2) the presence of ties, rather like those of clanship, conceived in terms of brotherhood and descent, linking segments of the village population with people of other villages; (3) the interweaving of different patrilineal groups in affinal and matrilateral relationships largely contained within the village. These multiple ties enable a large proportion of the village to have some part or interest in almost any large celebration. Traditionally each hamlet had only one men's house, although now most have more; the single house would have drawn our attention to the stress on hamlet solidarity still present within the village, especially in the performance of major rituals such as those of Tambin, or Panu'et which are based on a men's house. A particular hamlet holds the ritual, and the other hamlets come there to assist its celebration. Each year, the first eating of new *wadagep* (yams and taro) of that year is specifically a hamlet event whose timing is chosen by each hamlet for itself and feasted only by its members, eating together, particularly the children according to their like age and sex, sharing little fires and portions of food with those who have grown up with them.

Although one hamlet must inaugurate some major rite, and the rite be centred on its men's house, in cases such as the prolonged seclusion of young men in the initiating rites of Tambin, youths of other hamlets used to take part and be initiated then, which created a tie of ritual friendship between them: such ritual friends call each other *wusai* and have certain obligations towards each other. The term *wusai* – friend – is also used for a relationship, which was usually transmitted from father to son, between men of different villages. Any given man would have had one or two such *wusai* whom, if the villages were at that time enemies, he might meet secretly in the forest to exchange gifts of meat and news or warnings. Such *wusai* did not have ritual duties towards each other, nor was trade or formal ceremonial exchange done between them.

2
Environment and Disease

COMMENT ON METHOD AND INTENT

This chapter is about the environment in which the Gnau people live and their adaptation to it. I have emphasized natural features and social customs which affect their health and illness. It is designed to present a compressed account of their habitat, their seasonal and daily activities, and so to serve as a basis for understanding the conditions in which they fall ill. I describe first how things appear to the observer and second I have, in places, made comments on how they perceive them. The second part of the chapter deals with some medical aspects of their adaptation.

The lay-out is as follows:

A. Environment and adaptation
  1. General features of the environment
  2. Forest: vegetation and fauna, native perception and uses of the forest, hunting and gathering
  3. Gardening: seasonal and daily work, division of labour
  4. Travel and topography
  5. Village: layout, population, domestic units, meals and conviviality

B. Medical aspects
  1. Trauma and injury
  2. Chest disease, epidemic and contagious illness, diseases borne by insects and animals
  3. Sanitation
  4. Nutrition

The influences of the environment on health do not necessarily fit into the schemes of social inquiry or analysis. Heat and cold, or insect populations may, for example, be of greater consequence for human mortality than warfare or marriage arrangements, while native social recognition or adaptations to these natural facts are often undiscussed: the physical facts set conditions for and modify techniques of daily living although people may reflect little upon them and, of course, they may not know that some of them have any bearing on health. An inquiry into a dysentery epidemic or childhood mortality would demand careful study of sanitation, water supply and hygiene, or of mosquitoes, nursing, dietary rules and so on – the biological perspective would direct inquiries but it might require ancillary knowledge of socially haphazard though relevant practices or beliefs. The first intention of this chapter is to give a summary indication of some at least of these factors which will otherwise escape attention in later chapters. I have later to concentrate on illness which the Gnau regarded as severe. Such illnesses were not frequent although they occasioned explanations, treatments and responses which the anthropologist can analyse by the concepts and methods of his discipline. On the other hand, trivial ailments, like cuts, sores, colds or aches, do not provoke great concern or responses suitable for extended analyses in sociological terms. But these trivialities form the bulk of small medical misery. Environment, adaptation and the mode of life all contribute in different small ways to the pattern and incidence of these minor ailments, and I have tried to show how this comes about. The minor illnesses contribute most of what people bring to the attention of a resident doctor or an aidpost orderly, demanding the expenditure of much time and money in treatment if for example, a Public Health Department intends to provide facilities for their treatment.

I must here note briefly my own role in the treatment of patients. Soon after arriving in the village, I explained that as well as wishing to learn about their language, history and customs, I was a doctor and interested in their illnesses, equipped and prepared to treat them if they wished. Apart from humanitarian reasons for providing treatment, I did so in order to make clear my interest in studying their illness. It disclosed to them my motives in following cases of illness and I think brought to my notice more cases than would have been found if I had disguised my approach in order not to alter the prevailing situation.

I do not think they regarded me as a proper European doctor. At first, they were excited and hopeful that I would, as a white man, provide money, employment, a trade store, an airstrip, as had happened at mission stations near to them. Partly because of their position on top of and at the back of Anguganak Bluff, they had had less chance to earn money and find employment at the mission stations than many of the neighbouring people with whom they came into contact. They also believed that these people spoke of them as *buskanaka* and *haitan man* that is, as crude bush natives. They were sometimes proud of keeping to tradition, of hunting, of being bush men; and sometimes they were ashamed of their nakedness, their lack of letters, and they were earnest to change. Their first hopes of the benefits I would bring effervesced and were not damped by my explanations or disclaimers. After three or four months they began to realize and to accept their disappointment. Even so they helped me with my inquiries and they appeared with sores, burns and cuts for treatment. Missionaries, nurses and native aidpost orderlies commonly dress sores and give injections. In the Gnau people's experience, doctors are found at hospitals or at least they have one as their base. They did not consider me a doctor in this full sense, although they took to telling me who was ill and asking me for treatment, as well as asking me to dress their sores.

The focus of my research was sociological rather than biological. It will be apparent to a physical anthropologist or to a medical reader that I have not made a detailed inquiry into the physical and medical state of the Gnau. It was impracticable to undertake a survey single-handed, or to inquire into matters of special medical interest – such as blood pressures, anaemia or parasite loads. These are sufficiently complex matters to require well-planned study. To make amateur observations on them would have deflected me from the sociological purpose of my study.

Although much of the chapter is based on impression, I have also drawn on a study (Fountain undated) by a geographer, Mr O. C. Fountain, of the land and economy of a village, Wulukum, near to Anguganak. In description of the kinds and prevalence of local diseases, I have the benefit of Dr R. J. Sturt's survey of mortality and morbidity in an area around Anguganak, close to where I lived. The survey, which was planned as part of the New Guinea Mortality Survey, began late in 1961 and is still in progress (to 1969). The same 16 villages are visited twice each year to record the population, its changes and the present state of health in all inhabitants, about 3500 people. On some of the survey visits, particular matters are investigated such as respiratory function (by peak flow meter), or tuberculin sensitivity. Dr

Sturt has also recorded the diseases of patients treated at the hospital which he established at Anguganak. This is the only hospital with a doctor in the immediate area. The next nearest one is the Government hospital at Lumi 25 miles away. His information on 13,000 cases admitted there (Sturt undated) enables the limited data I obtained on illness from a single village over a short period (22 months) to be seen in perspective. I am much indebted to his extensive and detailed inquiries.

GENERAL FEATURES OF THE ENVIRONMENT

Gnau land comprises forested hills lying for the most part between two rivers, the Nopan and the Assini. From the long high axis of the range of the Torricelli mountains which lies to the north, hills and ridges slope down to lower hills along which the road past Yankok and the Anguganak Mission station now runs to Lumi. Then immediately south of Yankok, there is a steep conspicuous scarp, Anguganak Bluff, and the Nopan river curls south-westward round its base. The villages of Anguganak[1] and De'aiwusel are set on this high ridge which rises to about 2000 feet from 1000 feet above sea level and circles as a horseshoe south-eastward to Rauit village at about 1700 feet. South of this the land slopes down in sharp backed ridges. From the ridge of Rauit one can see when the atmosphere is clear over a huge expanse of hills and forest across the Sepik plain to the central chain of mountains rising on the other side, blue, indistinct and easily confused with cloud. The plain appears to be covered with dark forest, except for a few large paler patches of kunai grasslands from which smoke sometimes rises in the dry season. There is no visible sign or glint of the Sepik river and the Rauit villagers say they did not know of it until after European contact. They do not name or show interest in the distant land or mountains which they can see either to the north or the south of them. About their villages lie the gardens, stands of sago palm, and patches of regrown forest; two miles or so southwards forests begin which show no signs of previous cultivation, to an unpractised eye.

Much of the underlying rock in the area is obscured by deep soils which may be 20 feet deep, but 'the most common rock is a

[1] Elsewhere I have used its Gnau name, Nembugil, in order to distinguish the village from the mission station.

loosely compacted grey mudstone. This is easily and rapidly eroded to give rather striking flat-bottomed valleys with almost vertical walls wherever the bare rock is exposed. Sandstones, shales and clays with isolated granitic intrusions are found to the north on the upper slopes of the Torricelli mountains,' (Fountain undated, p. 23).

The climate is hot and humid. The wet season lasts from November to March but is not so clearly different from the dry season as on the coast or in the plain. The annual rainfall is less than 100 inches (72·5 inches in 1964 at Anguganak Mission station, although about 90 inches is average there). Fountain found in 1964 that 63·7 per cent of the rain fell in the 'wet' season and 36·3 per cent fell in the 'dry' season; but while 63·3 per cent of the total wet season days were rain days, as much as 42·0 per cent of the dry season days were rain days. As he puts it 'while slightly less than two out of every three days in the wet season have rain, more than one out of every three days in the dry season have this.' (Fountain undated, p. 24). Most falls of rain are brief, and days of protracted rain or drizzle are rare. Erosion is mostly a consequence of heavy downpours and the intensity of rain is greater in the wet than the dry season (3·3 times greater in December than in July). Landslips sometimes occur because of heavy storms and may destroy the exposed new planted gardens which are placed on steeply inclined slopes. Gardens were devastated by landslips once during my stay and gave cause to four families in Rauit for public mourning, announced by log drum and accompanied by a gathering for sympathy at which some smeared themselves with clay as though for death. Heavy falls of rain swell small rivers to impassable mud-coloured torrents which eat away at their banks and sweep trees and boulders in their spate.

The temperature varies only about 5°F during the year but the diurnal variation is greater with day temperatures reaching between 80° and 90°F and night temperatures dropping to between 60° and 75°F. The relative humidity is high throughout the year and follows a regular daily pattern. During the morning it falls to about 75 per cent, infrequently to as low as 50 per cent, but rises in the afternoon to reach 100 per cent at night so that leaves drip with dew in the early mornings. Fogs of the night are common in the village but disperse in the early morning. Almost every morning mist can be seen lying wispy or blanketed over low ground to the south.

FOREST: VEGETATION AND FAUNA

The climate supports a luxuriant and varied vegetation. Lowland tropical rain forest covers the greater part of Gnau land. The flora is very mixed with many different tree species. The ground cover is not so dense or thicketed in the forest as to make it difficult to walk through. Away from paths it is usually enough to thread one's way through and beside shrubs, young palms, keeping an eye open for stinging plants, and for those creepers, climbing rattans, or young palms which bear spines, thorns or rings of claws. Occasionally people have to cut at climbers or branches which bar passage and on slopes one sometimes meets tangled thick undergrowth.

Although it is usually easy to walk through the forest, there are no perspectives, no open views; a companion becomes lost to sight among leaves, stems, shadows and trunks when he has walked 20 yards away. A brown skinned person who makes no movement can hide easily. The light is dimmed and greenish. Through gaps in the canopy the sun shafts down to a patch of forest floor splashing it with bright scattered light. The air is still and it smells musty. A smell comes off on the hands if one touches the leaves of shrubs in passing, an odour of mould, leaves and dust peculiar to the forest. Occasionally one passes through a patch of unmoving air faintly scented by some plant like honeysuckle; one passes transient smells, of humus, of moist rotting wood or bruised fruits. The Gnau people are alert to smell; they learn which plants are aromatic and in some cases they use scent to decide the identification of trees or shrubs, scraping or cutting the bark or crushing a leaf.

The canopy and confusion of trees alters sounds and calls, limiting and muffling them, but as though enclosed in a leafy hall, the sharp screech or squawks from a nearby bird sound echoes in one's ears. I found the localization of forest sounds difficult, for example the evening cooing of pigeons hid high in the canopy, although the native people were accurate in pointing to the direction and finding them. They excel in identifying birds by call – for passerines and many other birds, the description attaching to a name is first, the imitation of its call or song, next its habitat, and then its plumage. They distinguish the patter, swish, and scuffle characteristics in animal movements and differentiate them in onomatopoeic speech.

The forests are crossed by main paths which are known to and used by all travellers. They are worn enough to be recognized except in distant hunting bush where they may be missed. Side or branch paths which lead from them are private to bush owners and may be distinguished by being left overgrown at the points where they diverge from the main path, or they may have taboo signs placed at their mouths. All the land which they use has names. In the more distant and wilder bush, the names cover larger tracts than those close to home. In the area of about 4·5 square miles surrounding Rauit village there are 251 named plots of land and they vary greatly in size. Most people know at least the larger tract names and their position. The land tracts follow, where possible, boundaries of slope and level, with limits marked by ridges, rivers and streams. Where the topography does not help, they may mark the boundary by planting certain kinds of trees, shrubs or a bamboo clump, or note some feature of soil, vegetation or rock. Instructions about a route to take, or descriptions of the events of a journey, are lost on someone who cannot recognize the species of trees. Bamboo, which also grows wild in some thick brakes in forest, is planted generously close to villages. By knowing the main features of ridge, slope, river, vegetation, and stream, they rarely get lost in the forest. When it happens that they are, they show little anxiety or haste, but are quite ready if necessary to sleep lost for the night, then work back by ridge and slope and tributary, towards the arterial rivers which can be followed and provide bearings. Once when lost with them, I saw them stop and listen at the faint cry of a kingfisher which lives by water, and we moved towards the sound and later they could make out the high piercing whine of a cicada found by streams, which indeed led us to the river.

The forests show to an unpractised eye no marks of previous habitation. However forests surround the sites of ancient villages. Some of these sites are quite abandoned and the forest looks as tall and immemorial as it does elsewhere. No one makes gardens at many of these distant sites. At others, there are bush camps. Even where they have long been uninhabited, one may find trees or bamboo brakes which people say were planted by ancestral hands. In a gloomy piece of forest, for example, below the ridge of Silip Pukaiyen which was left many generations ago, one may notice two of the orange and yellow paste-apple trees (*dapati*) standing by a dark marshy pool, witness to some ancient decorated grove of sago palms now all gone and overgrown. Another sign in the forest of previous events which the outsider will overlook is an unspotted and dark green small croton shrub which is planted to commemorate where someone stood to shoot a pig, or a man, and where his victim fell.

I assume that to a native eye the forest shows character and variations which I fail to perceive, lacking their ability to distinguish the kinds of trees, to recognize or orientate myself in it when I have passed by a place before. To hunt successfully, they must note and remember the habitual paths (*manipe*) of pigs or cassowaries; when they hunt by the method of encircling drive, the bowmen stand at points along these paths.

HUNTING AND GATHERING

The forests are the home of game resources which they hunt by various methods: for pigs, wallaby and cassowary – (1) by drive (*lagabil*); (2) by individual tracking or stalking (mainly in the early morning, rising before dawn) using bush craft and surprise, or a dog to find and corner the pig (*natu'alp*); (3) by waiting and watching at night for wild pig to feed either on fallen fruit or at prepared baits (*lategatep nem*); (4) by digging spiked pit traps on pig paths – none were being made while I was there (*lagel gig*); (5) by laying dead fall traps (*litalel nem*, or *lagao radetap*) for small ground-living mammals: these were also obtained by dogs chasing or finding them and men digging them out of holes in the ground or catching them in tree holes; (6) night hunting on silent moonlit excursions, slow moving and intently listening for marsupials which feed and rustle leaves, cracking fruit or nuts up in the trees. The men climb to kill them with knife or bow; also they wait in *taun* trees or breadfruit trees with a bow to shoot fruit bats. These trees are often planted just off the ridge edge by villages so that people can stand on the ridge conveniently close to the fruit-bearing crowns of trees and shoot. The night hunting, typically the slow, listening method is called *leirera ge'unit* (literally, they travel by the moon). For birds, they hunt by (7) making hides at water (*la'asil subag*) or hides at food trees or high up in branches (*la'asil wop wit* or *la'asil lup*).

Gathering in the forest provides some food. Men find eggs of the brush turkey (*Talegalla jobiensis*) by digging up the mounds of

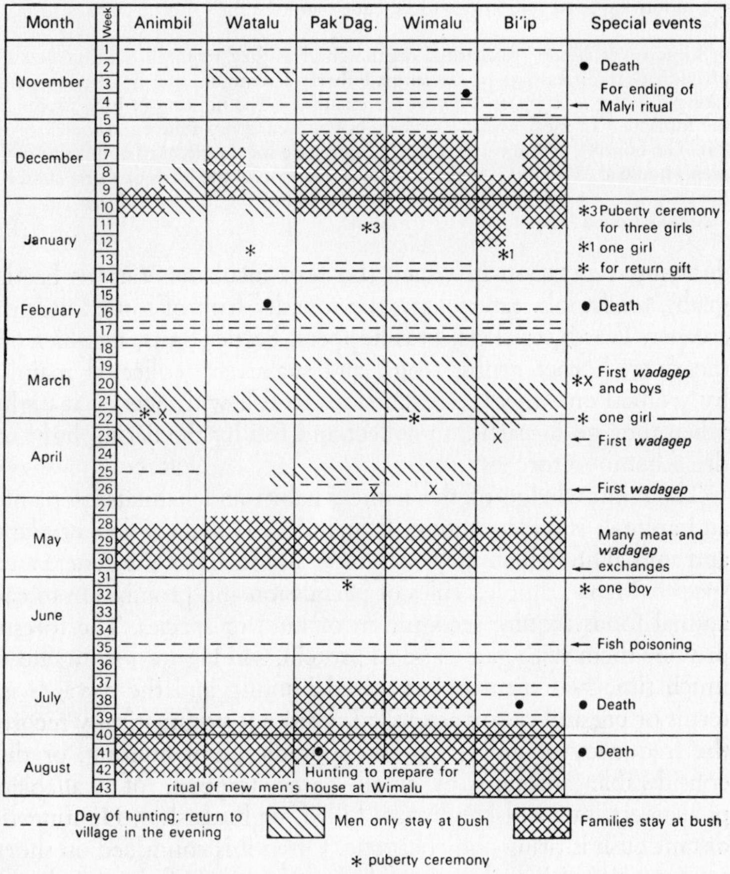

Month | Week | Animbil | Watalu | Pak'Dag. | Wimalu | Bi'ip | Special events

November
December
January
February
March
April
May
June
July
August

● Death
For ending of Malyi ritual
*3 Puberty ceremony for three girls
*1 one girl
* for return gift
● Death
*X First *wadagep* and boys
* one girl
First *wadagep*
First *wadagep*
Many meat and *wadagep* exchanges
* one boy
Fish poisoning
● Death
● Death

Hunting to prepare for ritual of new men's house at Wimalu

– – – – Day of hunting; return to village in the evening
Men only stay at bush
Families stay at bush
* puberty ceremony

Fig. 7. Frequency of organized hunting

Notes

Organized hunting refers primarily to the method of hunting by an encircling beat towards standing bowmen (now also towards men with shotguns). Where men stay at distant bush for days or weeks, they also hunt by individual stalking, trapping and by building hides to shoot birds.

I recorded systematically the kills of pig and cassowary. Numbers of wallabies and much small game were also taken. They add substantially to the amount of protein obtained from hunting. The total number of kills between November 1968 and August 1969 was:

wild pigs = 52 (killed piglets are not included)
cassowary = 18

I have indicated *deaths* of people on the chart because organized hunts must take place after a death so that the kill by a close kinsman of the deceased may enable the mourning food restrictions to be ended and the final mortuary rites to take place.

Some other rituals are marked on the chart as they required hunting first to provide meat for feasting, or exchange. Puberty ceremonies and the ceremony for eating the first *wadagep* of the year are examples. The hunting in June preceded the fulfilment of meat/*wadagep* exchanges between many affinal and matrilateral kin. The hunting in August was partly to prepare for the ritual of building a new men's house at Wimalu; and also for the celebration of the birth of a first child to the only son of an Animbil man (in fact the son of the former *Luluai*).

Smoked meat keeps for up to 3 months.

decaying vegetation in which the eggs incubate. Various beetle grubs, toadstools, caterpillars, the squashy fruit of some kinds of creeper, lizards, crickets, grasshoppers, beetles, nuts, mayflies on the river, hornet grubs, frogs, and snakes are collected mainly by women on either day excursions to fish with nets or at night when they go in parties to collect and fish by the flaring light of dried bamboo torches.

Their knowledge of the names, habits and habitats of plants and animals is wide-ranging. It includes the main orders of plant and animal life which they encounter and many of the genera and species. Many complex rules of permission and prohibition to eat animal foods require recognition of kind or species. The forests provide them with game and so protein, and Figure 7 shows how much time was spent in organized hunting and the rewards in terms of pig and cassowary killed. I did not systematically record the frequency of individual and sporadic night hunting, or the considerable amounts of small game trapped, of wallabies, phalangers, rats and bandicoots killed, or birds shot. Hunting in distant bush is tiring and energetic. Often it is continued on short rations and with little or fitful sleep because of the attacks of mosquitoes.

ENVIRONMENTAL CONTRAST

It takes time for someone unused to this environment to appreciate the differences between forest, garden and village because everywhere there are plenty of trees. The enclosing canopy of leaves, trees of great height, the dimmer light of the forest, the confusion of vegetation which stifles and limits the view, strike one most forcibly when breaking out of it to follow the river's course where flooding in the wet has cut a broad expanse of pebble, silt and mud flat in its flat reaches. Here the sun glares and shimmers. In the dry season, the Gnau sometimes follow its course for an hour or two of the walk back from the southern hunting camps, then they strike back again into the engulfing forest. As they get closer to the village, gardens begin and they pass in and out of clumps of forest, sunlit garden, through arcades of sago palms, by garden houses. The gardens have been cut out of the forest. The contrast I have mentioned is described in this extract from the text of a myth called the Python. The man has met someone mysterious in the forest who is in fact the Python though he appears to be a man. The Python asks him what part of the forest belongs to him and tells him to come to meet him there in a few days with gifts. The extract describes what happened.

The Python tricked him, sent him back to the village. It came and set there (in the forest he had named) a great pool, put it there, a round circle, rippling. The Python worked and cleared the forest round it and planted for him herbs with scented leaves, *dekerwai*, *woda*, *dyu'elbi*. It planted them for him around and encircling the pool; it planted sago palms and sago palms, and put *tulip* trees, *Pandanus* – planted all these things ready. And the man set off (from the village). He came and stood, stood some way off, and he looked at the place. His own land become beautiful. The light of the sun burst down upon and filled the place: it was just as when you clear a garden, cut down the trees there. He stood and looked saying to himself: 'The (Python) man met me he spoke to me, he came here and has cleared and planted these things for me.' He stood and saw the yellow orange paste-apple trees, sparkling circling round the pool. And the pool there rippled bul bil bul bil bul bil. It rippled with wavelets like the backs of many snakes. The man turned and fled.

GARDEN LAND

The valleys around the village have contained gardens for generations. The yam gardens are made new each year. In the second year after being cleared, they yield sugar cane, pitpit, pawpaw and bananas. By this time, weeds, long sharp grasses and wild pitpit invade them, and creepers and shrubs grow rank and tangled. In succeeding years the forest regrows. To judge from individual memories, land is not used again for yam gardens for 20 years or more after one garden is made there. I am using 'garden' as a short-hand way to refer to cultivated land in contrast to forest. The gardens contain other things besides yam gardens. Most nuclear families have gardens of some sort at about six different sites in any given year. Three or four of these have been planted with yams, two or three are from the previous year. The areas cleared for yam gardens vary in size from 20 × 20 yards to 150 × 300 yards. The areas vary because of slope and access. A very large area is usually cleared by members of several nuclear families if there is a good piece of flat land. Five or six families may then have contiguous plots for yam gardens. The co-operating families are hamlet, clan or lineage co-members.

A house or at least a shelter is built at each garden area. Most people have some widely distant gardens and these have their separate houses. The site of a garden house is often referred to as *wuyi'in adji* – your good place. Where a few neighbouring tracts of land touch, to all of which a given man has title, he may keep to one pleasant house site although he moves the yam gardens around the different nearby tracts of land. Thus some garden house sites have been in continued use for more than a generation. They have decorative shrubs and scented herbs around them, full grown areca palms, *tulip* and breadfruit trees (but never coconut palms), a little lawn of cut grass and a convenient small pool or stream nearby. The house is commonly placed on a dry hillock or mound near to a grove of sago palms and a thicket of Pandanus stands close by. The house is strong and well-made, similar in shape to a traditional village house, smaller but longer. But inside there is a rectangular box formed by long bamboos lashed in place – this is the storage enclosure of the yams for planting. The roofed but open shelters where there is no garden house may also have a yam storage enclosure. Each nuclear family builds a separate garden house. Now people frequently stay at these sites for a few days or weeks and wife, husband and children sleep together in the same house which they do not do in the village. A group of father and married sons, or of brothers, may build their garden houses fairly close together, a little garden hamlet of five houses. But they do not necessarily do so, and the separation of garden houses more commonly bears witness to the independence of nuclear families in gardening. Where the land is damp or marshy sago is planted, although it is also planted on dry seeming ground just off the main ridge and near to the hamlet settlements and it grows well. Small water holes are dug so that they will be convenient for women preparing sago. Some of the stands of sago have spread to form a long continuous line perhaps a quarter of a mile long but these are unusual and most stands are clumped over about 40 × 50 yards. Sago stands do not occur naturally in the forests but there are planted stands by some bush camps. The sago palm has apparently been introduced into the mountains and, as Fountain has pointed out, the relatively greater human settlement in a band along the southern hills of the Torricelli range may be partly explained by characteristics of soil and climate which have supported and favoured people who wished to grow both sago palms, yams and taro.

There are patches of forest but interrupted by the gardens. The area of gardens is scattered with planted trees which produce fruits or nuts, attract birds or are food plants for caterpillars and grubs, or else are decorative or have their special ritual uses. There are yam gardens, arcades of sago, stands of pitpit, thickets of Pandanus, clumps of bamboo. In contrast to the forest it is full of signs of cultivation, of human modifications, open to the sky, the bird cries are different. In the day you can hear the noise of other people's axes or the double bump of women chipping sago, and the echoing accented calls from ridge tops or ululated remarks coming and going between the families scattered among the gardens.

ANNUAL GARDEN CYCLE

Climate and season give a pattern to gardening. They influence what food is eaten and when (see Table 2). The most conspicuous pattern is related to growing edible tubers – *wadagep*, yams and taro – and particularly to growing the yam mami (*lawuti* in its many varieties). The garden cycle is basically an annual one and new gardens are cleared each year, burned towards the end of the dry season and planted from September onwards. In the second half of February, the broad-billed roller (*Eurostymus orientalis*) and the rainbow bee-eater (*Merops ornatus*) return. From their commanding perches the rollers career and swoop in elastic flight, the rainbow-coloured bee-eaters call shrilly 'teru-teru'. These two

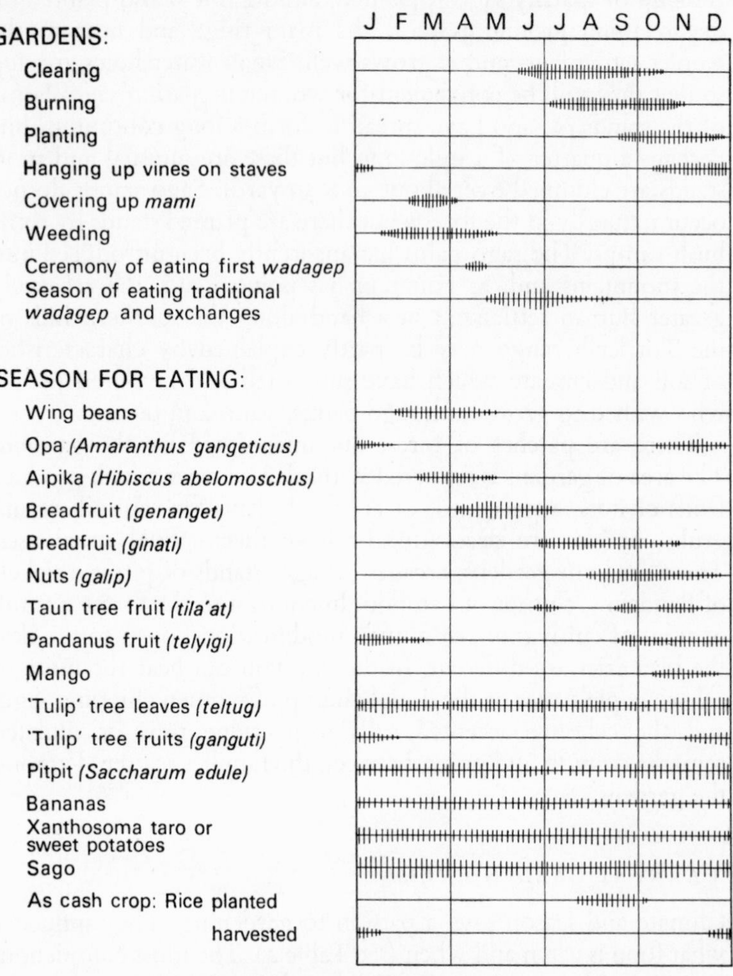

Table 2. Seasonal activities and crops

bird migrants, first arriving, are the signals to begin the covering over of *mami*, a period of hard garden work by men in which loose ground is heaped up and roughly enclosed around the base of the *mami* vine. The two migrant birds, and the swifts, the crested swift and martins which arrive later in this season, are all associated with growing the tubers and success in this; they are forbidden food to men until they are experienced and old because they say that to eat them would harm the man's success in gardening.

They go hunting in the second half of March, when most *mami* have been covered over. They find game for the celebration

Table 3. Division of labour

Task		*Women*	*Men*
General garden work:			
Felling large trees or palms			+
Clearing		+	+
Initial firing			+
Clearing debris and heaping debris for secondary burning		+	+
Weeding		+	(+)
Fencing (rarely)			+
Planting:			
Yam, taro, *mami*			+
Beans, *opa*, *aipika*, *pitpit*, sugar cane		+	(+)
Tobacco			+
Coconut, Betel nut, sago palm			+
Pandanus, banana		(+)	+
Taun tree, breadfruit, nut trees			+
Saior or *tulip* trees			+
Xanthosoma Taro, sweet potato		(+)	+
Harvesting:			
Digging up yam, taro, mami		+	(+)
Plucking leaves of *tulip*, *opa*, *aipika*, ferns		+	
Picking *pitpit*, breadfruit, nuts, *taun* fruit, mango		+	+
Climbing to pick coconuts	(young)	(+)	+
Special activities:			
Hanging up yam *mami* vines			+
Hanging up bean vines		+	(+)
Covering up the base of *mami* vines			+
Sago pounding and chopping		+	
Sago washing to leach out starch		+	
'Salt' ash preparation		+	
Lime preparation			+
Preparing tobacco			+

Table 3. Division of labour (*continued*)

Task	*Women*	*Men*
Hunting:		
All methods (drive, hides, night, trapping, tracking)		+
Butchery of game		+
Fishing:		
Net fishing	+	
Poison method		+
Collecting:		
Frogs, snakes, lizards, crickets, grasshoppers	+	children (+)
Splitting logs for sago or breadfruit beetle grubs		+
Cooking:		
Sago, leaves, meat	+	
Scraping or paring coconut		+
Boiling and mashing yam, *mami*, taro with coconut		+
Roasting tubers or bananas in fire	+	+
Roasting breadfruit	+	+
Baking game in leaves with hot stones and smoking it	+	(+)
Collecting and splitting firewood	+	
Fetching water	+	
House building: all activities		+
Government and Council work: road maintenance		+
Toilets	+	+
Digging water holes	(+)	+
Making all weapons, round baskets for smoking game, armbands, shell and feather decorations and formerly all implements except those used for working sago		+
Making string, net bags, fish nets, all sago working implements, Job's tears skirts, modern bead armbands and formerly clay pots	+	
Making Limbum containers, cutting bamboo for cooking	+	(+)

\+ Sex which does work.
(+) Sex which takes minor share in work, or sometimes does it.

in hamlet groups of eating the first tubers of that year which happens close to the beginning of April. Some at least of the first eaten tubers are certain varieties called in Pidgin *wailmami* (wild yam[1]) which are in fact cultivated, although I have been shown three of the 12 named varieties growing wild in forest. In the weeks following the ceremony of first-eating *wadagep*, people perform their duties of giving *wadagep* and reciprocating gifts with meat from the hunting in March. Before the introduction of *taro konkon* (Gnau, *keisan*; the *Xanthosoma* taro) and the sweet potato, tubers were eaten only from this time until about the end of September, when they began to hang the new next year's yam vines up on supporting staves, by which time the migrant birds had disappeared or were leaving. From this time they ate no more tubers and forbade them. The recently introduced tubers escape these restrictions.

As the dry season continues, the streams and rivers thin and the fish collect in remaining dips and pool-like depths along their courses. This is convenient for the net fishing and night fishing which women do. It is suitable for the rare collectively organized poisoning of streams, which I saw only once in a year. The men work and prepare the poison[2] to great effect: the fish rise to the surface stupefied or dead along a few hundred yards of stream. On the occasion I saw this done, enough small fish and eels were taken, from the night to the morning to cover the surfaces of four or five large kitchen tables.

Watering places in the forests dry up, and men build hides by the ones that remain where birds, especially of paradise, can be shot as they come to drink or bathe and ruffle their feathers in the water. In the driest part of the year bird-shooting hides are built by water, while at other times, by fruit fallen on the ground, by fruiting wild plantains or high up in the branches of food trees of the birds. The Gnau people do not fire grassland to obtain game and have no *kunai* grass fields on their land. They go to distant southern bush sites in the dry season to hunt.

There is a rough annual sequence[3] in the ripening of fruit bearing trees; these are named and shown in Tables 2 and 4.

[1] These varieties are said to produce seeds and some also have aerial tubers.

[2] The poison comes from the cortex of two trees and from two vines' roots.

[3] I am uncertain if it is quite regular and fixed or whether subject to some casual and equatorial confusion.

Table 4. Kinds of vegetable foods and their seasonal availability

Kind of food	Pidgin or English name	Latin name	Gnau name	No. of named varieties or species	Eaten throughout year	Eaten seasonally	Eaten sporadically
Starch	*saksak* sago	*Metroxylon rumphii*	*lawut*	4 spiny var.	+		
		M. sagu		4 non-spiny var.	+		
	Taro (traditional)	*Colocasia*	*nulape*	14 var.		+	
	Yam	*Dioscorea alata*	*wuningi*	19 var.		+	
	Mami	*D. nummularia + esculenta*	*lawuti*	9 var.		+	
	wailmami (aerial yam or seedbearing)	?	*wadagep*	(specific names) 12		+	
	banana	*Musa sapientum*	*tebawug*	27 var.	+		
	tapioc	?					+
Leaves							
(Trees)	*saior* or *tulip*	*Gnetum gnemon*	*teltug*	2 var.	+		
	kumu	*Ficus* spp.	*niyiwug*	5 var.			+
(Shrub)	*aipika*	*Hibiscus abelmoschus*	*nalyigup*	1		+	
(Herb)	*opa*	*Amaranthus gangeticus*	*benang*	1		+	
(Fern)	*Kumu*	? includes *Cyclosporus*	*subla'ap*	(specific names) 5 species			+
Inflorescence	Pitpit	*Saccharum edule*	*namut*	6 var.	+		
Stem	Sugar cane	*S. officinarum*	*biti*	5 var.			+
Beans	of *tulip* tree	*Gnetum gnemon*	*ganguti*	2 var.		+	
	winged bean	*Psophocarpus tetragonolobus*	*malgu'et*	5 var.		+	

Table 4. Kinds of vegetable foods and their seasonal availability (*continued*)

Kind of food	*Pidgin or English name*	*Latin name*	*Gnau name*	*No. of named varieties or species*	*Eaten throughout year*	*Eaten seasonally*	*Eaten sporadically*
Nuts	*Galip*	? *Canarium* spp.	*nimbalgut* (black pericarp)	5 species		+	
			melyi'it (crimson pericarp)			+	
			nulasibi (orange yellow pericarp)			+	
			mipugi				+
			nebalwun				+
	Coconut	*Cocos nucifera*	*we'at*	1	+		
Oily seeds	Screw pine Pandanus	*Pandanus* sp.	*telyigi*	8 var.		+	
Fruit	Breadfruit	*Artocarpus altilis*	*ginati* (yellow pulp and nut eaten)	8 var.		+	
		Artocarpus nobilis ?	*genanget* (nuts only eaten)			+	
	Taun tree	*Pometia pinnata*	*tila'at* (grey lychee-like pulp)	1		+	

Table 4. Kinds of vegetable foods and their seasonal availability (*continued*)

Kind of food	*Pidgin or English name*	*Latin name*	*Gnau name*	*No. of named varieties or species*	*Eaten throughout year*	*Eaten seasonally*	*Eaten sporadically*
	Mango	*Mangifera indica*	*nembibi*	1		+	
	Kumu	*Ficus*	*niyipe galuti*				+
	Muli	*Citrus* sp.	*lugeban*	2 var.			+
	Squashes growing wild in forest	?	*lambet langinet*	1 var.			+
			lambet tabalti	1 var.			+

Notes

Fungi: (Gnau, *telangep*) which grow on rotting sago pith are frequently eaten throughout the year. Some other species of fungi which grow on forest trees also eaten.

Spices: Various leaves or grasses with scent are boiled with food occasionally to give it a flavour. They include leaves of some *Zingiberaceae* (Gnau, *nilape*), other shrubs; rhizomes of ginger (*Zingiber* sp.); a small chili; the aromatic bark of some trees.

'*Salt*': An alkaline ash (Gnau, *nawugep*) is burnt from some aromatic tree barks (including *Plamchonia timorensis*) or the pods of the native winged bean. They had no salt, like ours, before European contact.

Lime: The lime eaten with betel nut was made of the ash of a small cone-shaped shell found in their rivers.

Daga: *Piper betle*, catkins and leaves are chewed with betel nut (*Areca catechu*).

Introduced plant foods:

The most important is *Xanthosoma* taro, eaten throughout the year. Sweet potatoes, sweet bananas and sweet corn are also widely eaten, as is the pawpaw. Other introduced foods are eaten sporadically but not liked or grown by all; these include tomatoes, pineapples, runner beans, cucumber, pumpkin or squash, chinese cabbage, shallot onions and chives. Rice is grown as a cash crop by many, but not all, men. Rice is eaten as a luxury. The rice eaten is almost always bought at a trade store.

As flying foxes and phalangers come to feed at night on breadfruit, mangoes, and the fruit of *taun* trees (*Pometia pinnata, tila'at*), night hunting follows the season of their ripening, although they may hunt for cuscus and phalangers on any brightly moonlit night for there are many forest trees with fruit or seeds to attract the marsupials. The ripening of various trees, especially the *taun* and a small fruited similar tree (*wulmakawun*) decides the times when most trapping is done because the fruits are used to bait deadfall traps for ground-living small game. They can bait them at other times with grubs and crickets.

The essential food of a Gnau meal, sago and *tulip* leaves of the tree *Gnetum gnemon*, are available throughout the year and vary little by season. Coconuts, bananas and *pitpit*, the edible inflorescence of *Saccharum edule*, a cane grass, can be had though in varying amounts all through the year. Sugar cane is used for refreshment at gardens. There are many occasional vegetables or fruit which appear sporadically in their diet, but without a marked season: these include kinds of ferns, the native citrus fruits, leaves and figs from *Ficus* spp. of trees. Other vegetables, more esteemed, are available by season: these include Pandanus fruit, three species of nut, the bean-like fruits of *Gnetum gnemon*; also some vegetables which are planted in new gardens at the time of planting *wadagep* and which become successively available – the leaves like spinach called *opa* in Pidgin (*Amaranthus gangeticus*); the mucilaginous leaves of *aipika* P.E. (*Hibiscus abelomoschus*); and the varieties of native wing bean (*Psophocarpus tetragonelobus*). Maize and runner beans, which have been introduced, are planted in new gardens and available chiefly in the first quarter of the year. Sweet potatoes are available during the whole year as is the introduced *taro konkon* which is widely planted and eaten. Other introduced foods (see note to Table 4) are planted by a few people but rarely eaten and in no special season. Pawpaw on the other hand is popular and planted for the refreshment of people working in the garden in the heat of the day.

In these various ways the seasons influence the supply of food but there is no recurring time of great shortage, and they do not appear to know famine. They sometimes lack enough food while on hunting expeditions; or lack ripe coconuts at home and starve themselves when ill. They forbid certain foods to infants which would improve their diet which lacks protein; and in general their diet is not well balanced by English standards. No one need starve. Usually they waste rather than conserve food; they throw away unfinished tubers, bananas that are part blemished or over ripe, a pawpaw if it has been pecked by birds, food that falls to the ground; sago uneaten at the end of a meal is given to pigs or thrown down the rubbish slope.

PATTERN OF THE DAY

The humid equatorial climate does not vary objectively very much during the year. People find the nights cold, particularly in the hours before dawn and the mornings with fog or rain and wind. They show signs of cold; their skins go goose-pimpled and they shiver. Convectional rain preceded by high winds sometimes occurs and is what they instance as most cold. On rare occasions a high wind and rain storm may be fierce and localized, causing broken branches, fallen trees which freakishly wreck a stretch of path in deep flat forest. On retiring at night almost invariably people make up a fire close beside which they sleep and they may wake two or three times in the night if cold to build it up or blow it into life. In a men's house with many beds in it, there are many small fires and much smoke. All the houses' doors are shut at night. Men always sleep raised above and beside the fire on beds made of the aligned hard and shining smooth midribs of sago leaves (P.E., *panggal*; Gnau, *brugetap*). Some women sleep on similar beds and some sleep on the ground on *limbum* – the broad leathery sheets of leaf bases from the *limbum* palm (Gnau, *biape*). They sleep beside a fire with their infant or toddler curled against them. Burns occur from men falling off the bed into the fire, or from women, and especially babies, rolling or being inadvertently pushed into the fire in sleep.

On rising in the early morning, women or girls go to fetch water and walk with a smouldering lump of wood held close to their chest to warm them. Men get up and go to sit beside their wives' cooking fires or else to sit under the roofed but open porch (*be'aipe*), or sit at the day-house (*warkao*) where they customarily sit at home. Here they make a fire while they wait to eat at some time between 7.30 and 8.30 a.m. If the sky is clouded over, they sit by the fire until the day is warm or on a clear morning people squat or sit dotted about the open places of the hamlet, their backs warming in the early sunbeams. They wait for the day to warm and then move off for work at between 8.30 and 9.30 a.m. This part of the morning is a time for chat, talking over any plans or going to talk with someone in another hamlet before he has gone off to the bush. They carry fire with them to the bush either as a slow smouldering lump of wood or preferably as fire creeper (*da'at lambet*) a dried forest liane about as thick as a garden hose pipe, which when lighted quietly smoulders along its length unless snuffed out intentionally. They work in the heat of the day; in gardens little sweat flies crowd on their backs. The pauses for rest are spent in shade or under the porch of a garden house. In the village, those who stay there taking the day off, or baby-minding sit, make things, doze in the shade of palm trees or porches or the day houses. The women return from sago working or the gardens from 4 o'clock onwards and before the men. Men and women usually wash at a pool on their way home; or if they have stayed in the village stroll off at about four for a wash before the sun goes down. Between 4.45 and 5 p.m. the kind of frog called *nundat* begins to pipe announcing the approach of evening. The women cook the evening meal. Men return to sit and chat. The sun lowers, the day cools. Between 6 and 7 p.m. people eat as the sun goes down. Late comers arrive just at dusk. After the evening meal they chew betel, smoke or chat by the fire until they go to bed. Most go off to sleep by about 8 or 9 o'clock taking with them a lighted dry bamboo flare or a burning log for the fire. Some frequently stay up until 10 or 11 o'clock to chat and this especially by bright moonlight; the children stay up as long as their mothers or fathers do, they scuffle, play or fall asleep while the grown-ups chat, then they have to be woken up and pulled up or carried off to bed.

Rain in the day often restricts people to where they are because they are reluctant to walk in it. If they are close to shelter when it begins to pour, they may run for it and I rarely saw adults, particularly men, run at any time. Rain can be heard approaching, a warning patter on the forest canopy growing louder and closer. Where there is neither the shelter of a village nor garden house, enough plantain or young palm leaves can often be cut in time and propped up to form a shelter or held for cover; or protection can be found among the huge buttressing flange roots of a *Ficus* tree. A storm may cut people off because a river, even a stream, has swollen wildly and they are cautious to cross it. Three Rauit villagers were drowned a few years ago by trying to cross a swollen river. Until the men learnt at plantations, they say none of them could swim: I have seen only young men and children swimming. Spearing fish while swimming under water with goggles is the prerogative of modern young men and boys.

VILLAGE

The third contrast is of village with bush, both garden and forest. The village seen from a distance is a line of coconut palms. These are not planted in gardens or forest. The village is on an eminence and the feathery crowns of palms seem to line continuously along its extent. The palms usually surround the hamlets so that clustered houses are not in danger from nuts falling on them. The ground where the houses are is worn or scraped bare. Bordering this are grassy places planted with coloured shrubs, scented or decorative herbs, *tulip* trees, *Ficus*, *taun*, and breadfruit trees. Right in the hamlets, or on their verges, bananas are planted sometimes as a grove, especially the *lyimungai* and some other varieties which are used in ritual and have special mention in myth.

Most houses are set on the ground despite instructions or suggestions by Administration officers that they should build houses on piles. Some people defend ground houses because they are warmer at night. Three traditional kinds of house were made: the men's ceremonial house (*gamaiyit*) which is tall and large compared to the others; a domestic house (*wunat*); a roofed day house (*warkao*) more or less open without walls – variable size. The *gamaiyit* in which men sleep is not open to women; it contains the slit-log gongs, hand drums and the decorated main post with face or body representations of a spirit or spirits. Formerly it was abundantly stocked with extra weapons and men slept with their shields on a rack over them.

There is no fixed orientation of houses, or formal pattern in their placing relative to each other, except that each hamlet had a men's house and its domestic and day houses were set within the hamlet ground. The men's house dominated other houses by size and height. In front of it was an open flat area of ground where they could dance. Three *gamaiying* built in the traditional style were destroyed during my stay. The current men's houses are built less tall and conspicuous and they are modified to have a square-ended overhanging porch. Instead of a single house for all hamlet men, hamlets now have a few rather ordinary looking houses to act as men's houses. The hamlet men are separated into smaller groups for sleeping. The domestic houses (*wunat*, pl. *wunangep*) are the wives' houses where they cook and sleep with their young children and daughters, or daughters-in-law. Only a son or husband would go through the door into a woman's house except for an exceptional reason. It is even unusual except during sickness, for other women to go inside another's house. Men keep valuable things in their wives' houses, their money locked in a red wood box (*paus*), feather and shell ornaments, formerly their shell valuables.

The domestic houses are sometimes set very close. The sharp ends of bamboo rafters are hidden by the thatch edges; someone who carelessly pushes under or past them may be deeply slashed. The domestic houses are not necessarily orientated towards the open space of ground in front of the *gamaiyit*. They usually cluster by lineage, for example, the wives of brothers and of sons. The day house of a lineage group of men is placed near the houses of their wives. Here if men gather they sit in the day or when visited and they usually eat here. The women either eat with their children beside their house, or sitting in a group on the ground in front of the *warkao* where the men are eating.

WATER

In the dry season, the pools which people use in or near the village may go dry, and women have to drudge carrying water from streams or springs which are in valleys, half an hour's climb in each direction. The usual water holes are excavated in declivities either in the hamlet or a few minutes' walk away. They are dug out expressly and are usually six to ten feet in diameter, straight-sided and about three to five feet deep. A few families, usually by lineage, share a water hole and for each hamlet there are now three or more water holes close by. Some people choose to dig separate holes to supply water for cooking or drinking; water to wash in, water to soak, mature and preserve sago flour in; but others will use one pool for all these purposes.

At Mandubil, there are two large pools in the middle of the village; at Rauit, the large water holes which were in the centre of hamlets have been filled in and are now dug at the periphery of hamlets.

To wash, people fill bamboos or other containers with water and pour it over their heads and themselves, bathing their whole body, rubbing the skin clean with their hands. They wash beside the pool and the water runs off them to the ground. They do not wash their feet or hands by dipping them directly in the pool, or washing the dirt off into it; they do not urinate into them, nor because of their steep sides do the dogs seem to drink from them or pigs to foul them. But the water is still and stagnant in the dry season. Some pools have weeds and slime in them and the water becomes more turbid, smelly and sour as the pool dries up. At Rauit one hamlet has a spring and a stream convenient for daily use.

In the gardens, someone working may drink water or eat pawpaw[1] or sugar cane, both of which are considered to refresh like water. These things with water, the milk of coconuts, are considered together to be cold as rain, and they may not be eaten after dark. This is a convention or rule which is formal like other food prohibitions and the consequences are specified as danger of illness by the cold of what is drunk.

But dangerous heat is the usual thermal element in illness: ideas of fever, of magical power, sorcery, snake poison, teeth of centipedes, hornet stings, burning destruction and fire are supporting images far more frequent and explicit in their account of the processes of illness than cold. Quite oppositely, the usual place of cold and water is as counter to illness, fever and mystical power. Cold and water are bold clear symbols for the intent and way of healing when the identified vehicle for attack in a sickness – often a plant – is uprooted, cut in pieces and thrown into water, especially into a flowing river to be made cold, inactive, to quench the patient's burning. The fear of illness from cold which is associated with the prohibition on drinking at night is contrary to the common pattern. They feel strongly enough about not drinking at night to refuse a gulp of water to help down a pill, on which instead they gag miserably.

1 Pawpaws are introduced fruits and they with water melons and tomatoes are classed among things essentially of water and cold. They say that when you eat them it is the same as eating water.

VILLAGE POPULATION

When I arrived in January 1968 the village contained 364 people. When I left in November 1969 there were 373 people. Between these dates there were 29 births (of which three were stillbirths) and 17 deaths. The composition of the village population is shown in Figure 8. The ages of people born before 1952 are guessed or estimated. After 1952, patrol officers recorded births and deaths,

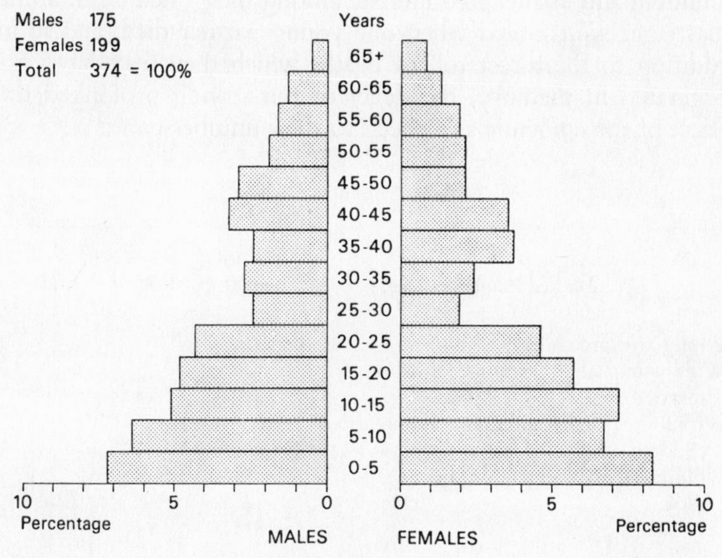

Fig. 8. Rauit village population

although their early records were incomplete. An earthquake in September 1935 (Marshall 1937), the visit of an oil-search surveyor, G. A. V. Stanley in 1936 and the War, 1942–5, provided some help in estimating ages. For recent births the child welfare and mission records provide some more accurate dates.

The shape of Figure 8 is a broad based pyramid, a form which reflects the high mortality of infants, and the greater risk there of dying in early or middle life compared to the risks in a country like England. From the data on a nearby population, some life expectancies were calculated by Sturt and Stanhope (1968): males at birth, 44·60 years; at 5 years, 47·79 years; females at birth, 40·64 years; at 5 years, 44·64 years. They found the masculinity ratio at birth to be 105/100. The disparity between Rauit males and females is not significant at the 5 per cent level for the numbers counted. The small size of the cohorts aged 25–29, and 30–34 is probably the result of an epidemic of dysentery in the late 1930s. A similar reduction has been noted by Dr Sturt in the population he surveyed (personal communication). According to what people recalled when they told me genealogies, about one-third of all the village's people then died in that epidemic. Children and infants predominate among their listed dead. Some marriages were ended when one young partner died, and so in addition to the direct toll of death, which they may have exaggerated in memory, the delay of remarrying prolonged the effect of the epidemic as a check to their numbers.

Table 5. Conjugal families

Married Adults	*Married couples*	*Widow*	*Widower*
Young with no child	12	—	—
With young children, none of whom yet married	40	2	2
With some married and some yet unmarried children	20	4	1
Children all grown up or dead	5	8	3
Childless	4	—	—
Total	81*	14	6

* There are 3 men with 2 living wives each, counted as 6 families: therefore there are 78 men and 81 women with living spouses; 14 widows and 6 widowers remain single.

The numbers of children or unmarried young people who have lost one or both parents is shown in Table 6.

Table 6. Orphans

	Male	*Female*
Full orphans	3	2
Fatherless	2	5
Motherless	10	6

DOMESTIC GROUPING

Family, domestic or dwelling group, and household are all terms involving problems of definition. In the tables above, I have shown the number of married couples and the numbers of those bereft of spouse or parent. There are no adults in the village who have not at some time married, except for 12 girls and 14 boys who have passed puberty only recently. The Gnau recognize marriage and parenthood in ways fairly similar to ours. A man acquires rights of exclusive sexual access to the woman he marries. Children born to her will be his children. He should be their only begetter; he is their father.[1] But members of a conjugal family do not eat together or sleep together. The wife's house where she cooks and sleeps with her daughters and small sons may not be in sight of the day-house where her husband eats in company with other men, or the men's house where he sleeps with his sons and brothers. The boys of the hamlet play around together in gangs. Where fathers are true brothers to each other, or closely related lineage kinsmen, some responsibilities for their children are jointly shared by the men and their wives: and men and women in a hamlet generally share some concern for the well-being and bringing-up of children of their hamlet. In garden work the conjugal family is clearly marked off. In village life, this smallest family unit can best be identified by observing which people a woman cooks for daily. In nearly all cases a

[1] If another man through adultery, is known to be the genitor of a child, he must indemnify the man who is married to the woman or be attacked and withstand his righteous anger. He may have to pay a large sum of wealth in compensation. In the only admitted case I recorded where a child was conceived in adultery, allowed to survive, and the couple had remained married despite the wife's adultery, the misbegotten daughter had two men as her 'father' using the lineal term *dakao* to both. It was said by the kin of the genitor that the compensation which he had paid (two-thirds of the standard bridewealth paid to the woman's husband) would give him and his descendants claim to half the eventual bridewealth given for the daughter. For the time being, she remained attached to her mother and therefore in the home of her mother and mother's husband, although sporadically the little girl ate and slept at the house of her genitor's mother who thereby kept it before the public that her son had some claim on the girl. Her son had meanwhile married; and become the proper husband of another woman and the father of a son. The peculiar jural position of this bastard daughter was hidden from strangers. The arrangement made to compensate the girl's mother's husband, and the survival of the child were unusual; they may reflect the changed circumstances in which infanticide is forbidden and violence with bloodshed liable to land one in gaol.

woman cooks regularly for herself, husband and unmarried children. She gives or sends food to her husband and he then may invite others to help him eat it: his wife does not just send food to swell a common pool at the men's house. Men must strictly abstain from eating food cooked by the wives of certain male kin; so when wives give food, they give it to their husbands directly to save confusion or mistake.

People commonly eat in groups composed of men and boys;[1] or of women, girls and small children. It is usual to see people sharing a leaf platter. Some actual examples of the variant family forms, arising from death, or change of spouse are shown by Figure 9.

Neither widows nor widowers necessarily seek to remarry. Remarriage of a widow is not automatic even though there will be no problem of bridewealth should a close male relative of her late husband marry her. If she had young children, her next husband would almost always explain that he married her to look after the interests of her children and care for them. In practice even if she does not marry again, her late husband's close male kin will feel strongly obliged to defend and maintain her children, to help her make gardens, plant them for her and her children. But those widows who have been strongest to resist men wanting to marry them, say they refused their suitors however importunate, for the very reason that they thought first of their children and feared for their sons' inheritance, that clear filial rights to their true father's gardens and trees might be obscured if a new husband assumed guardianship over them. In myths and stories – and I have heard it in real life – a dying husband may tell his wife to stay a widow and give herself up to caring for his children. If she obeys she will remain in his hamlet and his close male kin will provide such protection, food and male labour as she and her children need. They instruct and help her sons as the father would have done. If a widow married someone of another hamlet, she would take her first husband's young children with her. If they were boys, a conflict would later be likely between the boys' interest in their patrimony, their ties to their true father's male kin, and their affection or loyalty to their step-father who had cared for them and may have

[1] Some men quite often eat with wife and children but always from separate portions.

urged them to remain at his place. There were three recent examples of a widow with young children marrying into another

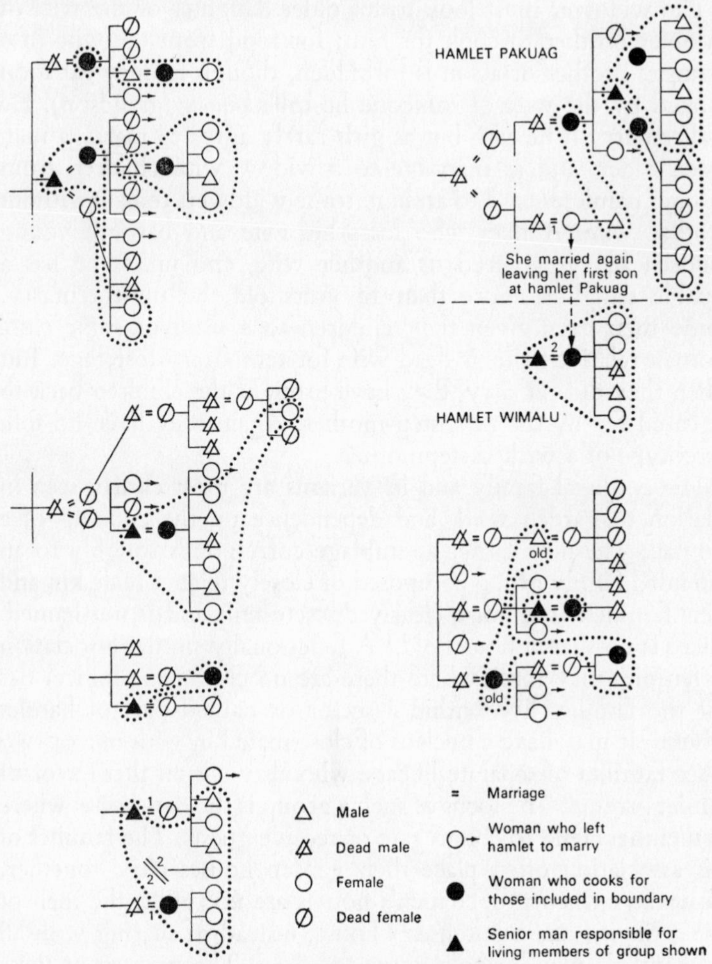

Fig. 9. Domestic groupings

hamlet. In one case only the son stayed attached to his step-father and half- or step-brothers; but he was descendant of an isolated lineage through a man who fled from Nembugil to Rauit two generations before and without other close kin. Fatherless children suffer little disadvantage; other male kin are ready and anxious to act as parents to them. Nothing suggested a stereotype of the wicked step-father.

The widower must look to his older daughter or the wife of an older brother to cook for him; for food from the wife of a younger brother or a son is forbidden, though he may eat food cooked by the wife of someone he calls *baluan* (grandson). He will remarry if he can, but as girls rarely agree to marry a man much older, and as marriage to a widow with children from another hamlet is hard to arrange, some widowers remain without another wife. A man who loses his wife and has still young children has great need of another wife, and unless he has a capable daughter more than 12 years old, he must remarry. Some men have given their children to a sister or some close woman relative of their dead wife for temporary fosterage. But when they did remarry, they have brought the children back to be cared for by the new step-mother. Again they have no folk stereotype of a wicked stepmother.

The conjugal family and its variants are most clearly seen in relation to garden work and dependence on the cooking of a woman. The next larger assemblage corresponds roughly to an extended family group composed of closely related male kin and their families. It is not a clearly discrete unit and is not named. There is no shared household.[1] A functionally similar association of families may form where there are no close genealogical ties but the families live within a sector or named part of hamlet ground. It may have a nucleus of close male kin with one or two other families of separate lineage who also live on that sector of hamlet ground. The focus of such a group is the day-house where its members tend to congregate or receive guests. The families of this association often place their garden houses close together. Nowadays when proper men's houses are not built, the men of this grouping share one men's house, instead of sharing with all the hamlet's men a single house for sleep. The women of these families associate with each other in sago working parties, preparing food for guests, and looking after each other's children. Such associations vary in how easy they are to distinguish at

[1] There is a rule which some follow that the wife of a second or more junior son shares the house of her mother-in-law. The wife of an eldest son should not share this house: she must have a separate house.

different hamlets. For example, a man may receive his guests from another village at a day-house he shares with a nucleus of brothers not of his lineage. But apart from special occasions, he would make his little fire and sit at a patch of ground under three coconut trees with his grown son and his family, where they have not bothered to make a day-house, although it is their special spot of ground close to the father's and the son's wives' houses and where they most often sit to take their ease.

The clearly separate active group above the conjugal family is made of all the hamlet's members, who have their houses within the hamlet area of ground and lead a close communal life. Their men hunt together, their womenfolk go fishing in parties, their children romp with each other and the hamlet people usually act in major ritual (i.e. those which are focussed on the men's house) as a unit. Previously men and youths would have slept at the same *gamaiyit*. Each hamlet celebrates its eating *wadagep* annually and independently as a hamlet celebration. The population sizes of the hamlets are closely similar (July 1969):

Hamlet		Population
Animbil		70
Watalu		70
Wimalu		73
Bi'ip		91
Pakuag	38	70[1]
Dagetasa	32	

The hamlet serves to demarcate a clear group of people; within it, the different sized smaller groups formed by conjugal families, extended families or associations of families can be distinguished less clearly. They have less explicit or less obvious identifying functions and the patterns of association are more variable, allowing for an interplay between ties of kinship, spatial position and friendship, according to context and occasion.

CONVIVIALITY

The occasions for people of different hamlets to gather and spend the day at leisure together are frequent and various. They are

[1] Dagetasa is a recent hamlet offshoot of Pakuag because the space there became too cramped. Some of the men whose wives or mothers live at Dagetasa sleep at Pakuag men's house.

common after the return of people from prolonged stays at the bush: especially at meals to celebrate the kills of pig or cassowary. They occur if someone is ill when, according to the severity of illness, people come repeatedly, or different hamlets come on different days. They occur at initiations of boys and girls, for events at which ritual takes place, such as breaking down a dilapidated men's house. If men foregather to discuss a marriage, to hear reports of council meetings, to discuss a dispute, they generally stay on and pass the day in chat. If a dog dies, there is a gathering to mourn it to which affinal or matrilateral kin come and those who come wear mourning clay (sometimes smeared around their mouths) in sign of their sorrow and gratitude for a dog which found much game that they received. Similarly there are gatherings to sympathize with those whose sons or brothers or husbands have left to work on a plantation or have been put in gaol; and for their return. The exchanges of meat/*wadagep* are also reasons to spend the day at leisure. Finally, however reluctant they have been to accept certain of the laws, customs and practices of Europeans, the institution of the weekend (Saturday and Sunday) has met with high approval. Women are even granted ease on Sunday morning – men and women forego the early morning meal, all eating at noon or in the afternoon and visiting in the village commonly takes place.

At all gatherings where men from different hamlets come together, it is usual for tubers, bananas or breadfruit to be cooked by men and eaten with scraped coconut soaked in its milk. The tubers (or bananas) are pounded into a mash mixed with the coconut. At ritual occasions, this is eaten by all, then the ritual takes place and is followed by a meal of sago jelly, leaves and meat. The more formal and feast-like the occasion, then the more exclusively does meat replace the ordinary daily leaf, *pitpit* and vegetable soup, which goes with sago.

The approval given to sharing food is evident in various ways: in the insisting of a latecomer to others who are already full up to come and help him eat; in the bantering and teasing remarks about eating alone, the act typical of selfishness and friendlessness; or the example of the evil wife, the one who refuses to provide food for her husband's friends. I asked people to describe an ugly man: after a catalogue of deformity, ills and sores, some would stress that such a man, foul-smelling and dirty, fungus covered and sore-ridden, is the man with whom no one will sit to eat, no one shares his food.

MEDICAL ASPECTS OF THEIR ENVIRONMENT AND ADAPTATION TO IT

Trauma and Injury

The forests do not present great natural hazards. One dangerous snake, the Papuan death adder (*Acanthopsis*) occurs there, and also in gardens. For people who spend so much time barefoot in bush garden and forest they are rarely bitten. During my stay two men said they were bitten while hunting by this snake – neither developed neurotoxic signs or serious localized reactions at the bitten site. Only one death by snake bite is recorded in their genealogies. Dr Sturt had nine admissions for snake bite, and two deaths from it in 426 recorded deaths. The dangers from wounded pigs on hunts are more serious and they usually check whether there is a tree nearby for escape when they station themselves on beats. They shoot at pig often from a range of only 3 to 5 yards. A lethal arrow shot traversing the pig's chest does not necessarily stop it charging; oblique arrow wounds, shots which hit but fail to kill are common and wild pig run with speed and tornado force. No one was savaged by a wild pig during my stay. Eight people on genealogies have died of savaging and many more have received bites or tusk wounds. Small mammals like bandicoots and rats bite particularly when people stamp on them to stop them escaping or put a hand in the hole to catch them. These bites fester. One man had the last joint of his middle finger bitten off by a lizard. Centipedes, hornets, black stinging flies or wasps occur and have painful bites or stings.

A risk involved in phalanger hunting is falling from trees. They take their great skill in climbing trees as a matter of course. In the forest with the hanging woody lianes, they rarely fail to find a way up, even though the big trees in forests may have no branches for the first 40 or 60 feet of their height. They change from a smaller tree into a larger tree high above the ground. For example during a hunt, someone happened to smell a cuscus and five young men took the nearest five tall trees which covered the area they thought it was in and each, by what seemed to me foolhardy daring, reached the big branches at about 70 feet above the ground on the off-chance of seeing where it was or cornering it – which they did not. They climb similar trees by moonlight and carrying a bow with arrows or an axe or a bushknife. During my stay one Mandubil man killed himself – he smashed his jaw and stove in his chest – by falling from a horizontal bough, standing at night to use two hands to strike at a bat while 40 feet or so above the ground. Rashness like that is rare. Women and children almost daily climb trees for leaves or fruit. Young men frequently climb in getting fruit, coconuts or hunting. Falls, considering this, are uncommon. The commonest tree to fall from, they say, is the *tulip* tree (*Gnetum gnemon*); this is probably because it is so often climbed but it is not tall; it has slender branches with the tender leaves at their extremities. During my stay I saw three Rauit people for bad falls from trees, none sustained fractures, but one had acute urinary retention following his fall. Two people in the village had had Colles' fractures of the wrist previously. I did not note other deformities suggestive of previous fractures. A man fractured his collar bone by a fall on to a boulder in the river in 1968. In the genealogies falls from trees and trees which fell or crushed people accounted for 11 deaths. Dr Sturt records 0·7 per cent of admissions with fractures.

Cuts, scratches and abrasions come from climbing and from forest walking. These are trivial for the most part, but they easily become infected and a proportion which would not lead to any trouble or concern in non-tropical climates, cause distress and pain because they fester. People are not clumsy or heedless in walking; indeed they are expert at avoiding spines and thorns, but they are continually exposed to minor injuries in their daily activities. The size or nature of the first injury may bear little relation to its outcome; no injury may have been noticed or remembered to explain the sore. Infected injuries become small sores. Some small sores become large and foul; some may be acutely inflamed with local swelling round the edges, itchy, hot, spreading and painful. The surface breaks down into pus and ulceration. Most of these ulcers would heal but after a period varying from a week to months or years. Large indolent ulcers were not common. This may well be a consequence of the hospital at Anguganak where previously many had gone to be treated for sores. Dr Sturt reports that 20 per cent of all his admissions there have been for tropical ulcer. This is the largest single cause of admission. But its incidence has dropped from 44·3 per cent in the first year of his records to 5·1 per cent in the ninth year. Dr Sturt suspects that the decrease is due to 'clearing up chronic cases (i.e. reservoirs of infection), prompter treatment of small sores and improvement in general health'.[1] He found that the overall admission rate for tropical ulcer was lowest in the months of December to February. He also found that the peak incidence for admission with tropical ulcer was 5–14 years of age.

At Rauit, two women had large and very chronic ulcers over the Achilles tendon. In both the underlying tendon had become fixed and shortened so that they walked on the ball of the foot, heel off the ground; in one of the women the changes were gross and the foot appeared adaptively deformed. No one else had an ulcer of even one year's standing. During my stay, I dressed sores and cuts and therefore I observed their incidence rather than the development and persistence of ulcers, although of course people sometimes failed to show me them until they had become eroded, pus-filled ulcers. There are mosquitoes, leeches, mites, various ants and biting flies which sting, puncture or irritate the skin. A shrub or tree (*Laportea* spp.) occurs in forest which stings and causes acute pain followed by itching and sores on a few people's skin, as does the most painful variety of nettle (?*Elatostemma* spp). Only some people are so susceptible as to come out in sores. Where insects or plants provoke itching or inflammation they add to the causes of skin infection found in the forest. Flies may spread the organisms particularly associated with tropical ulcer from one person to the cuts or sores of another. Village, rather than bush, flies buzz round and settle most persistently and annoyingly on sores.

The difficult paths are potentially dangerous for women who carry heavy loads of food and firewood. Women carry loads on their back tied on either side by a bark strap which loops up over the forehead. The weight of a heavy load (for example, one of 70 lb) is taken partly by her inclined back and partly by her head and neck as she walks bent forwards from her waist, eyes downcast. A sudden slip or fall, or the load caught in passing by a branch or creeper could jerk her head back or twist her neck sideways; the load will fall right off if her head is jerked back far

[1] The change in proportionate prevalence might also partly be because they now bring other complaints for treatment which before they did not choose to.

or if she falls backwards. So when walking with heavy loads, women usually hold the straps on either side at the back of their necks or clasp their hands at the back of the neck. They are watchful of obstacles; sure-footed and careful not to twist their necks but their bodies to look sideways or avoid an obstacle. Despite the strain and weight of the loads which they habitually carry, their necks are graceful and do not seem heavy muscled, nor did I find complaints of chronic or severe acute neck pain or stiffness, or signs suggesting cervical spine disease. In a few women the rubbing loads caused rough, almost shagreened skin on the back over the lumbar spine; and on many, sores.

The topography of where they live allied to the type of soil and rain thus demands agility, care and strong legs. When they speak of strength, of those like heroes in the past, of desired maturity, they speak of men or women with calves and thighs like tree-trunks. Conversely the first-mentioned attributes of a stunted man are his legs 'like bowel worms', or 'stick-like as the legs of pitta birds'. Illness and old age are alike in that they limit people to the village by weakness and shortness of breath. But despite the apparent rigours imposed by the shape of their land, what is surprising is that almost all of the grown people in a village of 370 were active and able to go to the gardens or on visits to distant bush sites. Even old men accompanied hunts in which the walking exhausted me, and old women carried loads up from gardens. Old people complained of aching backs or legs more than young people, and although a few old people were bent-backed (kyphotic) with the spinal changes of ageing, there were none with gross signs of osteoarthritis, none chronically crippled by hip or knee joint changes, none with gnarled and knotted hands, with Heberden's nodes. Acute joint injury, particularly of the knee, occurred after a stumble or twist while walking, and I saw a handful of men and women mostly in their forties with pain and effusion in a knee; two women came recurrently over two or three months. Dr Sturt found arthritis in 1·3 per cent of all his hospital cases, with 103 cases in the 15–44 age group (i.e. 2·1 per cent of admissions in this age group) and 46 cases accounting for 4·6 per cent of admissions in the 45 age group.

Breathlessness is feared in illness and old age, but only a few old people were clearly limited by it. Pregnant women and most of the old ably carried on daily garden work. A pregnant woman managed to keep up with our party of people walking for three hours over rough country at a usual pace and was delivered two hours afterwards of the first of her two 8 lb twins. Breathlessness which forced the subject to stay in the village was seen in acute chest infections and in two cases of heart failure. Apart from those with transient illness, there were two or three old women who were feeble, thin, poor sighted and walked slowly with bent backs; they rarely ventured away from their house or hamlet. One woman who was about 50 years old, still went to the gardens although she could walk only slowly and weakly because of motor neurone disease.[1] A more striking adaptation to deformity was seen in a married woman in her thirties, born with such severe club feet curled inwards that she had to walk on the outer dorsal not plantar surfaces of her feet; they had thickened into pads calloused as soles. She had difficulty in balancing and used a stick, but she managed to cope with her domestic duties (for a husband and one child), to prepare sago flour and to help with some garden work.

The slippery paths and steep slopes may seem to an outsider to be formidable for those who are disabled or aged but I noted few instances of decrepitude and I was more struck by activity preserved in the aged. The rugged terrain obliges people to carry infants and small children and so they are left behind in the village when their parents go to work in the gardens. Food prohibitions on pandanus fruit, leaf and spinach-like vegetables are lifted when the child in its third year is able to follow its parents to the gardens without being carried. Their reference to it marks it as a point in the development of the child and underlines to the observer its significance for them.[2]

Chest Infections, and Animal or Insect Borne Disease

A most serious cause of morbidity and mortality is infection of the lower respiratory tract, i.e. pneumonia and bronchitis. Dr Sturt has found it accounts for 36 per cent of all deaths in the

[1] It is possible that her neurological signs which were typical of motor neurone disease resulted from cervical spondylosis. I detected no sensory abnormalities: this would lend weight to a diagnosis of motor neurone disease.

[2] Also they alternatively say that these prohibitions, especially on pandanus fruit, are lifted when the child becomes able to go to the toilet by itself.

survey population and about 30 per cent of hospital admissions. The peak incidence for death from this cause was in infancy and old age; it accounted for 27 per cent of deaths in children under 12 months and 70 per cent of deaths in adults over 60. But he also found an almost linear relation between the age at death and the percentage of deaths from lower respiratory tract infection in both men and women between the ages of 25 and 60. Pneumonia was a major cause of serious illness and death amongst the people of the village where I worked; and indeed the same appears to be generally true throughout Papua-New Guinea. The factors which underlie this prevalence are at present uncertain. Dr Sturt has shown that there is no obvious relationship between season and death from pneumonia in this area and that pneumococci and *Haemophilus influenzae* are the most common pathogens to be isolated in respiratory infections. He has shown that the efficiency of people's lungs (tested by a Wright peak flow meter) falls significantly in 85 per cent of subjects after they have been exposed to the smoky atmosphere of their huts for 30 to 60 minutes. These are the huts in which they sleep. It is possible that their smoking habits also influence the efficiency of their lungs. The incidence of pneumonia rises in epidemics of influenza and measles; and dengue may possibly predispose to pneumonia. Dr Sturt also found evidence suggesting a high prevalence of chronic bronchitis (Sturt and Glasgow undated). All his findings are applicable to the village I studied, except that I found few men or women who could be considered to show clear evidence of chronic bronchitis if a habitual cough productive of much phlegm and an obvious reduced ability to climb up hills were to be accepted as criteria. I did not find any respiratory cripples of the emphysematous 'pink puffer' or the hypercapnic 'blue bloater' kinds, which are familiar to English doctors. What was most striking was the devastating and rapid effect of pneumonia in people who had before seemed active and vigorous; they developed high fever, were prostrated, feeble and tremulous. This occurred most noticeably in some men aged between 40 and 50. Men who smoked a lot often had a cough and some had adventitious sounds in their lungs on auscultation, but normally they did not expectorate sputum and were fit, to judge by their ability to walk strenuously. Of other chest diseases, tuberculosis was not found in the village where I was. Dr Sturt has admitted 31 with this diagnosis out of 13,000 patients. One woman in the village had recurrent attacks of asthma.

In early October 1968 a serious epidemic of influenza affected most people in the village and resulted in a number of cases of pneumonia. No one died in Rauit but a number of deaths occurred in surrounding villages. I discuss the social responses to the epidemic in Chapter 3. On three other occasions in two years a wave of colds or influenza passed through the village. The other illnesses which came as clusters of cases (10–30 people affected) were a mild conjunctivitis,[1] another illness presumably caused by a virus, in which some had fever, headache, general malaise, others had fever, malaise, colic and diarrhoea.

Rauit village:		Epidemic or clustered cases of illness
1968	February	Colds
	March	Conjunctivitis
	April	Influenza
	May	Anthrax in village pigs
	August	Conjunctivitis
	Sept.–October	Influenza
1969	February	Conjunctivitis
	April	Malaise, fever, and in some colic and diarrhoea
	June	Colds

No epidemics of measles, chicken pox or whooping cough occurred during my stay, although epidemics of measles and chicken pox were seen by Dr Sturt at the hospital in 1968. In nine years he has noted 18 epidemics (3 each of diarrhoea, influenza, conjunctivitis and chicken pox; 2 each of measles and whooping cough; 1 each of mumps and meningitis).

It is worth noting that the idea of infection may coexist with a cultural explanation in terms of a spirit which strikes down individuals. The devastating pre-War epidemic of dysentery was attributed to the spirit Taklei, which is also the spirit causing pig

[1] Trachoma is found in the Lumi Sub-district. I did not look specially for it. I did not see anyone with serious complications of trachoma involving the eyelids. Three old people had poor sight and corneal opacities, but I did not note corneal scarring or pannus on ophthalmoscopy.

anthrax. In their traditions, one of the ancient villages was abandoned because Taklei struck people down with a killing disease of skin sores. (Could this have been smallpox?) When the other epidemic, this time of dysentery, occurred, they recalled Taklei to explain the new epidemic. Thus Taklei would seem to be a spirit causing epidemics: Taklei (in some myths in company with his elder brother) chooses between men or village pigs; if village pigs die it is because he spared men, or was prevailed upon by his elder brother to accept village pigs instead of men. If he chooses to kill men then the wild pigs die with them and the village pigs survive. But as well as having this well-defined theory, people recognize that a sick pig may infect a healthy one and some take care to keep them separated.[1] At the time of the dysentery epidemic, it was recognized that close contact between patients and their families was dangerous for the uninfected and there are pathetic stories of fathers who told their children to abandon them lest they should catch the illness. In fact the idea of a spirit causing illness by jumping from one person to another is common; but this was not the phrasing of infection during the epidemic – it was in terms of sleeping in the same house, of physical contact and eating together. The spirit of Taklei is likened to a wind and is sometimes to be heard sighing and rustling the fronds of palms in the village.

Contagion as a reason for disease is evident to them in the skin disease caused by the fungus, *Tinea imbricata*, and in scabies. *T. imbricata* produces a grey scaling of skin (Pidgin, *grile*; Gnau, *warape*) which can spread over almost all the body in some people and may persist throughout their lives. The clear-skinned infant or child of a mother with *grile* more often develops the fungus than the children of unblemished parents. If neither parent has the condition, people will frequently indicate a playmate, nursemaid or close relative with *grile* from whom the child caught it. Until the age of 1½–2 years when the child can walk more steadily, it is being held nearly all night and day against someone's skin, most often the mother's or an elder sibling's. They use no cradles, and

[1] Epidemics of anthrax happen at intervals of a few years. The meat of diseased pigs is butchered and eaten but no cases of human anthrax have been found in this area by Dr Sturt – although he mentioned that a veterinary expert was infected when he did a post mortem examination on one of the pigs. The absence of human anthrax observed in the local population is curious and unaccounted for.

netbags are not made to hang babies up out of the way; but babies are hardly ever just dumped down on the ground, on a leaf or a bed to sleep, they are held, sat, curled or cradled against someone's arm, skin, back or hip. The first patches of *grile* usually begin before the age of 2 years. If a child does not have any patch of it by that age it is unlikely to develop *grile* later on. Despite close contact, children do not inevitably contract it. Some with it have only a patch which does not spread widely; such patches may appear later on than early childhood and may respond to treatment. *Grile* is thought ugly. It may last a lifetime, although in old people it looks burnt out, leaving dry, greyish skin without such scaliness as there was before. Formerly they had concoctions to rub on the skin to try to get rid of it: one woman is still nicknamed after her extensive *grile* which she rid herself of. A few younger men have lost it by *grile* lotion treatment at plantation. But as Schofield and Jeffrey (1963) showed, it commonly recurs after successful treatment when the New Guinea patient returns home or stops treatment. Their other common skin funguses (*T. circinata*, *T. pedis*, *Pityriasis versicolor*) are not so damaging to appearance, nor so persistent; some people have them and then lose them. They use a variety of mixed and specific herbs, tobacco juice, flying fox fat, marsupial smell glands, betel nut spitting to do so; and now use *grile* lotion. They are ready to spend money on the lotion because of the unsightliness of skin fungus.

Scabies (Pidgin, *Kaskas* – they say it is an introduced pest and call it by its Pidgin name, for it has no name in Gnau) clearly spreads by contact, especially among children and to parents who sleep bundled with their children. A child with the itch commonly infects his family. Children sprawl over each other,[1] sit against each other or their mothers. Men gathered for some meeting easily crowd and squash up without any finicky concern to preserve a distance between their skins. So scabies probably must spread. People do not share blankets or clothing. Some with it neglected to ask for treatment, waiting until they had widespread infected sores. Even then some never bothered, and the outcome in these cases was that the lesions disappeared without treatment, although the healing period varied, some lasting nine months.

[1] *Molluscum contagiosum* was seen on about five children in the toddler age group.

Most eventually followed someone's suggestion that they come to get benzyl benzoate lotion.

The other common ectoparasite is the head louse (Gnau, *mekutap*) which noticeably occurred in children. Infestation may be associated with a seborrhoeic dermatitis and secondary infection of the scalp, a filthy clotted exudate in the hair. The effective treatment they use is to shave the head. This exudative scalp condition was not seen in any except pre-adolescent children, mostly toddlers. By convention, children, girls and women nit and delouse each other while at leisure, and have head lice: men do not. Head lice seemed largely confined to the young: few men or women have them.

The other contagious diseases affecting skin to mention are leprosy and yaws. Leprosy appears to occur in the area as a consequence of outside plantation contact. It has spread recently in two nearby villages studied by Dr Sturt. One case was detected in Rauit, and three in Mandubil; they were undergoing treatment at Anguganak. Yaws was endemic,[1] but a thorough treatment campaign took place in 1960, although three cases were found in Rauit children in 1962. No cases were seen during my stay. Six people had what looked like collapse of the bridge of the nose.[2] This could have been the result of yaws, but no other deformities of bone skin or sole were seen suggesting tertiary yaws.

Mosquitoes are responsible for transmitting three of their endemic diseases; malaria, filariasis and dengue. The mosquitoes are not particularly troublesome at the height of the village (1700 feet above sea level). It is usually easy to sleep there without a net. There are, to be sure, almost always occasional mosquitoes to bite you in the night but you are not plagued. People assert that the mosquitoes mass and multiply as the moon waxes to the full. Often you hear them say this when they have been staying in the lower lying bush where the mosquitoes hum in large numbers and bite persistently. Malaria is the most serious endemic illness. It is uncontrolled, they have constantly repeated infection and

[1] Oddly they seemed to lack a specific term for the skin lesions of yaws: one name *wiyasiti* is applied to a large sore with heaped centre and pus, but no sore worthy of this name occurred while I was there – it was always, they said, a rare kind of sore to have.

[2] No stigmata of congenital syphilis and no syphilis were recorded – possibly because they are still largely protected by the relative immunity to syphilis which comes from yaws infection.

the population has a high degree of immunity. To judge by adult spleens and the almost inevitably palpable spleens of children, malaria is holoendemic there (cf. Schofield 1962 and Peters 1960, for Wam Wingei and Maprik areas nearby). Both *Plasmodium vivax* and *P. falciparum* malaria are common. Dr Sturt finds 80 per cent of positive blood films show *P. falciparum* and that malaria accounts for 44 per cent of deaths in children under 14 years; cerebral and algid forms of malaria are quite common. The first infections occurred in village children as young as 6 weeks old; but most clinical attacks were seen in children of 9 months to 4 years. By this later age most seem to have built up some immunity and clinical attacks become unusual; as they are in adults. In the critical time between 6 and 36 months old most children are not only malnourished, but also repeatedly infected by malaria.

Filariasis was diagnosed in a few villagers with fever, enlarged tender glands or lymphangitis. The microfilariae can be found in the day. Two men in the village also developed large hydrocoeles, one with orchitis: in both cases the hydrocoeles resolved spontaneously. There was no elephantiasis seen. The Gnau people say gross enlarged scrota more commonly occur in men who live south of them: I did notice a number of men with hydrocoeles on visits to these south-lying villages and also one man with thick legs suggesting elephantiasis. Dr Sturt has noted that microfilariae are demonstrated in the blood of about half his cases of deep muscle abscess: the deep abscess and filariasis may be related. I did not diagnose dengue: although Dr Sturt notes that 'every dry season there is a spate of P.U.O.'s which I interpret as dengue fever' (Sturt undated, p. 4).

Sanitation

The water holes are suited well to the spread of water-borne disease. In the late 1930s a severe epidemic of dysentery killed many people in villages of this area. Few of those in Rauit then escaped bloody diarrhoea. One hundred and sixty people named on genealogies are said to have died in that epidemic. The disease was presumably bacillary dysentery. If we suppose that the population of the village was what it now is – the village has not recently extended its limits – then almost half its members died. It is possible that they exaggerate the numbers by mistakenly ascribing the deaths of some, for example small children, to dysentery, but it was clearly devastating. The reduced size of the cohorts now aged 25–29 and 30–34 in the population pyramid (Figure 8), which Dr Sturt has also found in the population which he surveys, are presumably effects of this epidemic.

But epidemics of dysentery are not said to have occurred since then in the Gnau villages. Dr Sturt found diarrhoeal diseases to account for 5·1 per cent of hospital admissions and 59 per cent of these were in children under 4 years old. I did not hear of people with symptoms suggesting infective hepatitis, although the disease occurs in the Lumi Sub-district. Amoebiasis occurs but, according to Dr Sturt, is rare. The amoeba was present in the Rauit population, but during my stay did not present clinically as abscess or dysentery.

Among other reasons, faecal contamination may occur because people have insanitary habits and because of flies. Until the Gnau people were instructed by Government officials how to dig and use pit latrines – and then they were ordered to do so – it was customary for men and women to squat and defaecate on to the ground from a horizontal log perch on a felled tree trunk. The log perches (*balapibi*) were not far from the house but usually discretely downhill. Those for men and women were separate and each lineage had usually its own men's and its own women's perches. People now recall how these places stank, the blow flies, and spitting as they left to clear the foul smell from their mouths. The pigs also scavenged there. Most people now use pit latrines but a few of the traditionally minded quietly keep to a log perch. The others however preserve something of custom by building segregated latrines shared by only a few men, or a few wives or women of one lineage. The faeces of children are disposed of with care. Until the child is old enough to go to the toilet by himself, whoever is looking after him, most usually the mother, is called to come and clear up any mess he makes. It is rare for any one to do it for her, but it is common for someone to send a child to say or shout out that a child has made a mess at the other end of the hamlet – or further – for the mother to come and clear it up. The faeces of infants and toddlers must not be left for dogs or pigs to eat; they must be thrown down the steep rubbish slope named *talyipe*, where ashes, food refuse, sweepings are thrown. They can not be put in latrines, just as formerly they could not be thrown away at the parental perch lest the child fall ill with fever[1] from his faeces being covered over by those of adults. In warm moist conditions where as here, faeces can contaminate the soil, we would expect the possibility of hookworm infection. Many or most people are infected, but the worm loads appear to be moderate or small, insufficient to provoke clinical symptoms. Severe clinical anaemia was detected in few people. In Dr Sturt's 13,000 hospital cases, ancylostomiasis was the cause of admission in 0·3 per cent, anaemia in 0·8 per cent.

Despite what may seem insanitary to an observer in their arrangements, they are fastidious people in many ways. They hate to mire their feet, they like to wash daily, and food that falls to the ground is thrown away and not dusted, scraped and eaten. Daily they sweep their houses clean, and ashes and litter left by a gathering. They keep waste baskets of *limbum* in the day-houses for people to dispose of mess or chewed betel nut. They refuse to eat village mice and rats which are muck eaters and unclean; they will only pick them up with bamboo tongs or hold them at arm's length in fingertips with a protecting leaf.

In regard to chances for faecal contamination, I must note that they do not use their hands to clean themselves after defaecation. They wipe their bottoms by sliding the cleft against a tree or plantain stem. The specific Gnau verb for this is *nita'ambel*,[2] and although infants and toddlers have their bottoms wiped with excellent soft leaves of certain trees, adults say they do not use leaves but only the sliding method.

Some points remain about their water and drinking habits which are relevant to health. The first is that they do not drink water with meals and it is quite unusual to see them drink it in the

[1] This fear is mentioned by women to justify their reluctance to go down with an underweight child to the hospital for supplementary and supervized feeding. If the child goes to hospital, his excreta will be thrown into a common latrine there, and so they fear he will sicken.

[2] The myth of Marusi describes the relief of a monstrous person, an eater of uncooked food who had no anus – instead shaking faeces from the hands and legs. Marusi was cut an anus by trickery, on rubbing down against a plantain stem where a sharp sliver of stone had cunningly been set. The fine shell ring, a *wilagi*, with which Marusi repaid this great service is held by a family in Rauit. Rather similar myths have been recorded from the Mountain Arapesh (Fortune 1942, myth XLVII; also Mead (1949) part V, The Cassowary Wife), and the Mount Hagen Sub-district (Strathern 1970, p. 575) but these myths describe how a woman acquired a vagina.

village. They will drink cold water during hard garden work when the sun beats on their backs and they sweat. They drink occasionally from streams, springs or small natural pools when travelling but their ability to pass a day in hunting, in which they covered many miles of broken country, or to journey all day to a distant bush site without once drinking was usual, notable and intolerable to the thirsting anthropologist who sometimes accompanied them. Rather they would refresh their parched mouths by chewing betel which provokes a flow of saliva. Although they sweat less obviously than those not native to the place, they sweat. I did not make systematic observations on this. Despite sweating with exertion but drinking little, they do not show clinical signs of dehydration, exhaustion or disturbances of body salt and water balance. Stone formation in kidneys causing severe pain or kidney damage was not diagnosed or reported. Of Dr Sturt's 13,000 cases, some disorder of the urinary system was found in 36 and whether from renal stone was not specified.

They may drink little water, but they eat sago jelly in large quantities. The jelly is made by swirling boiling water into sago flour and turning or rocking it until the mixture gells. An individual consumes as sago jelly about two pints of water in the morning and again in the evening; and he also drinks the water or soup which comes with the vegetables. This would seem to explain why they do not need to drink more water. Also we may note that most water they drink is first boiled, which conceivably preserves them from some illness.

Nutrition

As can be seen from Figure 7 showing hunting activities, the duties associated with ritual for stages of the individual's life, the exchange obligations and annual ceremonies all act as spurs to co-ordinate hunting. The opportunity to hunt in south-lying bush provides the Gnau people with more protein than many of their northern neighbours. The physique of most adults is well-muscled and robust-looking, although only a few young women appear to have surplus fat. In comparison to their northern neighbours, one notes a small number of relatively taller men, some reaching between 5 ft 8 ins and 5 ft 10 ins. No clinical signs of vitamin deficiency were noted in adults. I have earlier indicated the variety of their foods: vegetable protein, particularly from *pitpit* and leaves, probably makes an important contribution to their diet. Fountain at Wulukum village found on measurement that sago contributed about two-thirds of the total weight of food consumed, greens provided a further one-sixth; roots, game meat, fruit and nuts the remaining one-sixth. He estimated that an average of 2·35 lb of dried sago flour was eaten per day by an average adult. The Gnau people probably eat a bit more meat and more tubers than the Wulukum people who have less opportunity to hunt and also devote more of their land to rice growing with a relative diminution in the amount of traditional yam and taro cultivation. The general pattern is probably similar. The frequency of felling sago palms by Rauit families (about two large palms over three months per nuclear family – e.g. two adults and two or three children) is similar to Fountain's carefully measured findings.

There would be little profit in my speculating on how adequate their nutrition is as I did not take measurements of their intake. However, I have noted that starvation does not occur except sometimes in illness where it is imposed by custom, as described in Chapter 4. In general, people behave as though they had more than enough food. Daily food, sago and vegetables, is given and taken without strict accounting: it is a duty to load food on visitors. One's relatives may casually take food (except for *wadagep*) from one's gardens: no man is so close to marginal subsistence that he must be parsimonious of his garden food or require return for it; it is, as they say, *nem gipi'im* – something nothing. But they should mention they have taken it to avoid suspicion against others of theft.

Despite this apparent plenty they are malnourished. Among other things, this is suggested by the late onset of puberty. The weights of infants are for the most part well below the tenth percentile of American standards, as can be seen in Figure 10. This scatter diagram was prepared from measurements at Rauit made by Child Welfare nurses from Anguganak Mission Hospital who usually visit the village once a month. But the attendance of mothers is irregular, and the precise dates of birth cannot be known with great certainty, although it is likely they are usually put in the right month. I have included all the measurements recorded where a birth date was given. The table shows a general trend deflecting further below the tenth percentile from about the sixth month onwards. The reason for their unsatisfactory progress is not so much that food is lacking but rather that the most suitable foods are forbidden them according to customary prohibitions,

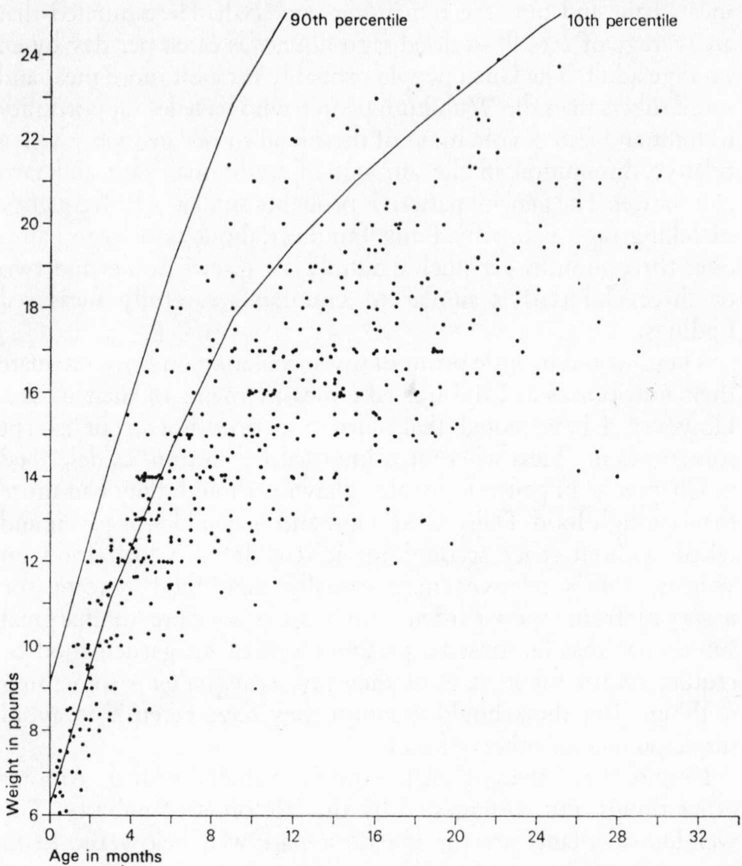

Fig. 10. Weights of Rauit infants

and the harm to their progress occasioned by exposure to malaria must also be remembered. The permitted order of introduction to new foods is shown in Table 7.

The rules are most strictly observed for first children and for these children the delay in widening the range of their diet may be longer. In the period between 6 months and about 2 years of age, which should be one of rapid growth, the children are particularly deprived of protein, iron and other nutrients. They depend on their mother's milk too exclusively and too long without other dietary supplements. Dr Sturt has admitted a few cases of scurvy to hospital in this age group. I did not observe kwashiorkor, marasmus or the gross skin changes of protein-calorie malnutrition. Soft straight hair with abnormal pigmentation (a reddish or yellow colouring that the Gnau call *gamani'it*) occurs in some children up to the age of 3 or 4 years. The hair,

Table. 7. Order of permitted introduction of food to infants

Food	*Indication of development*	*Approx. age*
Breast milk		From birth
Plain sago jelly	Sits, or first teeth	6 months
Water, coconut milk, coconut	Beginning to stand	10 months
Breadfruit (*genanget*)	First steps	14 months
Breadfruit (*ginati*), bananas, *pitpit*	Walks	16 months
Wadagep (all edible tubers), beans, meat	Talks, uses a few simple words correctly	2 years
Leaves of *tulip* tree, *opa*, Pandanus fruit	Walks well, beginning to walk on paths to gardens, can go to toilet independently	In third year

however, is not easily plucked out. Beriberi, rickets and vitamin A deficiency were not found. They can achieve an adequate diet only by eating a large bulk of vegetable foods: in toddlers a big protruberant belly is usual. This may partly be attributed to diet, partly to an enlarged spleen caused by repeated attacks of malaria. Throughout life most people's bellies appear rather round and domed by our standards.

When at about 2 years, they are allowed to eat meat, and starchy tubers, their diet improves and they are given many titbits. Little children play together in the day catching crickets, butterflies, grasshoppers and lizards round the hamlet which they roast on fires and share out. The older boys spend much time at hides to shoot birds, which by the rules against eating one's own kill, are usually cooked and shared among smaller children and sisters and provide frequent, sporadic morsels of protein apart from the less common occasions at which they, with adults, eat meat. I have commented on the disadvantages of dietary taboos for the infants and young children. It is inappropriate to try to explain taboos by their hygienic advantages but I would note that the taboos on wild pig (and cassowary) which are imposed on all men as soon as they have proved their skill in hunting (usually by about the age of 35 years), have the effect of distributing much of the best meat to the young and women. They consider meat to be essential for successful growth; their conception of its virtues in this respect was mentioned in regard to matrilateral duties in exchange. The bulk of the meat which men hunt tends to be smoked, kept and eaten at gatherings, and especially in feasting, rather than eaten as a regular part of daily meals. At such gatherings or feasts, the guests are given much food, and they often wrap up some of the meat to take home. A point of interest for their calcium intake is that they crunch and swallow the bones of most birds, fish, frogs, lizards and the smaller bones of animals.

The process of smoking game allows them to keep larger parts of meat for periods of up to three months. It is kept in a large round rattan basket hung over the wife's cooking fire-place in her house. The viscera of large animals must be removed and quickly eaten, small animals are gutted and the guts thrown away. The process of smoking appears to be effective and relatively safe as a preservative. On two occasions during my stay, a girl fell ill with abdominal pain. In one girl aged 5 years, an initial bloody diarrhoea was followed by ileus, constipation and a fortunate recovery after five days on medical treatment; in the other, aged 7 years, a sudden onset of colic and bloody diarrhoea was accompanied by prostration without fever, and she died within ten hours. Both these girls had eaten recently killed unsmoked village pig a few days before: a likely diagnosis in both cases was the necrotizing enteritis described mainly from the New Guinea highlands called *pig-bel* and caused by *Clostridium perfringens*. Otherwise there was little evidence to suggest food poisoning by decay and bacterial growth. Most food is cooked by boiling and sago is mixed with boiling water. Smoked meat is recooked and boiled before eating.

Apart from meat, the main food which is stored, rather than left in the ground or on a tree until eaten, is sago. When prepared from a large palm in quantity it can be stored for weeks by being left to soak in bamboo tubes at water holes: it seems to sour or ferment slightly – the sour smell is characteristic as you pass by the pools – and the stored sago, which is stuffed and impacted tight in the tubes, produces a denser opaque greyish-white (*gasinde*) jelly, which most people prefer to the pink yellowish rather translucent (*gangase*) jelly made with fresh sago flour. A housewife does not usually keep a provision of vegetable food at home. She must go to find leaves daily (many of the leaf providing trees are planted round the hamlet). She or her husband must go specially to dig up tubers if they want them. *Xanthosoma* taro has the advantage of keeping in the ground for longer than traditional tubers which, if overlooked, soon rot in the ground. At any gathering, the wives of the hosts have to work hard, going to fetch necessary or extra food in the morning and cooking it by the afternoon. Perhaps the most-quoted virtue in a wife is cheerful willingness to provide plenty of food for her husband's friends.

In eating, chewing, biting through vines or tough meat, crunching bones, people put their teeth to hard use and their teeth are good. A survey of all the villagers by a dentist (Mr F. Goldschmid) revealed very few cases of active dental caries. The few cases occurred in children and in some older women; teeth with arrested decay were also found in men. Some people had broken a tooth. Possibly the habit of chewing betel nut with lime may be a factor in preserving teeth from decay. It was formerly the rule that women and children could chew betel nut, but not with lime.[1] Many older women follow this rule still but it has effectively been given up by most younger women and young men, who also were forbidden the habitual use of lime until they had proved their hunting abilities. Like tobacco, betel nut and lime were controlled and mainly used by senior men. The rule foundered after men went to plantations where, away from the surveillance of their elders, they learnt new habits which have stuck.

The enjoyment of lime with betel nut and of tobacco were achieved after a man[2] had proved his hunting ability and under-

[1] They were allowed to chew it with the alkaline ash which is their native 'salt' – *nawugep*.

[2] Old women after they had grandchildren and had discarded their skirt in sign of age, were allowed to smoke.

gone the ritual for tabooing wild pig at which he learnt the full spells of hunting magic and was cut along the wrist. Chewing betel nut and smoking are relaxing pleasures or luxuries in their daily life: children and women now expect to be given their smaller share where before they received the occasional smoke or betel nut with a dash of lime as a treat rather than an allowance. At almost any gathering, bringing out areca nut or a tobacco tin provokes some clamour of demand and outstretched hands, for at least between men of roughly equal standing or within the circle of friends or the family such loud imperative requests are customary.

3
The Incidence and Prevalence of Illness

The environmental setting in which the Gnau live, and many aspects of their adaption to it, can be seen to have some bearing on the occurrence of disease. Their diet and subjection to malaria might claim our first notice if we were asked to name what things restrict or damage the general well-being of the people. The Gnau do not share our views on the causes of illness and some of the factors I referred to in the last chapter would not seem to them relevant. Even in those cases where they, as we, do consider that health might be damaged by something in the environment, or by something they might do, their interpretations of the dangers are often different from ours. Some rules, for example, concerning the use of food, or the disposal of faeces, are phrased with regard to risks of illness, but the risks they indicate are not the ones apparent to a nutritionist, or a sanitation inspector. The Gnau explanation of illness will be the subject of Chapters 5 and 6. In this one I present the data obtained on patterns of illness, a record of the incidence and prevalence of illnesses which, either acutely or by some marked alteration, interrupted the usual progress of people's lives. Although this account may be interesting to the epidemiologist because it comes from a kind of community rarely studied in this detail, it is chiefly given for other reasons.

The independent medical assessment of their sicknesses makes it possible to indicate what burden or severity of misfortune they respond to. The medical nature of an illness and the social response to it are interrelated. Without knowing the medical condition, it must remain partly uncertain which aspects of response have social or cultural roots rather than follow directly from the changes induced by disease. My present aim then is to make clear what medical conditions I observed so that they may later be matched against the responses to them. The account in this chapter takes the observer's viewpoint and attempts to define objectively the amount and severity of their illnesses. In the three following chapters I analyse their view of health and their explanations for illness. After these chapters I will return to the particular cases whose practical management and explanation I was able to witness. The total record of cases described in this chapter will be used in an analysis of how the Gnau applied their general theories about illness to these particular cases.

I tried to make a consistent and full record of illness over the extended period of my fieldwork, although it has certain limitations as I will indicate below. The anthropological value of the record is partly that a reasonably full account of the burden of illness was obtained, and it is partly that a 'universe' of misfortune was defined on external grounds and for this same 'universe' I am able to examine which theories they turned to for explanation and the choice of treatment, and thus to tell more precisely the conditions for applying them.

THE RECORDING METHODS USED AND THEIR LIMITATIONS

I remained based in the village between January 1968 and November 1969, although I was absent from it for a total of just over two months during this period. Throughout this time I recorded all illness that came to my notice, except for some transient fevers in infants and young children, minor sores and injuries, surface cuts and skin infections, vague aches in limbs or back, headaches, conjunctivitis and colds. However a number of cases of the above ailments appear in the general count of illness during my stay because they were severe or they interested me by the explanation or behaviour that was associated with individual cases. In these respects the figures which follow will underestimate the amount of these indispositions: all of them were not necessarily trivial since some of the passing fevers in infants were clinically malaria and I treated them as such. Between July and October 1969, I recorded all ailments, *including* the trivial ones mentioned above, to show the background of minor troubles which were not consistently recorded in the overall figures which follow. The other figures, referred to as the overall ones, do not include the trivial ills – apart from the exceptions I have mentioned – nor do they include the illnesses which occurred during an epidemic of influenza in October 1968, apart from six cases of pneumonia and four of severe bronchitis which occurred during it.

The adequacy of recording varied during my stay since my knowledge of the people and their language increased gradually just as did their familiarity with me and their wish or readiness to tell me when someone was ill. I depended on requests for attention, news and gossip to hear if someone was sick, if I did not chance upon them when going round the village. Those who were ill did not necessarily ask me to treat them, and it was customary for them to retreat from public gaze when ill. As the social patterning of behaviour in illness, the motives and expectations involved, require extended discussion, I only mention them here for their bearing on the collection of the data and I have reserved the analysis of their behaviour for the next chapter. The longer an illness lasted, or the more severe it was, the more likely I heard of it or saw the patient. Their views on what was appropriate to do also affected how quickly they told me about someone's illness (e.g. infants were readily brought for treatment; people liked to rub themselves with a strong-smelling turpentine liniment for aches or swellings, so they came to me for it if that was what troubled them).

In the latter part of this chapter I analyse the hamlet patterns in my records to show their inconsistencies. But some of the difficulties of making a consistent and complete record may be highlighted by an account of what happened in an epidemic of influenza which occurred at the beginning of October 1968. The circumstances were exceptional.

The epidemic spread from villages lying to the north and news came of the general illness and of deaths, the *garamuts* of other villages beating out the announcement of death. The first cases in Rauit occurred on 25 September, most between 27 September and 10 October. Many people had four or five days of fever, nasal congestion, headache, general malaise and aches, sore throats and an irritating cough; six people developed pneumonia (of whom three might have died without antibiotic treatment); four people had exacerbations of bronchitis which required treatment with antibiotics; between thirty and thirty-five people complained of transient painless, mostly unilateral, deafness which to otoscopy showed an inflamed ear drum.[1] A few of the first people affected by the influenza came to see me and were given cough linctus and aspirin: some of them offered particular explanations of why they were ill, but as more people came down with it, most accepted that it was a general malady for which they needed to give no special explanation to account for why they had it. It was like a wind passing through the village, they said. The usual course of the illness was understood and expected. The hamlets were littered with apathetic or miserable, supine bodies; people waiting to feel better. So many were affected that the daily fetching of food and water was a small problem for a time – but those who felt all right were able, with the sturdy help of children, to sort it out.

By 1 October, about twelve people had actually come to see me in search of treatment. On 2 October I visited every family. Out of 377 people in the village on that day, 206 had or had just got over symptoms of the illness. In the context of an epidemic, to go round, ask for symptoms and examine people whom I saw anyway, was more feasible than it would have been as a regularly repeated procedure for identifying all kinds of illness. The reasons for this are that healthy Gnau people, when asked out of the blue if they have been ill, tend to deny illness as they are proud to be well. In a slight way they are upset, anxious or put out of countenance if they have to admit to illness. The question is a difficult one to ask without suggesting that they look as though they should be or have been ill. To ask it repeatedly would either lead to annoying them or to their regarding it as a foolish or vacuous inquiry since if one lives with them, one should know the answer and therefore the question would not seem to many of them worth a careful answer. At one stage in my study, I tried systematically to find out past medical histories from well people and I found I got little useful information. The small number of people who actually came for treatment reflects the special circumstances of an influenza epidemic in which the brief though unpleasant illness has an expected course. The fact that many others were also sufferers removed for most people the

[1] I began by treating the first few of these deaf people with antibiotics but as almost none came for or took their medicine regularly, I gave no antibiotic treatment to the remaining 25 of these cases, and in all the deafness disappeared spontaneously within about five days and without complications.

anxiety to account for why one was singled out for illness. The treatment I offered was usually accepted although it made only a short-lived difference to how they felt; subsequently on visits to other villages they were voluble at boasting that none in Rauit had died during the epidemic because of the treatment they had had; however if actions speak louder than words, the responses of those affected later on in the epidemic showed little evidence of a general conviction of the benefit of cough linctus and aspirin.

At other times when a number of similar illnesses occurred together I did not do systematic village surveys. The total counts of 274 illnesses given in some of the tables in this chapter include only the 10 cases of pneumonia or severe bronchitis which occurred in the October epidemic but not the many other cases of influenza – thus the general method of finding cases remains the same throughout and is not unduly weighted by the large number of discovered cases which occurred during this outbreak. This outbreak was severe and widespread; the colds and conjunctivitis involved groups of twenty to thirty affected people or less.

THE KINDS OF ILLNESS: INCIDENCE

The picture of morbidity will be built up from various data, first from data on the kinds of illness that I diagnosed. I did not reach a high level of precision in giving diagnostic labels to the illnesses that occurred. I offered them a simple medical service and it was often not practicable, in the context of my other interests, and the facilities and skills I lacked, to establish and confirm each diagnosis – for example, I treated many cases of fever in small children on clinical grounds as malaria without taking blood specimens to establish whether or not malarial parasites could be found, although I did so on some occasions. Table 8 summarizes what I was able to tell of the medical nature of the illnesses which occurred between January 1968 and November 1969, i.e. the cases of the overall record.

I have grouped together all skin infections and injury, burns and trauma, since wherever the body surface is damaged there is a high risk of infection. The proportion of such cases included in Table 8 does not fully represent the amount of trivial cuts, skin sores, infected scabies, etc. As I was present in the village it was comparatively easy for them to get these cuts or sores treated early, and fewer cases became so seriously infected as to inconvenience those who had them. These were not included in my

Table 8. General categories of ailment (January 1968–November 1969)

Category	Cases	Subtotal
1. *Skin sepsis: injury and burns*		
A. Badly infected cuts, injuries and ulcers	33	85
B. Abscesses	19	
C. Animal bites	13	
D. Burns	7	
E. Trauma from assault, or falls with damage to joints, bones or bruising	13	
2. *Infection*		
A. Respiratory tract infection:		101
Lower tract – pneumonia, bronchitis, etc.	28	
Upper tract – sore throat, cold	15	
Middle ear infection	5	
B. General fevers which were identified or clinically diagnosed as malaria	27	
C. Other infections (e.g. filariasis, meningitis, urinary tract infection, etc.)	26	
3. *Symptom diagnoses*		
A. 'Rheumatism': pains unassociated with external signs of damage to muscle, joint or bone, though accompanied by functional limitation of movement or local pain	22	66
B. Pains in the head (headache, pain in jaw or eyes)	12	
C. Abdominal pain without fever with or without diarrhoea or vomiting	17	
D. Undiagnosed malaise	6	
E. States taken to be illness in which disturbed behaviour (*bengbeng*) was the abnormal sign; attempts at suicide	9	
4. *Miscellaneous medical conditions*		
(Including heart failure, severe arthritis, gynaecological disease, etc.)	15	22
Deaths from undiagnosed cause	7	
Total		274

Note: On this table, of the 246 cases of respiratory tract disease which I found in the influenza epidemic in October 1968, only 6 cases of pneumonia and 4 of severe bronchitis are included.

general count. I have compared (Table 9) the pattern of morbidity found by Dr Sturt in 13,000 hospital admissions (Sturt undated) and the pattern I recorded between July and October 1969 when I noted all ills including trivial ones, with that of my overall count. It can be seen that when everything was counted, injuries and skin infections comprised the largest percentage of complaints. Dr Sturt's figures show that 20·0 per cent of all cases were

Table 9. Comparison of morbidity data from three surveys

	Rauit overall count. 274 cases = 100% (Jan. 1968–Nov. 1969)	*Rauit detailed count. 164 cases = 100% (July–Nov. 1969)*	*Dr Sturt hospital admissions* 13,000 cases = 100% (1959–69)*
Skin sepsis and injury	31·8%	65·9%	40·7%
Infection (e.g. chest infection and malaria)	36·4%	20·1%	48·2%
Miscellaneous non-infectious medical conditions	29·3%	14·0%	11·1%
Deaths from undetermined cause	2·5%	—	—
Total	100%	100%	100%

* The detailed figures recorded by Dr Sturt are as follows – I have assembled them in the three categories used in the table above and in each instance the figure cited is the percentage of 13,000 cases: 1. *Skin sepsis and injury:* tropical ulcer 20·0; sepsis 11·8; trauma 4·1; burns 2·6; scabies 1·5; fractures 0·7. 2. *Infection:* chest infection 15·7; malaria 15·1; diarrhoeal disease 5·1; otitis media 2·6; measles 2·2; leprosy 1·8; eye infection 1·7; influenza 0·8; filariasis 0·7; yaws 0·5; ancylostomiasis 0·3; tuberculosis 0·2; miscell. infective conditions 1·5. 3. *Miscellaneous non-infective medical conditions:* malnutrition 3·2; arthritis 1·3; debility 0·7; anaemia 0·8; confinements 0·6; hernia 0·2; miscellaneous 4·3.

admitted with tropical ulcer: it was the largest single cause of hospital admission. In my overall figures, the proportion of miscellaneous medical ailments is large because it includes many symptom diagnoses, such as belly aches or 'rheumatism', which would not have merited hospital admission. The other general point to note is that respiratory disease and malaria make up a major part of all illness: combined they account for 34·4 per cent of Dr Sturt's hospital admissions and for 27·1 per cent of the cases in my overall count.

If one includes trivial ailments, aches and transitory indispositions, then in terms of numbers the cases of malaria and chest infection do not stand out so significantly; if on the other hand, one includes only severe or life-endangering illness then proportionately malaria and chest disease come to the fore. It must be recalled that malaria is so prevalent that children either die during early childhood or acquire a relative immunity to it.

The respective proportions of sick people in different age categories are shown for the three collections of data in Table 10.

Table 10. Age distribution of illness in three surveys

	0–4 years	*5–15 years*	*16–45 years*	*over 45 years*
Rauit overall 1968–9 N = 274	16·8%	11·3%	39·8%	32·1%
Rauit detailed July–October 1969 N = 164	20·7%	23·2%	32·9%	23·2%
Sturt hospital admissions N = 13,000	35·3%	20·0%	37·0%	7·7%

The numbers of patients provided by a particular age category depend on complex factors: for instance the number of people in the population who come in that category, the kind of illness, their mobility while ill. The hospital figures show a relatively small proportion of people over 45 years old: reasons for this may include the difficulty and expense of carriage to the hospital, their reluctance to go to an unfamiliar place, their relative lack of

Plate 1a. *The village: morning*. Preparing to go off to the bush. A bow and arrows rest against the house. Abdominal distension is obvious in the small children.

Plate 1b. *The village: evening*. The flat open space is where they dance. In the dark middle ground of the picture, one main post of the *gamaiyit* (men's house) they have recently destroyed still stands straight flanked by the two side posts. The children play and the grown-ups relax. The dodging boy holds a spinning top in his right hand. A woman in the foreground is making a string bag; fibre she has just rolled into string is on her thigh.

conviction that modern medicine will benefit them, and the feeling of relatives that the illnesses of old people are to be expected and the need to bring them for treatment less urgent. Babies and small children on the other hand are relatively easy to carry to hospital, the benefits of modern treatment for malaria or chest disease are clear and dramatic, especially with small children who quickly recover from what appears extreme illness. In comparison the figures from the village surveys show that old people provide a lot of cases – partly because they are prone to ailments, especially to chest disease and to aches and pains. These latter are often not severe – they would rarely merit a special visit in search of treatment at hospital – but they are ailments which receive attention and explanation in local terms. These infirmities account for time lost in illness and, though not severe, I have probably been more ready to note them down because their explanations were interesting anthropologically, while I failed to note some other aches in younger people though they were, in terms of pain and disability, similar in severity but lacked any attaching explanation.

DISTRIBUTION BY AGE AND SEX

The overall collection of cases comes from a single village and the population exposed to risk during the period of study was therefore known. In the following estimates of differences in the occurrence of illness by age and sex, I will show the relative

Plate 2a. *Women chipping sago.* One woman sits on the felled palm holding the angled bamboo *lyiwan* with which she pounds the pith; another *lyiwan* at the lower left corner rests on the upper *gelpi* half of the split trunk she sits on. The other woman puts pounded pith in a *limbum* palm leaf spathe: sheets of these spathes lie about on the ground.

Plate 2b. *Women leaching out the starch from sago pith.* Water is poured on pith in the palm leaf trough. A sieve-like coconut leaf fibre retains the pith. The dissolved starch runs down into the lower trough where the starch settles to the bottom.

Plate 2c. *A young woman with a large fishing net.* The sunlight catches her as she stands on boulders in the little stream: its brightness exaggerates the contrast with the gloomy forest bank behind her. She is pregnant. A swollen axillary tail of breast tissue, similar to the one at her armpit, was seen in a number of women.

amounts of illness in different segments of the population and their proneness to have illnesses of different kinds of severity. In most cases I present the proportion of illness of some specified kind which was provided by a given segment of the population, and then determine the relative proneness of that particular segment to that kind of illness by taking the ratio between the proportion of the illness they provided and the proportion of the total population that fell within that age or sex segment.[1] The proportion of some kind of illness that occurs in a segment of the population is obviously affected by how large the segment is. If young adults form a large one, even if they do not have a disproportionate amount of illness, it would still seem to the Gnau that a lot of all illness strikes young adults. Their perception of proneness to illness would, although this is a speculation, be unduly influenced by the fact that they most often hear that younger adults are ill and go to watch or assist at gatherings and treatment for them, rather than by a recognition of the balance or imbalance between the numbers exposed to risk and the number of cases.

Table 11 shows the distribution of the overall record of cases of illness by sex and age group. I have also included the number of

Table 11. Distribution of illness by age and sex (January 1968–November 1969)

	Males	*Females*	*A1* *0–4 years*	*A2* *5–15 years*	*A3* *16–45 years*	*A4* *over 45*	*Total all ages*
No. in population	160	195	48	112	133	62	355
Observed no. of ills	150	124	46	31	109	88	274
Expected no. of ills	124	150	37	86	103	48	274

cases expected if illness had a purely random distribution with no differences of susceptibility according to age or sex. This is, of course, not the case. The proportion of cases provided by each sex is shown in the accompanying histograms placed next to ones which show the percentage contribution to the total population exposed to risk.

[1] The population exposed to risk excludes men absent on labour at plantations, or in gaol. The figures also make allowance for births and deaths during the period of study, so that the average numbers exposed to risk over the whole period of study are the ones used in the calculations.

It can be seen that children (A2) have proportionately much less, and adults over 45 years old (A4) much more, illness in relation to their numbers in the population. The difference between observed and expected illness in males and females overall is significant at the 0·5 per cent level and this is due to a significant difference (chi-square = 13·1, d.f. = 1) only in the age group A4 (over 45 years old) in which the men contribute much more illness than the women. In the other age groups there is no such significant difference between males and females.

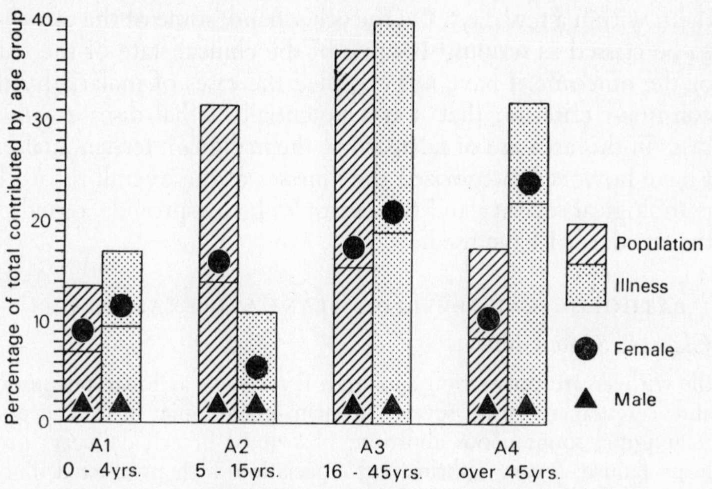

Fig. 11. Distribution of illness by age and sex

SEVERITY AND THE DISTRIBUTION OF ILLNESS

In the above I have made no discrimination of the kind or severity of illness and this must be done in order to appreciate the impact and burden of illness on the people. The estimate of severity is difficult to make even when as in this chapter, I consider disease from an external medical standpoint. There are two main criteria – (1) whether the disease is one to which we allocate on the basis of normal experience some threat of danger to life or of permanent damage to the person's well-being; and (2) whether the disease produces serious incapacity. The case of malaria, for example, is one of a deadly disease to which all Gnau people are recurrently exposed, which kills a high proportion of their young children, relatively speaking. Yet if they manage to survive its early attacks they acquire such resistance to it that it is uncommon to find an adult who seems ill because of it. The attacks in infancy are frequent and part of the ordinary process of growing up: in most cases the temporary fevers caused by malaria appear on the surface of everyday life as minor indispositions, but occasionally an affected child descends suddenly to extreme illness and may quickly die. In practice I have classed malarial attacks in infants as mild illnesses because I either treated them or kept watch on them without treatment to check that they got over them within a few days. On the other hand, some of the cases had to be classed as serious,[1] because of the clinical state of the child or the outcome. I have not classified the cases of malaria by the consistent criterion that it is a potentially lethal disease – most cases in this area are of falciparum, the malignant tertian, malaria. I have however categorized the illnesses of the overall record by pathological severity and the examples below provide a guide to the standards I have used.

PATHOLOGICAL SEVERITY. STANDARD EXAMPLES

Class A. Serious Illness

Ills with severe prostration and high fever such as lobar pneumonia and cerebral malaria; severe broncho-pneumonia in old people; meningitis; spontaneous abortion; obstructed breech delivery; gross heart failure; severe arthritis and emaciation with protracted illness; acute renal failure; the acute abdominal conditions diagnosed as *pig-bel*. The exclusions from this category are more debatable for they include treated malaria in infants (mostly classed as mild illness); some cases of broncho-pneumonia with signs of consolidation and pleurisy; iritis; a large breast abscess which took 68 days to heal as the patient did not care for regular treatment; a case of acute glomerular nephritis; all these were put in the moderate illness category. This group of A class ills also includes the illnesses which ended in death (17).

Class B. Moderately Severe Illness

Bronchopneumonia, acute bronchitis; otitis media leading to perforated eardrums; malaria with marked weakness and disturbance lasting

[1] As mentioned above, I did not record and investigate all infantile fevers: carefully designed and detailed sequential studies of the incidence and prevalence of malaria in village infants and small children in a holoendemic region have been made elsewhere (e.g. Marsden 1964; for the Sepik area see Schofield *et al.* 1964, and Peters 1960).

more than a few days; filariasis with acute hydrocoele, pain and fever; inflammation and suppuration of salivary glands; large suppurating abscesses; deep puncture wounds mainly caused by splinters or arrow heads planted to wound trespassers, which led to cellulitis and general inflammation of foot or hand; knee or wrist injuries restricting the sufferer to the village, or preventing performance of normal duties for more than 10 days; fractured clavicle; a woman with dysmenorrhoeic pelvic pain which was presumed due to endometriosis or fibroids; urinary infection. Conditions which in our society might have been included here, but I have not, are widespread purulent secondarily infected scabies; scalp infections secondary to head lice.

Class C. Mild or Trivial Illness

Sore throats; headaches; uncomplicated fevers due to malaria or filariasis; conjunctivitis; most of the heavily infected but superficial cuts and sores which were counted in the overall series and lasted two or three weeks but hardly restricted the activities of those who had them; animal, snake and centipede bites; bangs and bruises from falls or assault; burns of first or second degree; aches and rheumatic pains; colic and abdominal pain, accompanied or not by vomiting or diarrhoea, which lasted for less than one week and improved spontaneously.

Class D. Illness of Ill-Defined Severity

This class comprises those cases where the patients themselves (or their relatives) were anxious, and behaved (or were presented) as ill, but I could find no evidence of physical illness. In some of these cases the patients were incapacitated for more than two weeks; during this time they lay apathetic, refused food and said they felt pain or strange sensations although they showed neither fever, nor limitations of specific movements in the ways I would have expected from their description of the pain. The category includes these cases and others, for example, in close relatives of people who had just died, the parents of a child just dead saying that they or another child had pain or colic or had seen blood in a stool; people with complaints of diffuse malaise after an argument or a fight; or similar ills in young women who, following a dispute and a dramatic but prevented attempt at suicide by poison, afterwards fell ill in this way; women who showed the *bengbeng* behaviour described on p. 133 and after it were supposed ill or complained of malaise; men complaining of pains and weakness after they had accomplished a ritual task. Effectively this class includes illness in which the chief reason for inclusion in my study as far as I could tell was belief of illness. Inclusion in it could of course be due to my diagnostic errors.

The distribution of cases by severity is shown in Table 12. Nearly half of all the illnesses came in the mild class C and it will be noted that the men provide most such cases. More of the women's ills came into the moderately severe, B, class.

Table 12. Distribution of ills by sex of patient and class of pathological severity

Class	*Of total ills* (*N* = *274*) *n*	*%*	*Of total ills in males* (*N* = *150*) *n*	*%*	*Of total ills in females* (*N* = *124*) *n*	*%*	*% male contribution to class*
A	35	12·8	19	12·7	16	12·9	54·3
B	67	24·4	28	18·7	39	31·4	41·8
C	118	43·1	75	50·0	43	34·7	63·6
D	54	19·7	28	18·6	26	21·0	51·6

We may now distinguish in terms of this classing of illness whether there are differences in the incidence of illness according to age and sex. Thus in the C class of mild illness (total number of cases 118) I recorded 75 cases for males, and 43 cases for females. As there were 160 males in the population of 355 people exposed to risk, we would expect: $160/355 \times 118 = 53{\cdot}2$ cases from males, and $195/355 \times 118 = 64{\cdot}8$ cases from females, if mild illness should affect males and females indiscriminately. The difference between the observed and expected values is significant at the 0·5 per cent level (chi-square = 16·3, d.f. = 1). Therefore it would appear that mild illness in males was more frequently brought to my notice than for females. This could be because males had that sort of illness more often, or because they took it more seriously, or because women were reluctant to let me know about their mild illness. But similar tests showed that there was no significant[1] disparity between the contribution of the sexes in any other of the classes of severity of illness. The probable explanation then for the disparity in mild illness is that men bothered about their mild illnesses, and hence they came to my notice, while women did not do so. I will bring forward more evidence on the different patterns of attention to illness, which supports this view, when I deal with the types of incapacity shown in illness.

[1] Throughout this chapter I have taken the 5 per cent level as the minimum level for tests of significance.

It is well known that susceptibility varies with age in many kinds of illness. Figure 12 shows the proportionate amounts which different age and sex groups contribute to each separate category of severity. If the Gnau were to see severity in similar terms to the observer (in Chapter 7 I shall show that within certain limits this appears to be the case), Figure 12 would indicate roughly how illness seems to them to affect more or less commonly the people of different ages. I use proportions rather than percentages since the number of cases in some classes is small.[1]

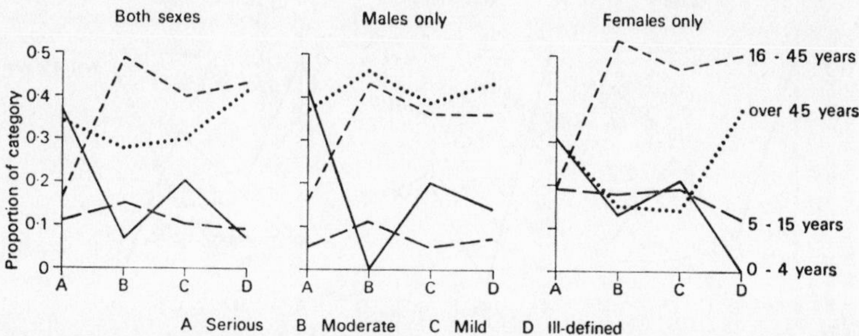

Fig. 12. Proportion of each category of medical severity contributed by different age and sex groups

Thus as we might expect, the figure shows that most serious illness (class A) occurs in infants and the older adults, and that the children rarely appear with the kinds of illness that I have classed as ill-defined, D.

But Figure 12 does not provide a measure of proneness to illness since the proportion of people in the population at risk differs according to age and sex. In order to show relative proneness to illness in these different categories of severity, I have, as mentioned, calculated the ratio between the proportion of illness and the proportion of people in the population who might contribute to it. Thus if each different population segment contributed illness in each medical severity class in strict proportion to its numbers and there were no differences of proneness, all the age and sex segment traces on a graph would be shown as straight lines at the level 1·0. The findings based on the overall record are given in Figure 13.

[1] The Appendix contains tables showing the basic data from which the various graphs and calculations in this chapter and Chapter 7 were taken.

It shows that the group of younger adults (16–45 years old) come nearest to a proportion in keeping with their numbers, although they tend to have less of severe A class illness. They are followed by the infants and toddlers (0–4 years) who, though they keep relatively close to a proportionate amount of illness when the severity of illness is undifferentiated, have a markedly disproportionate amount of severe illness, which I think reflects my selective recording of their severe illnesses as well as the actual great dangers they run from malaria in the period during which

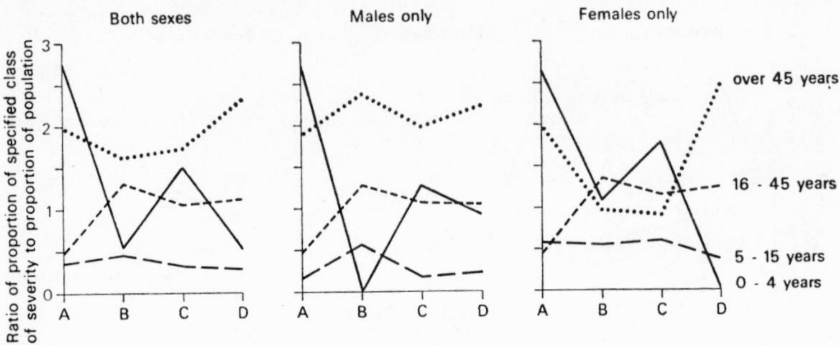

Fig. 13. Proneness to illness of differing severities in the various age and sex groups

they are acquiring a relative immunity to it.[1] Children surviving this age of risk have a period of relative freedom from illness; they keep below half what might be expected if illness of all kinds affected all ages and both sexes equally. The older adults (over 45 years) have nearly twice what might be expected on this basis; the differences are most marked in regard to severe illness (A class) and the class of ill-defined illness, D. The men of this age group have more illness of all sorts, and they show a consistently high level, while the women show it only in the classes A and D.

INCAPACITY IN ILLNESS

The significance of a particular disability varies with the demands put on the person by his situation; social considerations here weigh heavily on an estimate of severity and make it hard to

[1] The proneness of 0·8 for males of A1 in category D reflects parental anxiety and not, of course, the infant's belief that he was ill.

compare the gravity of pathologically similar ills in different societies – an injured knee may not matter much to a telephonist but be serious for a New Guinean wife. The physical demands of daily duties are fairly similar for men and women in a Gnau village. There are no marked occupational differences like those in our society. All well people go about their everyday business outside the village, therefore incapacity from illness effectively means restriction to the village. Unless people are very ill, they lie or sit around on the ground outside in the daytime when ill.

But there is another difficulty to the use of incapacity as a measure of the severity of illness. This comes from their conventions about how a sick person should behave, which I describe in detail in the following chapter. The convention that a person who feels ill should remain in the hamlet is generally observed, but the kind of illness or ailment which is taken to merit this restriction may not be objectively a severe one. The decision on what to do rests largely with the patient and his own perception of how serious the matter is. The illness may well oblige him to lie down. But if a man believes his headache is a sign or a portent of possibly great illness, he may show the marked behaviour of someone ill – he will certainly not leave his hamlet, he may shun company, refuse food and lie hidden from gaze in a hut with closed doors. If you go inside all you may be able to see at first is the gleam of light reflected from his white shell phallocrypt. He may talk very little and answer with a quavering voice. On the next day if his apprehension or his headache has gone, he may have strode off to hunt. On the other hand, equally apparent incapacity may result from lobar pneumonia, but the patient is really incapable, possibly incapable of crawling to the toilet; he must defaecate on the ground by his bed.

Incapacity measured by restriction is therefore an unreliable guide to the objective severity of an illness; it may indicate either the patient's interpretation of what he feels or what the illness forces on him, or both. If Gnau people were asked to measure incapacity, they would, I take it, count all cases of restriction by illness; the appropriate behaviour for sickness is the patient's responsibility and if he believes he is ill, other people do not claim in general to be able to know better than he does, or to judge that he feigns it or deludes himself. In one sense, the amount of incapacity caused by illness should include all the cases of restriction to the village for reason of sick behaviour: to deny this would be to stand close to the position of an English doctor who calls all people with hysteria or hysterical symptoms malingerers. Time lost by illness or by fears that this was illness, which I judged unwarranted, were equally to the Gnau time lost through illness.

The incapacity shown in illness makes a forceful impression on one: it influences one's general estimate of the impact of illness, for the sight of people lying listless about the village is direct and persuasive. Later one comes, like the inhabitants, to remark rather someone's conspicuous absence from public life, knowing that he or she is hidden because of grave illness.

The different patterns of behaviour during illness were categorized in four kinds, with a fifth one for babies as they were not old enough to make their own choices of behaviour during illness in the same way. The categories reflect both the nature of the illness involved and the patient's response to it or his interpretation of its significance. For this reason, I have discriminated one category (III) on the basis of my external viewpoint, although the Gnau themselves would not distinguish it in like fashion. The categories are:

Class I Not restricted to the village, but continuing normal activities despite illness.

Class II Remaining restricted to the village, not necessarily recumbent, change in manner slight, or not markedly inappropriate to the objective signs of disease or injury.

Class III Remaining restricted to the village, recumbent and conspicuously or demonstratively ill, begrimed, rejecting food, shunning company and conversation. But in my opinion, the response was markedly exaggerated and clearly inappropriate for the clinical signs of disease.

Class IV Restricted to the village; forced to be recumbent by severe debility. Physical state so poor that to walk unaided would have been impossible or a great hardship.

Class V Ill babies.

The distribution of cases by incapacity is shown in Table 13.

The main points to note are that most illness came in classes I and II; that men provided most of the II class of illness, while of all women's illnesses proportionately less came in that class; in comparison to the men a larger part of the women's illness came in the III class of demonstrative and inappropriate behaviour. The excess of male ills in class II is significant at the 0·1 per cent level (chi-square = 22·6, d.f. = 1) given the population exposed to risk, but the excess of females' class III ills does not differ significantly from the expected number. There is no significance to the differences between the sexes in the other classes.

When the age segments of the population are distinguished in

Table 13. Incapacity distribution by sex of patient and kind of incapacity

	Of total ills (N = 274)		*Of total ills in males (N = 150)*		*Of total ills in females (N = 124)*		*% male contribution to class*
Class	*n*	%	*n*	%	*n*	%	
I	93	33·9	49	32·7	44	35·5	52·7
II	82	29·9	58	38·7	24	19·4	70·7
III	36	13·1	14	9·3	22	17·7	38·9
IV	29	10·6	11	7·3	18	14·5	37·9
V	34	12·4	18	12·0	16	12·9	52·9

Figure 14,[1] a small amount of illness in each category belongs to children or toddlers because they had a relatively small amount of the illness recorded overall. But this is most marked in the III class, for children do not, except very rarely, show the demonstrative or conspicuous behaviour in illness, which is a learned behaviour shown for complex motives. The greater proportion of IV class illness in the older adult group reflects the more medically severe illnesses that they had. The interesting difference between the proportions of the conspicuous III class of behaviour in adults is the preponderance of younger women among females, and older men among males.[2]

By the same methods as used for pathological severity, Figure

[1] In this figure and the next one on incapacity, the calculations exclude babies, N = 34, who were classed separately in the V class containing 34 cases of illness.

[2] When adults as a whole, A3 plus A4, are compared, the larger proportion of women's versus men's ills in III as opposed to other categories is still significant at the 5 per cent level (chi-square = 5·2, d.f. = 1), although this finding must also reflect the fact that men's ills include a significantly large component in another class, viz. II.

15 was drawn to show the relative proneness of different segments of the population to different kinds of incapacity in illness. The figure reveals that older men are the most ready to show the

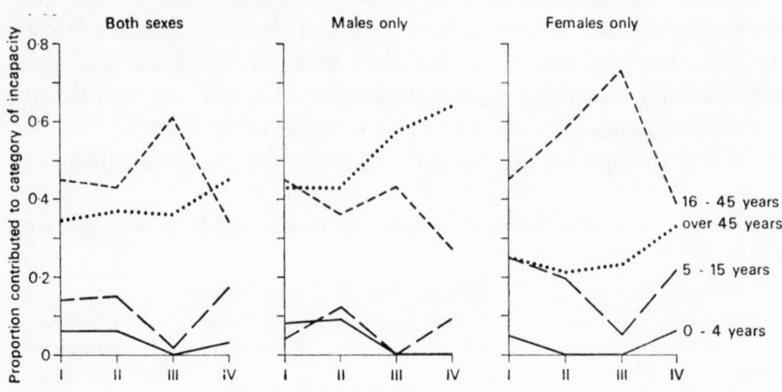

Fig. 14. Proportion of each category of incapacity contributed by different age and sex groups

conspicuous and inappropriate III kind of incapacity. The high IV ratios of older men and women reflect their severe illness. The younger women do show a marked tendency to III class

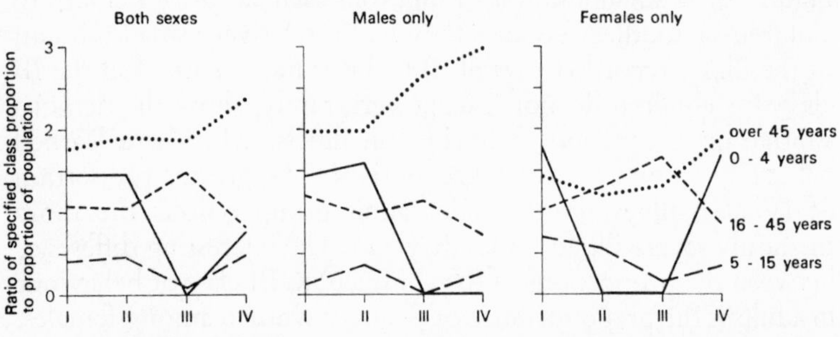

Fig. 15. Proneness to different types of incapacity in the various age and sex groups

incapacity which I suggest may stem from their need to justify taking time off from their domestic duties if they fall ill, since showing the behaviour is in effect an appeal for sympathy and help. A number of the cases followed quarrels with other people in the domestic setting into which they had married or a quarrel with their husband. This taken together with the finding of an excess of trivial or mild illness which men compared to women brought to my notice, indicates perhaps that women have greater pressures on them not to stop work for mild illness, and must justify abandoning their domestic duties by making clear how ill they are. In Chapter 7 I will show that the III class behaviour was associated with a very high level of elaborated explanation of the cause of illness in the case of men, but not so high a level in the case of women, which may suggest that showing such behaviour was in part for women (either consciously or not) an end in itself.

DURATION OF ILLNESS

This is the third aspect to the severity of an illness and it is largely set by the nature of the ill although it too may be affected by customary views about how long it is wise to remain as though ill or convalescent. The treatment I gave to the two men longest ill (for 236 and 220 days respectively) added to the time they lingered before dying, while other people's spells of sickness were also shortened or lengthened by my treatment. The measures I will cite do not therefore show the unaltered amounts of time which might be lost through illness in the village: I cite what happened, not what might have happened. In practice even so, duration is not simple to measure. Sometimes it must be decided whether what has happened counts as one long illness, or a series of episodes of the same illness, or different illnesses. For example, I have counted each of the attacks of bronchopneumonia occurring in an elderly man as an illness, if he was free from disability for more than one month between attacks; with a woman who repeatedly behaved as ill during and after she had a *bengbeng* attack,[1] I count the length of indisposition after the attack as that of one illness if she remained continuously unwell for more than a week, but the brief spells of a day or two's illness which occurred once a month for three months are counted as only one illness and the time given as spent ill is the summed few days of actual indisposition, not three months, since in between the episodes she behaved normally. Otherwise in most cases duration is decided by the length of uninterrupted indisposition or the time taken to

[1] *Bengbeng* is described on p. 133.

be healed. For the abscesses and acute heavily infected sores which I included in the overall count I have put down roughly how long they took to get better, e.g. an abscess formed in a groin gland causing marked pain and swelling over four days; it then suppurated and drained, the patient came and got it dressed and it began early healing in a further four days – the length of illness was counted as eight days although healing and resolution was not of course complete; a woman did not come for proper treatment when she had a large abscess in her breast, and it lasted for about

Table 14. Distribution of illness by duration and sex of patient

Class	*Of total ills (N = 274)* *n*	*%*	*Of total males' ills (N = 150)* *n*	*%*	*Of total females' ills (N = 124)* *n*	*%*	*% male contribution to class*
1	43	15·7	29	19·3	14	11·3	67·4
2	146	53·3	79	52·7	67	54·0	54·1
3	53	19·3	26	17·3	27	21·8	49·1
4	21	7·7	11	7·3	10	8·1	52·4
5	11	4·0	5	3·3	6	4·8	45·5

Class 1 = Illness lasting 1 day.
Class 2 = Illness lasting from 1 day to 1 week.
Class 3 = Illness lasting from 1 week to 2 weeks.
Class 4 = Illness lasting from 2 weeks to 1 month.
Class 5 = Illness lasting for more than 1 month.

68 days before the pus stopped draining and adequate healing began.[1] The distribution of illness by its duration is shown in Table 14.

Most of the illness was short-lasting. Men brought illness lasting a day or less to my notice significantly more often than women (0·5 per cent level, chi-square = 8·8, d.f. = 1), as they did with illness lasting a week or less (5 per cent level, chi-square = 4·8, d.f. = 1).

The record of duration can be used to calculate the amount of time lost through illness. To do this I have taken the total number

[1] I have, as mentioned, excluded from my overall count people with foul infected scabies who sometimes tolerated their condition for months before it healed more or less spontaneously or they accepted my treatment.

of days spent in the village for reason of sickness by those included in the classes of incapacity II, III, and IV (thus excluding babies who were ill, whose illnesses in fact meant that their mothers had to stay in the village with them) and to this total of 1664 days I have added 1170 man-days of illness which were produced by the 236 additional cases of influenza which occurred during the October 1968 epidemic and were not included in the overall record. An approximate measure of the prevalence of restricting sickness may then be made by dividing this total by the number of months of observation (22·5 months – the record continued until 10 November 1969), and the average size of the

Table 15. Time lost through illness

	Exposed to risk during study period (average number)	
	Men N = 85	*Women N = 110*
Total days of incapacity	1442	1005
Days per 100 persons in 12 months	905*	509

* The figures are based on the observed findings. It should be noted that two men had incapacitating illnesses lasting each for over 220 days; while no woman had one lasting for more than 55 days. The woman with a breast abscess continued normal activities and is thus not counted in these calculations. These cases which were lengthened because I treated them – both men eventually died – unduly weight the men's figures. How long they would have lived without treatment from me is hypothetical. If I just subtract the 457 days they contributed to the total days of incapacity and recalculate the same measure the answer is 618 days per 100 men in 12 months.

population exposed to risk during the period of study (355 − 35 babies = 320). I have expressed the result as the number of days of sickness occuring in 12 months per 100 persons.

2834/22·5 × 100/320 × 12 = 472 days per 100 persons in 12 months.

If adult men and women (i.e. those over 16 years old) are separated the measures are as shown in Table 15.

I should emphasize that my estimate is approximate and probably errs towards undercounting rather than overcounting the time spent in the village ostensibly ill. In a large-scale survey of sickness in England, the days of incapacity in an interviewed population were as shown in Table 16 (*Registrar General's Statistical Review for 1949*, H.M.S.O., p. 15).

Thus the Rauit men seem to lose almost ten times as much time in illness as English men (or about six times as much on the basis of the recalculation mentioned above); and Rauit women between five and six times as much as English women. Part of the greater amount of time that the Gnau people spend ill is due to the severe infectious diseases to which they are exposed and English people are not; they lack adequate treatment for ailments that are common, particularly respiratory diseases, injury and infection; as I was treating them, the situation would presumably be worse at other times. The contribution of malaria to adult illness is much

Table 16. Time lost through illness in an English population

	1948				*1949*			
	Age 16–64		*Over 65*		*Age 16–64*		*Over 65*	
	M	*F*	*M*	*F*	*M*	*F*	*M*	*F*
Days incapacity per 100 interviewed in 12 months	93	81	155	224	95	92	164	192

less than to the illness of small children. Because illness in infants is excluded from these calculations, most cases of malaria do not appear in the measures of time lost. But in part the greater amount of time lost is due to a different standard of what is appropriate behaviour in illness, a greater readiness to choose confinement to the village. A disparity between men and women can be attributed to two main factors; one is the greater incidence and length of illness from lower respiratory tract infection in men, most apparent over the age of 45 years; the other is the greater readiness of men to choose confinement to the village if they feel ill.

The significant preponderance of males (*a*) with mild C class illness, (*b*) with illness for which they stayed in the village though they were not in all the cases necessarily obliged to by its severity (some cases of II class illness), and (*c*) with illness of short duration (duration classes 1 and 2), also tends to support the view that men were more ready than women were to bother about mild short

Plate 3. *A sick man* (*i*). A sick man lies in the open porch of his house. His daughter is sitting near him. He is the man struck by the spirit Malyi when it was sent off from the village of Wititai (see p. 274).

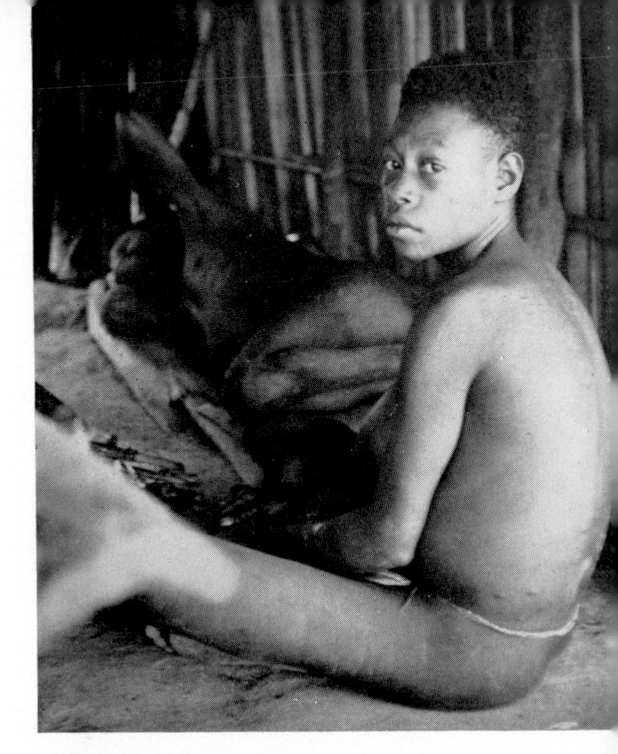

illnesses, to bring them to my notice and to take time off for them.

I have so far presented information on the kinds, incidence, prevalence and impact of illnesses in the village.[1] The impact of illness is not a clear concept; it can be taken to refer to objective damage and restriction, and to subjective suffering and anxiety: understood more generally the impact of illness is an effect not only on the patient who is ill but also on the people who live with him and may feel concern and fear for him when he is ill, and sometimes for themselves. The criteria of pathological severity and threat to life, the incapacity, and duration of illness, by which I have sought to measure the burden of illness objectively, also reflect a number of social considerations as I have pointed out.

Something so complex as the impact of illness can be appreciated more from the combination of these aspects than from their isolated presentation. An illness that is clearly damaging, incapacitating and lasts a long time, puts a different kind of stress on the patient, on his family and neighbours from one, for example, that comes without warning and swiftly destroys him. In order to give an overall visual summary of the data on the relative amounts (or burdens) of illness falling within different categories, I have combined the different aspects to severity in illness in Figure 16. The small numbers of some kinds of case and the nature of the categorizations preclude statistical tests of correlation between the various aspects to severity. But the association of serious pathological severity and forced recumbency can be seen in Figure 16, as can that between trivial or mild illness and continued activity. Many of the cases where I could not define what was wrong (D class) occurred in people who also had the demonstrative III kind of incapacity. This of course could be due partly to my diagnostic errors and the classification – if I was baffled or wrong in diagnosis, I therefore put people in fact

[1] In the Appendix I have included a note on mortality; the causes of death in the village, and on congenital or static defects and mutilations, which I noted in it.

Plate 4a. *A sick man (ii).*

Plate 4b. *A sick man before the spirit afflicting him.* Dauwaras, later struck by the same spirit, faces Malyi, the masked *tumbuan* figure, part of which can be seen from the back at the left of the picture. Dauwaras sits on an improvized chair, with dirt and ashes on his skin (see pp. 131 and 276).

with some illness, though ill-defined, into the category of those who showed an inappropriate response for their clinical signs: examples of the kinds of cases classed as ill-defined have already been cited.

	A Serious	B Moderate	C Mild	D Ill-defined
I Active unrestricted		222 333333 4444 555	11111111111 222222222222222 222222222222222 33333333 444444	1111111111 22222222222
II Restricted to village	2 3	2222222222 3333333333333 44 55	11111111 222222222222222 222222222222 3333	222222222222 3
III Demonstratively ill		22222 3 4444	1 222222	111 22222222222 33 4 55
IV Forced recumbency	1111 222 3333333 4444 555	2222 333 5		
V Ill babies	111 222222 333	22 333	11 222222222222222	

Duration

1 one day
2 one day to one week
3 one to two weeks
4 two weeks to one month
5 over one month

Fig. 16. Composite summary of the distribution of recorded cases by severity

HAMLET VARIATIONS IN THE RECORD

I learned of illness in the village in various ways but the overall record I made depended a lot on whether people told me about their own or other people's illness. The data will now be examined to show the different contributions of the various hamlets. I lived at the hamlet of Watalu and I tended to see more of its daily goings on, and to be most familiar with the people who lived there. This hamlet provided just over twice as many cases of illness as any other single hamlet. The figures are given in Table 17.

Table 17. Illness by hamlet

Hamlet	*People exposed to risk* No.	%	*Ills* No.	%
Animbil	66	18·6	43	15·7
Watalu	67	18·9	98	35·8
Pakuag and Dagetasa*	68	19·0	44	16·1
Wimalu	70	19·6	47	15·0
Bi'ip	84	23·5	48	17·5

* Pakuag is the hamlet from which Dagetasa had recently been formed (see p. 73n) and some of those whose day house was at Dagetasa normally slept at Pakuag. I have therefore combined the two physically separate but socially interwoven hamlets for the purposes of this analysis.

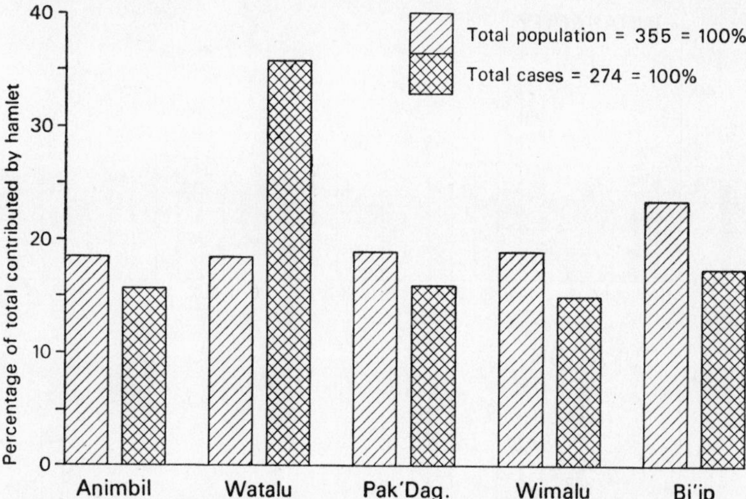

Fig. 17. Hamlet contribution to total population and total collection of cases

In Figure 18 the histograms show what the different hamlets contributed to each category of illness according to the various classifications I have been using. The preponderance of Watalu in almost all the categories is clear, although the use of percentages in comparison of categories with small numbers exaggerates its appearance. The actual numbers of cases are given in the Appendix. The preponderance of Watalu proves to be significantly above what would be expected if illness were distributed randomly, at the 0·5 per cent level in all classes except those of:

serious A class illness; forced recumbency (IV class) and the illnesses of babies (V class); illnesses lasting over two weeks

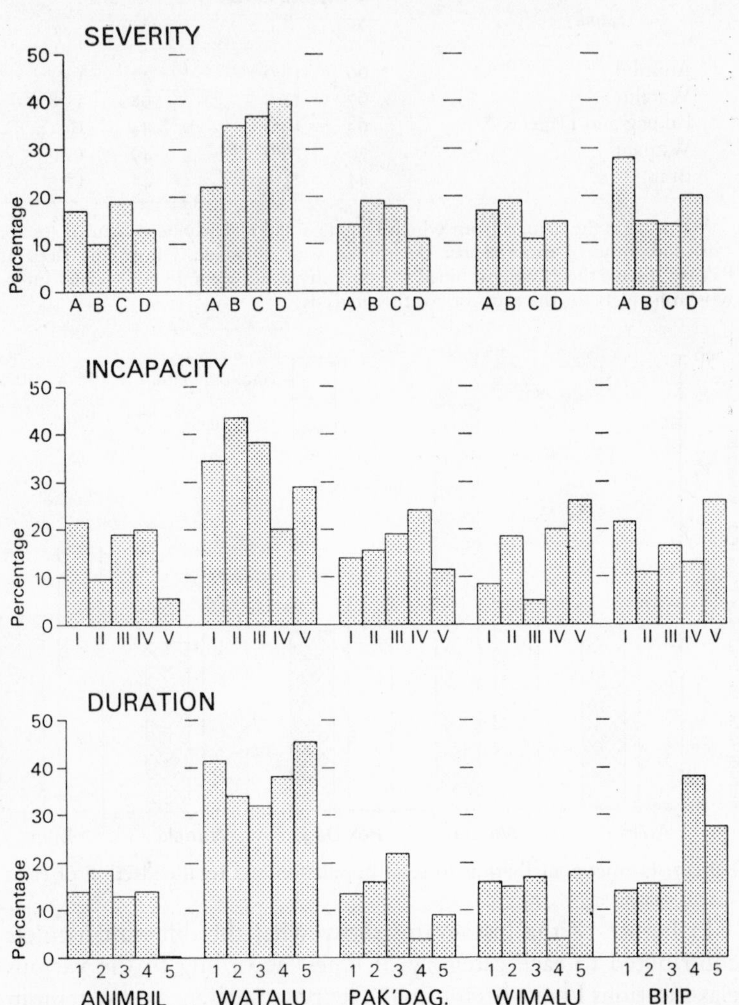

Fig. 18. Percentage contribution by hamlet to each category of illness

(duration classes 4 and 5 – in which the numbers are too small for the tests to be worthwhile); while in illness lasting between one and two weeks (duration class 3) it is significant at the 5 per cent but not the 0·5 per cent level.

I probably learnt about nearly all serious illness in the village, and it was unlikely that I heard nothing of illnesses which lasted two weeks or more in any hamlet unless they happened while the patients stayed at a distant hunting camp. On the other hand, I may sometimes have underestimated the length of illnesses because I was told of them or found them only later on in the illness and sometimes it was hard to be clear when they had begun. This would alter consistency in recording minor more than serious indispositions for it was more likely with the latter that they came quickly to find me. In Watalu where I lived, it was easy for someone to drop in to see me because of a vague ache which did not last – in consequence I recorded more short-lasting and mild ills from this hamlet than others. One reason for the higher number of fairly long-lasting ills (duration classes 4 and 5) at Bi'ip, which include some badly infected leg cuts, is that this hamlet was about 20 minutes' walk away and it was less convenient for people to come from there quickly or regularly to have a sore dressed than for people in the other hamlets all clustered in the main body of the village. The proportion of serious A class ills at Bi'ip looks large: in fact there are eight cases of which four were provided by babies who died soon after birth. Apart from my missing cases through lack of observation and familiarity, the large number of Watalu cases also indicates, I think, the greater frequency of mutual dependence and personal contact within a given hamlet which, even though the hamlets are set physically close together, tends to circumscribe the communication of information about illness as about other matters to those who live within the hamlet.

The percentage of ills contributed by either sex from each hamlet does not vary much by hamlet: no hamlet provided significantly less illness in females than the others; in other words the women do not appear to have concealed their illnesses from me more in some hamlets than in others. The proportion of ills occurring in either sex is shown for the hamlet in Figure 19.

The contribution of illness from different age groups in each hamlet is shown in Figure 20 by means of the ratios between the proportion of illnesses contributed and the proportion of people exposed in the hamlet to a risk of illness. The numbers of people in each hamlet in the age groups A1 (0–4 years) and A4 (over 45 years) are small. Figure 20 shows a general similarity of pattern in the age distribution of illness in the hamlets. The following points may be noted: the high ratios from Watalu differ from those of other hamlets in the A3 and A4 adult groups, and in men more than women. In the A3 group this chiefly results from the fevers diagnosed as filariasis which the young adults,

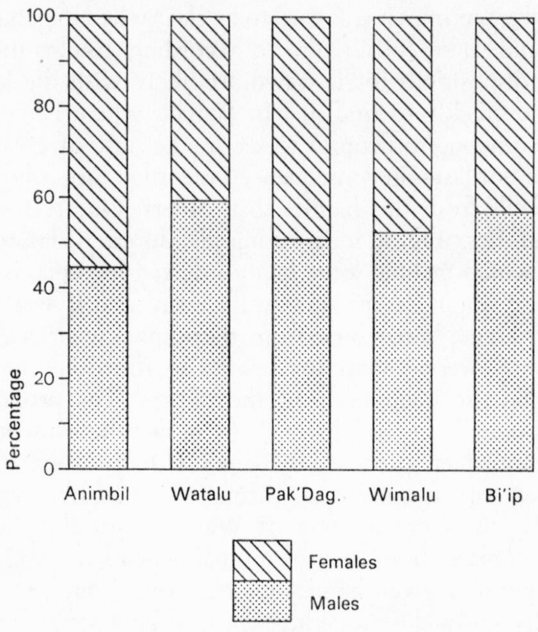

Fig. 19. Proportion of male to female illness contributed at each hamlet

especially the men, at Watalu brought to my attention while I rarely heard of them in other hamlets. In general, brief fevers or malaise came to my attention more often in Watalu than elsewhere. The large proportions in the A4 group at Watalu are also due to mild aches and pains for which they came to get liniment while older people in other hamlets less often bothered to come for it. The difference between men and women in the A4 group is marked and consistent, except in A4 women from Watalu and Animbil. At Animbil the high ratio is due to three very old and feeble women who each had serious illness, and also to their relatives who expected them to die and sought treatment from me or other people for them if there was cause for anxiety. The

A1 ratios at Watalu are high probably because it was so easy for a mother to ask me about any illness in her baby, while at Wimalu the very high ratio for baby girls is due to a small average number exposed to risk (two babies) and the special anxieties of a man from the village of Libuat who came to live at Wimalu for a year during my study because his previous babies had died in infancy, as he thought, by harm from the spirit of a man he had killed on a path just beside Libuat; therefore he came with his first surviving baby to Wimalu to escape this danger at his home.

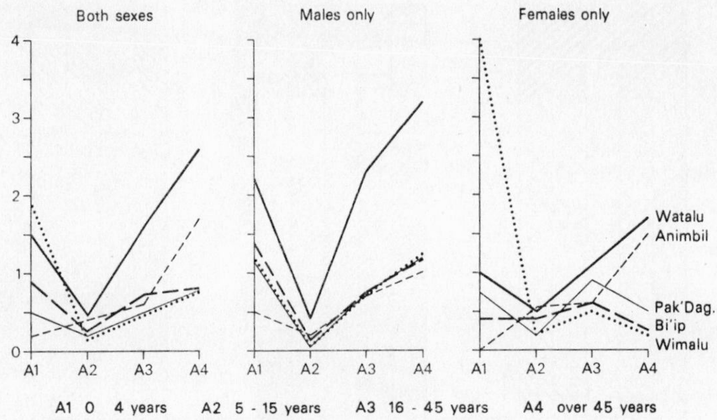

Fig. 20. Contribution of illness by different age and sex groups at each hamlet

Finally in Figure 21 I have compared the proportionate contribution of each category of illness to the total illness recorded at each hamlet. The general patterns of recording are fairly similar for all the hamlets as regards medical severity although the serious A and moderately severe B classes in Pakuag, Wimalu and Bi'ip are slightly higher than at the other two hamlets. In the incapacity comparisons, the III type behaviour contribution is small at Wimalu and this is probably because I missed observing its occurrence at some stage in some illnesses. Again the high ratio of babies' illnesses (and the concern about them) appears as a large V component at Wimalu, while the deaths of newborn infants at Bi'ip add to this component there. The different hamlets all contribute very similar amounts of I plus II incapacity illnesses. In the duration comparisons, the proportionate amounts of illness lasting less than one week (i.e. 1 and 2 class illnesses) are similar; the larger proportion of long lasting illness at the distant hamlet of Bi'ip (duration classes 4 and 5) has already been commented on.

The impression these comparisons give is of fairly consistent patterns in all the hamlets, bearing in mind that the numbers involved are small. But I recorded twice as much illness from

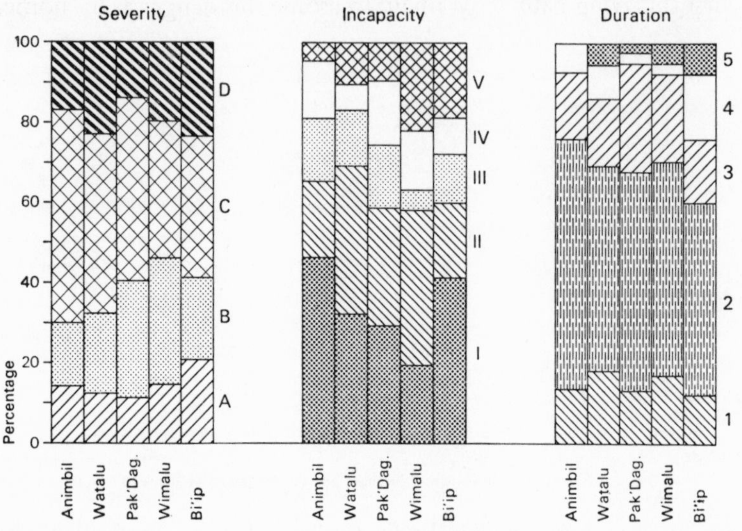

Fig. 21. Proportion contributed by each category of illness to the total recorded at each hamlet

Watalu as from any other hamlet. The other hamlets were very similar to each other in amounts of illness. Thus the lack of greater proportionate differences among categories of illness at Watalu compared to the other hamlets suggests that I obtained a more complete picture of illness at Watalu, rather than that I got a very different selection of the kinds of illness at that hamlet compared to the others.

SUMMARY

I have presented a general account from an observer's point of view of the impact and burden of illness in one Gnau village over

22 months. I have shown the differential distribution of illness by age and sex, the greater attention paid to trivial or mild illness in men, the greater amount of severe illness in infants and the older adults, and the relative freedom of children from illness. The behaviour of younger women in illness appeared to reflect a need they felt to emphasize the severity of their illness and so to justify not fulfilling their heavy domestic duties. The overall amount of time lost through illness by the village's people is much greater than in an industrial society (as in England), but this is due not only to the kinds and more severe consequences of illness in New Guinea, but also to different standards of appropriate conduct during illness. The men appear more ready to indulge their mild illnesses than women by taking time off when they are ill.

Examination of the record to show up discrepancies suggests that it is more complete for the hamlet in which I lived, and therefore that the overall record undercounts the total amount of illness. There were no gross disparities produced by a selective recording of illness in certain age or sex categories from particular hamlets, apart from the preponderance of the hamlet mentioned. This, as well as confirming that I learnt most about those whom I lived closer to, also may reflect a native and natural tendency for knowledge of illness and its care to be somewhat localized to the hamlet.

Behind this characterization of the patterns and prevalence of Gnau illness lies the intention to discover the associations between the medical facts of illness and the patterns of explanation and treatment used by the Gnau in response to them. The account given in this chapter will form the basis for later analysis of their responses to illness (Chapter 7) after I have discussed the principles underlying their behaviour and understanding of illness.

4
The Recognition of Illness

The aim of this chapter is to characterize a view of illness held by Gnau villagers. My concern is with their understanding of illness in general as a kind of state or condition in which people find themselves from time to time, rather than with their understanding of the various particulars of different illnesses or their specific causes. Indeed I shall include very little on their beliefs about the causes of illness. Illness and health are clearly contrasted for us as general concepts but we sometimes find it hard to draw a strict line and say on which side a particular case falls. Health and illness indicate either end or a continuum. Diseases show themselves in diverse ways but we see something common to them which allows us to put them within the general fold of illness while we consent to exclude from it other peculiarities occurring in people (such as gluttony, menstruation, white hair, nostalgia and love-sickness). Our view of what should be done when someone is ill and of how he should behave is guided by our understanding of the nature and significance of illness. We rarely find it necessary to define or specify the general and essential features of illness but they inform our responses to it. These general features are implied in behaviour perhaps more than they are formulated in words. They tend to elude exact statement.

This is also true of the Gnau view which I will try to characterize, and so I must describe the behaviour of Gnau people in illness, particularly in illness which they regard as serious or potentially so. Part of my interest in this behaviour was prompted by the ways in which it did not conform to how I expected a sick person to behave. The privileges of questioning and access to the sick person's body which I have taken for granted as a medical practitioner in my own country were not similarly given to me among the Gnau. In part this was to be expected from our mutual strangeness but just as with us the relations between doctor and patient are based on common assumptions concerning the situation so with the Gnau the sick person and those who care for him share certain assumptions and these do not provide an identical basis to ours for the relationship between patient and healer. That I deal with illness in general rather than in various particulars reflects an aspect of their assumptions; that I deal with the sick person and say little about the healer reflects another aspect. The role of specialist in treatment or expert healer is not sharply differentiated by them; almost any adult may on some specific occasion be considered the appropriate person to perform a part in treating a sick person, although senior men do most in treatment.

After describing the behaviour of someone sick, I will examine some of the words by which they refer to sickness. These words imply or suggest a link between illness and death and I go on to relate this link to their view of the normal course of life and the vulnerability of someone sick. One question lying behind my account of the Gnau view of illness is to know how it corresponds to ours, whether we find that they bring together a similar or different assembly of human states to those which we include within the domain of illness. The anthropologist who intends to study illness in another society from his own will want to decide what comes within the scope of his inquiry. If he also aims to understand social factors which influence the prevalence, course and outcome of illness there, or to show the problem of disease and how it is faced in that society, he should also in my opinion try to keep in mind a distinction between disease defined by external modern medical criteria and illness as it happens to be recognized in the society he studies. By preserving this conceptual separation between social or cultural factors and medical or biological ones, he will be better placed to observe their interrelations. I try to explain this distinction, though briefly, in the later part of this chapter before coming back to a final comment on what contrasts with illness – the Gnau view of health.

ILLNESS TO THE GNAU: THE MAIN DISTINCTIONS

The point of departure for a study of medicine in another society will be the patient, as it is what has happened to him that must be explained. What do the Gnau see as illness? While I was among them, I did not find or treat a wide variety of ailments. I treated people where I was able to and if they wished; I was also brought pigs and dogs to treat on occasion. In a most general sense nearly all of the conditions I saw, which we hold to be disorders of the body are admitted under the heading of things 'undesired', the word they use is *wola*. This is the only word which will net or include all these conditions. But *wola* is an adjective which would correspond to our word 'bad' – I could gloss it as 'ill' but it can also mean bad, evil, wretched, harmful and forbidden, powerfully dangerous, and it is also the only word they have for aged or old (although usually in this reference it is used with a completed action marker *bi* – i.e. *biwola*). I wish to note then that they lack a covering word which would differentiate illness in general from other undesirables as 'sickness' and 'illness' do in English.

But first it must be said that 'bad' or 'undesired' is not very different from the English word 'ill'. We apply the contrasting concepts of health and illness in everyday life and often we apply them with naive certainty. The manner in which they seem black and white, clear and straightforward as general concepts but yet at times prove obscure, subtle and uncertain when we ask how they apply to particular cases resembles the application of other judgements of value, like ones of moral good and bad. Long before medicine became scientific, health and illness existed as concepts related to basic values such as life and capacity for performance. Doctors work with a knowledge of the range of normal functions and the evidences of normal structure; but the knowledge of different organs or systems varies greatly. 'Medical science does not consist in elaborating these normal standards to arrive at a general concept of illness any more than it feels it should discover a single remedy for all its cases. The doctor's function rather consists in ascertaining what precise kind of state or event is presenting itself, on what it depends, how it proceeds and what will affect it. In the great variety of states and events called "disease" almost the only common factor is that disease implies something "harmful, unwanted and of an inferior character" ' (Jaspers 1963, p. 780). Thus with *wola* as their comprehensive term for ills the Gnau differ little from ourselves. It may be worth noting that the Pidgin English '*sik*' has been very readily assimilated by them and even by speakers who have only five or ten Pidgin words in all: but they certainly do *not* misuse *sik* for non-bodily misfortune.

When they applied *wola* to their ailments, I noted that someone could say either that his part was ill (a limb, tissue or organ), or that he himself was ill. In trivial things, like a cut or sore, the man is well, but a part of his skin is ill. In more severe disorders, a crucial distinction is made by the sick individual. It involves his perception of himself, his body image, for he may say either that it is he who is ill; or he may say that it is the part which is ill while he himself is well. This might seem to read things into a mere form of words but it was indeed the supplication repeated over weeks of a man, sorely ill, each time that he was brought forward to confront his afflicting spirit, Malyi, that it was not he but his joints only that were ill: and the figure Malyi would, quivering, bow, bending at the legs, then rise tall and stamp its foot in sign of acquiescence. The simple phrasing of these supplications was of this general form: 'I am a fit man (literally, a good man): it is my knees and my shoulders that hurt, they are ill – I am well. You must not kill me; it is only my knees not me, I am well'. It was also repeated and called out by the other men who surrounded and supported him as he faced the spirit.

The distinction of illness of the self and not only of a part of the body has far reaching consequences for their behaviour when ill. They distinguish part of the wide field of things we call illness with an intransitive verb which means 'to be sick' – *neyigeg* – he is sick. He suffers in his person as a whole. It applies to illnesses which are, for the most part, ones we would call internal, ones accompanied by pain, fever, nausea, debility or disturbances of breathing, of the bowels and so on. It does not cover external ailments like skin diseases, nor does it cover conditions which are long-standing states of disorder, for example limb deformities or stunted growth, mental defect; nor insidious illness – it was not applied to a woman with a slowly progressive nerve disease of paralysis and wasting muscles, or to a man with gradual worsening heart failure. Of these insidious diseases and the long-standing disorders, they said that those who had them were 'ruined', 'wretched', not that they were 'sick' (*leyigeg*) – they used the word *biwola*, the same word as that for 'old', 'aged' (i.e. *wola* with its completed action marker). Ills of the body may therefore be seen as ills of a part, or ills of the person; and the ills of the person may either be a present critical state, or a completed finite condition.

BEHAVIOUR IN SERIOUS ILLNESS

When someone is sick in the critical sense of *neyigeg*, his behaviour is conspicuously changed. It is not only altered by the physical effects of the disease, but also by conventions for behaviour – he shuns company and conversation; he lies apart, miserable in the dirt or inside a dark hut, the door shut; he rejects certain kinds of normal food, tobacco and areca nut; he eats alone; he begrimes himself with dust and ashes. Further degrees of this behaviour are seen in severe illness; more extreme restrictions of food are applied, men discard the phallocrypt and lie stark naked (although in all normal life as when bathing they would always hide their naked penises).

The first thing to note about this pattern of behaviour is that it involves a decision and one which the patient himself takes. The illnesses in which this behaviour is assumed vary greatly in objective severity but if someone regards himself as critically sick in his person, he adopts the behaviour. It is shown by both men and women. And he keeps it up until he thinks he is safely well. An ash-grimed man lies in the dirt and others say he is ill. I might be urged to go and treat him but on some occasions the patient would tell me in a low and confidential voice: 'I will be well tomorrow. I feel all right and have felt so for a few days but I stayed ill like this for a little more to be sure.'

Disease may be considered from the point of view of the observer or the patient reflecting on himself. As Charcot, the great nineteenth-century neurologist, observed: 'There is a particular moment between health and sickness when everything depends on the patient, the borderline between a discomfort which is accepted and the decision "I am ill" ' (Jaspers 1963, p. 425). This borderline is sharply defined by Gnau behaviour, and the decision is left, except for children, to the patient. In marked contrast to ourselves they do not expect others or specialists to discern for them whether or not they are ill, or when they are better. That is not the doctor's job.

What I have described represents the stereotype of how a Gnau patient should behave. Clearly the behaviour is patterned on common features of bad illness, and some people do not need to act or mime its signs. The things which most mark it as conventional, rather than a spontaneous expression of subjective feeling, are the conspicuous and rapid griming with dirt and ashes, the marked alteration in speaking voice, the disinclination to hold conversation, the placing apart from others, even were it only to lie outside in the sun where others anyway were gathered; and the consistent association of the essential signs when shown. In addition to these, the other signs mark an illness as more or less severe: the grading of severity is shown in greater reluctance to take part in conversation, the quavering thin voice, withdrawal into a hut with shut doors, avoidance of a wider range of foods, the anxiety and fears shown in trembling and agitation when many women gather near to a sick man; abandonment by men of all attire, including the phallocrypt; eventually, and this on the part of the patient's relatives, the fencing off of a part of ground round the patient with bamboo poles, magicked with leaves and spells, so that someone bearing ill to the patient will be struck or a spirit barred off should one seek to pass the magical barrier. The barrier also serves to alert and keep away people who might be carrying foods bringing dangers through the association of spirits with food.

In general the type of behaviour is withdrawal into a passive and wretched state: noisy, active or agitated signs of illness are uncommon and when someone ill groans or shouts with pain, as occasionally happens, it makes by contrast a more remarkable impression on other people. Women sometimes provide an exception to the general type of passive behaviour in illness when they show *bengbeng* behaviour. Gnau people say that this behaviour was first learnt in the early 1950s when a cargo cult spread to their villages. The behaviour was so characteristic of the cult, and shown by men and women, that when the Administration came to suppress the cult and in the course of doing this, gaoled a few men, although none from the Gnau villages, the interpretation of Gnau people was that the men were gaoled for *bengbeng*, that the behaviour itself is forbidden by the Administration, carrying the penalty of gaol. Sometimes *bengbeng* is accompanied by speech and revelations in the persona of a spirit, but not necessarily. Where I observed it in women as an early and arresting event in their illness, the chief features were frantic and uneven breathing while rapid cries were seemingly jerked out of them that rose and fell incontinently with their uneven breathing (the cries were often hus! hus! hus! hus! or he! he! he! he!). If they sat their bodies jerked in time to the cries or they strode round chanting incomprehensibly, or spoke messages from dead spirits or warnings. The cries or jerks could crescendo to a point of collapse called 'death', or else fade and fall silent; the woman then sat blank and tired out but in touch with her surroundings. I witnessed the point of collapse once, but *bengbeng* without obvious deep trance or collapse about fifteen times. In Gnau theory, *bengbeng* is due to possession by a spirit and the behaviour is not due to illness nor itself an illness; it may however reveal illness. Some women, after it had occurred, were regarded as ill and behaved in the appropriate withdrawn manner. They were treated but the treatment was not for the *bengbeng* which is not itself harmful, but for whatever it was that they were supposed to be afflicted with or by.

Thus *bengbeng* to the outside observer can appear as an additional way in which attention is drawn to illness, although to the Gnau what shows it is the withdrawn behaviour which follows: that is the general rule of illness. The showing of the withdrawn behaviour constitutes an appeal for help, a demonstration which obliges others, particularly the patient's closest relatives, to find out and treat his illness. As this was the appropriate form of a request for treatment by the patient, it was difficult to count requests for consultation in a way that could be compared with those, for example, of English patients. Actual requests or suggestions that I should visit someone ill came from a variety of people; if illness affected someone notable or was severe, I would be told to go recurrently through the day or days of his illness by all sorts of people, some of them perhaps had not been to his hamlet since he was ill, or did not know that I had already been. People rely largely on the silent showing of illness, and this works in a village where everyday life is public and the spread of news within it rapid. People quickly learn when someone is ill and if they have any sense of obligation, they come to find out what the matter is and how they can help.

COMMUNICATION WITH THE SICK PERSON

In critical illness, they become inert and withdrawn – others must take action to bring about their recovery. I was sometimes baffled and exasperated by this – few of those 'sick' themselves came for treatment at any time during my stay. But a random succession of their relatives, or of casual passers-by, would tell me to go and see whoever it was. If I asked how the patient was sick, they most often answered by generalities; or by symptoms which were not confirmed by the patient; or telling me sites of pain which were diffuse or proved inaccurate; or they occasionally said wrongly that the patient, even when this was their wife or father, had blood in the urine or had gone deaf. The most common answer was 'I don't know but he is very sick, sick all over'. Direct inquiries of the patient were often frustrated because he was showing rather than explaining how he was sick: he lay listless, head hanging and stared silently at the ground, he indicated sites of pain with indiscriminate gestures scattered over his body. A question to him was often answered for him by someone watching, and the sick man would rarely then bother to answer for himself or correct what others said.

Illness is displayed rather than described. I have emphasized this as it was one factor behind the apparent indifference to recounting symptoms which surprised me when I began. I could rarely get beyond learning that they were sick and had pain and fever. Later I collected over a hundred anatomical terms and I assembled from descriptions of symptoms and illness a vocabulary which was adequate to the precise and detailed description of pain in its varieties, and functional disturbances, and so on. Even though I knew the language better, it was always rare and difficult to obtain a subjective analytic account of symptoms from an ill person during his illness. But they can describe the changes occurring in illness. I would emphasize that their range of words reveals a perceptual awareness of pain, weakness, nausea, and so forth, which is in essentials like our own.

There is no ground to suppose that they fail to suffer physically in illness as we do. For most people in the world and over long stretches of time in our own history, ill health has meant feeling ill, suffering pain or incapacity and going in danger of death or mutilation. Whether this state could be traced to some structural change in the cells of the body did not enter into consideration in deciding whether a man was healthy or ill. Illness is recognized by the Gnau patient subjectively. It is communicated to others in a conventional manner which relies on non-verbal rather than verbal behaviour. They have a verb meaning to 'examine some-

K

thing carefully or closely' (e.g. to look at the engraved pattern on an arrow shaft which might identify its maker) but they do not apply the verb 'examine' to looking at a patient; one just 'sees' or 'looks at' him (root – *nakel*). The examining aspect of my medical approach was only cautiously accepted by them.

THE VERBS FOR SICKNESS AND THEIR IMPLICATIONS

When they talk of the kind of illness, which with them implies its cause, this is distinct from what they say of the manner of illness, indicating constraint, suffering and limitation. If you wish to know what kind of illness the patient has, you may be told the name of one of various agents causing illness, but this tells you virtually nothing about the clinical form or pathology of the illness. In so far as the answer is concerned with the cause, it corresponds to an aetiology, but as particular agents are not, or rarely, held to produce specified symptoms or signs of illness, one cannot deduce the kind of illness from knowing its cause. A few limited exceptions to this will be brought forward later on. By reference to the manner of illness then, I mean description of its observed form and kind as something roughly parallel to what we would call its clinical description, or else its pathology. It is in this respect that verbal distinctions about kinds of illness are lacking in Gnau. They have the necessary vocabulary to define the site and features of a disease but they do not ordinarily refer to it to analyse and define how someone is ill.

Instead this is indicated in only general terms through the discriminations of certain verbs. It is characteristic of their language that these discriminations are made by verbs. I should note that they rarely have substantives or nouns for things like emotions, particular rites, acts of ritual, sorcery: all these concepts are identified in verbs. Three verb roots can be related to expressions for health and illness. They are *-p-*, *-t-*, *-g-*, which are easier to grasp in third person masculine present tense forms: viz.:

nap – he lives; *nat* – he sleeps; *nag* – he dies;

and

nap – he stays; *nat* – he lies; *nag* – he is inert.

The live and sleep roots *-p-* and *-t-* are both used to say of things that they 'exist', 'are somewhere', 'stay'; the root used depends on context as to the more active or passive quality of staying (for instance as between nuts staying on the branch, and the nuts staying (put) in the bag). Only *nap* is used to mean 'he lives'. *Nag* means 'he dies' but is used of a man fallen unconscious, even though they know he will come to in a moment and get up. The root *-g-* is also used for the moment when sago flour being mixed with boiling water and swirled round, suddenly goes solid, it gells, it 'dies' (*wag*). The future tense form of *nag* is *neyig* – 'he will die'.

root	3rd masc. sing.	verbs of sickness		
		syllabic reduplication	incomplete action marker *-mb-*	both
-p-	*nap* 'lives'			
-t-	*nat* 'sleeps'	*natet*	*nambet*	*nambatet*
-g-	*nag* 'dies'	*nageg*	*nambeg*	
	neyig 'will die'	*neyigeg*		

In Gnau, emphasis, exertion, repetitiveness can be introduced into the action described in a verb by reduplication of a component syllable, for instance: *nalep* – 'he went', *nalelep* – 'he went on and on', or *nap a'an* – 'he stayed in the bush', *napap a'an* – 'he stayed on and on in the bush'. In the verbs for sickness we find a series of syllabic reduplications of the verb roots for sleeping and dying. The basic verb for 'he is sick' (*neyigeg*) is a reduplicated form from *neyig* – 'he will die'. There are also forms which incorporate the incompleted action marker *-mb-*. The reduplication of the root of the verb 'to die' modifies its action rather than intensifies it, as is usual. The verbs for sickness are specific; I learnt them to mean sickness as synonyms for *neyigeg* without discerning distinctive meanings for them at first or noticing their morphological relationships to the 'sleep' and 'die' verb roots. *Neyigeg* is the verb for 'he is sick': it does not by itself imply degree of illness. *Natet* and *nambet* and *nambatet* are used to suggest continuing illness either severe or minor and they may be qualified adverbially. *Nambeg* and *nageg* imply severe illness. The use of simple behavioural description to indicate more complex human conditions, emotions or responses is characteristic of Gnau idiom – for example in a phrase such as 'they said to him "Eat!"; he sat', the words 'he sat' are understood to mean he refused the offer. The form of verbs for sickness seems to link sleep, lying, constraint, dying, the risk of death and sickness.

It is not easy to determine by questions in the abstract whether one is right to infer such a conceptual link from the forms of verbs. If you turn to look at their food taboos you find that the sanctions for many of them are given in terms of constraint – implying illness – if you eat this or that which is forbidden you will be heavy, you will be confined to the village – by implication illness will take from you activity, freedom and movement; they do not usually specify how, although if you ask it is most often said by breathlessness and weak and painful limbs. If now you look to the overall pattern of food taboos you find that at each stage of life those foods which are forbidden are called *wola*. There are two peaks of restriction when food taboos are most complicated and extensive. One is from birth to the age of about three to four years (objectively a dangerous period of their lives judged by their infant and toddler mortality rates). The second peak is from puberty until a man or woman has grown up children (the restrictions are most marked for a couple with its first infant) and after this time more of the forbidden 'bad' foods are permitted until, in old age, virtually all that was classed *wola* becomes permissible. Thus the quality of 'bad' is not attributed to food as an absolute or inherent quality (except where that which might be eaten is never classed as 'food'), but as a quality relative to the status, biological or social, of the person.

I am trying to get at their view, implicit, perhaps ill-defined or vague, of the relation of sickness to the normal course of life. As they see it, people develop to a stage of full maturity not at but after puberty at about the time when they have their first children. This is the stage when a person is fully entire or complete – the word they use is *nembli* (it means 'entire' in the sense, say, of a sprig of nettle leaves before you have plucked off any of the leaves). From this whole and untried state, a person does things like having children, learning to plant new things, shooting pigs; and in regard to performing all sorts of activities like planting something he has not done before, or shooting a cassowary, he is *nemblin* – 'whole, untried' in that respect. The attitude towards achievement is similar to that implied by the much more formal recognition given by Iatmul to achievement or first performance through *naven* behaviour (Bateson 1936, Chap. 2). Progressively as the Gnau man proves himself in these things, the restrictions protecting him are lifted. Progressively he moves towards that eventual state of old age which they call *biwola*. Thus his first child is said to be *nemblisa* – the child of his 'wholeness', or of his whole blood, and each subsequent child is relatively less the child of his whole blood than the one before; and the sanctions for the taboos between siblings which depend on birth order are phrased by reference to this diminishing completeness of their source. As the individual moves from maturity in this *nembli* sense, he declines towards old age, *biwolen*, and he is allowed more and more of the things which were *wola*, which would before have endangered him with illness, a premature decrepitude. So for a death which comes in old age, they do not so usually search out an explanation by some particular cause.

THE MOTIVES OF GNAU BEHAVIOUR IN ILLNESS

For them illness is a state in which many factors may play a part. The conventions of their behaviour when ill give a general uniformity to the outward show of illness and tend to mask the different and distinguishing signs of syndromes or symptom complexes. The sick appear most wretched and degraded: they are cut off from normal life. They are well able to describe the intention of this behaviour and they explain it in this general way: 'If you are ill you are in danger of continued or aggravated illness from which you could die. You are in danger of attracting the attention of many spirits, and you are weak. You must abstain from foods which you know spirits are likely to be watching over and especially if you know which spirit is at work in your illness, you must not eat any of those foods with which it is particularly associated. If you ate them, it might say "Have I not warned you already and you go eating my things again?" You withdraw from normal activity and conversation because other people may bring with them dangerous influences either from their sexual or ritual condition, or from spirits which follow or watch over them and may turn their eyes towards you or smell you out in your weakness and turn aside to strike you and compound your illness. Once ill you are in greater danger of further and cumulative attack. You must appear wretched for in this way you may deceive a spirit into thinking its aim, which is your bodily ruin, accomplished and it may leave you.' The chief features then are the patient's vulnerability, his need to avoid drawing attention to himself and to appear wretched. Sympathy gatherings are held for sick people but the patient is not participant at them or often visible, nor do visitors go to see him. People should not be loose-tongued in speaking a sick man's name; in some circumstances it is forbidden. Sometimes I have seen a very ill man twitch with agitation and tremble because women crowded too close around him. In many ways their behaviour when ill resembles a rite of passage; it is indeed a life crisis. The end of illness and the return to normal life is marked by the patient going to bathe and wash away the filth of his illness – the usual way they say 'I am better' is in fact by the implication of the phrase 'I have washed'.

ILLNESS AS A 'RITE DE PASSAGE'

The form is close to that of a *rite de passage*, containing elements of separation, marginality and aggregation (e.g. the changes of attire, the withdrawal, silence, food abstention, the final purifying wash). It is expressive and conventionalized. In illness, the person passes through a crisis: as with puberty or childbirth or death, the timing of the events is, at least to our view, set by nature rather than society. The word 'crisis' applies aptly to illness with its accompanying threat of loss of life, mutilation or such damage as will deprive the sufferer of his independence and fitness to fulfil his obligations and his hopes, or deprive him of his previous status. The behaviour emphasizes marginality: withdrawal from danger, abstention from normal life in the hope that it will protect the victim from a bad or the worst outcome. But in contrast to the rites for puberty, maturity, birth, marriage or death, the crisis of illness is not usually among the Gnau the prelude to assumption of a new social status, but rather by the illness itself, the victim is unfitted or forced from his usual position in society. The conventionalized aspects of the behaviour in illness underline or signal this unfit state, an unwelcomed change, to other people. If the patient survives it, he hopes to return to his previous status, not to some new one. In some other societies, the illness is itself the passport to a new status, or the possibility of achieving it: in the Ndembu cults of affliction described by Turner certain rights of participation and roles are open only to those who have passed through the illness and its treatment (Turner 1968). An illness interpreted as possession by pathogenic spirits is often 'the normal road to the assumption of the shaman's calling' (I. M. Lewis 1971, p. 54 and Chap. 3). Among the Gnau this view of affliction is almost absent; but primacy in holding one large ritual (that of Malyi), which was acquired by the Gnau from a neighbouring tribe, is given to the lineage descendants of the man who was first struck down by the spirit and for whose treatment it was bought and learnt: his descendants are those who now direct and officiate in the performance of this ritual. But those who themselves have been struck down by the spirit remain, in their opinion, at greater risk than others from it, and take care not to approach the spirit's image, or to eat in the men's house where it is housed, or go to sing there for it when its full ritual is performed.

THE CLASSIFICATION OF ILLNESS

Apart from the general nature of illness, there is the question of the classification of kinds of illness. I have already indicated that the Gnau do not depend on observations of the physical signs or symptoms of illness to discriminate between them; in this, they differ from Subanun (Frake 1961) Azande (Evans-Pritchard 1937), or Lunda people (Turner 1963) and ourselves, who each have a more precise scheme for illnesses differentiated by their clinical signs.[1] In our system of medicine, signs or symptoms are the indicators of disease; the disease can be inferred from these observations. Although Gnau people could describe pains or physiological disorders, such descriptions were rarely given by patients.

A collection of descriptions of symptoms is not the same as a set of disease names: it does not necessarily imply a classification – at least not in the systematic or conceptual sense. The contrast or distinction is that between percept and concept: one can describe one's perceptions of illness without necessarily organizing

[1] Skin diseases must be excepted for the Gnau distinguish finely between different skin fungus diseases, and name variously some defects of the skin. Incidentally it is interesting, when we recall where and how they live, to note that they do not distinguish between cut, abrasion or injury to the skin surface and infected cut or sore: they are all called *maniwolem*.

these by some conceptual scheme of kinds of illness. Classification is used to organize knowledge and the selection of features used in a classification is usually significant for some purpose: the subject matter comes to be organized into a system. In study of the principles of division in a classification we hope to discover something of what others judge to be significant and relevant.

The Gnau used a few verbs to differentiate the severity of sickness; they also distinguished sickness of the whole person from that of a part. However they did classify illness further not at the level of its manifestations, but instead at that of its causes. Once someone had become sick in the serious sense of *neyigeg*, it was common for them to refer to what had happened, or was happening to him, by naming the cause. Treatment depended on identifying it. Since in their view causes were not discernible from the clinical signs, exact description of these was not relevant. Cause and remedy were to be revealed by other evidence than that of the body's state. One might be tempted to say of the Gnau that they have no word to distinguish illness from other afflictions or misfortunes: the word *wola* does not do so. On the other hand, they have a verb (*neyigeg*) which is quite specific for the critical field of illness.[1] At what level of interpretation is it right to say that some people do not distinguish bodily from other affliction? I doubt that anyone intends to imply it in the literal sense and suggest that they lack perceptual sensory awareness of the boundary between self and things outside themselves. Lévy Bruhl proposed that primitive man's outlook on the world differed from ours because various collective representations so ordered his understanding that he conceived there sometimes was a mystical participation between himself and certain things of the outside world. He did not argue that the senses or cerebral structure of primitive man differed from ours. Piaget from his studies of child cognition also put the view forward that a child does not distinguish clearly between his self and the outside world; the physical world is not sharply divided off as material and inanimate but instead is treated as though it were alive, responsive and willing. Both have suggested that people can have

[1] The names for objects, events or kin relationships are easier to study and classify – or perhaps just more obvious – than verbs: at least it is nearly always nouns, occasionally adjectives, which appear in the taxonomies analysed by anthropologists.

blurred views of the distinction between self and outside world, but they analyse cognitive conceptions of the relationships between self and outside things; it is not suggested that there is failure to sense (perceive) the distinction between a blow struck on one's self and one which struck one's discarded clothing or a tree. When it is said that illness is not discriminated from other afflictions what is meant, I take it, is that the causes and explanations for both kinds of misfortune are thought to be the same. However the outstanding and universal subjective property of illness is that it afflicts the individual person. In behaviour, in the conventional withdrawal of the Gnau patient, the personal crisis of illness is sharply differentiated from other misfortune.

A clinical classification of disease as detailed as the one described by Frake (1961) for the Subanun of the Philippines provokes question of the reason for so many names: he recorded 186 human disease names; 132 of these were single word labels for diagnostic categories, the rest standard descriptive categories like 'stomach ache' or 'swollen liver'. One might expect that, if diseases are named by reference to their clinical manifestations, then these signs are significant either because they indicate a cause or because they have a bearing on the treatment to be used. In the reports of Evans-Pritchard (1937) on Zande leechcraft, and of Turner (1963) on Lunda medicine, this seems to be the case. In both examples they describe treatment by specifics, by herbs and medicines whose appropriate composition depends on recognizing the kind of illness by its symptoms. The fact that they have herbal remedies, or some explanation for the nature of symptoms, does not necessarily replace a set of explanations or remedies on a different level, for instance explanation by witchcraft. The analysis of how such a system involving explanation at different levels worked was of course a central theme of Evans-Pritchard's book on the Azande. Although Frake was dealing with Subanun diagnosis not treatment, he mentions that 'everyone is his own herbalist' and that 'diagnosis – the decision of what name to apply to an instance of being sick – is a pivotal cognitive step in the selection of culturally appropriate responses to illness by the Subanun. It bears on the selection of ordinary botanically derived medicinal remedies from 724 recorded alternatives' (Frake 1961, p. 132). In comparison the Gnau are pitiful herbalists. They rely on stinging nettle leaves as counter-irritants, or razor cuts over sites of pain. They have some bark and sap dressings for cuts and sores, and on these they also put occasionally white silt from the river, lime or urine. They prepare bark poultices for painful joints, they chew ginger for colds or sore throats (or another aromatic bark). But in serious illness, only nettle leaves are commonly used. They use no specific herbs in the sense of plants whose medicinal use depends on the clinical signs observed. But there are many plants which must be used in ritual treatment, although few are eaten or rubbed or plastered on the patient's body: their use is dependent on identification of cause and on knowledge of the complex relationships between spirits and plants.

RESPONSIBILITY IN ASSUMING SICK BEHAVIOUR

I would like to go over some of the more striking features of these observations. When a Gnau person thinks his illness involves a threat to himself as a whole, he behaves in a way that indicates this clearly to others. Sickness in this sense is thought to be critical because they believe that it involves a threat to life – the recognition 'he will die' implied in the etymology[1] of the verb *neyigeg*. The causes said to produce it, such as spirits, destructive magic and sorcery, are explicitly and conventionally held to cause lethal illness, not just illness, and the outcome will be death unless appropriate and effective treatment can be performed. Once ill, the sick person is more vulnerable to further attack and compounded illness. His isolation and withdrawal from normal life contains an important element of prudence.

The decision that his illness is critical rests with the sick person. He is judge of when he is at risk, and he discerns this mainly on subjective grounds – his sense of being ill – but he may also take into account the dangers he has exposed himself to and any signs or revelations such as those of dreams or strange events. Recognition of critical illness is in principle held to be private to the individual, not questionable or requiring legitimation or proof in objective physical signs in the clinical sense. However children must at first depend on the judgement of others when they fall ill and people do assess by general appearance how seriously ill

[1] Which perhaps I should note escaped me for a long time during my fieldwork.

someone else is and also sometimes give advice to others to be more careful; they may comment on or question the severity of someone's illness when they talk to other people about it. The conventions for sick behaviour mask differences in the objective effects of various illnesses and make it hard to assess severity. The intention to dissemble, to appear more wretched and ill than one feels, to trick a spirit into leaving, is an explicit element in this behaviour – again it is a matter of prudence. The outward appearance of illness may be deceptive. This the Gnau know but they are not convinced that the way to find this out is by inspection and examination of the sick person. Malingering, the complete pretence of severe illness, was mentioned to me a number of times as a trick used commonly by those who intended to erupt in the disguise of evil ancestors (*mami wolendem*) at night during the performance of a particular dance ritual (*Wolpililyiwa*), and also occasionally by those who planned a murder.

If one accepts their opinion that the individual knows if he is critically ill and that others cannot really tell true from pretended illness by objective clinical signs, and if illness is also a legitimate ground for avoiding normal obligation, one may ask what stops them from pretending illness often to evade unpleasant duty? The question is connected with the more subtle one of deciding whether their conventions about illness tend to encourage the valetudinarian, or to allow illness to become an indulgence. The social isolation, starving, dirt and abject lot of someone who is critically sick seemed to me very discouraging. There are few comforts for the sick. A man whose serious illness dragged on for many weeks lay much of the time naked, silent and alone in a small smoky hut with the door shut, therefore in the dark, hearing people's voices outside but not talked to; sometimes for part of the day he had to lie on his excrement; late in his illness he developed a toxic psychosis and he was visited at times by people who came to wail over him at his approaching death. His isolation and debility were pitiful.

With the decision to behave as critically ill comes dependence on others as well as exemption from some obligations. The responsibility for providing treatment, for searching out and bringing someone to do it if necessary, rests with close kin primarily and then the wider circle of co-villagers. Rarely the patient himself may perform some small treatment ritual for himself; commonly he will give some indication of what he thinks needs doing. In part his behaviour while ill – his deceptive wretchedness, abstinence from certain foods, for example – is intended to be protective and remedial, self-determined treatment. But in general the sick person must submit to the decisions of others, he cannot go to find someone if he wants him to treat him, he cannot fetch the ritual plants he needs. He appears apathetic and miserable. If others decide to do some treatment for him, he submits, perhaps without knowing the deductions which have led them to choose to do it, for it is not necessarily discussed with him beforehand. If his mother's brothers persuade his brothers that he has a better chance of recovery if he is moved to their hamlet, then off he is taken. The energy and urgency with which other people arrange to treat someone who is ill, the gatherings in sympathy at the hamlet where he lies, provide an index of their feeling and esteem, their sense of obligation, for him. In the case of at least one man, the neglect and indifference shown by his relatives and neighbours was very bitter to him.

As inferences about the cause of an illness are not considered by them to come from physical examination there is no reason to pay special attention to clinical signs or to grant the healer special rights to examine the patient's body. The patient waits for people to treat him, for his relatives to arrange this or send for someone. He submits to treatment rather than co-operates in it.

PROBLEMS OF COMPARISON: ILLNESS AND DISEASE

At the outset I wrote that only the word *wola* would cover all their ailments. The word means 'bad' and can be used in many other and much wider contexts than only ailment: a man who has recently taken part in ritual is *wolen* in the sense of being dangerous to others; a woman menstruating is *wola*, both dangerous to men and vulnerable herself. Her withdrawal from normal life, her purifying wash after her menstrual period is ended, offer parallels to the behaviour of someone sick in the *neyigeg* sense; but she is not spoken of as *weyigeg*, only as *wola*. The same would apply to a woman in and after childbirth. The area of ills of the person or self, not merely the part, is the one circumscribed by *neyigeg* and it denotes present active critical illness. The medical correlates of *neyigeg* vary greatly: it may only be a headache. It excludes long-standing, slowly changing disorders or completed ones;[1] instead they describe people with these as *biwola* – wretched, ruined or old. These are not seen as critical destroying illnesses.

In attempting to compare the boundaries they give to illness with our own, we may be led to ask if our view has clear limits. Do we define the field of medicine clearly? It may be futile or frustrating to look for equivalents for medicine in other societies if medicine is a vague concept and peculiar to our way of thinking.

In English 'medicine' can be given the traditional meaning of the art of healing. There have been sick people ever since man inhabited the earth. Or medicine can be given the meaning it has come to have now, that is, study of the diagnosis, treatment and prevention of disease. The traditional sense, the art of healing, implies that medicine is concerned with people or patients; with conditions of man; while the modern sense, study and control of disease implies rather study of a thing, disease. The change of emphasis from conditions of people to a study of disease entities is attested to in the history of European medicine. It is associated especially with Thomas Sydenham who repudiated the general supposition 'that diseases are no more than the confused and irregular operations of disordered and debilitated nature and consequently that it is fruitless to labour to endeavour to give a just description of them'. Instead he maintained that 'Nature, in the production of disease, is uniform and consistent . . . The self same phenomenon that you observe in the Sickness of a Socrates, you would observe in the Sickness of a simpleton' (Sydenham 1676). Sydenham's view has come to dominate nosology. Before him, disease had been considered as a deviation from the normal in which a healthy man through the influence of any number of factors – physical or mental – was changed and suffered. Following Cohen (1961) we could formulate this view as $A \xrightarrow{\searrow\downarrow\swarrow} A^1$ where A was a healthy man. The later view was that disease was a distinct entity. In the second view when a healthy man A fell ill, he became A+B, where B is a disease $(A \xrightarrow{B} A+B)$ This view maintained that there were innumerable Bs, each with

[1] Perhaps rather similarly we do not usually speak of mental defect or certain congenital anomalies as illnesses.

its individual and recognizable characteristics. The recognition of disease entities through patterns of symptoms and signs is not of course restricted to Europe. Evans-Pritchard for example, wrote of the Azande: 'In such cases the disease had to be diagnosed and named and a specific remedy applied. This very naming and identification of the disease objectifies and gives it a reality of its own independent of witchcraft . . .' (Evans-Pritchard 1937, p. 508). But the Gnau view is not like that.

Our diagnostic nomenclature is largely a taxonomy by pathological anatomy; it classifies morphological form not clinical function; disease, but not people or illness; it is a classification by clinical inference rather than one by clinical observation. At the end of examination, the doctor covers over all the clinical detail by giving a diagnostic label to the patient's illness. I summarize the analysis of Feinstein (1967) who, in his critique of clinical judgement, calls for a clinician's nomenclature which should classify a host, *and* an illness, *and* a disease. Either the traditional view of medicine or the modern one, obliges us to look further – if medicine is the art of healing, what is the state or process in man that is to be healed? The answer 'sickness', then what is 'sickness'? Or if we take the second view then we must define disease.

I will briefly consider what is implied by the scientific notion of disease. It is unusual to find a general concept of disease made explicit in medical writing: such writing abounds instead with the concepts of particular diseases. From a biological standpoint, certain kinds of change in any living species may be called disease. In global perspective such changes may be seen to result from varied causes such as genetic change, maladaptation to environment; environmental change; the predatory, parasitic and competitive habits of different organisms – bacteria for instance. The concept of disease is focussed on the individual of a species. The delicate spirochaete of syphilis must have precisely set conditions to live and these are given by the human body: it is in terms of its effects on individuals of the human species that we call syphilis a disease. We call it a disease because it alters the physiological and psychological functions of the individual man or woman and these functional changes reduce the capacity of the affected individual to survive or reproduce. These are the essential features of a biological view of disease. I assert then that doctors recognize disease through disorder of physiological and psychological function.

Man, unlike trees or beasts, can reflect on and talk about changes in himself. I have used the word 'disease' to set it in a biological frame and I will use the word 'illness' to distinguish – and perhaps artificially to emphasize – that people recognize either in themselves or others, certain changes of body or mind as undesired, as ills, and that what particular people so recognize may vary. I wish to contrast, on the one hand, 'disease' defined by criteria of a biological nature, and applying generally to the human species, with, on the other hand, 'illness' which will be determined by the views of particular individuals or cultures – it is of a social and psychological nature. By using disease in the biological sense we set bounds about the field relevant to our inquiry. By reference to 'illness' we examine how individuals perceive and interpret changes in their condition. The reason for making this distinction is to clarify what we are about if, for example, we wish to examine the nebulous view that disease may affect culture and culture affect disease. A social anthropologist may quite well find that some diseases are not regarded as 'illness' by those he studies; he may find illness of the body apparently undifferentiated from other misfortunes such as a house catching fire or drought. He may urge then that medicine is a category like 'magic' or 'religion' tainted by our particular conceptual bias; hard to use in comparative study.

The sphere thought proper to medicine depends on the conceptions of health and illness which prevail in the society; these suggest for example what people expect doctors to treat. In Samuel Butler's *Erewhon* you find the problem in a nutshell:

> In that country, if a man . . . catches any disorder, or fails bodily in any way before he is seventy years old, he is tried before a jury of his country men, and if convicted is held up to public scorn and sentenced more or less severely as the case may be . . . But if a man forges a cheque or sets his house on fire or robs with violence from the person or does any other such things as are criminal in our country, he is either taken to a hospital or most carefully tended at the public expense, or if he is in good circumstances, he lets it be known to all his friends that he is suffering from a severe fit of immorality . . . and they come and visit him with great solicitude, and inquire with interest how

it all came about, what symptoms first showed themselves and so forth.

Erewhon was of course nowhere, but the problem it suggests is this: Should the medical ethnographer in *Erewhon* concentrate on the management of embezzlers or dyspeptics? In my view he should study the dyspeptics.

The grounds for accepting that disease in modern medicine is conceived in biological and objective terms and lacks any essential social features have been discussed – especially in reference to mental illness and criminal responsibility (see Paul Halmos 1957, Chap. 2; A. J. Lewis 1953; Wootton 1959, Chaps. 7 and 8). I will not present the case in detail here, but only indicate some of the crucial issues presented by the authors I have just referred to. I think a strong case in favour of this view can be made. If such a view is valid, then we have the means to keep social well-being apart from health and disease separate from social deviance or maladjustment: if we keep them distinct conceptually we are better placed to observe their interrelations. Even if disease criteria are in essence physiological and psychological, we must often be highly dependent on knowing the social and cultural background in order to appraise the conduct and efficiency of these functions. We cannot ignore social considerations when we assess their adequacy but we are not bound to consider whether the behaviour is socially deviant in order to decide if disease is present. The point of the argument is that some have proposed social adaptation as a yardstick for health or mental health. But how do we decide success or failure in social adaptation? Who sets the criteria or indications of maladaptation? If social disapproval plays a large part in deciding what is called maladaptation then this will vary from group to group who express the disapproval. Then the decision on whether disease was present would depend on which group expressed the disapproval. The demarcation of health and disease would be shifting – for example with the state and saturation of the employment market if the ability to hold a job were a criterion of social adaptation and therefore health. If social adaptation is the criterion of health it is possible that the valued and desired state which adaptation is to attain or maintain may itself turn out to be health: as far as that is true social adaptation will be a tautology for health. For these chief reasons I think we are wise to accept external biological criteria of disease and compare these with the concepts of illness which prevail in a particular society, rather than to depend solely on sociological definitions of illness.

HEALTH

In most of what I have written so far, my explicit concern has been with illness, with the recognition of disease. The other side of the coin is health. The biological view of disease, which I briefly presented, in effect implied that for practical purposes health may be defined as the absence of identifiable disease or infirmity – a negative view. But among us health has much more commonly received recognition as an ideal, for example, by the World Health Organization whose Constitution begins: 'Health is a state of complete physical, mental and social well-being and not merely the absence of disease or infirmity'. Ideals involve notions that go beyond what is to what ought to be. Since their claim is to formulate what ought to be rather than what is, they cannot be verified in the sense of being shown to correspond to fact. The doctor proceeds from knowledge of the range of normal function and the evidences of normal structure; but the knowledge of different organs and systems varies greatly. The criteria of normality in medicine are both statistical and ideal; they are ideal in the sense that the proper functioning of different organs is conceived with the help of teleology – the scientist tries to determine what the relationships of different organs are, what purposes they serve; it entails the notion of proper function adequate to a purpose. Many of the most important functions of the organism are those which regulate and integrate the working of separate systems; some ideal of integration and balance, and the separate contributions of different parts to this whole comes to be involved in judgements of adequacy. In practice the doctor has no reliable positive indications of when ideal balance is achieved; instead he considers healthy the man who is free from any evidence of disease or infirmity. Health in the positive sense is an ideal 'approached but not attained' (Polgar 1968). Polgar distinguishes this asymptotic view of health from two other kinds, which he terms the elastic concept and the open-ended view. The elastic view holds that health is an accumulated resistance to potential dangers. The view adopted is a preventive one which foresees illness as likely to happen in some form. In the open-ended view, health has no definite limits; put briefly, health is anything better than death. The implicit view of health which the Gnau would appear to hold comes closest to the elastic view in which illness is part of living or a risk of living. There is a normal course to life in which vigour and strength to resist illness waxes and then wanes; such a view makes the deaths of infants and the old more ordinary than those of people in their prime. Many of their rules of behaviour, especially their taboos, are phrased as rules of prudence by which health may be preserved. As I went round the village during the October epidemic of influenza, I came to one man sitting in his hamlet, where there were many lying scattered about miserable in the dirt, and he said: 'I have not got it. I am a hardwood post. I am well.' The idea of resistance was expressed clearly and with pride. Similarly the notion of variable resistance can be deduced from the tentative, testing way people try out the foods that were specially forbidden them when ill, and the progressive way in which foods that were once taboo become permissible after someone has shown that he can do something, or has passed the stage of vulnerability. In old age the most enduring food taboos are raised, but people argue uncertainly that this is either because the food will not harm them, or because they are already past their prime, the food will not matter if it debilitates them since enfeeblement and weakening are natural to old age; the old are not expected to maintain or in the same way to husband their health. The old men have fulfilled their duties and should stand aside to watch the young men kill their game. To quote the words of a Gnau man as he invoked his ancestral dead at a hunting ritual for a grandchild:

> Now we two have long been full grown men; no longer will we kill pigs – no, these young men are growing up to hunt, we now eat forbidden foods, we have begotten children who are now grown up and adult . . . Our children have borne children. The things of hunting are for us no longer; we eat the forbidden foods which scare game away. Shall we still kill? These young men, they must kill; they, young men, rise up and kill their game because they are still men with the good smell, the smell of youth.

The notion of health as resistance still allows it the quality of an ideal; it is desired and admired. Men and women take pride in good health, as I mentioned when explaining the difficulties of inquiring about past illness. But they imagine that the malicious spirits may sometimes look on a vigorous person and say, 'there is a young man, flaunting himself, I will make him shout with pain', and strike him down in preference to a decrepit unappealing old man. I can quote a tape-recorded example of this kind of thinking, though it was expressed in joke – an old man riposting to a young man who had teased him;

When I am dead and you come along my path I will fasten tight round you – fine young man! you come along my path – I will strike you and when the old dry yam-mami [i.e. an old man] comes along I'll let him be, that appetising one there, that's the one my eyes will rest on – aargh! strike him down, that one!

5
Classes of Cause

The preceding chapter was primarily concerned with the sick person and the changes occurring in him by which illness was recognized. I described the typical features of their responses when illness was considered serious or potentially serious. In doing so, I made no analysis of the questions which most urgently concern them in this situation – the likely cause of the illness and its correct treatment. The identification of a specific cause often indicates the line of particular treatment required. Its identification depends on a general understanding of the nature and dispositions of various spirit causes, the powers available to men using magic and sorcery; and the dangers of breaking taboos. The recent movements, activities and social relations of the patient are then usually reviewed in an attempt to reason out the most likely source of his sickness. Many different people may speculate about the cause of someone's illness if he or she appears seriously ill or if the sick person is someone important. Revelations contained in dreams or strange events may also indicate it and sometimes the cause is searched out by divination. There need be no public declaration of cause, no statement of final conclusions and no general consensus. The evident resolve to find out and decide about the cause varies greatly with persons and illnesses. If a person of no concern to one's interlocutor is ill, the sick person may be said by him to be 'just sick' (*neyigeg gipi'i* – he is sick nothingly) or, even if he has died after an illness, he may be said 'just to have died' (*nag diyi* – he died for no reason, by no cause or purpose).

The common form of diagnosis by the Gnau is a diagnosis of the cause and not the manner or clinical type of illness. It is in this sense that they may be said to classify and distinguish between illnesses. The present chapter and the next one will analyse their understanding of the causation of illness mainly from a cognitive and theoretical point of view. After these two chapters, I will present my findings on the cases of illness which happened during my field study where I was able to observe what they did and question them about the diagnosis and thereby see how they applied their theories of illness to actual instances. In this chapter and the next I will not therefore examine the practice but rather the theories which lie behind their 'system' of medicine. I put 'system' in inverted commas because their beliefs about illness do not constitute a clearly bounded field of knowledge co-ordinated and organized as a whole around illness as the central subject. Instead a statement in detail concerning all illnesses would need to describe their ideas about a wide variety of human pursuits and supernatural powers in which there are possible consequences for health and illness. In this chapter I concern myself only with the main classes of cause in an attempt first, to make plain their general nature and second, to show how some of the causes are associated particularly with certain individuals, with groups of persons or with people in particular relationships. I approach the general nature of spirits in Gnau thought through the distinctions they make between human beings and different types of spirit, and the extent to which spirits are personified. I give some detail on the difficulty I experienced in determining differences between spirits and on the links they recognize associating people and spirits. The question of spiritual differences and identities is a familiar anthropologist's problem (see for example Evans-Pritchard 1954); my concern with it here is chiefly to bring out how the identity and name of a spirit may be more or less precisely defined. The complexity in this, the fluidity or sequence of definition of named identities and their more limited associations, allows for a diagnosis to be refined and made precise or altered during the progress of an illness or after the more elaborate disclosure of the forces possibly at work in it.

It is necessary to understand the general principles by which they link spirits and their concerns with people so as to be able to follow why they turn to a particular person as the appropriate healer or ritual officiant, and on what grounds they deduce that certain activities of the sick person may have exposed him to harm. I have not space here to give a full account of Gnau religious ideas: in the section on Panu'et (pp. 169–80) I have provided an illustration of the variety of identifications and concerns of one of their major spirits which shows the complexity I have mentioned. I will list the main concerns of various spirits in the course of this chapter to show in outline the putative divisions of labour and responsibility among spirits which bear on diagnosis. The general nature of views on magic, sorcery and then taboo are presented after that. In the next chapter, I take up the question of how they interpret the effects of causes on people and I will consider then some general aspects of evidence in diagnosis.

SPIRITS

The Gnau distinguish human beings (*matildel*) from all kinds of spirit (*malet*).

Matilden – a human being: *malet* – a spirit

The most comprehensive distinction between human beings and spirits is made with the two words above. As a species, human beings in the singular are given a suffixed ending appropriate to sex and '*matil*' can be used adjectivally to mean 'human'. *Matilden* refers also to the whole body of a dead person which remains at death to be put in the ground to rot. *Malet* is the most general word for spirit, and it can be used of any of the kinds of spirit which they recognize although it may denote a restricted class among these spirits in certain contexts. Its general application to spirits is shown by usages like *malet-belyi'it* or *malet-gelputi* where it is compounded with a second word for a particular class of spirit. But this word *malet* for spirit cannot apply to any attribute of the living human person.[1]

Matilden – human being: *malauda* – shadow: *gelputi* – shade

Indeed the Gnau do not formulate a clear doctrine that living people have spirits or souls. In life the individual is a human being (*matilden*); the word also referring to the body which he leaves behind at death. The living person has a shadow (*malauda*) which the sun casts upon the ground. *Malauda* is also his tiny image in another's eye, his reflection in a pool. In dreams if you see other living men, you as a *malauda* meet their similar reflections. Although they did not think to bring it up in the times I ques-

[1] In one text I took down about a method of destructive magic, the stylized representation of a living person's face, cut into a tree trunk, was referred to as that person's *malet*. On other occasions, pictures or representations of living people referred to as *malauda* – 'shadow' or 'reflection'.

tioned them as to a living spirit, the *malauda* is detachable: three times I saw leaves of cordyline shrubs placed at intervals on paths, twice to guide back the errant *malauda* of very sick men, once prophylactically for that of a newborn child whose mother had rashly carried it with her to the gardens. At death, if you press for an answer, the *malauda*, the shadow disappears into the ground. There is no transformation of *malauda* into spirit after death.

But people become spirits after death. The spirit of an individual after death is called *gelputi*: the word *gelputi* is also used for the colour of things which are very dark or black and most appropriately I would translate *gelputi* as shade of the dead. No living person has a shade (*gelputi*), this is the spirit he becomes after death. If you ask what or where it was before death, they do not seem to take the sense of the question, to see what problem you have in mind. There is no doctrine of transformation of shadow (*malauda*) into shade (*gelputi*).[1] They said the shade stayed at first close to the body and the hamlet of the dead person, low to the ground, and it was dangerous so that on the first day or two after a death people must sleep many together, mutually protecting each other, not one alone, lest the new *gelputi* strike down someone, especially a close relative or friend, so as to have a loved companion as companion shade with it. A period of mourning and of food restrictions continues until a close relative of the dead person kills some large game animal, usually a wild pig. Very soon after a death, there are a series of organized hunts. The animal killed is given to certain relatives of the dead person (especially for a man or a child to matrilateral ones; for a married woman to her brothers or their inheritors). The food prohibitions are ended with a ceremony at which the bed and a few intimate possessions of the dead person are burnt, clothing or a blanket. Formerly when the body was smoked on a platform, it was at this ceremony that the body was broken up and the bones were taken, some thrown away with a few small shell valuables of the dead person, other bones of a man were distributed and kept. The shade is then exhorted to leave, to go high

[1] On a single occasion, however, I heard someone use the word *malauda* for a dead man's spirit in the interim between death and the second stage of a funeral ceremony where his *gelputi* shade is sent off to a clap of thunder. Apart from this single occasion, people answered questions and spoke as if with death, the individual's *gelputi* came at that moment into existence.

up and to watch over and help his relatives. When the shade leaves and goes high into the air (or into the sky – *gape nemblipe*, sky cloud), they say there may be a clap of thunder as it goes up; and at one such ceremony I attended there was indeed a clap of thunder and they were pleased to recognize the proper sign of departure.

Gelputi – shade of a dead person: *malet* – myth spirit: *belyi'it* – song spirit.

In certain aspects the spirits are conceived with human attributes and personified. The abstracted, faceted, partial elements of analogy used to interpret the actions of spirits may help to give them the peculiar quality of being other than human. Their conception of spirits was not so crudely that of invisible disembodied persons as I often found myself supposing if I took the personifying analogies too simply. In Chapter 1 I mentioned briefly that the Gnau have long genealogical narratives which are often begun by recounting some mythological event. In fact the word *malet* is used to refer to a genealogical narrative, and also to any myth – to myths about great spirits who taught certain rites and to myths about witch-like spirits which are told as diverting horror stories. Someone who tells a myth badly is said to tell the *malet* badly (*dji sap malet geburkai*). A mere listing of the names of one's lineal ancestors down to the present is referred to as 'telling one's *malet*' (*sap malet*). Lineage, or the united collection of lineages from a common place of origin, is meant by implication in phrases of the sort *malet adoa wuteba* – 'we (inclusive) are of one spirit or story'. Although *malet* in the usual sense of 'spirit' takes the plural form *maleg*, if many spirits are spoken of with particular reference to ancestors as a collectivity, the singular form *malet* is used – e.g. *malet adeg wagao lawug eitam* – 'my ancestors planted those sago palms'. This special use of *malet* for the collection of one's ancestors stands out noticeably since *gelputi/gelpug* (pl.) could be used, but is not usually, for the spirits of particular dead people in this context. The meanings myth and spirit may seem more distinct to us than to them. There is also a distinguishing term *belyi'it* which is preferred for certain great spirits whenever they are thought of in connection with major song rituals. Such a spirit may have many names; some names tend to be used when particular aspects of the spirit are thought of (e.g. Panu'et and sago; Panu'et and Dilyiwan and illness); while other names tend to be used when the spirit is thought of in the context of its major song rites (e.g. Panu'et is usually called Maden, Wolpawei, Bulti Lagep, or Gamultug in connection with the rites to celebrate the building of a new *gamaiyit* at which the ritual ash used in hunting is prepared). Panu'et or Dilyiwan would usually be called *malet*, while Maden usually *belyi'it* because Maden identifies the song ritual. The verb root for 'sing' and 'dance' *-rag-* is the same: initially I had difficulty in making clear for example that I wanted the words of the song (*lyirag nunt gipi'i* – literally, they sing-dance voice nothing – i.e. they just sing). To perform the major rites of a great spirit is phrased as 'they sing-dance the spirit' (*lyirag belyi'it*): it would equally be possible to translate *lyirag belyi'it* as 'they sing-dance the song'. The point I am getting at is that *belyi'it* means (1) song, (2) spirit, just as *malet* means (1) myth and (2) spirit. They have no word that I learnt apart from *belyi'it* which could mean 'song', no word apart from *malet* which could mean 'myth' or 'tale'. For a long while I could not understand what criteria made some but not all *malet* spirits *belyi'it* spirits as well; I saw the meaning 'song' and the link of the term *belyi'it* to spirits with the major song rites only after I had realized the myth-spirit-*malet* linkage and this linkage too took me some time to perceive. The translation of '*malet*' by 'spirit' was soon clear but not the translation 'myth' or 'story'. The time I took to understand reflects the ease with which I could assimilate concepts of personified spirits but the difficulty I had in grasping the concept that a spirit and a myth, or a spirit and a ritual song are in some sense the same thing. The word identity of 'myth' or 'song' and 'spirit' in Gnau recalls the 'dreaming' of Australian aboriginals (Stanner 1956) in which a power, cause or force believed to exist independently of men is *verbally* identified with some class of actual human experience at particular times or places, something men think, roughly narrative and abstract, in the sense of being composed of mental images or words and meanings.

Something can be both *malet* and *belyi'it*: but while all *belyi'it* (pl. *belyipeg*) are *malet* (pl. *maleg*) not all *maleg* are *belyipeg*. *Gelputi* (pl. *gelpug*) I have glossed as 'shade of the dead', and this term is fairly strictly and consistently used for 'shades' of the relatively recent dead individuals; occasionally one is alternatively called a *malet* but, in contexts where an individual's *gelputi* is not specifically being referred to, the conjunction *malet-gelputi* or *gelputi-malet* is quite common. Next, as I have mentioned with regard to *malet*, ancestors as a collectivity are referred to as *malet* and the singular form is always used in the collective sense of the group of ancestors from whom one is descended. While the recent dead are remembered by names as individuals (*gelpug* – plural), the

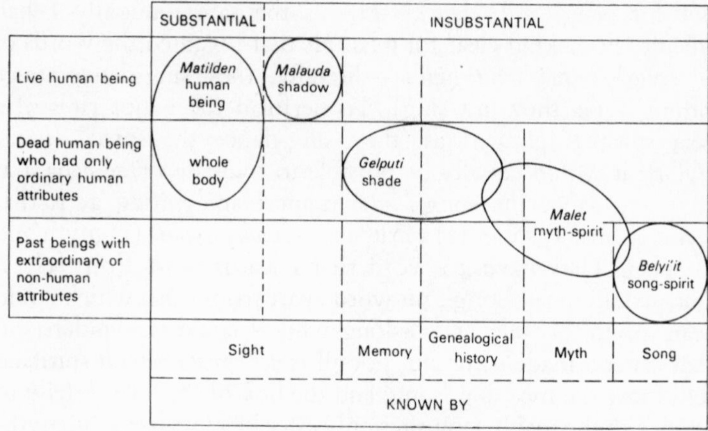

Fig. 22. Identification of spirit attributes

collective body of remote ancestors, though names are given in geneaologies, become *malet adji* (your myth-spirit ancestor). *Malet* and *gelputi* are not discrete. The shade of a dead ancestor may be said to 'go down into' a great spirit (*malet* or *belyi'it*) and activate it. The spirits of a clan or lineage, the collectivity of all its dead, may be said to 'stay' in the image made of the *belyi'it* Tambin or Panu'et placed on the centre post of the *gamaiyit* (men's house). The image is the *belyi'it* Tambin or Panu'et, they say, and our ancestors 'stay in it – *wape*. Remote ancestors have lost their individuality as remembered past people with faces, personal characteristics, and thus forgotten, become vaguely assimilated or confused with the myth or the individual mythical person whose extraordinary doings are recounted at the beginning of it. By this interpretation of the ways they use *gelputi* (singular), *gelpug* (plural), or *malet*, I am suggesting psychological reasons which allow for their fusion of shades with a spirit and I must add that what I do is to rationalize linguistic usages which they did not unravel or analyse and explain like that.

Figure 22 shows the terms I have so far discussed and summarizes their salient distinctive aspects.

PROBLEM OF SPIRIT IDENTITIES AND THEIR LINKS WITH SOCIAL GROUPS

For each distinction between spirit terms, there are aspects to the Gnau use of terms which complicate and blur the separations I have made between them. The problems of one identity behind many different names and a variety of myths which may share no common features is one which does not seem to be a problem for them as it is for me. Like Zeus, one of their spirits may change form; but it can change name, sex, and number as well. Within one village, there may be a small number of different myths and slightly different ritual practices for the spirit celebrated at the building of a men's house: to the Gnau, these represent owned clan attributes, equally valid as relating to the spirit but proper to that clan, although others may sometimes use them during celebrations in the village. The names and rites for the spirit celebrated at the building of the men's house are one important aspect of this spirit which also has a variety of other concerns under some additional or different names and rites. However the sets of activities, rites, myths and names which go together as subsumed under one identity are consistently parcelled out; the divisions of spiritual labour are fairly clearly drawn by the Gnau.

When the Gnau consider the different clan-linked rituals and myths, they assume that they are all aspects of the same spirit and that the differences stem from the differing past origins and migrations of the people who are now collected in their village. Rituals and myths are associated with groups of people and there may be secret parts to them which are not supposed to be revealed except to those who have a right by birth to know them. Pedigrees provide the charters for these rights and the links of genealogy lead back to the myth; distant shades of the dead become assimilated into the myth. They regard myths and rituals as property, and for this reason think it improper for someone to tell a myth which does not belong to him, or even the other man's genealogy: it is in a sense use of someone else's property – so for example when I asked a man, who knew it well, to tell me someone else's myth he said 'you go and ask X; if I tell it he will be angry and say that I say his land is mine'. But the myth in question gave no specific grounds of legitimacy for the other group's ownership of any particular bit of land. Because the myths, like rituals or the distinctive aspects of some ritual, are in theory restricted, they serve to maintain the identity of groups of people, and being so restricted are one of the ways by which people discriminate and show their legitimate claim to whatever other rights come from position by birth or descent. Detailed knowledge of the pedigree which leads down from the myth also supports one's rightful claim to other things and this is one element in the emphasis given to genealogical knowledge. Thus the connections between spirit, myth, ritual, genealogy and the problem of maintaining the identity and rights of particular social groups are fairly overt and straightforward.

But the above presents only part of the picture. Genealogy cannot in theory be acquired or bought, but rituals can. Some major song rituals are said to belong to one group first and another second. Within the village a performance of some major ritual is put on by one group, usually a hamlet, and the other hamlets 'come to help them with it' (*lali lisambelda*). As they interpret the distant past, the acquisition or learning of a ritual from another group is similarly understood as the result of living with the other group or coming to participate in their ritual. In the relatively recent past, new rites have been acquired from other villages and these are said to have been bought with shell valuables (*lager mingep ala lagaiyam* – they took shell valuables to buy them). The example of Malyi, a major song rite, is cited below: the rites were acquired because a man was diagnosed as struck by the spirit Malyi and, as no one in Rauit knew the rites by which to heal him, his kin sent for men of another village to come and do the full ritual for them, paying them for the performance in their hamlet, participating in it and thereby learning it. Now the descendants of the man who was ill are those who hold it first (*garut*) in Rauit and they have performed it for people in other hamlets who now help with it as second-holders (*lalut*). In passing I would note that it is consistent with the general account I have already given of how they understand illness that new causes may be recognized and the appropriate rituals to heal them added to what is already known independently of any discerned change in the clinical pattern of symptoms and signs of diseases.

Malyi is the only relatively recent example of acquiring a major song ritual: it was bought for the illness of a man in the grandparental generation of people now aged over 60 years old. His present descendants, none of whom was alive when it was bought, still lead its performance and receive some payment, in whatever the hamlet it is done. The issue of payment to the *garut* first-holders in Malyi is a special case because the ritual is only performed for the primary purpose of healing someone and it has been recently acquired. In other cases where some group holds the ritual *garut*, the *lalut* second-holders do not pay the *garut* holders if they perform it; their acquisition of it belongs to the distant past, and if there is an associated myth they may also tell it. Sometimes the right to perform is spoken of as having come through marriage to a woman of the *garut* holders and they suggest that her coming and the shell valuables they gave when she came secured their right to perform it.

In contrast to acquiring new rituals, old ones may be forgotten. The *garamut* rhythm which is used to identify the clan Saikel is called Wawut; this is the name of a forgotten song ritual which the fathers of the oldest Saikel men now alive last performed and their sons never learnt it even though they say that it was the distinctive Saikel song ritual. They are therefore left without the distinctive song ritual which they held as *garut* – hair of the head. Therefore if they put on a major ritual performance, they must use one of those which they share as *lalut* – jaw holders with some other group.

Sharing or participating in the rituals of others who live in the village, and especially in the same hamlet, and thereby acquiring the rituals *lalut* is accepted and evident. It conflicts with the notion that the ownership of myths and rituals should be transmitted only by descent just as the assumption that only people of common descent should reside in the same hamlet conflicts with the finding that in practice many hamlets contain groups of different descent. The putative units of the four clan-like groupings cannot be seen in their present holding of ritual, and again the discrepancies stem from the difference between using descent as the linking or determining principle and using a place or territory to link people.

In more general terms the ambivalence comes from linking ritual and myth with persons or with places. I have so far been concerned with how groups of people have rituals and myths associated with them, ideally through descent, in practice also by residence and joint participation. In parallel, some spirits show a similar ambivalence according to their unfixed or fixed locality associations. Myths may identify some site, or an object (for instance, a strange stone formation) as the place where the mythical events happened and if this is so, the place is spoken of as the special local habitation of the spirit. An example of this is the tie of Tambin with the site now called Pakuag with its strange stones. The emphasis given by the *lalut* Wuninangiwut clan to Tambin is bound up with their return to this site: as I interpret it, the *garut* Wimalu clan who did not return to the site have in part ceded their identification with Tambin because of this. But apart from a few bad witch-like spirits, the *maleg wolendem* I mention later, fixed and exclusive association to a place is not a characteristic feature of Gnau views on spirits: in contrast to the reports of some other Sepik peoples such as the Mountain Arapesh (Mead 1940), particularized bush spirits fixed to some pool or forest play little part in the explanation of illness. Instead the major song spirits are putatively unfixed, universalistic and free-floating. They have special interests and responsibilities such as interests in particular plant foods but the Gnau suppose that the spirit which cares, for instance, for sago is essentially the same one whatever different names it has among other people. As spirits are unfixed to place so rituals do not require performance at a special site but the major ritual can serve to bring near or concentrate the spirit wherever it is done.

THE DISTRIBUTION OF RESPONSIBILITIES AMONG SPIRITS

The imputation or assumption that the major spirits are universal comes out clearly in their allocation of interests in plant foods to spirits. There is general consensus over the distribution of interests among the spirits and this assumption conflicts with the ascription of particular spirits to particular social groups. The plant foods which grow well in theory because people perform the proper ritual for the spirit concerned are foods which everyone must plant. Thus everyone in the village must participate in the rituals and so gain benefit from them for plants which they all grow: this is ostensibly an additional motive for others to come and help in their performance and again it breaks down the exclusive nature of the tie by descent to a myth, ritual and the spirit. In ritual, the village has organic rather than mechanical solidarity.

The association of the major spirits with plant foods is shown in Table 18. It will be noted that the spirit interests in plant foods,

Table 18. Plant food concerns of spirits

Panu'et:	sago; mushrooms which grow on sago pith; Pandanus fruit; water from pools; the walnut *nimbalgut* – with a black pericarp; breadfruit; the *tila'at* or *taun* tree fruit
Tambin:	all tubers; bananas; sugar cane; *pitpit*; spinach-like greens (*benang*, *nalyigup*) the nut *melyi'it* with a purple pericarp
Malyi:	all tubers; bananas; all edible fungi; *pitpit*; spinach greens; sugar cane; (according to some people) coconut
Wunitap:	if one asks for the things associated with Wunitap, they name no foods but tell you the inedible things which someone struck (mad) by Wunitap is impelled to eat. Wild plantains; the fruits and leaves of certain forest trees (*lu subagdem*, *magasiwug*, *digawug*); white silt and earth

though divided with overlaps among them, together cover nearly all the habitual foods of the Gnau: the only important exception is the leaf (*teltug*) of the tree *teltati* – *Gnemon gnetum* – I did not hear, nor could I deduce, a reason for this.

A compendium of the spirits recognized by the Gnau and their chief significance or associations is given below.

Panu'et

This spirit watches over the following foods: sago; the mushrooms which grow on sago pith; Pandanus fruit (*telyigi*); breadfruit (the *genanget* kind which grows in groves); the *taun* tree fruit (*tila'at*); *nimbalgut* – the walnut with a black pericarp. The spirit is associated with groves of sago and waterpools, marshes and the mud around pools. It belongs to garden places, especially to the *wuyi'in adji* – 'your good place' with the garden house and the grass sward. Its major rites take place for the building of a new men's house (*lyirag gamaiyit*) during which hunting ash is ritually prepared. In one aspect, the spirit is held to be of particular benefit in hunting tree-living marsupials. Finally Panu'et is pre-eminent as a cause of illness and is associated with a number of special ritual techniques of healing. A more detailed account of the spirit Panu'et is given below (see pp. 169–80).

Tambin

The spirit watches over the foods: *wadagep* (yam, mami and taro), bananas, *benang* (*Amaranthus gangeticus*), *nalyigup* (*Hibiscus abelmoschus*). Its major rites involved the prolonged seclusion and initiation of young men whereby they became entitled to assume the head-dress of men. The complex of spells for the growth, strength and health of young people are particularly associated with Tambin, as is the ritual of penis bleeding. Of their rites, those of Tambin more than any other, were considered to bring men success in hunting. The rituals of hunting tend to be assimilated to the name of Tambin. Although Tambin may be cited to account for any illness, it has a special association with madness (see p. 213). Tambin in contrast to Panu'et is associated with the hamlet, rather than the gardens.

Malyi

Malyi is a spirit whose rites were acquired and learnt at Rauit for the purpose of treating illness caused by the spirit. Among neighbouring people, the major rites of Malyi are used for the seclusion and initiation of young men as the Tambin rites are used among Gnau. Like Tambin, Malyi is held to watch over *wadagep* and bananas. The major rites of Malyi are performed for sickness at Rauit; if they are performed people take advantage of the spirit's presence to seek benefit from it in planting yams and taro. Otherwise it is only mentioned for the harm it does.

Wunitap

It is linked with wild incomestible things, not foods, and with bush rather than hamlet or garden. Its major rites are performed to bring success in hunting: young men and boys sleep in the men's house during them to seek this benefit. Those who have done so may use the help of, or invoke, Wunitap in certain curses against those they hate, especially people whom they are bound to by ties of kinship. Wunitap provokes a special type of madness (see p. 212). One curious point about Wunitap is that some of the names cited for it are female names and sometimes people stress that Wunitap in contrast to all the above major spirits is female rather than male.

Malet

Apart from the description of the general meaning of *malet* which I have already given, there are some additional special uses of the term.

(1) They do not necessarily consider that a spirit has a name and identification. They may say of the origin of some things like bats, hornbills, some kinds of wild plants 'the spirit put them there' (*malet wopelem*). To the question 'what spirit makes the foetus of the child inside the mother?', they may answer, 'the spirit makes it' (*malet webariye*). In neither statement do they attempt to identify it. Some illnesses are ascribed to *malet* without identifications.

(2) In cases of bad witch-like spirits (*maleg wolendem*), it is rare that the myths identify them by name; they are identified by the name of the place they inhabit – they are 'the spirit of X place' (*malet beiya X*). One of their manifestations may be as phosphorescent toadstools. The localization or concentration of the power of a spirit at a place or in a strange natural form of stone at some place is also a feature ascribed to named important spirits associated with myths too.

(3) Among the materials used in hunting magic, there are some peculiar small stones of special virtue. The stones have the names of some persons who appear in related myths (Berwada, Pilka, Yuwer) but in this special context the isolated word '*malet*' means the stones themselves (e.g. *lager malet*, *lager gelputi*, *lager geplagep* – literally, they take the spirit, they take the shade of the dead, they take the scraped raw magical substances, but it means, 'they take the stones, they take scrapings of an ancestor's jawbones, they take the scraped raw magical substances').

(4) There are a number of things which have *maleg* inevitably associated with them, e.g. the *mama* (watching spirit) of yams and taro; the unnamed *malet* of the snake creeper (*lambet bulti*), the wild aroids called *mandaper*, *piyem*, certain ferns, etc. Any of these may be suggested to explain illness.

(5) There are some isolated but unlocalized general type

spirits. The spirit python (*Bulti* or *malet Bulti*) which sometimes is the explanation suggested for a child's stunting. *Wiswis*, the name of something dangerous like a great worm, that is particularly associated with the paths of big game (of pigs and cassowaries) and the success of men who stand in hunting with bows by these paths. The underground worm spirits are sometimes heard or felt as a cracking or rumbling in the earth (cf. Bulmer 1968). Certain natural things and forces are spoken of as (manifestations of) spirits, notably *mungil* (earthquake), *dyulin* (comet i.e. a moving star which in the associated myth has a long tail): falling stars *nungabuti*, share their name with fireflies and both are associated with or thought to be manifestations of spirits of the dead; phosphorescent toadstools are said to be signs of evil spirits which go 'low' to the ground. The *ge'unit* – moon is spoken of as a spirit; *ge'uwan* – the big star (morning or evening star) which 'moves with the moon, the *wauwi* (mother's brother) of the moon'.

(6) One identified *malet* requires special mention because of its association with epidemic illness (see pp. 81–2). Its chief name is Taklei, with the alternative names Wolape and Wogereg. Wolape and Taklei are the names in the myth, but *Wolape* also serves as name for the disease, anthrax in pigs. *Wogereg* is the name for a pustular condition of the skin which by one myth tradition occurred and caused the death of many people (? smallpox). I did not see a case though some Gnau people say they have seen people with *wogereg* which did not lead to death. In the theory of Taklei, village pigs are struck down but people escape; if people are struck down, village pigs escape but the wild pigs like people are struck down. *Wolape* – anthrax in pigs – is the clearest example of a disease inevitably ascribed to a particular agent. I have stressed at length that the physical signs and symptoms of a given disease in our terms do not imply a particular cause in Gnau terms. Pig anthrax is effectively an exception to this statement; and to a limited extent linkages such as madness with Tambin, a kind of madness with Wunitap, the identifying behaviour of someone struck by *langasutap* or by sorcery on sexual leavings, or bleeding from the nose or anus at death through sorcery of body leavings are in theory links which make the physical signs of disease show the kind of agent which causes it. But the point I emphasize is that in practice, the physical signs

are not necessary to the diagnosis; in fact the diagnoses are more often made in the absence of these signs than in their presence. In theory, the human illness caused by Taklei is pustular *wogereg*, but the outstanding attribute of Taklei is the epidemic and lethal nature of the illness it causes. The epidemic of dysentery mentioned on p. 81 was put down to Taklei and because of the very large number of individuals who were said to have been struck by Taklei in the recent past and had died of dysentery, I made the mistaken initial inference that dysentery, the disease bloody diarrhoea, was caused by Taklei. But when in fact one or two people had bloody diarrhoea there was never any suggestion that Taklei was the cause because the cases were isolated.

THE ATTRIBUTES OF THE SPIRIT PANU'ET

The intent of this section is to show the complexity of attributes grouped together as aspects or refractions of one major spirit. I choose Panu'et because it is the most frequently named spirit involved in illness. Unless I state specifically to the contrary, the names and aspects which I will describe can be taken to be, for the Gnau, in some sense attributes of the one spirit Panu'et. In brief the chief things which are associated with Panu'et are illness and certain techniques used in diagnosis and healing; sago, ponds, streams and marshes associated with working sago; building a new men's house (*gamaiyit*), an image on the central post (*sulat munganda*); the hunting of tree-living marsupials (i.e. phalangers – *mareg wisem* 'the high game').

What I have included as 'attributes' of the spirit are clearly very different kinds of thing. Among many names some are used only or mostly to refer to the spirit in one context (e.g. as the spirit giving success in phalanger hunting) while others are names for rites primarily, although they are occasionally used as though they named a spirit; still others are names for persons who appear in myths. The name Panu'et has general currency and any of the other named identifications can be converted to Panu'et to explain to someone like myself who or what it is that is being talked about; Wolpawei is the only other name which comes close to achieving this general substitutability. A group of other identifications closely associated to rites, myths or songs belong to particular clans ('clans' in the sense discussed in Chapter 1). The idea of Panu'et is given visible man-made form in a carved face (called Face or Man); in a body made of plants, usually with a painted face (called Panu'et); or Panu'et can be collected in the amorphous shreds of the plants used on other occasions to make its body: in each case, by ritual the image is said 'to be' Panu'et (i.e. the image is called it) or to 'stay in' (*wape*) the image.

Thus they have a concept which can be represented visibly in man-made form. The other attributes are things which belong to the spirit in a sense rather like that of ownership establishing a link between a person and a thing. The spirit either 'watches over' (*wenarep*) or 'stays in' (*wap*) the thing concerned. There are places like the groves of sago palms, or pools of water, where Panu'et is localized or likely to be present and watching. There are the plant foods of men in which the spirit is interested and may stay as a man stays in his house. The foods with which the spirit is concerned grow well, it is thought, because of the spirit's concern and certain rituals are done by men to propitiate or please the spirit so that it will be bountiful in these foods which men tend or plant. The spirit is also concerned with certain things that people do: the rituals practised when a new men's house is built are 'things of Panu'et" (*nem beiya Panu'et*) or 'Panu'et its things' (*Panu'et aridem*) and so are certain techniques for healing sickness. In Table 19 I have listed the names and things of Panu'et which are used, known or shared by Gnau people generally rather than linked to a particular clan.

There is no myth in which a person with the name Panu'et does things; Panu'et is the name of the spirit (*malet*) which anyone may use, but the name is most closely associated with its aspects as the spirit watching over sago and pools, and as a spirit causing illness. There is a particular body of knowledge about certain spells and methods for 'smelling out' an afflicting spirit and removing minute 'arrow-heads' with which spirits strike people: men who have acquired this knowledge are said to 'know' Panu'et (*la'am Panu'et*). They acquire it by passing through a ritual during which they must 'die' (go into trance): this ritual is only done at the end of ceremonies for building a new men's house and only then on rare occasions. Men who have acquired this knowledge are thus the experts in healing and diagnosis in so far as these special Panu'et abilities are thought to be particularly useful and effective. There is a secret myth associated with this knowledge describing how it was obtained: there are three secret names used in invoking Panu'et which are the names of persons in the myth – Saiwan, Margadin and Dilyiwan. Dilyiwan is used also for a charm sometimes hung round a person's neck to ward

Table 19. Names and attributes of Panu'et

Names: Panu'et. Wolpawei. Masipe (Face). Legin (Man). Dilyiwan. Malet gemen (Eagle spirit). Malet de'aipe (Wind spirit).

Places where spirit localized:
Groves of sago palms. Water pools, marshes, mud of water pools. Garden places, especially *wuyi'in adji* – 'your good place' with the garden house and the grass sward. (Panu'et. Wolpawei. Occasionally malet de'aipe.)

Foods which the spirit cares for:
Sago; the mushrooms which grow on sago pith; breadfruit (the *ganganget* kind which grows in groves; the *taun* tree fruit (*tila'at*); *nimbalgut* – the walnut with a black pericarp. (Panu'et. Wolpawei.) Some also say the areca palm.

Things: Images of the spirit – carved wooden face (Masipe or Wolpawei), the cigar-shaped large image made of plants (Panu'et or Legin); the shredded plants used in the image (Panu'et).

Ritual and human activities:
(1) Ritual for the building of a new men's house (*lyirag gamaiyit*) and the preparation of hunting ash (*nawugep*). (Clan specific names or Panu'et for these major rites.)
(2) Hunting of tree-living phalangers (Malet gemen or malet de'aipe).
(3) Rituals for the healing of illness (Panu'et principally; also Masipe or Legin, Dilyiwan and sometimes clan specific names).

off sickness by Panu'et. The myth about Dilyiwan has a link to the myth called Gamulti (the Bird of Paradise) which belongs to a clan group and will be considered in a moment. Apart from the special esoteric knowledge of *la'am Panu'et*, there are various healing practices which are commonly used and generally known to all adult men. In these practices, Panu'et is collected and brought into an image made for the purpose of healing. There are many different plants which must be collected to form the image, and among these plants, certain kinds are specified as parts of (the body of) Panu'et (e.g. its heart, ribs, lungs, backbone and faeces). The full image is called Panu'et; to make it is to 'fasten up Panu'et (*lamberyi Panu'et*). A smaller version of the rite may be tried first in which the plants are collected but not made into an image formed in the pattern of the human body. The plants are collected and mixed, shredded and rubbed together – this is called *lauweru'a Panu'et* – 'they mix and shred Panu'et' (very occasionally they refer to the shredded leaves as *Panungep* – that is Panu'et given a plural ending). Another synonym of Panu'et used in connection with illness is the name Legin – the word *legin* means 'man' – but it may equally well be said of a particular illness either 'Panu'et struck him' or 'Legin struck him'. Among the esoteric techniques of Panu'et experts is the ability to 'extract' by mouth suction or manually certain tiny stones said to be coloured red (I have not seen them) called *legini*. In these treatments of illness caused by Panu'et, the body of the spells used and in some cases openly sung during certain of the kinds of treatment are in fact verses of the song ritual sung during the building of a new men's house.

Panu'et is particularly associated with sago and the pools of marshy places where sago grows, with the mushrooms which grow on the heaps of discarded sago pith. Less important is its association with pandanus fruit (*telyigi*); occasionally mentioned, with areca palms, and the kind of breadfruit trees which grow more commonly collected together in groves (the breadfruit *genanget*). The watching presence of Panu'et benefits the growth of sago palms. When the spirit is told to depart at the end of treatment for illness, the people call out to it to go away to the bush of some of their named clan relatives. This is not because they wish harm to them but because, while they want relief for the sufferer from its afflicting presence, they say they only want it to leave them temporarily and if so to go off to benefit the sago of their relatives rather than anyone else. The plants collected to make Panu'et must come from the gardens and sago places of the person who is ill. In this sense it is a spirit of garden places, of *tuwi gargitasa*, of the good bush places *wuyi'in adji* (your good place) where garden houses are built. Panu'et contrasts in this respect with the other spirit, Tambin, which in treatment, must be made of plant materials from the *hamlet*, and with the other spirit Wunitap associated with things of the wild bush (*tuwi sinape*).

The third general aspect of Panu'et is its association with phalanger hunting; in this regard its distinctive name is *malet gemen* or *gemen* – the Eagle (or hawk) spirit. The second largest bird of prey they identify is called *gemen beiya wuge'ai mawugep* – which means 'the eagle[1] which cooks hunting ash'. The magical hunting ash (*nawugep*) may only be prepared in the rites celebrating the building of a new men's house; its preparation is one of the chief aims in accomplishing these rites, and to participate in them is supposed to bring benefit especially in hunting tree phalangers, although in common with all the major song rites (except perhaps that of Malyi) they expect success in hunting generally to follow their performance. The eagle, they say, preys on phalangers high in the trees and flies high with the wind: if they use the name, *malet de'aipe* – Wind spirit, they mean Panu'et.

The names and aspects of Panu'et given above are all used and belong in common to all Gnau people. I must now come to those which are diacritical of the way Panu'et is recognized by different social groups, although the people concerned consider them to be differences of convention about the same thing. The diacritical features related to the rituals done for the building of a new men's house are shown for the Rauit clans in Table 20.

The myths of some of the different clans have names which are said to be names for Panu'et. The myths themselves are of varied character: most lead into the quasi-historical genealogical accounts of lineage which I have described elsewhere. Thus the name of the Maru myth – Gamulti or Gamultug (the Birds of Paradise); of the Wuninangiwut myth Marusi; and names contained within such myths such as the name Wolpawei in the myth of Lamu-Wolpawei; or the unnamed spirit of the place in the myth of Delubaten, or the one in the myth called *Belu'et wamberiyel* (the Pig turned them mad) or Malet Tuwape, which describes the end of the first settlement of Rauit, are all at times said to be names or manifestations of Panu'et. Wolpawei, among these names has a special place as it is used by people of any clan for Panu'et, although the actual myth of Lamu-Wolpawei belongs to only one of the lineages. Wolpawei more than any other single name is given as the alternative name for Panu'et. Even

[1] I have not identified the species. The tarsi of *gemen* on hunting bags which I saw were feathered to the toes, suggesting that it is an eagle, ? *Harpyopsis*.

Table 20. Clan-linked attributes of Panu'et

Clan name	*Distinctive name for ritual of building a new men's house*	*Myth – name of related myth*	*Garamut signal rhythm name*	*Diacritical features of the ritual performance*		*Secret spell names*
Olu subdivision (Bi'ip hamlet)	Bulti Lagep (Bones of the snake)	Lamu-Wolpawei (two names)	Bulti Lagep	Face called Wolpawei: post with the carved face called the Snake's post	the high parts (*wisem*); the crown (*bena'at*): the image of Panu'et long (*lugi*)	?
WIMALU						
Maru subdivision (Wimalu hamlet)	Gamultug (Birds of Paradise)	Gamulti (Bird of Paradise)	—	Post with the carved face called the Eagle's post:		Wolpawei Maolyi (may have others)
WUNINANGIWUT	Lawe'ut (Dry Sago)	Marusi (a name)	—	Face called Masipe	the low parts (*tasem*); the base (*beli*): the image of Panu'et short (*dila*)	Seinaur Wapei
SAIKEL	Maden (a name)	—	Maden			Tawei Maiket
NEMBU	—	—	—			

further complicating things, different clans have various additional secret names for Panu'et which they use to attach to the spells when they whisper them in treatments for illness – the names used in the secret spells are in pairs of husband/wife, i.e. a man and a woman's name – some clans use Wolpawei as the male name, but for the woman's name they use another name than either of the names of the two women he marries in the Lamu-Wolpawei myth.

I mentioned that performance of major song-rites is called *lyirag* – they sing-dance. In the case of all the other *belyi'it* spirits except Panu'et, performance of their major rites is indicated by putting the chief name of the spirit after *lyirag*, e.g. *lyirag* Tambin, *lyirag* Malyi, *lyirag* Wunitap. In the case of Panu'et the phrase *lyirag* Panu'et is very rarely used; if it is used it applies to the major ritual for the building of a new men's house, but the common phrase which indicates *any* hamlet's performance of this ritual is *lyirag gamaiyit* (they sing-dance for the men's house). Otherwise the phrase used for this ritual will imply the particular lineage or clan or hamlet which performs it, since their rites and songs are slightly different and called differently: Wimalu clan at Rauit observes two forms of *gamaiyit* ritual – the Maru part do 'Birds of Paradise' (*lyirag* Gamultug); the Olu part do 'Bones of the Snake' (*lyirag* Bulti Lagep); the Saikel clan do Maden (a name); the Pakuag-Wuninangiwut clan do Dry Sago' (*lyirag* Lawe'ut); I did not learn a special name for the Nembu clan's performance.

In the Maru case, Gamulti or Gamultug refers both to myth and rite; in the Olu case Lamu-Wolpawei names the myth, Bulti Lagep the rite; Lawe'ut, Maden refer to rite. The rhythms beaten out at certain of the major rituals are called by the name of the spirit and are used as identifying calls for the clans primarily associated with the ritual: only Bulti Lagep and Maden among these Panu'et rites have identifying signal rhythms attached to their name.

In the details of performance there are differences in the verses of the song series Gamultug, Bulti Lagep, Lawe'ut and Maden. But at performances of the ritual, the whole village comes to take part and verses from different song series are sung on the same night, though precedence is given to the series belonging to the celebrating clan. The most apparent difference in the ritual is the height of the image containing all the plants of Panu'et which is bound about the central post of the new men's house. All Wimalu make this image tall, but especially so in the Bulti Lagep rites. In contrast Saikel and Pakuag Wuninangiwut are said to make a short image. This diacritical difference provides a way of distinguishing how the full rites are performed: thus Wimalu 'know' (*la'am*) the crown (*bena'at* – crown of a palm or tree), and Saikel Pakuag the 'stump or base' (*beli* – tree stump or base) of Panu'et; Wimalu know the 'high parts' (*wisem*), the others 'the low parts' (*tasem*); Wimalu make Panu'et 'long' (*lugi*), the others 'short' (*dila*). Wimalu women supposedly store prepared sago in long bamboo containers, while the others in short containers. The central post around which Panu'et is bound in vegetable form receives also a wooden carved image representing a stylized face – this image of the face is called Wolpawei by those who celebrate Bulti Lagep; by the others, the similar looking image is called Masipe which means Face; and Masipe may also be used as synonym (or euphemism) for Panu'et (e.g. *Masipe wa'ab* – 'the Face struck her (with illness)). As the men's house is symmetrical, there is a central post at either end; the post to which the face is tied is called in this ritual reference *sulat gemenda* (the Eagle's post) by all except those who celebrate Bulti Lagep, who call Wolpawei's post (with the face on it) *sulat bultida* (the Snake's post) and the other post they call *sulat gemenda* (the Eagle's post). The two sides of the roof of the *gamaiyit* are called 'wings' of the house (*naplawug*).

Thus even without following the full details of the different myths and rites, of the lists of plant needed to prepare the image of Panu'et or the ritual soups, the multitudinous complexity of the spirit can be grasped. Although the spirit is personified in some aspects, it also comprehends elements drawn from analogy with bird, plant and wind. There are so many associations and concerns of the spirit Panu'et that it is possible for them in almost any illness to produce a reasoned hypothesis which links the immediate or recent circumstances of the patient's life with some interest or exposure to the attention of the spirit.

The larger scale treatment rituals involve making an image of the spirit. Such treatment is public and organized. The image is made from vegetable materials and the form of the image is conceived in analogy to that of the human body. Many different plants are used, among which ones with aromatic or powerful scent predominate. The materials for the image must be sought at appropriate places. In the case of Tambin certain of them must come from within the village. In the case of the spirit Panu'et the materials must come from the garden place and sago stands where the patient was supposed to have been struck. The image is made at the bush, by male kin of the patient, hamlet co-residents, often helped by affinal or matrilateral kin of the patient. The young men are expected to collect the materials and do most of the work of making it, although a few older men go with them to supervise. The materials collected in the morning are brought to an arranged meeting place at the bush, where as they prepare the spirit's image, a meal is cooked which includes some game. Any women who have gone to the bush must return ahead before the making of the image is begun. The men also prepare an offertory platform and when the image is ready, but undecorated, they eat together and place an offering with an invocation to the dead who watch over that tract of land, an offering of part of the food, areca nut and tobacco also for the spirit. It is for the spirit Panu'et and to the spirits of the dead. The image is about five or six feet long and cigar-shaped. At the same time as it is being made, some of the men prepare scraped shredded herbs, root ginger and certain substances (including mud from the Panu'et linked water holes beside which sago is worked, a brown glutinous sap exuded by certain trees which they call tree faeces). These comprise the materials from which a ritual soup (*wa'agep*) will be cooked on arrival at the village. The image is then carried into the village and the hamlet where the patient lies. Here the women and senior men who have gathered to sit in sympathy have passed the day in relaxation and eating. A face is painted on sago palm leaf spathe and attached to the undecorated image; shell valuables and furs and feathers are tied about the image according to the pattern of ceremonial male Gnau attire. The ritual soup is cooked. It is only then that a senior man must come to say the secret spells over the ritual soup and blow them into the head-dress, the ears and base of the image so that the spirit will enter it. It is said to feel heavy once this has happened. The man who does this bespelling is usually a senior man from within the patient's hamlet, although it might be a woman's brother who had come to take part. There was no rule determining by kinship which man it should be; nor was the man who did it necessarily someone with special knowledge of Panu'et diagnostic or healing techniques even if such a man might be present.

At this point, the sick person appears on the scene, having until then remained withdrawn or disregarded. A betel quid prepared with some of the shredded ritual substances is given to him (or her) to chew as the image is carried up to him. He faces the image whose nettle-covered base points at him. A circle of men surround him (or her), and they call out in invocation to the dead and to the spirit and say who the patient is, when struck, and they demand that the spirit leave the patient. They sing certain of the verses of the ritual song which belongs to the spirit while the nettle-covered base of the image is touched over the body and head of the patient for a minute or two. Then the base of the image is suddenly struck down into the ground to startle off the spirit. It is carried to the side and cut open at its heart (this is explicitly 'striking' or 'killing' the spirit – *la'ab*, they kill it – and let the cold into it). Some of its insides are taken and shreds of fur and feather from its decorations; they are placed on a betel-bespat banana leaf in which are stuck two hibiscus flowers. In major ritual for any purpose, at some crucial point of the ritual such a leaf is prepared and torn lengthwise down the midrib as tobacco smoke is blown over it from over a handful of hearth ash held on a small patch of banana leaf. The leaf is held over either the thing or the person for whom benefit is sought. The answers they gave in explanation for this act were only that it was done so that the ritual might be good in the sense that its desired aim might be achieved. However, the myth which accounts for the making of all men at a certain hill, Delubaten, near the village, a myth which does not belong to a particular clan, describes exactly this action with the leaf at the crucial point in the story of how men were made, although in much questioning on the interpretation of this action no one spontaneously adverted to it to justify or interpret the act.

In the Panu'et healing ritual, the shreds from the insides and the decorations of the image are placed on the leaf which is held over the standing patient; the dead are invoked, the spirit again called on to leave the patient and the leaf is suddenly torn so that the shreds of material fall down over the patient's body as the spirit is ordered to leave and go off. The leaf is casually thrown down. The patient is fed a morsel of the ritual soup (*wa'agep*) by a senior man who blows the spirit's spells into it. This may be done by one or more of the men present in succession, who each then take a nettle leaf, bespell it and rub it down the patient's arms, ending at the hands which are firmly grasped, the fingers sharply pulled and bent to see whether the knuckles crack in sign that the sickness has gone. The patient stamps and shakes himself to shake off his sickness and sits down. Hot water in a bamboo is first brought and poured over the patient, washing off his dirt and grime; then cold water. It is then sometimes that a marked change of manner is shown by the patient. Having hardly spoken until now, and then in a small often quavering voice, having been till then grimed and head downcast, he may begin to chat and talk to others in a normal voice. This is not always so, since the patient may be tired by standing for the rite and soon retire to his hut. The rest of the ritual soup (*wa'agep*) is given to many people, especially to the children and women present; sometimes a dog may be fed a bit. The soup is said to strengthen them and protect them from possible harm from the spirit. Later that day or the next, the remains of the image are taken and thrown away down the hamlet rubbish slope.

Certain features of this form of treatment, though it takes only the day to do, are arranged in the same way as they are in the rarely performed and prolonged major rituals for healing, such as the one for Malyi; and indeed these elements of pattern recur in all major ritual. These are: the making of the spirit by men outside the village; the offering placed on a platform there; the entry of the image into the village undecorated; its welcoming and decoration with valuables; bringing the spirit into the image; the singing or celebration of its song (in major prolonged ritual the singing goes on for whole days or whole nights, sporadically over many weeks, interspersed by the brief crucial performance of specific ritual acts in a set order, and it is only for the few minutes that these acts take to perform that the patient comes before the spirit; the rest of the time he remains secluded at a distance from the spirit and the singing or the dancing, withdrawn from the danger of contact or proximity to it); the concluding rites in which the spirit's image is symbolically killed and the spirit, concentrated or fixed by ritual at the village, is released, ordered to depart (indeed at major prolonged ritual it is sent off to *garamuts* beating the rhythm for showing anger or crossness).

The wide distribution of the ritual soup to strengthen or benefit many others present at the Panu'et ritual I described above, is analogous to the way in which those who perform or are present at the performance of major ritual to cure someone are also said to acquire benefits for themselves, sometimes specified ones such as success in hunting or gardening. Only one major prolonged ritual, that of Malyi, was performed for curing during my stay in the village. The smaller day-long rituals were performed on eight occasions for Panu'et.

There is also a simpler version of the Panu'et day-long ritual which can be performed by one man alone, or by one or two men. The same plants are collected ('the body of Panu'et') but no image is made, no *wa'agep* soup made. Instead the herbs and plants are brought into the village, shredded, crumpled and mixed, bespelled and placed with heated stones in a large palm spathe container. The patient comes and receives a betel quid prepared with the ritual scraped substances and water is poured with invocations over the plants of the spirit and the stones so that scented steam billows over the patient. He is then rubbed with nettles and washed as before. This simpler form of treatment may be tried first, judged inadequate and the more elaborate one done in a few days.

THE SECOND MAIN CLASS OF CAUSES IN ILLNESS: MAGIC OR SORCERY

Spirits as a class of cause differ conspicuously from magic and sorcery in that they are invisible agents while in magic and sorcery the agent is putatively another person. The techniques of destructive magic are the same in general kind as those used in productive magic. These also use materials and blown spells whispered. Productive magic is also 'worked': you 'work' yams so they will grow big; you 'work' a man so he will hunt successfully. Magic may be put to destructive or productive ends. It is a technique of power and whether you regard its use against a man as evil or good, legitimate or not, depends on your point of view: it may be to protect your property, or it may be someone out to kill you from jealous spite. Magic in itself is morally neutral or rather the moral evaluation depends on particular context and view-point. When a man of consequence dies and they announce his death on the signalling *garamut*, they beat out the list of his achievements in life; they commemorate first the number of men he shot in warfare, second the men he killed by magic and sorcery; third the cassowaries he shot, then the pigs; and so on.

In contrast to this 'worked' destructive magic there are the kinds of *sanguma* sorcery which are always reviled: *langasutap* and *minmin*. Many of the anthropologists who worked in Africa have conformed in their use of the words 'magic', 'sorcery' and 'witchcraft' to the distinctions which Evans-Pritchard proposed. Sorcery indicated only destructive magic applied antisocially and illegitimately. Most of those who worked in Melanesia called destructive magic, whether socially approved or not, sorcery. *Sanguma* sorcery is sorcery in the Africanist sense; no one openly admits to knowing or practising it; it inspires horror; it provides the bogeyman for small children; it is feared and despised. The distinction between them is carried into the Gnau usage of Pidgin English: destructive magic is *poisin*, sorcery *sanguma*. The *sanguma* sorceries in contrast to destructive magic have substantive names *langasutap*, *minmin*. The verbs relate them to the victim: *langasutap* 'strikes him', *minmin* 'hangs up on him'. Their theory of *langasutap* attributes to those who possess it abilities which ordinary men do not have: those with *sanguma* can move without trace, conceal themselves in tree cracks, become invisible; cut someone open and eviscerate him without leaving a mark; they may eat human flesh. When destructive magic is used, men 'work it'; where *langasutap* is used, although men bend it to their evil whims and 'hold it' (*natao*), it is the *langasutap* which strikes, not the man.[1] However *langasutap* is a learnt technique, with spells, and not an inborn quality or substance. When there is a rumour of *langasutap*, men go out with bows and arrows to hunt down its bearers.

But magic and spirits are quite often not so clearly set in separate domains as I may have made them seem by my first division between them. Nadel wrote: 'The efficacy of ritual lies in the whole procedure and not in any of its elements, not even in the language employed on such occasions' (Nadel 1954, p. 16). Few otherwise, magical acts of the Gnau are not accompanied by invocations to spirits. Almost all their ritual activities used two

[1] In verbal usage: I describe in the next chapter the usage by which men holding *sanguma* are conventionally spoken to as a 'shade of the dead' – *gelputi*.

verbal forms successively: one was the bunched close, whispered or choked – even sometimes only thought – fixed formula spell with its mixture of secret names, 'ancestral' language, and trills; and the other was the loud, declarative, head-raised invocation (free-form and in normal Gnau language) to named ancestors, usually those among the relatively recent dead, saying out the reason, intent and hopes attaching to what they were doing. The two types of verbal act can be clearly distinguished in some tape-recordings I took of magical ritual. Gnau people call them 'little voice-speech' *nunt seki'in*, and 'big voice or speech' *nunt bu*. With the exception of a few cases, it is not difficult to decide whether they ascribe the cause either to spirits or magic in the given instance. In practice, one takes the ritual and identifies a relative emphasis on the technique employed and the ideas they hold about how it works. Where magic is in question, the emphasis looked for is that it is a human technique or art, rather than an appeal to spirits to act, but, as has often been pointed out, the distinction is not necessarily clear cut. The tendency to isolate an element of the ritual and to write of it as its essence, in the sense of source of its efficaciousness, is most apparent in the analysis of magic: that is why I quoted Nadel's comment as a reminder. When the essence is abstracted from the other ritual elements, what seems to happen then is that the student comes to analyse the magic in terms of its essence alone. In this way, the writer slips so that a problem is created, *viz*. the intrinsic quality of power in spells or magical materials ('medicines'), its latency or potentiality. At first sight, the use of a poison which truly poisons, or of a medicine like aspirin, is not magical unless accompanied by ritual manipulations. Gnau people with a sore throat might just chew ginger because it made their throat feel better: ginger, eminently hot, and classed by them as 'hot' in a ritual sense, was also an obligatory ingredient in a number of ritually prepared potions. Ginger for a sore throat was not used more magically than we use aspirin. What makes me call its use in potions 'magical' were the ritual actions necessarily accompanying its use. The people would say they chewed it for a sore throat because chewing it made their throats feel better directly; they did not refer to its hotness in a ritual sense.

It has been a commonplace of anthropology that Melanesian magic relies on spells, but African magic relies on material substances. If one abstracts an element as the essence, and then considers whether power is 'inherent' in the substance, one might also have to compare the inherent, automatic but damaging effectiveness of contact with a taboo object and discern in what sense the object and action in regard to it (the taboo thing) are different from inherent magical power. The isolation of the power in spell or substance does not seem to help in discussing the peculiar nature of magic although the relative stress is highly relevant to the discussion of style in magic. Just as the inherent danger in a taboo object could be regarded, in the terms of the taboo believer as a statement of an invariant and uniform effect of nature, given certain conditions (like that of snake poison), so the inherent beneficial quality of aspirin is regarded as a uniform effect of nature by the empirical scientific believer. But the substances or spells are effective through the whole ritual, while people talking about it may only stress one or other part as its essence.

Certain of the circumstances for ritual performance may lead people to call to mind a part rather than the whole. One possible facet to the emphasis which native Melanesian interpreters give to the spell may be its secrecy; the reason is functional – they stress what is peculiar to the knowledge of their own exclusive group – *viz.* the particular spell formula. The Gnau transmit certain magical knowledge strictly within a kinship group. What is unique to the group is the formula with secret names and words. The pattern of ritual actions and the material substances used are often common to the different groups. But people would say the exclusive special knowledge which they learnt was the spell, and this was the secret essential knowledge. On the other hand, they observed and acknowledged that other people living with them, for example, planted yams with closely similar rites and, although they knew different spells and secrets, yet they grew them just as successfully. In the context of this latter sort of conversation, people might lay primacy on the shared common ritual pattern, rather than on a particular form of words, which they knew differed for each group.

Part of the problem of interpreting how people view magic and isolate its essence comes perhaps from the difficulty of translation. Evans-Pritchard (1937) writes that *ngua* stands for the notion of (1) magic (as technique); (2) medicine (any object in which mystical power is supposed to reside and which is used in magic rites); as well as (3) leechcraft, and (4) closed associations for the practice of communal magic rites. Is magic a thing or an activity? The Gnau had three words, all three of which stand out to me conspicuously as words whose meaning I found peculiarly elusive: I took a long while to grasp the general sense behind particular uses of the words which were shown me. These words were: (1) *belyigep* – spells; (2) *geplagep* – scraped raw magical or ritual substances; (3) *wa'agep* – cooked magical or ritual substances or 'soups'. None of these words served as a general term for magic, nor was I told or given the impression that one was essential, the others ancillary to magical acts. There was no general term which demarcated a domain corresponding to 'magic'. The usual general phrasing for magical activity was with the common verbs for 'working', 'doing' or 'blowing'.

The magical knowledge which is necessarily transmitted within a kinship group is for the most part productive magic concerned with planting or hunting. The destructive magic is not of this kind. It is taught to individual men at the discretion of other individual men who already know it: in deciding whether to teach it, they are influenced by various considerations such as friendship, desire to help someone to protect or revenge himself, recognition of the ability and good sense of a younger man who later will have to take responsibility. Such considerations make it most likely that the knowledge is transmitted to other relatives but it does not necessarily follow that because a man knows it, he will pass it on to his son. Other relatives such as a mother's brother, may teach destructive magic while they would not do so with yam-planting magic which is linked to the descent group and the different inherited lines of yam they plant. People may also seek out someone knowledgeable and pay to learn destructive magic, particularly as the knowledge of the destructive magic must necessarily include both how to harm and how to heal. Thus in each clan there is a scatter of men who know the different kinds of destructive magic, but it is difficult to get reliable information on the full distribution of such knowledge. Most of the men who either admitted knowledge, or were pointed out to me as knowing particular techniques, were senior men. The men who had been notably effective in hunting or fighting were most often instanced as knowing destructive magic. The youngest of the men whom I learnt knew any of the important techniques were in their middle thirties and they were both eldest sons, notably effective hunters, serious or determined in general manner, and rather less light-hearted and talkative than some of their age equals.

TABOO

The third general class of causes is breaking a taboo. It may be noted that the first two main classes of cause (spirits and magic) involve agents acting against the sick person: he is their victim. In this third class, however, the actor and victim are usually the same. In this general class, the relationship of cause, patient and effect is differently phrased, since where taboo is concerned, it is assumed in general that everyone knows what are the points of danger or the dangerous actions. Taboo serves to narrow down, identify and localize danger, as Franz Steiner (1967) said. In type the phrasing is: the sick man has done this or that thing, so then, or therefore (*wa*) he is ill. But as they assume knowledge of what is taboo, it is often enough to say: 'he did that' (whatever it may have been) – the relevance for them of stating the act done by the patient is clear without naming the consequence.

We have the cause side, X, and the effect side, Y, linked by a conjunction indicating consequence *wa*: X *wa* Y. On the X side, the causes are doing things you know you should not (*yir wuna'at* – do not think to do) but instead the man has disobeyed or refused to listen (*naren patet* – he disobeys). There are taboos about kinds of food, those which are good (*wuyim*) – he eats (*nanu* – he eats), those which are bad (*wolem*) he must not eat (*nagao* – literally, he dislikes); but instead, 'he eats forbidden foods' (*nanu wolem* – he eats bad things) or the name of the food may be said and to an informed Gnau person, all is clear. There are people standing in certain relationships to you whose food must be avoided; instead he 'has eaten it from him' (*nanuan gapabeg* – literally 'he has eaten his body dirt'). A place or person is dangerous and forbidden, or it may be that an action such as standing above him, walking over him or it, touching his hair, sitting in his seat, drinking before him is forbidden; then if it is done, it is said he has 'gone over' him or it (*nauwererapen* – he goes over/crosses over him). This is the verb commonly used to express a general concept – it can be used actively in the sense of *degauwererapyi* – 'I go over you' and it is you who suffer because I am a menstruating woman and you a man, or it can be used passively in the sense *li wowererapeg* – 'she goes over me' and it is I a man, who suffers because she is a menstruating woman. It is thus also possible for someone through ignorance, thoughtlessness, or malevolence to cause harm to another person by breaking a taboo.

A person by the act of breaking a taboo may either wreck himself (*neburkai tambit aren* – literally 'he wrecks self his') or he wrecks another man or women (*neburkaiyen* – he wrecks him). The other specifications of the cause side, X, are precise descriptions of the forbidden acts, such as, 'he said the name of' (*nage'in*).

The effect side, Y, commonly contains non-specific descriptions of illness, but certain consequences are rather often said to follow a broken taboo, or imply a particular infraction. Breaking rules of precedence or food avoidance which forbid the senior to touch or eat what has been touched or grown by the junior lead to *dape wola* – 'breathlessness' (literally 'bad respiration or wind') in the senior. Eating forbidden food or being 'gone over' leads to constraint, *nar matagep* – he is heavy; eating certain things which you have planted which must be at first not eaten by you but others leads to dim eyes which miss the game (*nembe'it ari wure'aiyi nambeg* – (the tree) its sap covers over your eyes); or if ever you eat of sago or a coconut which you have planted, you will only sit in the village (*lawut/we'at we'umemyi* – the sago/coconut sits heavily on you – literally 'sits' with reduplicated syllable). Various other effects are described more or less specifically.

In the course of this chapter I have discussed the general kinds of cause they recognize without giving detail on particular spirits or techniques of magic. If they diagnose an illness in terms of one of these causes, they specify the spirit involved, often by name, or they speculate on the technique of magic or sorcery used, who may have done it and why. The ways they describe or speak of these causes when they attribute someone's illness to them imply views of the reasons for and means by which the causes act to produce illness. In the following chapter I will examine these views to show what knowledge they refer to in considering the evidence on which to base a particular treatment. Below I provide a full annotated list of the Gnau expressions relating cause to patient where the cause is either spirit or magic.

STATEMENTS OF THE CAUSE IN ILLNESS: SPIRITS AND MAGIC

I have collected together the various forms of expression they used to state a relation between different kinds of cause and the sick person. These expressions were compiled from recorded texts and notes of conversations both with me and among themselves. The translations are fairly close or literal.

Spirits

Spirits make up the first general class of cause which may be indicated by expressions that are generally applicable, not specifically limited to any named spirit. These are the expressions used, divided into groups which suggest different ways of acting.

I.

A. Verbs suggesting the nature of contact made by the spirit.

1. *wa'ab/wanem/waleb* – it strikes her/him/them. This is the most common and typical expression. The verb, grammatically irregular, is the usual one for to hit, shoot, strike or kill. The subsequent examples will assume a single male patient and have the appropriate post-fixed agreement.
2. *wogeren* – it took him
3. *wapen* – it stays in/with him (common)
4. *wewagen* – it goes down into him (this is used for possession and displacement of the man's own personality by the spirit; rarely it is also used for what has happened to someone in an illness not necessarily accompanied by spirit possession. Commonly it can be used for entry of the spirit into its own man-made image; or in a particular concept for the entry of a named ancestor spirit into a great or universal spirit, which has another name, thereby activating the latter).
5. *watipepan* – it crushes, treads on him (common)
6. *watitepan* – it holds him
7. *wamberyipen* – it fastens round him (common)
8. *wamunteten* – it ties him up (common)
9. *webaryi'en wulin wulin* – it holds him tight close (literally, it does him closely closely)
10. *wete'aiyen* – it pulls him to it
11. *wangu'en* – it pulls him (away)

B. Verbs suggesting attention of the spirit to the person it afflicts. By sight:

1. *wagaopen nambeg* – it puts its eyes on him (common)
2. *webalen nambeg* – it gives eyes to him (common)
3. *witamalawipen* – it spies him out

By smell:

4. *watemitapen* – it smells him (most often used of the bad witch-like spirits in tales; though also occasionally for spirits causing illness and especially for the prospect of a spirit smelling a man already sick).

By speech:

5. *wosapen* – it speaks of him
6. *woge'in* – it says his name
7. *wogenanpen* – it calls out to him

C. Verbs suggesting more specific or elaborate actions by spirits.

1. *wanu'en wamberiyen* – it eats him and swallows him (this is rarely used except of evil witch-like spirits in tales; but a few people used it for what a spirit killing someone would do; or in imperative form as an example of what someone might say addressing a spirit that he wished to kill another person).

2. *watebipa tu/daget beiya natiteben ao nerat* – it blocks up the throat/the passage by which he urinates or defaecates (according to particular case).

3. *wosigeren tuwat tuwug* – it slices up his lungs (said of a spirit by someone watching beside her semi-conscious husband as he was dying with pneumonia).

4. *wegateten webalen napiget* – it cuts him in bits it adzes him (from statement of a hypothetical case).

5. *wambelupan ala bewog daget woleda* – it draws his blood for going off (i.e. it with the blood) down the bad path.

6. *X wetaupen Y* – X throws him to Y. (This means that a first spirit X has struck him with illness and then throws him to Y, another spirit, to afflict him further.)

Only where I have indicated it in parenthesis does the verb offer an implication about the kind of afflicting spirit, otherwise any of the verbs might be used of any spirit. I have noted (common) beside those verbs which I heard often used.

Magic and Sorcery

II.

The second general class of causes *are human methods of destructive magic or sorcery*. As the typical verb for spirit affliction was *wa'ab* – it strikes, so the typical verb for sorcery/magic is *nebariyen* – he (the sorcerer) works him (the victim). The verb root *-bari-* is the common verb for to work, do or make. Almost as common and typical is the verb *nasupepen* – he blows or bespells him, which is based on the root *-su-* to blow with an object marker *-p-* and the emphatic reduplication *-supep-* although it can still mean he blows magic or sorcery without reduplication – *nasupen*. There is no generic noun for destructive magic, sorcery or sorcerer – the concept is expressed by verb and there are various techniques, many of which I list below. Nearly all involve blowing spells into or onto materials or things, hence the alternative verb root *-su-*.

A. Verbs indicating destructive magic or sorcery in general, rather than a specific variety.

1. *nebariyen* – he works him (common)
2. *nasupen* or *nasupepen* – he blow-bespells him (common)
3. *napepilden nem* – he puts down for him things (common)
4. *wataowen* – she takes (has, holds) him. This verb usually carries the specific implication of a woman who works sorcery on a man's sexual matter leavings, but it can be used without this specific implication and it can be used where a man is the sorcerer e.g. *nataopen* – he takes (holds) him; it does not necessarily mean that sexual leavings have been used.

B. Verbs or complex phrases which indicate the specific method of sorcery or magic.

Sorcery (Pidgin – *sanguma*) always evil and horrible; use never legitimate.

1a. *Langasutap* – *sanguma* – a noun of obligatory plural form, the name of the sorcery

b. *langusutap manem* – *l-sanguma* struck him (common expression)

c. *natao langasutap ala manem* – he (the sorceror) took *l-sanguma* for striking (the victim) (less common expression)

2a. *minmin* – the name of the *sanguma* previously known to be practised by people distant to the south west of the Gnau; while I was there, use spreading and coming close

b. *minmin watewunpen* – *m-sanguma* hung up on him (common expression)

c. *minmin wogeren gungi* – *m-sanguma* took his blood (rare)

Destructive magic (Pidgin – *poisin*) – used with specific intent to damage someone else or in revenge; in general, thought of as evil, but in particular instances, the user and those who support him regard it as a right and legitimate method for redress of wrong.

3. *lebari lambet* – they work the creeper: rarely referred to, a most virulent sorcery in their theory to be used to destroy many people, a whole village or a hamlet.

4a. *nebari dambep* – he works body leavings. I am not sure whether *dambep* is a name for the technique or for the class of things 'body leavings'; it also can be said *nebari dambep gisa'awug* where *gisa'awug* is the name of tiny ants which sting painfully: *dambep* is more probably the name of the sorcery techniques. Examples of *dambep* they cited are various body leavings, food left over. In essence the method is to dig a hole (typically by the main post of the men's house) put in the leavings and red hot stones, cover the hole and keep a fire burning over it until the victim dies.

b. Alternative phrasing may be *nebari ba'anangep/gibeg* – he works faeces or urine or other specified material; *namunteten ba'anangep* – he tied up his faeces.

5a. *nag nunt X ala nasupepen* (*Y*) – he uses spell X for blow-bespelling him (or his Y), where X is the name of the kind of spell; Y the kind of body leaving or material vehicle for transmitting, conveying the effect of the spell.

b. *nasu nunt X* – he blow-bespells with spell X. *Nunt* means mouth, speech, language or spell. The spells of destructive magic have identifying names as do those of much other magic. The main names of the destructive magic spells are:

i. *nunt wola*: evil spell. Worked with lime gourd or apparatus of betel nut chewing such as the spatula or sharp bone with which lime is withdrawn from the gourd, or a morsel of the betel pepper catkin which was eaten by the victim. Sorcerer bespells his own lime gourd, spatula or pepper, gives some to victim and keeps the rest.

ii. *nunt ginati*: the heart spell. Worked on meat, eggs or grubs part of which given to or eaten by the victim or on betel nut or betel pepper.

iii. *nunt nulape*: 'wild taro' spell: worked with body leavings brought into contact with certain varieties of 'wild taro' aroids.

C. The magic may be referred to by the actions characteristic of it, not by spell name.

1. *nager lugati na'ana* – he takes cane grass (arrow shaft) plants it; or *negatet lugati* – he breaks, cuts cane grass shaft: destructive magic worked on a cane grass shaft which is bespelled and later cut.

2. *nagelen wa'albi nembipe* – he broke his betel pepper catkin: *nagel kuti* – he broke the lime spatula. Alternative ways to specify the magic of 5b. i or ii above.

3. *napel dauwalyi* – he put down cordyline: method of hiding or putting a cordyline leaf on a likely path, watching for the victim to walk over or touch it with his foot, the leaf then used. A few other plant leaves may be used.

4. *wuge'ai ba'anangep/gibeg* – she cooks faeces/urine. Sorcery of a women to kill the infant of another women she hates; faeces or urine of the child bespelled and cooked in clay pot.

5. *na'abapel wambep* – they beat their footprints (literally feet): destructive magic with particular spell and special tree materials with which footprints of intended victim, or a trespasser are beaten.

Protective magic – generally approved magic to produce harm which is used to protect property or warn people away – if used as warning it is openly marked by some sign.

6. *nasupep nembigug* – he bespells wands (*nembigug* – 'wands' are in fact the leaf stalks or petioles of the compound leaves of the *taun* tree (*tila'at* in Gnau, scientific name, *Pometia pinnata*): they can be more than a foot long). They may be hidden in gardens or openly placed on fences as a warning. There is a particular spell for them.

7. *nasupep wamei'ing* – he spells bamboo fence poles. The particular spells blown on a horizontal fence pole which the victim walks under or over. Warning cordyline or croton leaves may be, or not, tied onto it.

8. *natebebip nem* – he blocks (places taboo) on things. Signs are put up as warning; sometimes croton or cordyline leaves are bespelled with spells which may have various names (ones of 5b. i, ii, iii might be used or others whose names I have not cited). There are other methods:

i. *nitalepa sari/sarep* – he lays down *sari*-grass. Certain other kinds of grass or fern can also be used. A hank of the grass placed on a palm frond at the opening to a path off from the main path.

ii. *namunt tamberun* – he fastens *tamberun* – a whole coconut palm leaf plaited round the base of an areca or coconut palm.

As these methods use warning signs (tantamount to taboo markers) the implied onus of responsibility for illness may be put on the victim, so they may say:

iii. a. *natipepem* – he trod on things

b. *nauwerapem* – he walked over things, implying the victim had touched against or walked over the bespelled materials.

Finally there are some causes which do not fit straightforwardly into one of the categories above.

The Gnau commonly accompany magical acts by loud invocations to spirits telling them what they are about. But the harmful magic rituals referred to under heading II are effective themselves without help from spirits even though they are often invoked. There are however other rituals by which men instigate harmful action against other men by spirits. This kind of ill-doing against another man by setting spirits on him is referred to as:

1. *nasapen narin* – he speaks his ruin. In some contexts it would be correct to translate this as 'he curses him', but in others, complex ritual acts are necessary as well as cursing.

2. *nagerpen wolem* – he brings ill to him.

3. *nag nunt nagilpen wolem* – he invokes ancestral spirits to do him ill.

It is harder to decide how to class illness attributed to:

4. *belyipeg wolendem manem* – literally 'evil spirits struck him'. *Belyipeg wolendem* includes the plural form of the special word *belyi'it* used of the class of great spirits associated with long ritual songs; but the Gnau take the form *belyipeg wolendem* to refer to a manner of afflicting people, which as they know it, is closely

like that of destructive magic. Men prepare a harmful paint by specific techniques and put it on food or into water. They speak of men 'working' the victim (*lebariyen*) or putting things down for him (*lapilpendem*) as in other destructive magic. The detail of how this is said to be done makes it resemble destructive magic. The manner of its curing, which has to be contrived by Au speaking villagers, who are the people to whom the ritual belongs, resembles a ritual for the healing of spirit-caused illness, with songs, and masked figures.[1] *Belyipeg wolendem* are not indigenous to the Gnau – they present it as though it were sorcery; the Au people, to whom the rituals belong, appear to consider them as spirits which cause illness: there are two Au names for *belyipeg wolendem*: (*a*) *wunu wuna'ak*; which some say may also be called *wasu neki*; (*b*) *kinpau*.

5. *Lambet bulti wanem* – the snake creeper struck him. The snake creeper is given as an example of a type of cause which I have not so far mentioned. Certain species of plants are held to be dangerous and if someone touches or cuts them, he risks illness: apart from the snake creeper, the prominent members of this class of cause are some giant wild taros (*mandaper*, *pi'em*), and a tall fern (*nembe'et*). The difficulty about classing these causes is this: while in general such species of plants may be spoken of as automatically dangerous, in particular cases where such a cause is considered they refer to a spirit, perhaps some particular named one, associated with the plant and watching over it. That particular spirits watch over plants is one of their cardinal views; a host of plants may be watched over by spirits temporarily or from the time of their planting. The difference between this host and the snake creeper class is that all members of the species in the snake creeper class are inevitably and always dangerous, while the other plant species, which sometimes have spirits guarding them, are not necessarily or always dangerous.

6. *bulti watuwongen* – the snake coils about him. This phrase which stands rather on its own among those identifying the causes of illness, is used of children who are feeble and stunted:

[1] The ritual involves dancing with long gourd phallocrypts which are made to bounce up and down clicking against the belt. In this respect they resemble the dancing described by Alfred Gell from the Waina Sawonda. It may be worth noting the further parallel that the magical substance used is body paint (Gell 1971).

also they usually have a pot belly. To explain the phrase, they say the child must have walked under a spirit python and so been harmed; either the harm is likened to coils which fasten about him and constrict his growth; or the bloated belly and its writhing intestines are said to mark harm by the snake.

6
Causality in Illness

As disease is a distressing but inevitable part of life, we are sure to find some explanation of it in every society. In the preceding chapter I described the general causes for illness recognized by the Gnau without providing indications of how they were supposed to produce their effects. The beliefs I deal with in this chapter are those interposed between a general understanding of the nature of the causes and the recognition that someone has fallen ill: collected together, they comprise what I learnt of Gnau opinion on how illness was made to happen. Their evaluations of moral responsibility in illness and of the justice or injustice of the suffering entailed will not be analysed until the following chapter in which I present my observations of particular illnesses. For the moment my primary objective is to convey the theories and knowledge or interpretations they draw on to work out the cause for someone's illness, and to preserve people in everyday life from avoidable or imprudent exposure to harm.

The empirical fact of serious illness which may bring suffering, the threat of death and the disruption of social relationships, is directly distressing and significant at the level of human relations and emotions to the sick person and those who live with him. It is therefore important to distinguish how, and on what grounds, these events are not taken as inexplicable but instead, perhaps, intelligible in the wider and reasoned terms of a particular cosmology. Such ascriptions to causes may be more or less precise. If the cause and the illness are closely and dogmatically linked in theory, the perceived significance of that cause or power must be coloured by the frequency with which the particular illness occurs and the distress it occasions. The inquiry here described into the means whereby illness is produced will take me some of the way further towards an assessment of the part illness plays in Gnau culture: with few exceptions, the causes to which illness is referred have relevance in other spheres of life and social activity besides illness. They are not exclusively known because there is illness and they account for it. Illness is but one of their aspects: other functions and interests are attributed to them but we have here to see how illness is tied to them. With this understood, we can then move on in the next and the concluding chapters to reconsider the place of illness as a distressing manifestation or sign of forces which have neither substance nor visibility in a straightforward sense and must therefore be known in certain privileged or indirect ways, among which illness is an emotionally and socially significant one.

In this chapter I discuss first the applicability of the notions 'normal' and 'natural' to Gnau beliefs before going on to a more detailed discussion of certain processes of harm which are held to be common to many kinds of sickness. These processes illustrate the ambivalence for good or bad that can be found associated with many of the substances or forces which the Gnau believe to be powerful. Gnau statements relating the causes to the sick person are frequently based on analogies with familiar human actions and I examine their assertions and behaviour to see how they mean these analogies to be taken, and what insight they provide into their beliefs about causation. Finally I discuss the general problems of evidence and precision of diagnosis in the Gnau context. This context offers distinctive possibilities for altering and adding to a diagnosis which can become one of multiple causes. As the Gnau do not have clearly recognized medical experts, an authoritative diagnosis is rarely decided on, the emphasis is rather on the testing out of diagnosis through the empirical results of treatment.

NATURAL CAUSES

The everyday notion of cause in our own culture is that a cause produces an effect. But in the stricter terms of logic, the word 'produces' is held to be unsatisfactory. For in alleged instances of causality, often what can be discovered in the instance in question is only that there is an invariable relation between two or more processes. A brick meets the window with a certain force; the window always breaks. This is the general notion of causality in the developed sciences – the analysis of invariant relations. In this sense, the field of taboo resembles statements of invariant relations, of uniform 'natural' laws. The danger in breaking a taboo is inherent and automatic; an analytic distinction may be made between the conceptions of the causes (spirits and sorcery) which produce or intend effects; and the causes (taboo) which involve statements of belief in natural law – invariant relations. This distinction parallels the one commonly made between personal and impersonal forces.

The Gnau say of some illnesses that they just come: *neyigeg gipi'i* – he is sick nothingly, *nag diyi* – he died by no purpose or intent. Some maladies come and go, like colds, which usually need no explanation, although particular individuals may offer one for them. Of others, for example as happened in the influenza epidemic, people say 'everyone has it' it has a normal course and because so many have it they do not seek to provide an explanation of why particular people have it. Ackerknecht (1946) felt that such views as these were not so much examples where illness was rationally accepted as a natural phenomenon, as examples of illness unexplained. We speak of illness as the result of natural processes that will pursue their course according to certain kinds of regular pattern which we can study by the scientific method: it is a systematic method of learning by experience. This interpretation of illness is not a matter of merely accepting that certain illnesses just occur, or expressive of a lack of concern and interest, but part of a view which is consciously held, applying equally to trivial and to tragic ailments. Although it may be analysed by only some members of our society in terms of the precise assumptions and methods by which we can find out about illness, the view prevails nonetheless as a general assumption about illness. Individual people in our society may not accept it as fully adequate to account for illness and seek religious or moral reasons for the illnesses of particular people, or even for illness in general; or individuals may feel an obscure yet deep emotional dissatisfaction with explanation purely in natural terms, but the general view remains. Our view that illness can be investigated in a purposeful, constructive, testing search for 'such general laws as can be used to link together the observed phenomena' (Singer 1926, p. 89) is thus very different in sweep and consistency from the Gnau view I have just cited that illness sometimes just occurs. On a few occasions, women came to me for treatment with large discharging breast abscesses; these, it was said, sometimes happened if a child had died in early infancy; the milk swelled the breast, it was blocked and changed to pus. They did not suggest it was caused by something. It happened; they gave examples of other women to whom it had happened. The women, though some with pain and much discomfort, would continue to do their habitual jobs. I would regard this as an example of a distressing ailment accepted as a natural event. I happened to try and treat a young woman whose breast abscess was large, painful and long-lasting, and I was much surprised that no one, even when prompted by my questions about spirits, sorcery and the death of her child, ventured beyond the quite detailed natural explanation I have given for her abscess. She went about her daily life as a well person would, with none of the care and caution which someone believing herself ill by spirits or sorcery would take. The abscess, despite its size and pain, was a mishap of ordinary life as an infected sore would be.

The abscess appeared to me sufficiently abnormal for me to expect from them some particular explanation, which I did not obtain. They regarded it as ordinary in the way that most infected sores are ordinary. The identification of a particular cause in practice depends on a variety of factors not solely linked to the immediate nature of the illness. Even common sores may in some circumstances be considered the sign of mystical harm. Perceptions of the observable cause, of the usual outcome and severity in visible ailments, like sores or burns, affect the kind of attention paid them and the degree of urgency to account for them. The words we are tempted to use in referring to such interpretations, the words 'normal' or 'natural', do not mean exactly the same, and the distinctions between them, as well as between their opposites, need a moment's care. The troubles in using the dichotomies natural/supernatural and normal/abnormal come in part because the words in English are complex and ambiguous: the concepts associated with them have changed in the course of their use, and from this comes some ambiguity. There are two aspects to normal, an ideal and an average one: the ambiguity may easily be recalled by remembering that dental caries are pathological but not abnormal: great strength and

Plate 5. *Making Panu'et: at the garden.* The shredded plants lie on *wuna'algi* palm leaves (the rib-cage). The two upstanding cordyline leaves (its lungs) can also be seen in the finished image shown in Plate 6b.

intelligence are abnormal but not pathological. Normality in the sense of health often implies the ideal aspect rather than the average to people such as the Gnau. In discussing the concept of health and illness (p. 151), I have noted that this is a common view of health and one taken by most people in our society too. The Gnau rules on correct behaviour, proper food, the dangers in objects, animals, trees, represent an ordering, or a collection of precepts which one should follow to achieve the ideal normal life.

If we take the Gnau, or indeed almost any people studied by anthropologists, we can find examples of processes like puberty or yam growth, in which the normal outcome, in the sense of average, is success yet the activities or processes are surrounded by ritual controls and restraints. The Gnau example which springs to my mind is a short ritual done for children aged about one year so that they will learn to walk: a magical cassowary spell is blown on to nettle leaves with which the child's knees are beaten. It is difficult to maintain that magic to make a child walk has arisen from a perceived chanciness in the normal outcome, that on average only a few infants will learn to walk and that therefore magic occurs here to assure a doubtful outcome, or express anxiety about it. On the other hand, it may express something about normal development in terms of an ideal outcome or the value set on its achievement. The Gnau do not have a word which corresponds to 'normal' as part of a concept of 'normality'; although clearly considerations of commonness or triviality, of what can be expected or understood as a direct visible sequence of dependent events, lie behind their statements that things 'just happen', in terms of *gipi'i* – nothingly, or happen without intention or some cause willing or contriving their occurrence, as with *diyi* – without cause or purpose.

The problems in using natural/supernatural have been more heavily trampled over by anthropologists. They are concisely

Plate 6a. *Decoration of the image: at the village.* The young men have finished painting the face and are attaching the head-dress.

Plate 6b. *The finished image.* The sick woman's husband holds the image. The boar's tusks and the hibiscus flower symbolize, as for a man, that Panu'et is a killer. The dimpled scar at the man's epigastrium marks the site of his *wuna'at* where in youth he was burnt in the ritual of *litau wani wani* to strengthen his *wuna'at* and make him grow well.

stated by Evans-Pritchard: 'We use the word "supernatural" when speaking of some native belief, because that is what it would mean for us, but far from increasing our understanding of it, we are likely by the use of this word to misunderstand it. We have the concept of natural law, and the word "supernatural" conveys to us something outside the ordinary operation of cause and effect, but it may not at all times have that sense for primitive man. For instance, many peoples are convinced that deaths are caused by witchcraft. To speak of witchcraft being for these peoples a supernatural agency, hardly reflects their own view of the matter, since from their point of view nothing could be more natural' (Evans-Pritchard 1965, pp. 109–10). The idea is turned upside down: it can be done, I think, because of our entangled conception of 'nature'. First, nature has its original sense of an essential quality in things – the inborn element of its Latin origin, *natus*, *natura*. What was first looked for in nature was some essential principle. Second, there is 'nature' viewed as the existing system of things in space and time – natural phenomena. Third, there is nature viewed as a universe acting according to rules or laws. The major ambiguity is the antithesis of nature passive and created (the phenomena we see, touch, etc.), and nature as active or creative (the system of laws or rules by which phenomena happen). By the first of the three senses, it may often be right to say that some people consider that there *is* a difference of essential nature between men and spirits. Spirits are not subject to the same limitations of space and time as are human beings and so on. By the second sense, that of existing phenomena, it can sometimes be said that spirits live in a sphere above or beyond the ordinary perceived universe of nature; or on the other hand it may be, as Peter Lawrence writes, that: 'We must dismiss at once the concept of the Supernatural: a realm of existence not only apart from but also on a higher plane than the physical world. Gods, spirits and totems were regarded as a real, if not always visible, part of the ordinary physical environment' (Lawrence 1964, p. 12). The third sense, that of active Nature with laws or rules, is the most tricky, for the particular assumptions we make about natural processes and natural laws are (i) that they may be described in their own terms without any prior assumption of purpose or design; and (ii) that nature is uniform. The assumption of uniformity is crucial: it enables us to say that, under a sufficient degree of similarity of circumstance, what happened once will happen again: it enables us to say that something is impossible, i.e. not naturally possible. The assumption that nature is uniform is not an axiom in many societies, or taught there as an explicit doctrine – there may be areas of explanation in which it is assumed, for example, in regard to taboo, the invariant relations I have mentioned – but these are only segments of experience, in others it is not found. A general view of nature in which events obey impersonal laws is one that sustains the division between what is thought possible and what is thought impossible, according to present knowledge. It differs greatly from a view that various forces intervene irregularly, variously willing and intending events. By the first view of regularity, rare events may seem so phenomenal and extraordinary that special attention must immediately be paid to them, by their very strangeness and rarity – while by the second view such rare events may not necessarily constitute such a problem since there is not the same expectation of regularity. People in simple societies have occasionally been noted to be indifferent to phenomenal natural occurrences. Attention which is selective is in part determined by what is understood of possibility and impossibility. People in societies like that of the Gnau often make an assumption of purpose or design behind events and by these assumptions 'the Acts of God', or of gods or spirits, or the effects of sorcery are then seen as natural even though they are not normal. Despite this distinction between the view I have called 'ours' and scientific, and the view I have called 'theirs' and might call 'primitive' or magical, there is fundamentally a similarity in that both views, ours and theirs, search for some ordering or reason in events. Events are not accepted in either view as chaotic and anarchic matters of chance. Both look to make sense of things so that people may be able to deal more effectively with them, and decide what if anything can or needs to be done.

The above deals with part, not all, of the complexity in our ideas of nature: I have not touched on the conceptual separation of man from nature – the dichotomy of the nature/culture antithesis. Our modern conception of illness and disease by which we treat it as natural and biological rests on the assumption that man is not separate from nature but part of it and likewise subject to its laws.

THE PROCESSES OF HARM IN ILLNESS

In general there is a gap between the agent acting and the exact nature of the harm it causes: to use our medical jargon, Gnau statements tell something about aetiology but little about pathogenesis or pathology. This of course fits with the general lack of precision about clinical state which I described in Chapter 4. However there are certain descriptions of what happens in illness which lie intermediate between pathology and pathogenesis, statements half of what is happening, half of how it happened: they bridge the gap in understanding how the agent works upon its victim, and also provide some rationale for finding and interpreting evidence of the mode of harm and the agent. These statements concern three main subject areas – blood, heat and the vital centre – which I shall describe successively, preceding the discussion of the vital centre by an account of the pathology of sorcery, which they explain more elaborately than that of most other illness.

Blood

In those views which come closest to pathology, blood is the disordered element. In the normal person, blood should lie still beneath the skin, filling it out and making it glossy. In the old it is dried up and the skin wrinkles and goes dark and dull. If blood 'dies' (*gungi wag*) in a young person, he remains stunted and ill-favoured. In illness with diffuse malaise and aches, the blood 'courses and flows about' (*gungi wegatemeg* – literally, blood follows in me), a description often unaccompanied by gestures of the hand running up and down the skin. With bad aches, the blood throbs (*gungi wor lugluglug* – onomatopoeic); the head aches with the blood 'gone into it' (*gungi wogegem* – literally blood goes, reduplicated syllable, to them, i.e. heads because the head is idiosyncratically spoken of in plural form); in aching bumps and swellings, the blood 'collects' (*gungi wape* – blood stays there). For swelling and headaches, they nick the skin with multiple little cuts to let the blood out. The blood is bad, stale or polluted – it may be by forbidden foods which have been eaten (the discussion of penis bleeding contains more information on this, see pp. 36–9). Where a spirit 'strikes' it may stay (*wap*) in a knee which then is painful and swollen because the blood 'collects' there –

if you were to cut it open, they say, you would see only blood and congested flesh; the multiple little cuts aid by letting the blocked blood flow out. There is nothing to see of the spirit; but the literal sense of its staying and its localization in the knee may be implied in a treatment when the 'stinking creeper' (*lambet gunpe* – which smells of faeces and rotting toadstools) is tied around the affected joint to stink out the spirit.

Blood shows the ambiguity which Gnau see in many things they consider powerful. Blood is vital stuff; it is lost in death by wounds. They say they fear the loss of blood to blood suckers like the mosquito or the leech: that by these even they may be withered or diminished and dried up before their time. Yet oppositely, they nick the skin or bleed the penis to let out 'bad' blood to make them strong or well again. Or they say blood throbs and courses (*wegatemeg*) in pain and illness, yet to draw the bow with power, they say they must force blood to course down (*wegatem*) into their arms and give them strength which they do by breathing deeply in and shutting their mouth with the upper teeth clamped down over the indrawn lower lip, forcing breath against its blocked outlet. Or the blood let from the penis is 'bad' blood, but the penile blood smeared on or fed the youth is said to do him great good. A similar ambiguity can be seen in heat which burns and destroys in illness, but is spoken of as the principle of desirable ritual power and effectiveness; or in cold, where making 'cold' is the usual imagery for healing sickness yet cold, as with water drunk in the night, may also be a cause of sickness. Food, particularly foods sometimes tabooed, have this ambiguity – they are 'bad' for those forbidden them, but 'good' when they become permitted; and the people who state the rules like this have all the interest of unsatisfied appetites for the foods which, many of them, are uncommon, succulent and meaty. The conflicting contrast of power to do good and to harm is also in their view of spirits which I will mention again later, and in the view of destructive magic as a good thing or a bad thing to know and use. A comprehensive list of such ambiguous attitudes would be a long one: when I first wrote of the word for 'bad' (*wola*), discussing the Gnau concept of illness (p. 130) I noted that among its meanings was clearly that of 'powerful, fine, awful, terrific'. Thus a man, boasting loudly of his own magnificent decoration, of his tremendous singing, of his fierce shot or hard work, will nearly always, when carried on the flood of rhetoric, use *wola* ('bad') to indicate how admirably good he was.

The association of blood with life and health is also implied in the notion that spirits and especially *minmin* sorcery work by 'drawing out' blood of the victim (*wambelupan* – it draws out his blood); and in the idea that the birds which sing loudly after death have fed on the blood of the dead (*wanu gungi* – literally, it eats blood; a figure of speech for loud singing by birds); in neither of these notions do they look to see actual blood drawn out.

Heat

Blood by its shining beauty, colour and containment within the skin, its spurting and loss with hurt and mortal wounds, is suited to be a symbol. So too perhaps is fire which flares, consumes and destroys; it burns and hurts and the body in illness is commonly hot to touch. The idea of heat as a metaphor for ritual power is widespread: fire is used in sorcery, and the imagery of fire and blood can be seen in this account by someone of his brother's death:

> They dug a hole, heated stones; they took his body leavings and cooked them in the hole. They made a fire and lighted it to cover over his leavings. Ah! that was the end. Sabuta ruined, the heat consumed him; he lay for a few nights, not many. Blood struck him, here and here (on his body); it flared in him, his face, and he was ruined; crusts of white lime sordes bespattered his lips, puked up on his lips and teeth (i.e. a sign of the lime spatula which was used in the sorcery; the victim, Sabuta had sucked it) . . . He spoke to me 'Purkiten, you will remain, I am ruined, I am dying I am very ill'. Ah! the blood struck him in the head, down there, the ribs, the back there and there, the vital chest, the heart, the fires burned him.

Blood which is vomited forth from the mouth and nose, or from the anus or the vulva, just before death is held in theory to mark death by destructive magic. To burst into sweat at the moment of dying likewise marks sorcery on sexual leavings. Cold, not only heat, may harm (see p. 66): *magi wogelen nansipe wuna'ambelen* – literally, cold went through him earth covered over him – a phrase for coldness and stiff aching joints. The shivering of coldness (*nasegegin* – he trembles) is also noted by them. But the most specific feature to do with cold, which marks the sick person struck down by *langasutap* sorcery, is refusal of hot food. He has been struck down, eviscerated, but made whole apparently, estranged and dumfounded: he returns as one dizzy, staggering, he mumbles or speaks nothing and when given hot food, he cannot touch or eat it – he can swallow only cold things until, after lingering a day or two, he dies.

'PATHOLOGY' OF SORCERY

The beliefs about *langasutap* sorcery are more defined than in other sorts of ill: they correspond in type to that described by Seligman and Fortune under the name of *vada* (cf. Fortune 1932, Appendix II). The victim is hit on the back of the neck (*wawa bawagi* – it hits the back of the neck, which is to them also a vulnerable spot). He falls unconscious or staggers vertiginously; he is struck again and falls. The *langasutap* ties his throat and tongue so that he cannot cry out: then the men (for they work in pairs or small groups) take points of bat bone or sago spines and stab him in the vital point of the chest (*wuna'at*); the point enters his heart. The men stick the points under the victim's nails. Then with a finger nail, one of the men cuts him open, removes internal organs; he may replace them with points inserted into them or he may keep them to eat. He cuts over the flesh muscles of the thigh or arms and works there little pockets in the flesh in which he places more points of bat bone. He then passes his hand over the wounds and they are made as whole. The man then stands a short way off from his victim and stamps with his foot on the ground. The victim wakes, tries, staggering, to stand. The man calls 'Who am I? name me ' If the victim makes to answer, he is again struck down, for his throat and tongue to be made dumb. He is wakened again and stands; then lastly the man holding *langasutap*, calls out to him 'I am a shade of the dead; you a man, you go back now to your village'. And so the man staggers home. A man who holds *langasutap* to use it becomes, they say, a shade (*gelputi*) rather than a human being (*matilden*). If Gnau walk by night, or even in day, and they hear suspicious rustles or crackles in the bush, they call out 'You a shade or a human being?': if no voice answers 'I am a human being' then they will be ready to shoot. When a girl thought she saw *langasutap*, a man she did not know standing immobile a little way off, silent, she fled back to be asked over and over again, 'Was it a man or a shade you saw?'

If from the manner of his death, *langasutap* is suspected, a particular method of divination will reveal it. The body is laid out and covered; his relatives await those who come to mourn. The visitors, if they dare this test and exposure, rub the skin of the dead man's body with leaves and the bark called *dungug*. Under the stroke of the man who used *langasutap*, cracks will appear on the dead man's skin where the points were inserted and from the fissures, blood and putrefying liquids will ooze.

I should make clear that for the moment I am relating their theories about illness and not their application in particular instances of illness, where such signs and marvellous marks as these occur most rarely, if at all: yet it is not rare for the causes of which I write to be discussed.

The traditional theory of *minmin* sorcery was that a man, knowing it, aimed at his victim and the blood was drawn out of his body into the special aiming arrow. While I was in the field, there was a scare about *minmin* which added to and altered the already-held ideas about this sorcery, which before had been spoken of rarely and only as a remote danger. There was a veiled speech about it in July 1968 at a big gathering on the final day of a prolonged ritual for Malyi in the village of Wititai. In late September and October 1968, the epidemic of influenza which resulted in an unusual number of deaths helped to recall and feed these fears: the *garamuts* announcing deaths beat out, there were gatherings for mourning and inevitably speculation about their cause. Out of discussion of these deaths and the exchange of views at mourning gatherings, the understanding of *minmin* sorcery became clearer and it was distinguished by certain methods. It could also be worked by pointing a finger, a stick or a comb. Arrow heads entered the body. The arrow heads that I saw 'extracted' were 1½ inches long and of sharp smooth wood which looked like bone. An adult in theory might feel the moment of being shot, and in contrast to a child, he might manage to wriggle so that the arrow missed a vital spot and he survived to have them withdrawn. A blank exhausted woman, who later on that day, had three such *minmin* arrow heads 'extracted' from her chest, described to me what she felt when struck. She was in the branches of a tree collecting leaves for supper.

I did not see them; you cannot see them and they stand a long way off. I was up in the tree. My ears went deaf. I felt dizzy and sweat came out over my body. I went to wash in cold water. I felt the pain in my chest and the back of my neck.

She went back to the village and was there possessed by the spirit of a dead relative of her husband who revealed what had happened.

I heard only one subjective account of *langasutap*, and that is a doubtful one: I was told that a sick man I knew had, a few years before, been struck by *langasutap* – to be told this contradicts theory from the start for, in theory, *langasutap* is always fatal. I asked him about it. The victim's account, which I wrote down but not verbatim, was this:

He said he did not know if it had been *langasutap* or spirit attack. He had been cutting sago for his wife to work. Late in the afternoon she returned home ahead of him. He finished cutting the sago palm, took the sago grubs he had collected earlier and went to cut some bamboo for cooking tubes. While he was cutting these, he felt suddenly dizzy (*worwor*). He gathered his bamboo tubes, his axe, a packet of leaves and the grubs. It was evening. He began to go home – the bush was called Pilikawun – at a stream, he fell unconscious (*degadag tebawin* – literally I fell down dead). He must have remained unconscious for some time because when he came to his senses, it was raining heavily, thunder and lightening. The stream was not one with a spirit staying there (a common reason for storms is that men go by certain water places associated with a spirit). He lay there. The bamboo tubes, the grubs, the packet of leaves and the axe had fallen by the water. His wife was alarmed – men had gone out to find him. His brothers-in-law found him, lying in the stream - he was not crying out or in pain. One shouted out at him: '*Dji Saitan ao Sulaiman ao dji masi?*' (literally 'You Satan or Solomon or who are you? – a nice touch – Satan is quite commonly used of evil spirits and for *sanguma* men in Pidgin, the man talking to me however knew little Pidgin, and he was speaking Gnau to me. I never heard anyone else bring in Solomon). He replied '*Saitan gnau – deg matilden*' (Not Satan – I am a human being). They came up to him, picked him up and carried him on their backs and put him down at the porch of his wife's house. They lighted fires around him, made sago jelly for him and scraped him coconuts and these he ate. In the morning, his wife went to fetch the things that had fallen by the stream and they were there. The others said to him 'what struck you, was it *langasutap* or a spirit?'. He said 'I don't know. I went unconscious – I think probably a spirit.' (To me) Could it have been *langasutap*? it only happened to him once like that.

WUNA'AT: THE VITAL CENTRE – ITS NORMAL AND DISORDERED STATE

I have now twice mentioned alterations in conciousness given in retrospect dreadful significance. The way they spoke of the disordering was by referring to 'shut ears', 'fastened mouth' to 'dizziness or befuddlement' (*worwor* – an allusive or onomatopoeic sound which is used of something turning round and round and is especially used of the subjective state in *bengbeng* behaviour, see p. 133), and to falling unconscious (falling down 'dead'). To clarify these views, I must explain their concept of the *wuna'at*, the vital centre of thought and being. To begin with the material and work towards the immaterial: the *wuna'at* is at the front and not the back; it lies centrally just below the breastbone, at the epigastrium. The word for body orientation by the front is *wuna'at*. Most of the various ritual applications which strengthen or affect it are applied with sharp blows to the patch of skin just above the solar plexus, some men bear scars from these at this point. They can distinguish it as a surface marking by another word (*malu'api*). In the generous elaboration of their vocabulary for graphic descriptions of fighting and wounds, the same place can also be referred to as *gasipe* or *perper* which allude to the panting and beating indicative of life. Breathless and panting at the top of a hill, I showed my bad *wuna'at* (*lin wuna'at wola* – he is breathless): it went *per per per*. The *wuna'at* is the vital centre: if it is observably inert the man is dead. But if he was cut open one would not see something to call the *wuna'at*, but a heart, lungs, blood and so on. The location seems to shift slightly and indeed sometimes people include a good heart with the good *wuna'at* when they urge you to take care and think what you are doing (*tao wuna'at ginati wuyi* – hold/bring a good *wuna'at* and heart).

For as well as being the vital centre, *wuna'at* is the centre of thought and emotion. Your *wuna'at* speaks of the man (*wuna'at wosapen*): you are sorry for him; your *wuna'at* speaks (*asa wuna'at adji*): it is your wish or desire; your *wuna'at* marks it (*wun'at watitila*): you think of it; it boils (*wuna'at wetatetub*): you are angry. These idioms and the forms of verbs for forgetting (*wuna'at wati*); remembering (*ger wuna'at* – take *wuna'at*); being ignorant of (*wuna'at genauden* – be without *wuna'at*); not thinking of doing something (*yir wuna'at* – do not think to); disliking (*wuna'at wagao* – *wuna'at* dislikes) are all combinations with *wuna'at* in them.

TRANCE

The Gnau also refer to the blank or empty *wuna'at* (*wuna'at gipi'i* – the empty *wuna'at*). This was a state induced at one stage in the ritual for having killed someone and for purposes of fighting. If a killing was made, many men tried to shoot arrows or throw spears into the body; if the body lay conveniently close by mothers, fathers, mother's brothers brought even the little boys and, if necessary, held or helped their hands to stick some weapon in it. Those who had struck or killed him could receive the wild aroid plants considered of virtue for fighting. A small boy received only a little of the first 'soup' after which his mother's brother might put his shield over him and sit on it and the boy, so that the boy might grow to be steadfast and unafraid in later life. But the youths and men entered the men's house for the rituals of successful killing. Inside the house with doors shut, senior men made a mixture of certain wild aroids, crotons, root ginger, scrapings of hornbills, of the blood on the arrows which had shot the man, and of ancestral bones and gave them to those who had shot him, especially to the youths and younger men. The raw wild aroids, most hot and powerful, made their mouths and throats burn, their lips frothed, some vomited but the strong retained it. Repeatedly they were beaten or, if big men, beat themselves with the fierce nettles called *ningi nengupe*. For the actual killers, the nettles were stuck in their ears and anuses as well as rubbed on their *wuna'at*, their scrota were pulled backwards to their anuses, and the young men's tongues were cut with bamboo slivers after which ritual hunting ash was rubbed into the cuts. All this occurred to the beating of log *garamuts* triumphally announcing the killing and the rituals and to singing. The beating with nettles continued until tremors began running through their bodies and some younger men eventually fell to the ground, either trembling or as dead. The log *garamuts* or large *kundu* drums were placed on top of their prostrate bodies until they slept or their eyes again appeared good, clear, no longer vacant, and they heard speech showing that the *wuna'at* had returned to its proper place in the front. The trembling, even unto 'death' (verbally they make no distinction between this and physical death) was the chief sign of *wuna'at gipi'i*. The wild aroids and the nettles were to turn round the *wuna'at* (*wuna'at wamberyi*) or to turn and send it into the back (*wuna'at wamberyi walep tapi'it* – *wuna'at* – front turns round it goes into the back). While in this state of trembling *wuna'at gipi'i* they were as though blind and deaf; if the doors of the house were not shut they might rush out and kill whoever came close to them.

Although trance was induced after killings, they did not speak of it as a rite to cleanse or purify someone from a danger he incurred by the fact of having killed a person. It, like the hunting rituals done after killing a pig or cassowary, was said to strengthen him and make him more sure of future success. If they had stuck some weapon into even the dead body, young boys received some of the aroid potion and young men went through the rites, so that they might become strong, steadfast, and fearless. We will now see that although displacement of the *wuna'at* is a way to become able, and desired or sought out even if it is dangerous to others, its displacement is ambiguous, and can also be a harmful thing for the individual.

DISPLACEMENT OF THE WUNA'AT AS ILLNESS

The turning round of the *wuna'at* and sending it to the back identified the process of *wuna'at gipi'i*. Trance was sought out by these techniques but exactly the same theory that the *wuna'at* had turned round and gone to the back may be advanced as an explanation in almost any illness: the view of *wuna'at* as a vital centre, rather than as a thinking centre then seems foremost. Betel nut juice in rituals for treating illness is typically spat on the back of the patient just over the scapulae for the given reason that the vital centre has shifted there and must be treated there to get it to return to its proper place. Such shifts in illness are not necessarily associated with any disordered consciousness. Because the *wuna'at* is a vital centre the arrow heads of *minmin* and the points of *langasutap* are aimed there to kill.

Wuna'at names the part of the body where are localized vitality, thought and emotion – functions which by this shared localization seem bound or intermingled in the way that our folk concept of 'consciousness' supposes a quite similar complex of involved functions sited in the head or brain, although their recognition of associated vitality is rather different and more marked. Reference to the *wuna'at* to explain states of lowered vitality (illness), altered consciousness and also madness are consistent with this view; and the mechanism of displacement from a proper location explains for them its pathology: for them localization is a clear attribute of consciousness while for our folk concept this is not so in the same way. Our thought and language are imbued with the duality of mind and body; our intellectual traditions include subtle bewildering debate of the relation between consciousness, self-awareness, the individual's spirit or soul and its link to or independence of the body. The duality of mind and body is not shown in Gnau language as it is in English. Emotions and states of mind are not made abstractions but identified by verbs describing characteristic gestures, or movements of the skin or *wuna'at* – crudely they remind one of William James's pragmatic theory of emotions. The *wuna'at* has no link to spirit or soul.

THE WUNA'AT, MADNESS AND SPIRIT POSSESSION

Wuna'at gipi'i, the empty *wuna'at* of trance, comes within the wider category of madness. It is one state within it. The words which I translate by madness, *wora wuna'at*, apply to all the entranced and strange behaviour states, to epilepsy and febrile fits, though not to the simpleton or mental defective who is spoken of as *wuna'at genauden* (him with no thinking centre). The main feature implied in *wora wuna'at* is lack of awareness. *Wora wuna'at* means literally 'unthinking of it' – quite commonly the expression is *worel wuna'at* – 'thoughtless of them' (persons); and the analogous expression *worel nambeg* is suggestive: it means to flick your eyes restlessly from person to person without fixing on any one. Beside the trance of *wuna'at gipi'i*, there are two other forms of what we would call 'trance' which are said by Gnau to come from striking by spirits, and the further form of behaviour whose interpretation is spirit possession (see p. 134).

We need to consider what has been meant by possession. The point where I think ambiguity can creep in is at the distinction between entering and possessing. Our own, rather our own ancestors', cultural version of spirit possession like that of many other cultures would emphasize that the spirit occupies, dominates, controls or actuates the possessed person. As Oesterreich described it: 'The first and most striking characteristic of someone possessed in the strict sense is that "he appears to be invaded by a new personality, governed by a strange soul". The external signs of his possession are that he takes on a new face with altered features, his voice speaks not according to the spirit of his normal personality but that of a new one. These phenomena are usually but not always accompanied by others, foremost among which are motor ones. The affective disorder of the possessed is translated by his movements which may equal those of veritable raving madmen and consist in a disordered agitation of the limbs with contortions and dislocations in the most impossible directions' (Oesterreich 1930, p. 32). The *bengbeng* behaviour is interpreted as possession in the sense of the requirement, 'that the actions of the person affected are thought to be either those of the spirit or to be immediately dictated by the spirit'.

The two remaining forms of trance in the terms of native explanation are ambiguous as to whether spirit entry or possession is involved. The spirits strike men with the madness of transient 'death'. These spirits are of the kind called both *malet*, the generic term for spirit, and they can also be called *belyi'it*. Two different spirits, who in this context are called Tambin and Wunitap provoke madness in men. 'The spirit struck so that he was mad' (*belyi'it wanem wa lin wora wuna'at*).

The madness of Wunitap sends someone so that he runs away into the wild bush, he eats in his rush certain wild incomestible plants, he climbs high into trees or straight down mountain sides and as his relatives chase after him calling to him, he whistles a peculiar short bird cry or calls back 'here I am' (*deg yitena*). And when they reach the spot he is no longer there, they call again, and his cry reaches them from a further tree and so on. The behaviour is highly specific. It occurred once in the village 20 years ago in a youth about 15 years old, the man now says he does not know what he felt and did during it, but it happened as he stayed in the ritual house during the singing of Wunitap; the others say they chased his cries until at last he was caught by his father at the top of a high tree on the edge of the precipice called Wau. He was brought down, carried to the village and treated with flames, spitting, nettles, etc.

Tambin, the other spirit I mentioned, is the one perhaps most associated with madness and is the usual explanation for epilepsy and febrile convulsions. It further inflicts a dangerous madness in which the afflicted does not recognize his brothers or his friends, and would kill anyone if he were not restrained. Some men within memory have been struck in this way; the affliction of one of these men precipitated the removal of a section of one hamlet to form a new one (Pakuag to form Dagetasa). He is now about 65, an eccentric withdrawn man with some killings to his credit, to whom in the past women were attracted. The killings were not ascribed to his Tambin madness and indeed no killings were ascribed to such affliction. To get rid of it the full ritual of Tambin – which takes several months – was performed. This kind of Tambin madness is rare – of the three recent cases, although they happened before the War, two occurred in men who had not long before had a near relative shot (a wife and a father respectively) but there is no pattern seen by Gnau people in this or other events to explain their madness; all the men involved are remembered as fierce impetuous fighters. I should mention that Tambin may also strike to produce a variety of ailments besides madness.

The madnesses, then, of Tambin and Wunitap seem to fall into the category of spirit possession but I said earlier that they were ambiguous. The spontaneous description is of the spirit striking with madness. Perhaps implicitly the spirit is present, enters, provokes the abnormal behaviour and is besought to leave in treatment but this is implicit rather than ostensibly stated or elaborated, although direct questions along these lines would be answered 'yes it is so'. In brief the people are concerned with aetiology or pathogenesis rather than pathology, that is with the particular explanation of why this case occurred, which can be answered by saying Tambin struck him, rather than with the abnormal mechanisms which produce the kind of behaviour he showed, that is with a theory of spirit possession. A spirit which strikes people mad as though by a blow is a recurrent theme of their myths, particularly those which tell of the cataclysms which led men to be dispersed. A spirit is stabbed and killed, the earth quakes, the people in the ancient village go mad, turning, trembling, turning round (*lambererigel*), some change to stone, some rush crazed about and so disperse to new places. The identifying verb in myths for this event is *wambereryiyel* – it (the spirit) turned them round and round. Another theme in myths is the spirit which strikes someone dead then teaches him spells, makes him to arise after which he knows the spells and ritual. Again the idea of a spirit striking with madness though not possessing or entering occurs in the ritual work of hunting magic. One aim in this is to persuade a *gelputi*, shade of the dead, to tell a man in dreams where and when he will find game, a pig, say. What he hopes is that the pig so revealed, will in fact when he hunts, come towards him struck by the spirit or the dream (commonly they say 'the dream struck it' – *nansibep ma'ab*). The pig will come, head nodding, *wora wuna'at*, neither seeing nor hearing him, straight towards him.

Clear distinctions between striking as with a blow, sending something like an arrow or a poison into someone, or the spirit taking over and directing the behaviour of the person often can not be made from their account. To suggest that they necessarily make them would be misleading since they are not particularly concerned with this question of the processes involved in the production of symptoms or signs.

INTERPRETATIONS OF CAUSE BY ANALOGY

In their talk of causation in illness, the Gnau frequently use verbs with everyday meanings like 'strike' or 'do' to indicate the relation between cause and patient, but in this context the phrases are precisely allocated to different kinds of cause. I have already provided a full annotated list of these statements (p. 187). The everyday meanings suggest analogies for the action of the cause

Plate 7a. *Transfer of a spell.* Divination in the forest at the outset of a day's hunt. The man bends close blowing and whispering a spell into the *wuna'algi* palm frond which has been stuck into the ground.

Plate 7b. *Invocation.* He calls on his ancestors for aid and bends the frond at the point bespelled to see if by a clean effortless break the frond will show that their hunting on that day will be successful.

and analogy is universally used to help interpret experience and provide a means to understanding. Even in random observation we have to make hypotheses and guesses by analogies in order to interpret what it is we are sensing – we have seen and have touched solid objects in the past, we see something in the distance and we suppose it will be solid if we touch it. We cannot take a step forward in an inquiry or in interpreting some obscure and pressing problem like sickness unless we begin with a suggested explanation. Such tentative explanations are suggested to us by something in the subject matter, and by our previous knowledge. In order to produce suggested explanations we start from something familiar. We have to go from analogies or resemblances which we note between the facts we are trying to explain and other facts whose explanation we already know. Thus in any explanatory system, scientific or other, we tend to make hypotheses by analogy (cf. Cohen and Nagel 1934, Chap. 11).

The verbs the Gnau use to indicate the action of a cause draw upon common experience in order to move by analogy from the level of empirical observation (a sick person) to a suggested cause. The analogies are from human behaviour – particularly from ways to harm, shooting by bow and arrow, striking; or from giving attention to someone (speaking, looking, smelling). A problem then is whether in making this jump from the facts of observation to explanatory theory, the verbs are understood

Plate 8a. *Hunting ritual: transfer*. The young man has killed a cassowary for the first time. On return, inside the men's house, his father performs a stage in his advance towards full acquisition of the ritual knowledge for hunting. His father blows and spits the spell and herbs with betel juice into a nettle leaf with which he is about to strike his son at the *wuna'at*. A dark blot of betel juice below the son's armpit marks another vital spot (*nalgiti*) where he has already been struck. The father wears a hibiscus flower showing that his son has just killed a cassowary: his son cannot wear it because it was the first time he had killed one.

Plate 8b. *Hunting ritual: annointed image*. The ritual in Plate 8a used the blood from the cassowary carefully brought back from the forest where it was killed. When the young man had been treated, the carved figure of Tambin was annointed with this blood on the forehead and at the *wuna'at:* which show black and shining in the photograph. The image here is undecorated as it had not long before been moved to a temporary men's house when the dilapidated *gamaiyit* was destroyed. Arrows and bows rest beside the figure.

literally by the people or whether they are intended purely as metaphors or figures of speech. We have looked at those views intermediate between cause and the patient which partly account for the nature or mechanism of the harm present in the patient. I have remarked that Gnau people are most concerned with aetiology, less with pathogenesis and less still with pathology. In looking now at the question of literal understanding, I shall take what is shown by behaviour or said generally, rather than speculate on what goes on in the minds of individuals. So I would cite the 'extraction' of a bone *minmin* arrow head from a woman's chest as an example in which the statement that *minmin* sorcery is shot (by arrows) into the victim, appears to be understood literally or intended to be (whatever those individuals who 'extract' the arrow heads know and believe about it). In contrast the view that the roots of a tree crush down a patient, because he cut that tree down, is metaphorical in the sense that they (as we can) see that the man is in one place and the roots of the tree remain stuck in the ground at some other place. These examples illustrate a difference between literal and metaphorical suggestions more clear than can be seen in many of their other statements. In following out the general range of comment and behaviour I can often not resolve the problem of whether they suppose or mean the cause acts literally as they say it does, or not.

Entry

Their statements on spirit causes suggest first the nature of contact made by the spirit – viz. striking, staying in, going into, crushing, tying up, pulling, etc.

To strike or shoot him (*wanem*) is sometimes understood in a literal sense: harm from the spirit is due to arrow heads they have shot into him (*sigap wapen* – arrow heads stay in him). In the case of the spirit Panu'et (*malet* and *belyi'it*) associated with pools and sago, or the spirits which watch over yams, these are tiny spicule arrow heads. Some men know techniques to 'remove' them by suction and they do so, spitting out and then searching in the dust for the tiny fragments which are then shown in evidence that the treatment has been successfully accomplished. At other times the spirit is said to 'strike' but they do not assume it has shot particles into the victim or that he has felt the hurt of a blow. Where they say that a spirit 'stays in' the patient they may also do a variety of things which suggest a literal interpretation. They may tie a stinking creeper to the affected part to stink out the spirit; they may sear the patient's skin with flaming coconut fronds to drive it out by heat. They may try to knock or startle off the spirit by applying a treatment, such as one with bespelled nettle leaves with heavy blows to the patient's body, ears, chest, or head. At the end of treatment, the bespelled nettle leaves are stroked with great care down over the affected part with gestures of gathering together, clutching and enclosing, and then standing and throwing out the arm suddenly in the peculiar gawky overarm throw gesture to throw something (spirit or harm) off with the leaves, calling out to the spirit to depart from the patient. At the end of almost all treatments, the healer (it can also be the patient himself) takes the patient's hand, grasps the finger and bends them (*lagelapen bigep*) to see if the knuckles will crack (*bigep bimapepu* – the fingers have cracked). If they do, it is taken as a good sign. With the gawky overhand throwing gesture they hope to and sometimes do, make the elbow or shoulder joint crack as similar sign. They may also try to make leg joints crack by kicking out straight. By contrast in illness, the fingers are tried and bent in this way; that they will not crack confirms to them the continuing state of illness. At the end of treatment, the patient stamps on the ground, shakes his head, suddenly throws out his arm, or kicks out his leg to see if the joints will crack. One man had severe heart failure: his son got hold of some gunpowder. He came up in the evening as his father slept beside a fire and dropped the gunpowder in the fire. It should have startled the spirit away.

In addition they state belief as 'it stays in him' (*wapen*) and during treatment they call out loud to the spirit to go clear from or leave him (*suwipen* – you leave him); to leave him alone (*ta'apen* – you let him be!). These actions and words do not so far impute more than entry into the patient. Explicit diagnosis of spirit entry without possession in the stricter sense is shown by the case of a sick woman who, a few days before had leaned down to take her bamboos filled with sago, stretched out her hand and they said, in retrospect, then the spirit had jumped into her fingers from the pool. With gesture and speech, they discussed how the spirit tracked up her arm to her neck and then down to her pubis, where it stayed causing great pain. The woman had been in fact briefly spirit possessed during this illness but by a different spirit, one of her husband's recent dead, which through her explained how and why she had been struck by the other spirit staying in her and causing her pain. When I asked in my ignorance if the spirit possessing her had been treated, I was clearly told 'no' for it was not that spirit which made her ill, but the one from the pool which had gone into her pubis. The form *wewagen* 'it goes down into him' is the verb used for possession and/or displacement of the man's own personality by the spirit. It is not strictly used for illness. The root – *wag* – means to 'go down' for instance, a tree or a hill. Used with a human suffix, it can ordinarily mean to 'visit someone'. Apart from its use for spirits possessing people, spirits also are described as 'going down into' their man-made images or a bamboo pole or stick used in divination (*wewaga* – it goes down into it); or occasionally a shade of the dead (*gelputi*) is said to 'go down into' a great spirit (*malet*) like Panu'et and thereby activate and instigate its actions. When a spirit goes into a held man-made image or stick, they say, the image or stick then feels heavy, implying that they feel something has added to its weight. To be heavy with illness (*nar matagep* – he is heavy) is a frequent comment on any bad illness whatever the cause.

Constraint

The idea that the spirit constrains and restricts the patient may be expressed through the verbs crush, hold, fasten, tie up, hold tight, pull to or pull. This may be an interpretation of the feeling of constraint and limitation which comes with the feebleness and lassitude of illness. These analogies are sometimes elaborated. The general type of their elaborated explanation can be exemplified from a case: a man was 'crushed down' by illness (he had pneumonia); he was crushed down because he had eaten grubs from a certain palm; the palm had been cut down in order to extract the grubs; the shade of the dead man who had planted it and watched over it was cross that it had been cut down; the shade crushed him down with the roots. The sick man's sons went and hacked out the roots, cut them in pieces and threw them in a cold running stream to try to remedy his illness. Another example from treatment during the prolonged ritual of Malyi is the sequence in which a long creeper is tied to the figure of Malyi who dances to the patient and the creeper is wound round and round him, then ritually cut in pieces from about him. Despite the suggestive name given the creeper in this rite (*dugi* – umbilical cord) the explicit interpretation of it is with this analogy; 'a tree or a sago palm with many vines and creepers on it is tied so that it cannot spread as it grows. The sick man is the same. When Malyi, the spirit, struck him, his self (*tambit* – skin, self) became tight, he could not walk about, he could only sit as the tree must sit when vines and creepers tie it down. Later they come and cut the vines; that's it, the branches open out; the man gets up now.' The view that a particular plant – a tree, a palm, fern, or creeper – is the immediate and necessary link between a cause and a patient is commonly brought forward, and treatments depend on uprooting all of the right particular plant, cutting it in pieces and throwing it in the river.

Localization

Spirit entry or possession in contrast to striking, crushing, tying round, etc. may prompt us to question how they localize, limit or imagine the identity of a spirit: if a spirit 'stays in' a patient, can it be somewhere else as well? To the question, put in this form, they answer clearly that a spirit can be in more than one place at once: spirits are like wind (*de'aipe*) and can be at one and other places simultaneously. But their ideas on movements, the time and place of spirits provide points for reference and citation when they discuss probabilities in diagnosis. No spirit is everywhere *and* always: neither is wind. They imply varieties of limitation. The important concept which associates spirits to places is the one that they 'watch over' things (*wenarep* – it watches over): watching over in the sense of looking after or caring for things. The verb root – *narep* – means this and is used for the ownership or stewardship of inherited land, or other things, by people, for caring for one's own or step-children; it is also the usual verb for to watch something or watch over it. The real things like foods, trees, land, pools and rivers, and people which spirits are said to 'watch over/look after' provide the link between invisible spirits and people who fall sick, the link for understanding or adducing evidence about which spirit is involved. The varieties of limitation, or localization in this matter, apply to the different kinds of spirit.

The great spirits, of the *belyi'it* kind, linked to song rituals, are associated with care for certain kinds of vegetable food, with their successful growth and vaguely with their origin; they are jealous of the foods which they watch over, requiring men to observe respect and moderation in their use of them, particularly outstandingly good or large specimens of the food in question, wherein the spirit may lodge as a man lives in his *gamaiyit* – men's house. One aspect of the assumption of identity of certain spirits despite their many different names is that wherever these foods are grown the great spirit watching over them is the same one. They know that neighbouring people, speaking different languages have other names for them. In this sense they attribute universality to some of the spirits. The seasons of ripening and for eating certain foods are the times when it is likely that people suggest the associated spirits as the causes of the illnesses. When one of the spirits is celebrated through performance of its major rites, the general pattern is that the spirit is sought out and brought into the village where the rites are performed in its presence. Men who sleep in the *gamaiyit* (men's house) which is the focus of the rites are said to 'stay in the *belyi'it* – spirit' (*lap belyi'it* – they stay in the spirit) or to 'sleep in the *belyi'it*' – (*lat belyi'it*). At the end of the rites, the spirit is sent off, told to depart thence, sometimes after rites which enact its killing. The presence of such a spirit in the village is thought dangerous and therefore they must observe certain precautions. At the time they send off a spirit they have been celebrating, people in nearby villages fear it will come and strike them. Such ideas of the localized presence run counter to the view also held that the spirit is everywhere watching over certain foods – the idea of presence and localization is perhaps closer to that of concentration than to the either/or of presence/absence.

Shades of the dead (*gelputi* s., *gelpug* pl.) are more limited than the great spirits in where they act. They are in theory shades of dead individuals and usually said to stay close to the places where they lived, particularly tall trees, sago or stands of bamboo they planted, or by land which they gardened or hunted over, or in the hamlet where they lived, especially in the main posts of the men's house where men of that line may 'go down into' the central post (*munganda* – of the husbands) and women who married into the line go into one or other of the two flanking posts (*wolmisa* – of the wives). Bones of the dead (especially the jawbone) are carried by descendants to assure themselves that the shade of their ancestor accompanies them to watch over them if they make a distant journey, or (formerly) go off to fight. The protective relationship between ancestor and descendant also may indicate another man or woman as the link between a patient and the harm of that person's ancestor. Since people invoke ancestral aid when they plant or grow food and hunt, food again may be the substance which points to the diagnosis of a particular shade of the dead.

Food is a very common focus in discussion of the source or agent causing illness. The food is taken as the vehicle through which the spirit harms the patient. In some cases, it is only said that the spirit watching has its attention drawn to the victim because he has taken or eaten the food. In other cases, there is explicit statement that the spirit being in the food enters with the eating, or jumps into the person who has touched the food.

They have thus a constellation of theories involving contact, incorporation, presence and attention which may be flexibly drawn in the unravelling of evidence for the diagnosis of a particular case.

Attention

The verbs suggesting attention by the spirit to the person it afflicts involve sight, smell and speech. Whether they are understood literally or are only figures of speech cannot be asked or discerned in a clear sense; the words demonstrate some of the terms by which spirits are personified in analogy to human beings. The elements of withdrawal, of intended deception by looking worse than one feels, and the occasional prohibitions on speaking a patient's name, which I described of behaviour during illness, are consistent with these statements of how spirits take note of people. Only in dreams do people say they have seen or heard the voices of spirits and spoken with them.

In the above comments I have considered the mode of attention but not the quality of attention, in the sense of affective quality, motive or intention. I implied earlier that they consider spirits are jealous on some occasions and demand respect. When someone is struck for taking food which a spirit watches over, it is often argued that the spirit is cross or annoyed (*wutelap nem ari* – it is cross about its things). I have also said that ancestral shades protect their descendants and may strike down those who do witting or unwitting ill to their descendants, and do so, I must emphasize, *whether or not* the descendant who is hard done by wishes them to retaliate. The fact that the ancestral shades are often held to have acted independently of their descendants is important to remember when considering the consequences for village harmony of the diagnosis that an individual's ancestor is the spirit causing the illness.

However these circumstances do not exhaust their views on the motives of spirits. The great spirits are held to be powerful; people observe correct procedures in dealing with them, yet they are still struck down. In this sense, they are capricious or unpredictable: for people observe the correct procedures in order to derive benefit from the spirit (e.g. successful yams, good hunting) and most of the time they assert the spirit helps them. Two verbs, to 'benefit' (*wasuwilen* – it benefits him) and to 'do ill' (*wadinge'apen* – it does him ill), express these ideas without necessarily implying motive or intention on the part of the actor – e.g. a pig which stands unaware in a clear space 'benefits' the shooter; if still unaware it moves to a position where he cannot shoot without revealing himself, it 'does him ill'. On the other hand, the verbs can be used in contexts where the actor's intention to help or harm is assumed. The other capricious side to spirits is the suggestion that one may afflict someone and then toss him aside to some other spirit to continue his affliction. The putative intention of the spirit may be to strike to warn people and remind them to respect it. The sequence of certain healing rites goes on until the spirit 'approves' (*wawilpa*) or is propitiated by what is offered or done for it, and then leaves the patient alone. Where the diagnosis is made that the spirit struck the patient through the patient's own food, or that it is a husband's ancestral shade which is at work, the form of appeal to it is: 'Have you not looked to see who it is you strike? Do you not know him (her)? It is So-and-So (who belongs here, to whom the food belongs) our So-and-So. Use your eyes. Leave him be! Leave him!' as though the spirit had lashed out indiscriminately.

The last important motive ascribed to spirits is a poignant one: the spirit of someone recently dead is lonely and grieves for the company of those he loved, therefore it may strike down someone close so that they shall not be separated by death.

Thus it cannot be said that spirits only cause illness in people from malice or malevolence towards individuals. In so far as they attribute some illness to the caprice or unpredictability of spirits with great power, their interpretations of illness come close to the view that it is a result of forces present in nature which are independent of and unconcerned with moral right and wrong in man's behaviour.

EVIDENCE IN DIAGNOSIS

I have given this account of ideas about the nature of causes of illness so that it can serve as a general basis for understanding how they set about looking for evidence in diagnosis, for reasoning out the cause of an illness, and thereby the appropriate kind of treatment. In the example I gave of the man with pneumonia crushed down by the palm tree roots, it may be noted that it involved a sequence of levels of explanation, from the time, place and vehicle of entry (eating grubs); to the mechanism (crushing down by tree roots – in imagery not in fact); to the agent (spirit of the man who had planted it). In an illuminating comparison of African traditional thought and Western science R. Horton (1967) analysed explanation, and the similarity in mode between Western science and African thought whereby both in making the jump to theory from the limited vision of natural causes provided by common sense widen the contexts in which the thing to be explained is seen; whether this be in terms of some general nuclear theory or of a theory about the supernatural. They both start from the world of everyday things and people, and go beyond these to the causes which are outside the grasp of simple or unaided perception. The question then is upon what evidence are these different contexts or levels of explanation linked to each other? How are the hidden paths between them to be revealed? As the context is widened so more and more becomes relevant to the cause. For example, a man is knocked down by a car: did the car fail to stop because the road was wet, the brakes faulty, the driver drunk? Was the man knocked down because he chose to cross at that moment and the reason he chose to cross that he wanted cigarettes from the machine across the road and so on. I take this example from E. H. Carr's discussion of Cleopatra's nose in *What is History?* (1961, Chap. 4). In illness one may be faced with a plurality of causes and wish to distinguish between what is incidental or necessary, predisposing or indispensable in some chain of cause. I have given three main classes of cause the remote or abstract level of explanation which the Gnau would hold to be the most significant but I must qualify this immediately by saying that for actual illnesses this level of abstraction is often not reached. As Horton and others before him have pointed out, in the developed sciences the precision reached in analysing observations depends greatly on how exactly some effect to be explained is distinguished. As the differences between effects are distinguished so the inquiry may pursue the explanation of these differences. Where cause-effect links are less discriminated, it is possible for many causes to produce the same apparently single effect. Horton applied this reasoning to the working of a system of divination or diagnosis.

If E is some effect of illness, say elephantiasis, and is unambiguously ascribable to cause A, then if action is taken to rid the patient of E by manipulating or appealing to A and fails; then the most obvious verdict is that A ⟶ E (the theory) is invalid, or alternatively that the treatment is wrong. If the theory is however of the second converging type then things are very different. The theory is protected; you ascribe it to A, take measures and fail, then the causes B, C and D are still available: the theory itself remains unscathed. Horton's point was that many traditional African theories were of this second type, but that they presented in real life this problem; a man with elephantiasis did not want to be told that he might be afflicted by A, B, C or D – he wanted a definite causal verdict and divination in many societies was in essence a mechanism for resolving this conflict. He then wrote of how the divined verdict has an 'aura of fallibility' about it which may have to be made plain to account for failure in some instances.

The Gnau did not use their methods of divination until after the death of a patient and I will give a reason for this later. As they make little discrimination of the symptoms and signs of serious illness, so serious illness appears as the common effect of virtually any of the many causes which they recognize. The relations between causes and effect are of the converging type.

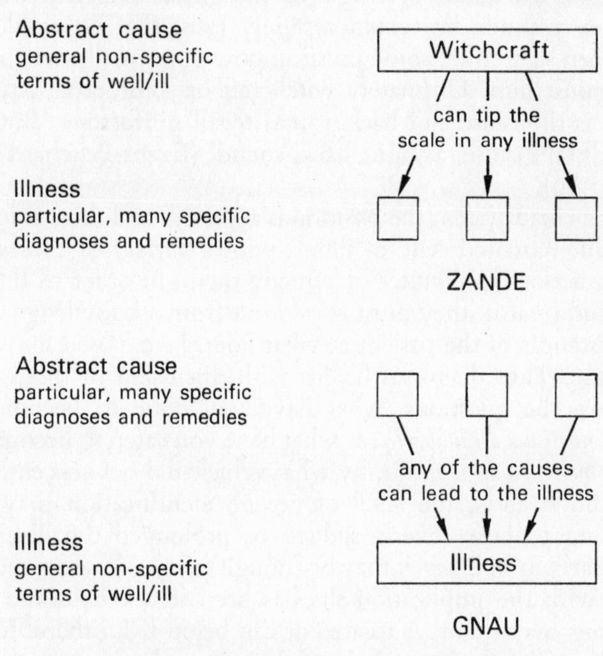

Fig. 23. Illness and cause: Gnau and Azande contrasted

But they converge in a way which may be worth contrasting briefly with the Zande system. The Azande distinguish symptoms and signs and name their illnesses: some of these diseases are said to have specific causes and proper treatments. In a given case, they may explain and treat it with success on this level. If the treatment fails, they may then move to explain failure by reference to a more general theory; they sometimes call it 'the second spear', the theory of witchcraft. Witchcraft and action against witchcraft take place at one level and affect the outcome of treatment in the general terms of good/bad: well/ill: success/failure. The action to control the illness can proceed by reference to explanation at two levels, by reference to what Evans-Pritchard called dual causality. However he makes clear that there are varieties of behaviour and opinion which defy rigid classification because they shade into one another in a complicated pattern of interconnections. Even 'when supernatural causation ceases to be explicit – i.e. referred in social behaviour and notions to the actions of witchcraft or magic or the ghosts – if you were to question a Zande he would certainly insist that he would not have been sick unless some mystical power, normally witchcraft, was against him. Ultimately witchcraft or some other mystical power is the cause and background to all misfortune. But here it is a distant cause, a vague background' (Evans-Pritchard 1937, pp. 509–10).

In the Gnau system the position is reversed, and there is instead an undifferentiated state of illness with a variety of causes, and specific actions to counter or remedy them. In order to find the cause and treat it, they must reason out from a knowledge of the circumstances of the patient at what point he exposed himself to the cause. Thus diagnosis begins with discussion of these possibilities – the questions 'what have you done to become ill?' (*Gagai meni wa dji wolen?*) or 'what have you eaten to become ill?' (*Ganu meni wa dji wolen?*), by what vehicle did sickness enter? As with the Azande, the level of precise identification may vary according to how severe, sudden or prolonged the illness has been. Early in an illness it may be enough to say, 'she ate someone's yams' with the implication she has been struck by some spirit watching over them. A treatment can begin from there. It fails; then they ask which precisely of the ancestral spirits invoked by the man who planted them is behind it, the spirit must be found out, decided on and appealed to: this fails. Then the major spirit concerned with yams in general is recognized and the appropriate rituals undertaken: these fail. Then there is the path she walked on which had a concealed sign placed at its entrance which she must have brushed against and this leads through another chain of cause and remedy. As each possible cause is discerned the appropriate treatment is tried and if it fails, this reveals that there are other things at work. In one sense, their treatments are tests of diagnosis resembling a divination through treatment: the trying out of treatment gives an empirical quality to their approach.

To move, as I intend, from the description of a theoretical system to its use in explaining why certain people have fallen ill, brings me face to face with serious problems of method. If I take a specific answer: 'I am ill because I cut down that sago palm', it implies cause at a low level of precision, assuming we are acquainted with Gnau views. By pushing my Gnau informant with questions, he would probably define and refine his answer further, but this is an artifact of questioning because in normal circumstances someone could take action to treat the patient without doing so. If this failed, then he could go on to specify the cause more precisely. Although I have written that a diagnosis is tested by the outcome of a treatment, a number of treatments resting on different theories of cause may be applied in quick succession. If the patient gets better, it can be a matter of choice which of the treatments is held to have been the decisive one. The fact that the patient is better removes the pressure to explain the event, and people only rarely comment retrospectively on the illness to decide its definite cause. People do not necessarily exchange views or come to a collective decision on cause; the patient may undergo a series of independent treatments. It is a reflection of his social withdrawal and silence, that a sick man underwent unsuccessful treatment based on the scandalous supposition, untrue in fact according to the subsequent account of the patient, that he had eaten a forbidden lizard. The analysis of explanations of cause requires qualification on how the diagnosis was made, one's own part and interest in pursuing different people with questions, on how one heard or overheard it, who from and so on. Again the timing in relation to the illness is significant since retrospective questions months afterwards may receive quite altered explanations.

One reason for the relative difficulty in handling this material is that the roles of diviner or healer are not more specialized: diagnosis, explanation and treatment are done by nearly all men, and to a lesser extent by women too. There is not, as in many other societies, a clearly defined source, either through diviner, oracle or healer, for authoritative decisions to be reached during an illness. The difficulty of telling about or counting the diagnoses and successful treatments of the Gnau is like that of answering who was right and who in the wrong in the disputes of a people without courts to adjudicate between them.

This is the case during illness: the evidence for diagnosis resting on knowledge of the patient's activities; his visits to other places or the forest, to strangers, the work involving ritual he has done recently, his contacts with women, with other sick people; or the recently dead. The interplay of their ideas of contagion and infection or the related ones of the binding or localization of spirits to a place or a person, and their release: the part played in diagnosis by strange signs (a parrot screaming in the night), the revelations of dreams or spirit possession: a host of things to be considered if the cause must be brought to light.

The evidence of circumstance is complex. Those who bring it forward are not primarily concerned with mutual consistency between different chains of reasoning but with finding a reasoned basis for treatment. In general, it is said that spirits, destructive magic and sorcery all cause death. The treatments for illness due to spirits will make or persuade the spirit to desist, they say 'to recognize who the sick person is, and turn its eyes away from him and leave him'. Destructive magic can be removed only by the man who has worked it; if he is from outside the village, they assume (or used to) that he cannot be persuaded to desist. They do not now, nor did they in the past, attempt to buy off the sorcerer from outside. (Until recently, warfare continued: there were many villages into which men from one village would not venture.) *Langasutap* sorcery is lethal. Thus treatment is directed to controlling spirits and to making sure that the patient does not suffer from inadvertent contact with destructive magic worked by people in the village. So the patient receives counter-magic from co-villagers whose protective magic might have caused his illness: personal malice between the co-villager whose magic is thought to be at work and the patient is not, at least on the surface, suggested.

When someone dies, on the other hand, the very fact of death in someone who was young or full of vigour points to sorcery, the work of destructive magic from outside. After death, divinations and ordeals to reveal a sorcerer may be enacted. Divination, because it is to reveal a sorcerer, is not used in life for the sorcerer cannot be dissuaded from his evil, nor his sorcery countered except by his wish.

7

The Explanation of Actual Illness

INTRODUCTION

The two chapters preceding this one have introduced the general frame within which the Gnau seek to understand how and why illness occurs. The aim of this chapter is to look at the body of cases of illness which occurred while I was in the village, and examine how they interpreted them. I will draw together the medical and social data obtained in order to try and discern the relevant factors which led them to explain an illness or leave it unexplained. I will illustrate some of the characteristics found by example but the sustained intensive study of a small population allows me also to attempt an analysis of general patterns found from all their sickness. Certain illnesses by their severity or the unusual character of an explanation, make a striking impression on an observer: the analysis of all the observed cases is intended to balance and correct such selective impressions. I recall illness explained rather than illness not so; yet for 57 per cent of the 274 cases of sickness recorded (whose medical nature was described in Chapter 3), no explanation was offered me in terms that went beyond mere acknowledgment of the disorder or a matter of fact description of the circumstances in which it occurred. I shall try to show the range and varied precision of explanation in the different illnesses I studied and discover what led to these variations.

Clearly these are ambitious objectives: failure or success in achieving them would be dependent first on the adequacy of my information. This is deficient in various respects and I will point out the more obvious of these. In the analysis I have tried to give a precise picture of what I recorded of the application of their ideas to events. The methods I have used for this may also be of interest in the context of anthropological study of belief systems. By these methods I will support some of my conclusions about the differing saliency of their various explanations of misfortune, and about the part illness plays in the wider context of their world-view.

My preliminary task is to make explicit some of the limitations of the record. By analysis of the incidence and prevalence of illness in each hamlet, I showed that the record of illness from the hamlet where I lived (Watalu) was significantly larger than that from other hamlets, given the sizes of the populations exposed to risk, and since the proportions of cases by severity, incapacity and duration on the whole resembled the proportions in other hamlets, it seemed likely that I obtained a fuller picture of illness at

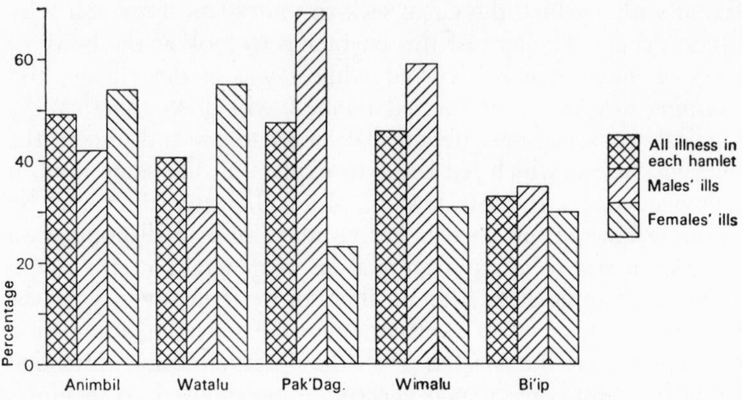

Fig. 24. Percentage of 'explained' illness in each hamlet

Watalu than in the other hamlets. The larger number of Watalu cases compared to other hamlets probably reflected a native and natural tendency for knowledge of illness to be localized to hamlet members, as well as a tendency for my knowledge to be greatest of those who lived closest to me. It might be expected that similarly I learnt more of explanation in illness at the hamlet where I lived. I will describe below (p. 234) what I mean by an 'explanation' of illness in contrast to illness 'unexplained', but first I have prepared tables comparing the relative proportions of illness 'explained' and 'unexplained', according to these criteria for each different hamlet. Figure 24 records the percentage of all illnesses in the hamlets which were 'explained', with the sexes taken together and then separately. It shows that the proportionate records of 'explanation' in illness is fairly similar in all the hamlets with rather less recorded overall at Watalu and Bi'ip.

If, as I shall show, medically trivial illness is more rarely 'explained' the greater numbers of trivial ailments recorded from Watalu would probably account for its lower percentage of 'explanation'. The reason for Bi'ip's low record will be shown below. Figure 24 also reveals that there is no consistent difference between males and females in regard to 'explained' illness. The most marked difference occurs at Pakuag where the relative lack of 'explanation' for women's ills compared to those of men is

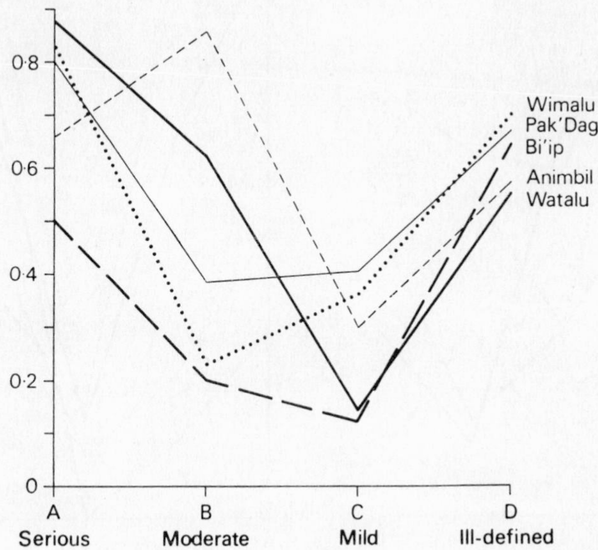

Fig. 25. Proportion of 'explained' illness of different classes of medical severity at each hamlet

significantly[1] different at the 5 per cent level (chi-square = 4·4, d.f. = 1) from all other hamlets: the most likely explanation of this is defective information.

The second approach I have used to find inconsistencies is to compare the proportion of illnesses of a certain class of severity which were 'explained' at each hamlet. The numbers in some classes are small and I have therefore expressed those 'explained' out of the total in that class at the hamlet as a proportion rather than a percentage. Figure 25 shows that half or more of all A class

[1] In this chapter, as before, I have taken the 5 per cent level as the minimum level of significance when I refer to the results of tests of significance.

illnesses (serious illness) were explained in every hamlet, and this was also true of the D class, illness of ill-defined severity. The D class included mainly illness in which I could not find clinical evidence to bear out the complaints of the patient, and thus the

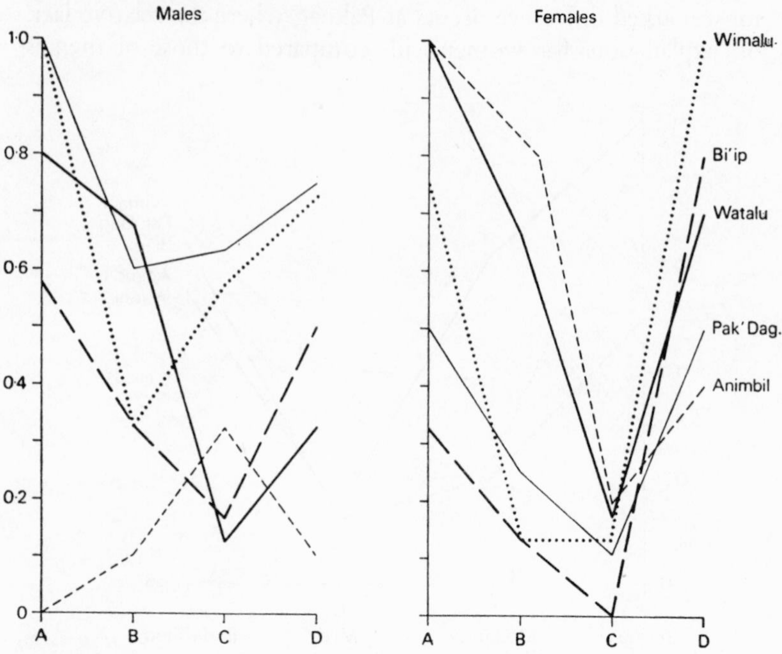

Fig. 26. Proportion of 'explained' illness in males and females at each hamlet: classes of medical severity separated

belief of the patient that he or she was ill was the chief ground for calling it an illness. 'Explanation' in such instances might be expected. The scatter of 'explanation' in the B class (moderately severe illness) is wide; in the C class (trivial or mild illness) it is narrow; in all hamlets less than half of C class cases were 'explained'. The proportion of 'explanations' at Bi'ip is low for all classes and suggests that in general I found out less about their 'explanations' there.

When the illnesses of males are compared separately from those of females (Figure 26) it can be seen that the patterns for females are more consistent than those for males and that no single hamlet stands out clearly as quite different from the others in one general way, except for the lower traces from Bi'ip.[1] Taking all the hamlets in Figure 26 the proportions of 'explanation' show:

Severity	Over half 'explained'	Under half 'explained'
A (serious)	7 instances	3 instances
D (ill-defined severity)	6 instances	4 instances
B (moderate severity)	5 instances	5 instances
C (mild illness)	2 instances	8 instances

Such differences as these in 'explanation' by sex and class of illness will be analysed below. My purpose so far has been to show that the hamlets do not differ so much from each other in their supply of 'explanations' as to make it necessary to keep each one separate or to discard one or more from the analysis because I learnt too little from it. I will not further distinguish between the hamlets but take all the recorded illness together: the larger numbers of cases involved give greater chances for distinguishing pattern and significance.

QUESTIONING

The next major factor affecting the record of 'explanation' is the part my varying grasp of their language and culture played and how my questions and probing altered it. I began ignorant and became progressively less so. As illness was the chief focus of my inquiry and as from the start I provided a simple medical service, I soon learnt the rudiments for talking to patients and asking about illness, but I did not know the implications behind some of the answers I received or how to ask the right probing questions until much later. The assessment of explanation to be given below is based on what I was told, not on guesses at the implications of answers, unless I specifically mention it. Thus some of the illnesses I recorded as a newcomer were no doubt explained but I remained in ignorance. I learnt to ask as they did: 'You are ill. What have you done to become ill?' (*Dji wola. Gagai meni wa dji wola?*) If unsatisfied by the answer to that question, then I often asked

[1] A class at Animbil in males has 2 'unexplained' cases only.

'What has struck you or do you not know?' (*Meni wayiab ao garape wuna'at*?) If they still seemed doubtful or hesitant I sometimes asked 'Do you think it might be a spirit, or what, or are you just ill (i.e. with no cause)?' (*Dji asa malet ao meni, ao dji asa geyigeg gipi'i?*) I used this general approach fairly consistently throughout the study, either with the patient directly or when talking about him or her to someone else. Individual responses of course varied greatly: sometimes illnesses were presented from the outset with an accompanying detailed explanation; sometimes later on I was able to grasp a hint and follow it up. At times and with variation during the course of our mutual study of each other, they must have given me answers to satisfy my curiosity or what they supposed I wanted to know, or duped me, or not bothered with what I could not understand. Similarly my readiness to accept a disclaimer of knowledge, a matter-of-fact description of circumstance, a casual answer, varied too with the kind of illness and my insight into what was to be expected. Opinions on cause were not necessarily made public, and different people often held their own differing private views about the same illness. Most of the explanations on which my analysis is based came either from the sick person or from his or her near relative, because in most cases I saw or went to see or treat the patient. I shall include some comment later on the explanations of those more distantly involved in a case of illness. In summary the many personal factors involved here, of which some are subtle and highly variable, make for uncertainty. I am most likely to have failed to learn of explanations but apart from that, the reader can only guess at my judgement and understanding of their answers and must rely on the evidence I present here.

I am using the word 'explanation' to refer to explanation of an illness in terms of causes. The causes which are involved are any of the three general kinds of cause I described in the previous two chapters, i.e. spirits; sorcery or destructive magic; breaking a taboo. The 'unexplained' illness is one in which they said they did not know why it occurred, or in which knowledge of any cause was denied, or in which the illness was accounted for solely by an observable directly connected sequence of ordinary events (e.g. my skin is burnt because I tipped boiling water over my leg). Thus illness in which the answer to 'what have you done to become ill?' was a description of the direct causing of the harm was called illness 'unexplained'. If spirits, magic or sorcery, or breaking a taboo were specifically indicated as the cause, then the illness was put in the category 'explained' illness. In a later section of the chapter, I examine the detail of explanation and what is entailed in it, but for the moment 'explanation' between inverted commas refers to explanation in this limited, specific and undifferentiated sense of explanation by one or more of their three main kinds of cause.

SEVERITY AND THE 'EXPLANATION' OF ILLNESS

In discussing their behaviour when ill, I have stressed their lack of attention to the clinical features of an illness. I categorized in a rough way the severity of their illnesses in modern medical terms (the A, B, C and D classes). The 'explanation' of these different classes of illness is shown below (Tables 21 and 22).

Table 21. Medical severity and 'explanation' of the cause

	A (*Serious*)	*B* (*Moderate*)	*C* (*Mild*)	*D* (*Ill-defined*)	*Total*
'Explained'	25	31	28	33	117
'Unexplained'	10	36	90	21	157
Total	35	67	118	54	274

Table 22. Proportion of cases 'explained'

		Chi-square (*d.f.* = 1)	*Significance level*
Class	A>B	5·88	5%
Class	B>C	10·00	0·5%
Class	D>C	22·62	0·1%
Class	(A+B)>(C+D)	9·89	0·5%
Class	(A+B+D)>C	30·49	0·1%
Class	D>B	2·64	n.s.
Class	A>D	1·00	n.s.

Although they did not attend to the clinical details, they did assess by general appearance the seriousness of someone's illness. If it were argued that 'explanation' is more likely in serious illness, then this is borne out by the findings. Serious illness in the observer's terms came into classes A and B rather than in C or D, and in the former two classes 'explanation' was significantly more common. But in Gnau terms the class of illness D (ill-defined) might just as well be called serious, and if the classes A, B and D are taken together, or separately, in contrast to C class, their greater 'explanation' is also significant. The A and B classes are not significantly different from the D class in 'explanation'. If it is taken to reflect a view of the severity of illness, then there would seem to be some common ground between the observer's and the Gnau peoples' views of severity. The findings suggest that the lack of differentiation I have discussed is not complete, and that they do make some general assessment of severity.

DURATION OF ILLNESS AND 'EXPLANATION'

From some of the serious, long-lasting illnesses I formed a strong impression that the length of time an illness went on would be linked with whether it was 'explained'. The variety and number of 'explanations' I obtained for a few of the lengthy illnesses is high, but if the undifferentiated criterion 'explained'/'unexplained' is applied to the whole record, I find no significant association between length of illness and 'explanation', comparing the proximate classes, although there is a small gradual rise in the percentage of 'explanation' with increasing duration (see Table 23).

Table 23. Duration and 'explanation' of the cause

	Duration Class					
	1 (*1 day*)	*2* (*1 wk*)	*3* (*2 wks*)	*4* (*1 mth*)	*5* (*over 1 mth*)	*Total*
'Explained'	16	62	23	10	6	117
'Unexplained'	27	84	30	11	5	157
Total	43	146	53	21	11	274
% 'explained'	37·2	42·5	43·4	47·6	54·5	42·7

SYMPTOMATIC FEATURES OF ILLNESS AND 'EXPLANATION'

I classified all the illnesses which occurred into four groups according to the following crude symptomatic features:

Z1 Internal illness characterized by malaise or physiological dysfunction, but without marked pain or fever. These illnesses appear to come of themselves, so to speak. I have included here sudden death, cases of oedema, *pig-bel*, abdominal disorders with diarrhoea or vomiting, complaints of passing blood in the stool or urine, obstetric or gynaecological disorder, and diffuse non-specific malaise of undetermined origin, such as was associated with some of the D class illness, where *bengbeng* behaviour heralded illness.

Total 65 cases.

Z2 Internal illness characterized by marked fever and malaise rather than by marked pain. Respiratory tract infections, malaria, and filariasis provided most of the cases.

Total 73 cases.

Z3 Ailments characterized by the complaint of pain but without a visible cause for it. This group includes diffuse, internal aches and pains, as well as others such as headaches, eye-pains, painful joints or teeth.

Total 49 cases.

Z4 Ailments in which there is pain consequent on injury, assault, bites or falls; or else in which pain is localized to a visible external source such as an abscess or wound.

Total 87 cases.

Thus Z1, Z2 and Z3 represent 'intrinsic' illness as opposed to Z4 'extrinsic' illness, in which there is a superficial observable or visible reason for the pain or ailment.

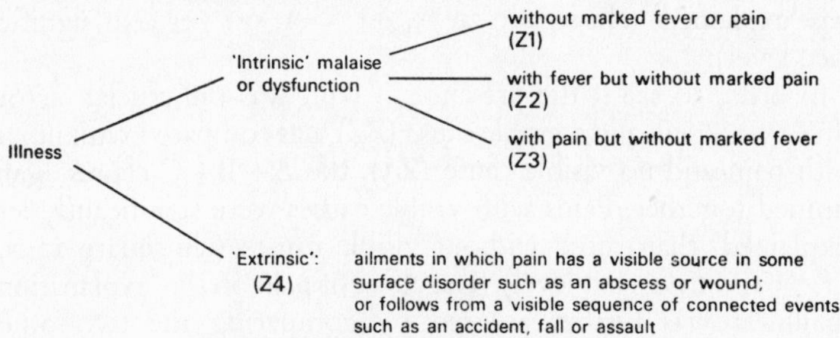

Fig. 27. 'Intrinsic' and 'extrinsic' illness

I have set out in Table 24 the numbers of cases 'explained' and 'unexplained' in order to test whether there are differences in 'explanation' according to the rather general characteristics used, i.e. intrinsic versus extrinsic; pain versus no pain; fever versus no fever. The distribution of medical severity among these Z groups obviously differs greatly and I have therefore separated them according to medical severity on the basis of the A, B, C and D categories used before. It should be noted that Z4, where there is some visible cause or reason for pain, is unlikely to occur in the D class, and where fever was present (Z2) I deduced or diagnosed an illness rather than call it ill-defined (D).

Table 24. Symptomatic features and 'explanation' of the cause

Symptom categories	*Medical severity class* *A*	*B*	*C*	*D*	*Total*
Z1 'explained'	8	9	3	16	36
'unexplained'	8	0	9	12	29
Z2 'explained'	13	11	14	1	39
'unexplained'	2	6	26	0	34
Z3 'explained'	2	5	5	16	28
'unexplained'	0	3	9	9	21
Z4 'explained'	2	6	6	0	14
'unexplained'	0	27	46	0	73
Total	35	67	118	54	274

Comparison of 'intrinsic' illness (Z1+Z2+Z3) with 'extrinsically' produced illness (Z4), taking the A, B and C severity classes together, showed that an immediate or superficial and visible reason for illness made it significantly less likely that the illness was 'explained' (chi-square 29·75, d.f. = 1, 0·1 per cent significance level).

In order to see if the presence of pain was the crucial factor, illness with pain and a visible cause (Z4) was compared with illness with pain and no visible cause (Z3), the A+B+C classes again lumped together. Pains with visible causes were significantly less 'explained' than those without visible causes (chi-square 12·06, d.f. = 1, 0·1 per cent level). The effect of pain on the 'explanation' of illness was further assessed by comparing the two other 'intrinsic' illness groups without pain as a marked feature (Z1 + Z2) with the group (Z3) of intrinsic illness and pain. Comparing all classes of severity taken together, there is no significant difference; nor is there any difference between the D classes of the two categories. The D class was separately tested to find whether the complaint of pain, which may be hysterical or assumed, was more common in the ill-defined and 'explained' cases; in other words, where illness was, I thought, grounded in belief of illness rather than objective disorder (D class) was a complaint of pain significantly commoner than a complaint of general malaise? The answer was no (chi-square 0·016; d.f. = 1). Finally I tested whether the presence of fever (a sign they commonly noted) made any difference to 'explanation' by comparing 'intrinsic' illness without marked pain or fever (Z1) with 'intrinsic' illness without marked pain but with fever (Z2). The A, B and C classes lumped together in both cases show no difference (chi-square = 0·016; d.f. = 1).

The small numbers of like cases of different kinds of diseases make a more detailed statistical comparison of clinical features and 'explanation' impossible. The crude symptom comparisons made above tend, though not very convincingly, to confirm my earlier conclusion that the Gnau differentiate little on clinical grounds between illnesses. The significant finding which emerges here is that a visible cause or an observable reason for illness or pain makes 'explanation' less likely. This would seem a fairly obvious or expected finding, especially as many of the illnesses in the 'extrinsically' produced group are common, or trivial.

SEX AND AGE AND THE 'EXPLANATION' OF ILLNESS

The differences in 'explanation' between the sexes are shown in Table 25 with the classes of medical severity separated.

Table 25. Sex and 'explanation' of the cause

		Medical severity				
		A	*B*	*C*	*D*	*Total*
Males	'explained'	13	15	21	16	65
	'unexplained'	6	13	54	12	85
Females	'explained'	12	16	7	17	52
	'unexplained'	4	23	36	9	72

The illnesses of males are not significantly more 'explained' than those of females; nor does any class of severity show a significant difference in 'explanation' between the sexes. Age must be taken into account before the difference of sex takes on significance.

Table 26. Age and 'explanation'

	0–4 years A1			*5–15 years A2*			*16–45 years A3*			*over 45 years A4*		
	M	*F*	*T*	*M*	*F*	*T*	*M*	*F*	*T*	*M*	*F*	*T*
'Explained'	10	7	17	5	10	15	14	19	33	36	16	52
'Unexplained'	17	12	29	5	11	16	38	38	76	25	11	36
Total	27	19	46	10	21	31	52	57	109	61	27	88

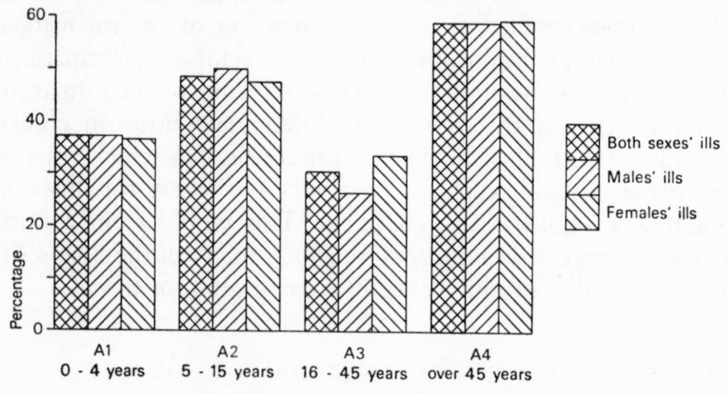

Fig. 28. Age and 'explanation' according to sex

It is clear from Table 26 and Figure 28 that there are differences in 'explanation' according to age. There is no significance to the difference in explanation between children as a whole (A1+A2) and adults as a whole (A3+A4); or between infants and toddlers (A1) and older children (A2); but there are significant differences between various adult groups. The results are set out in Table 27.

Since we know that men over 45 years old have relatively high proportionate amounts of all illnesses, and compared to the others notably a high proportion of illness in the severity classes A, B and D, which are more often 'explained', their proportionate high 'explanation' is to be expected. But by taking B and C class illness separately and distinguishing men over 45 from all other adults we can discover whether this difference is maintained even when only illnesses of similar severity are compared. The men over 45 are still significantly different in regard to C class illness, but not for B class illness (B cases, chi-square 3·11; d.f. = 1; C cases chi-square = 12·10; d.f. = 1, 0·1 per cent level). But in

Table 27. Comparisons of proportionate 'explanation' of illness in different age and sex groups

'Explained' illness		*Chi-square d.f. = 1*	*Significance level*
Adults (A3+A4)	> Children (A1+A2)	0·06	n.s.
Over 45 (A4)	> the rest (A1+A2+A3)	14·23	0·1%
Men over 45	> Women over 45	0·00	n.s.
Men over 45	> Other males	8·54	0·5%
Women over 45	> the rest	3·36	n.s.
Women over 45	> Other females	4·25	5%
Men under 45	< Male children	1·82	n.s.
Women under 45	< Other females	3.20	n.s.

men and women over 45 years taken together, both B and C class illness is more 'explained' than in adults under 45 years. (B cases chi-square 7·86; d.f. = 1, 1 per cent level; C cases chi-square = 6·64, d.f. = 1, 1 per cent level of significance.) As the older group of adults differed in these ways, the younger group of adults was compared similarly with the children and there was no significant difference between them in 'explanation', taken together or with the sexes separated.

INCAPACITY AND 'EXPLANATION'

The classing of behaviour during illness according to the different kinds of incapacity shown is the most complex of the criteria used. It reflects both what the physical disorder forces on someone and his appreciation of its significance. When, for example, the disease is seriously disabling, the sick person is forced by its severity to lie down (class IV) and also because of its severity we may expect an 'explanation'. In class III, which contains those who seemed to me to overact their show of illness grossly, I expected and found that there was usually an 'explanation' for their illness. The proportion of women in this III class, for whose illness an 'explanation' emerged is less than for men: this, I think, is due to cases in women where the showing of illness appeared as a way partly to gain sympathy, partly to sulk, after a fight, a

Table 28. Incapacity and 'explanation' of cause

		Incapacity class					
		I	*II*	*III*	*IV*	*V*	*Total*
Males	'explained'	12	25	13	9	6	65
	'unexplained'	37	33	1	2	12	85
Females	'explained'	9	10	15	12	6	52
	'unexplained'	35	14	7	6	10	72

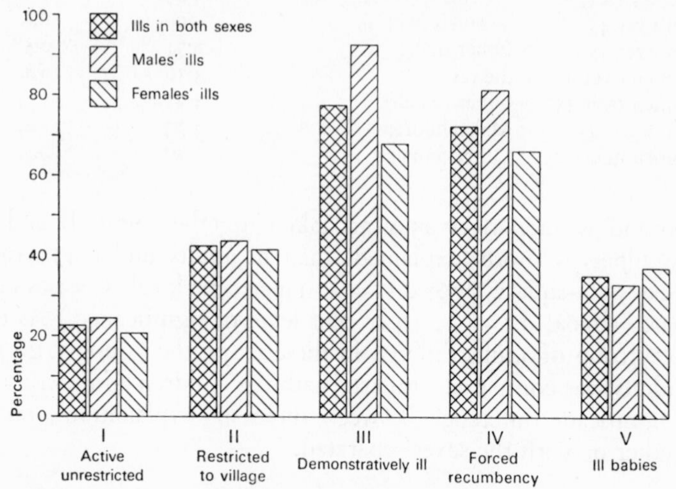

Fig. 29. Percentage of 'explained' illness in the different classes of incapacity

quarrel or a threat of suicide. The relative lack of 'explanation' in these cases makes it seem as though the behaviour was (either consciously or not) an end in itself. The percentages of 'explanation' in the different classes of incapacity are shown in Table 28 and Figure 29.

In class I where people remained active there was less 'explanation' than in class II, but the medical character of ailments was less severe in the former. If people decide for themselves when they are sick and therefore to behave as ill, it would be interesting to know whether their decision was influenced by their knowledge or suspicion of its cause. In a subsequent section I will present more evidence about this and the question cannot be simply answered from these figures. At times some people behaved as ill yet said they knew of no cause for their illness, while others said they knew the cause and were going to remain as ill until they were sure they were in no danger. An attempt to see if behaviour was associated with 'explanation' was made by comparing relative 'explanation' according to class of incapacity I or II or III within each of the separate classes of medical severity B, C, and D.[1] Significant differences were found only in the greater 'explanation' of C II compared to C I class illness (chi-square = 10·90, d.f. = 1, significance level 0·1 per cent); B III compared to B I+B II (0·1 per cent level), but not between B II and B I; or between any of the D classes I, II and III; although within each severity class the proportions of 'explained' cases all went III> II> I (except for D II> D III). The data tend to confirm my impression that people acted as ill in part according to what they supposed was at work to make them ill. But there are so many factors involved – such as who gave the 'explanation' and the time in the illness at which it was expressed – that the crude dichotomy I have used ('explained'/'unexplained') means that these findings can have little weight. A similar comparison of illness with (Z4) and without (Z1+Z2+Z3) visible cause in class I, where people remained active, still showed a significant association (chi-square = 11·34, d.f. = 1, 0·1 per cent level significance) between 'explanation' and a lack of visible cause, even though the people involved did not choose to keep to the village. An 'explanation' did not inevitably lead to confinement to the village: such people did not regard themselves as ill in themselves, only a part was affected.

SUMMARY OF STATISTICAL FINDINGS

In summary, the main findings of this general and statistical survey are that not all illness is 'explained'; that women do not differ from men in general as regards 'explanation' of their illness – their illness is not in this sense disregarded; that men over 45 years old (and probably women over 45 years) are more

[1] 'Explanation' was not better correlated with the classification by medical severity than that by incapacity: a variance ratio test showed no significant difference between the two classifications.

likely to have their illness 'explained'. 'Explanation' is more likely as illness becomes more severe, but in illness with an obvious cause or visible source it is less likely. Evidently they do discriminate the general severity of illness but there is a group of illnesses without physical signs of the disorder complained of (the D class) which they take seriously and 'explain' as much as the most medically serious of their illness. From this general background, I now move on to look in greater detail at what is involved in 'explanation'.

CAUSE AND ILLNESS

I have not so far distinguished the precision, source, or number of assertions underlying 'explanation', or its relation to treatment. From now on I will use explanation without inverted commas: it is not intended to have a limited and special sense. The points already made about the lack of necessary connection between clinical signs and the attribution to a cause may be illustrated from my observations in three ways:

(1) *A given cause is not linked to a particular clinical kind of illness* – for example, the spirit Malyi was named as a cause in these illnesses: fall leading to acute renal failure and subsequent urinary infection; severe arthritis; congestive heart failure; pneumonia; infected hand from a deep splinter wound; perirectal abscess; abdominal colic and diarrhoea; abscess in the groin; a cold; hip and thigh aches.

(2) The reverse of the above: *a given clinical kind of illness does not imply a specific kind of cause* – for example in 25 cases of pneumonia or bronchopneumonia, the following causes were explicitly suggested: named great spirits Panu'et (7 cases), Tambin, Malyi, the *mama* spirit of *wadagep* (tubers), the bad spirit of a particular water hole (all once each); undifferentiated spirits of the dead of a specific lineage or clan (11 cases); named dead individuals (6 cases); broken prohibitions (5 cases); sorcery (4 cases); no explicit cause recorded at all (4 cases). Obviously in some of these cases of pneumonia, more than one cause was suggested. This is the third point.

(3) *A given clinical illness may be attributed to a variety of causes* – for example, an old man's pneumonia (the explanations are given in the sequence in which they were brought forward): the spirit

Panu'et because he had eaten mushrooms his daughter had collected from a pile of sago pith rotting beside a pool; he broke a prohibition by eating a snake killed on land belonging to his matrilateral relatives; the ancestral spirits of the Local Government Councillor of Mandubil at whom a month before he had drawn his bow, threatening to shoot him (a covert implication of possible sorcery is involved here, not explicitly stated until after his death); the spirit of the man who had planted a palm from which he had eaten beetle grubs; the spirit of his own dead wife; ancestral spirits watching over a tract of land from which he had eaten bananas, the land having been the ground for a virulent dispute between his clan and a group of Mandubil men just over a year and a half before.

A MEDICAL SYSTEM?

Presented thus, Gnau attributions of cause in illness may appear wayward, without rhyme or reason. I have suggested that they lack a medical system in the sense of lacking a special department of co-ordinated knowledge and practice concerned specifically with the understanding and treatment of illness. In Western medicine, the natural or biological conditions necessary for diseases to occur are investigated. Illness is explained as a phenomenon whose causes apply to people independently of their moral or ritual[1] state. The boundaries of what comes within this sphere of medicine, of what the doctor should deal with, have altered in our history, as has the specialization of the doctor's role, and the separation of medical institutions (in the sociological sense) from those other institutions which before were closely involved in the care of the sick.

The fact that in certain circumstances a man with madness or smallpox may also find that his illness has legal consequences, does not make the judge a doctor or the law a department of our medical system. We see medicine as that part of dealing with illness which is primarily concerned with the natural processes involved and the job of the doctor is to acquaint himself with these and manage them. Ostensibly he should set aside from his professional duties any moral, religious or social judgements

[1] To apply terms we use for others to ourselves.

about the patient and his illness. In his professional training in medicine he learns about the nature, causes and treatment of illness as natural biological processes; moral, religious and social wisdom are not explicitly taught as part of this training except where occasionally they somehow bear on certain aspects of the natural processes involved in illness, or to make clear the ethical and legal bounds to his future practice.

This central focus on human sickness and the definition of a field held relevant to it, the co-ordination and integration of knowledge according to its value for understanding and treating sickness, is what gives some unity to 'medicine' in our society and allows us to separate it off as an institutional system. In other societies there may be no separation of a department of knowledge and practice specifically orientated towards human sickness. Illness may be treated by religious or other specialists as one of their many duties; the explanations to account for it may stem from theories or premises that have much wider relevance than to sickness alone, and whose chief significance is other than explaining illness. In such circumstances illnesses may well be managed in a rational and ordered manner. The explanations and treatment may follow logically from the ideas involved, yet to speak of a 'medical' system as a separable system would, I think, be unwarranted for the primary or central focus of the ideas and practices is not sickness. It is not necessary for all kinds or treatments of illness in some society to come within a single or comprehensive systematic frame of knowledge; it is not necessary for the explanations or treatments of the system to correspond to what we would call natural or empirical ones: all that is required is the primary orientating focus on human illness. Thus for example, I would call Zande leechcraft a medical system, but not the organized body of ideas and practices concerned with witchcraft, even though of course they are often relevant to the management and understanding of illness in that society.

In the case of the Gnau there is very little to call leechcraft, or to put forward specifically as a medical system. What is interesting however is to see how variously they manage illness, and into how many different areas of understanding and behaviour the possibilities and chance events of actual illness are thought to ramify; and in its turn the actual occurrence of illness may reflect back upon these ideas and practices.

ILLNESS AND SELECTIVE ATTENTION

An illness, if serious, can not easily be disregarded. It may provoke Gnau people to reconsider recent events, activities, and social relationships with a heightened awareness: it may alter their perceptions of significance, for what might have been passed over in the changing flow of everyday life, takes on a different light after the illness has occurred. Attention is concentrated to pick out the actions that were wrong or rash, the coincidences that become, in retrospect, significant. The illness, according to its nature and severity, may also require that other people recognize their obligations to the patient and show that they do. Emotion, affection and duty are no doubt variously interwoven in this. The occasion of the illness perhaps provides a test of social worth and the opportunity to re-assess the strength of social bonds. Thus illness offers certain parallels to ritual.

For ritual has been held, among other things, to confirm, or alter, or restructure peoples' perceptions of their relationships to each other, and the relationships and significance of activities or objects that they know. Within a ritual context, these may be picked out and emphasized selectively, as though framed by the ritual. Likewise an illness may alert their attention to what was before it merely experienced, accepted without comment. The metaphor of framing fits quite aptly to the way they review past circumstances trying first a narrow frame of time and circumstance, examining and selecting events within the picture according to their ideas of cause and evidence, then perhaps finding it inadequate, widening it to include a greater range of time and event which might have bearing on the illness. The detail of explanation in actual illnesses enables us to follow how they have selected from their theories of cause and evidence, applied them and articulated them with the events of ordinary life. Since there is a wide range of possible explanation, in looking at the choice and selection they made in actual illness I have had a number of questions in mind which I will mention before proceeding to my findings.

The most general of these is the question of whether explanation is indispensable to the management of illness. There are two issues involved: one is explanation as a means to understand the significance of the event, the other is explanation as a means to guide decisions about treatment. Both are interwoven so often that isolation of one or other issue would more likely show the bias of interest or interpretation in the observer rather than in the observed. But where explanation comes with later reflection on a past illness or follows after a death, the concern to understand the event appears detached from any bearing on treatment, as the patient has by then recovered or is dead. During an illness people may suggest various reasons for it, some of which could provide the grounds for an appropriate treatment, yet no action is taken; in some of these cases the speculative aspect appears uppermost, and not the practical question of the choice of treatment. Matters such as the cogency of one theory of cause, or apparent indifference to another, the commitment of belief for intellectual reasons in contrast to the emotional content implicit in some explanatory view (for example, one relating to a previous death), require some attention if we wish to understand the selections they make in their diagnoses.

THE ARTICULATION OF CIRCUMSTANCES AND DIAGNOSIS

As their diagnoses do not follow from clinical signs, the process of linking the patient and his circumstances, what is or was to be observed, with the theories about causes which are not ordinarily visible, leads us to examine the evidence and knowledge they use to discover these causes and the flexibility, coherence or prepotency of the reasoning involved. The level at which they first seek to understand an illness is straightforward and matter-of-fact in most cases. They consider the recent circumstances of the patient and try to deduce what might be the likely cause. From accounts which to the observer seem to be factual descriptions of recent events, certain foci of attention become clear either because they are conspicuously associated with risk, or because without one or more of them the diagnosis could not have reached a certain point of definition or precision; or the treatment could not have been performed as it was. The difficulty the observer sometimes faced in deciding whether he had just heard a plain description of recent facts, or a statement by implication about the supernatural causes of an illness, suggests that the gap or difference of conceptual level between natural and supernatural was not made in the same terms as the observer used and did not necessarily entail a jump to a different level of reasoning.

Diagnosis of the cause from circumstance and description of past events is their common method but such a retrospective search is not their only deductive approach. Current ritual or some recent death, for example, may provoke anxiety or anticipatory concern, so that a slight indisposition is quickly seen to confirm the supposed risk. And revelation or divination may also provide a diagnosis, the event of illness altering their notice of dreams or natural phenomena to give them a special significance in relation to the illness. The techniques of divination are special modes of knowledge. They are remotely parallel to those diagnostic methods, like biochemical analyses of blood or X-rays, which we similarly use to reveal what cannot be perceived unaided.

During an illness, the detail of progress in deduction, the points at which talking stops and treatment starts, the times when discussion must be resumed, the specificity of the links between a diagnosis and a treatment, variously reflect the practical importance of their theories about cause, as well as intellectual commitment to them. In Figure 30 I have summarized as a set of alternative paths, the possible relations between interpretation of cause and treatment in the Gnau context. At the top, patient's condition → treatment represents the sequence: recognition of a kind of ailment by clinical signs – therefore kind of treatment. This is the usual method of Western medicine but the Gnau adopt it only for the treatment of superficial wounds, burns, abscesses, skin infections, and a few other conditions including snakebite, swelling and colds. Otherwise a decision about the likely cause guides the choice of healer and treatment, of what should be done and where. Such decisions about the cause are neither conclusive nor exclusive. I have remarked already on their empirical approach in treatment whereby recovery in theory shows that a diagnosis was correct yet cannot prove it incorrect since more than one cause may be at work simultaneously or in sequence during a single illness.

Thus they face a number of problems in deciding how to treat someone. If they try one treatment, it may fail because the diagnosis was wrong, or because there were other unrecognized causes needing remedy. If a treatment is performed and the patient continues ill, it may be because they have not waited long enough for it to take effect, or because there is another cause so far untreated. As they do not differentiate the kinds of illness by

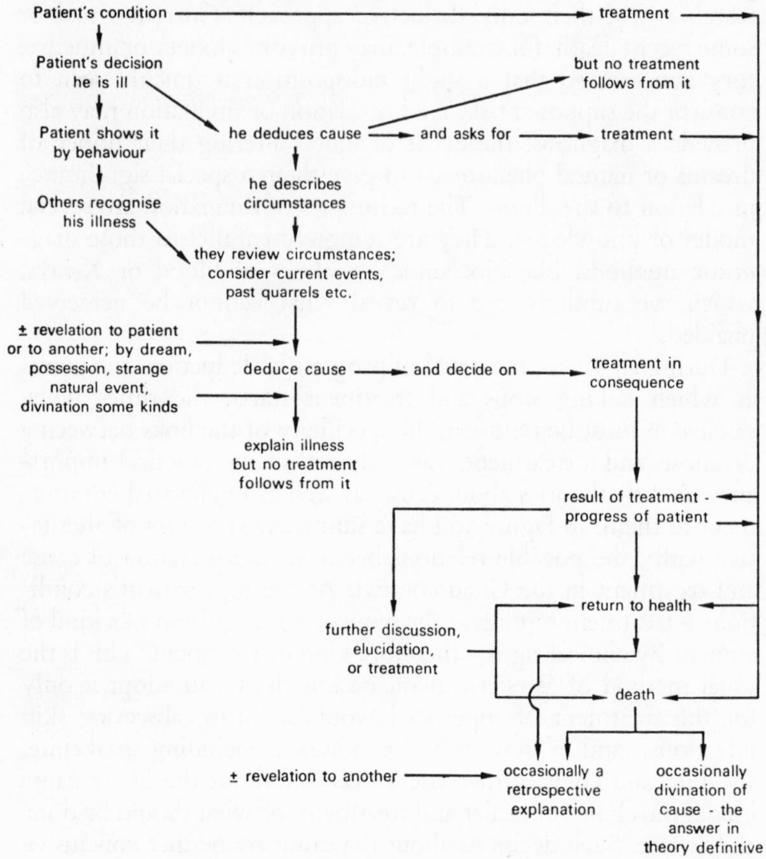

Fig. 30. Paths in the interpretation and treatment of illness

clinical signs so they have great difficulty with prognosis, with foreseeing what course someone's illness will take. The lack of a clinical classification of sickness tends to prevent knowledge accumulating about the usual progress and outcome of different illnesses. If they wish to compare the similarity of two illnesses in terms of how they affected patients, they must name the patients in question and rely on the listener's familiarity with the cases.

Individuals vary in how much they know about other people's illnesses. It is difficult for them to collate knowledge since there are so many opportunities for confusion. So prognosis is difficult, and the withdrawal and conventions for behaviour when ill also obscure the differences in physical state. An idea of what to expect is the surest basis from which to tell whether a treatment works or indeed makes any difference. Because they lack such guides, failure of a treatment is less easily discerned; judgement about the urgency of doing something else must depend on their general assessment of severity and on their impression of whether the patient is worsening or improving. They do not expect that a treatment will necessarily effect a sudden or rapid improvement. They therefore must wait to see, but the problem is: how long?

In general terms of strategy for a severe illness they would rather try a number of treatments in quick succession, if there is some indication for them, than examine, refute or reconcile competing, different explanations and the evidence and reasoning that suggested them. Thus many treatments, indifference to the inconsistencies between alternative diagnoses, removal of concern when the patient gets better, which in theory should show the cause because the treatment worked, together combine to obscure definitive decisions about the causes of particular illnesses. There is no arbiter to announce a final verdict on the illness, no regular occasion or reason to decide about it publicly and reach consensus after recovery. So people's eventual views about what caused an illness remain largely undisclosed, often uncertain and sometimes various.

During many illnesses, people may hold different views about the causes and if there is no large gathering for sympathy, their different views are not generally discussed. Instead they remain private opinions, sometimes exchanged between a few people who happen to bring up the subject of the patient when they are sitting together; or if someone is related or obligated to the patient and must therefore go to see him, the visitor may say what he thinks. He may perform, if the action is appropriate to his explanation, some small act of ritual treatment, typically an invocation to his lineage dead accompanied by spitting over or on to the patient, asking for the patient to be healed. The modes of discussing diagnosis and arriving at decisions about cause and treatment may now be best grasped from description. The four following selected examples all concern fairly serious events but differ in how suddenly the illnesses began.

FOUR CASE HISTORIES

(1) Saoga, aged between 35 and 40 years. Dysmenorrhoea.[1] She was born at Bi'ip and married to a Wuninangiwut man living at Watalu. On 7 December 1968 she felt pain. Her husband and her closest neighbours knowing she had gone the previous day to bush where but a day before her husband's classificatory son, Ulibel, had planted yams and taro, immediately assumed it was the lineage dead spirits watching over the yams and taro who afflicted her, for there is a prohibition on people, especially a woman, going through a garden newly planted. The spirits were supposedly angry with her. The classificatory son invoked the spirits, explaining that she had not realized that he had just been planting, and he spat on her therapeutically at a small gathering composed of some people from Watalu and her brothers, who had come from Bi'ip. The next day the pain had gone and the day after that she resumed normal life. But on the following day, 10 December, she again had pain. In the evening, she became agitated and began striding round making the hus! hus! hus! noises of *bengbeng* behaviour. It lasted about 20 minutes and she retired inside her house where she had occasional brief further outbursts during the next two and a half hours. She did not communicate any messages during her *bengbeng*, but the behaviour was attributed by the Watalu people to the spirit of her husband's dead elder brother. Some Wuninangiwut people came down from Pakuag to see what was the matter. The wife of one Pakuag man (also Saoga's classificatory elder sister) told me next day that the spirit had been that of Saoga's husband's father. Saoga slept the night

[1] I am uncertain of the diagnosis of her illness. She had been married to three different men yet was never pregnant by one. When I first asked another Watalu woman about Saoga's menstrual periods, the woman, who was about 55 years old herself, said we neither of us menstruate now, we are both senior women. Saoga said she had had no period for many months and that before this her periods had been irregular and spaced at long intervals. She denied having had similar pains before. It is possible that her symptoms were caused either by endometriosis or by uterine fibroids. I was specifically asked to treat her first after the initial Panu'et ritual was done. I was able to examine her externally and found nothing abnormal. She refused vaginal examination and did not wish to go for further investigation of the bleeding to the Mission Hospital.

in her house accompanied by two other Watalu wives. In the middle of the night she again began crying out with *bengbeng*. The husband of one of the wives, who is expert in the Panu'et diagnostic techniques (see p. 170) came and 'smelt out' (*natemitepa*) her illness and found (*nagegera*) Panu'et. He performed no treatment. She slept again.

The next morning I asked if she had been treated for the spirit possessing her and was told no, the spirit was only making her *bengbeng*, not sick. One of the wives who had stayed with her for the night told me Saoga's pains were in her pubis and buttocks and added that it was illness from Panu'et. Saoga's brothers and their families came to Watalu that day and sat in sympathy. It was decided to perform treatment for Panu'et on the next day. Again that night, Saoga moaned and cried out with pain.

On the morning of 12 December, at about 7 a.m. people from Bi'ip, Animbil and Pakuag began to assemble at the day-house at Gabagi in Watalu. Saoga was inside her house. The visitors, arriving intermittently, sat down in the day-house and discussed her illness. Most of the talk at first involved repetitive assertion and agreement that she had been struck at the tract of garden bush called Walyibat, by a *malet*: sometimes they referred to it as *malet*, *maleg* or Panu'et, sometimes as Marusi. These namings were taken as referring to the same thing or cause, and were accepted as consistent. No one contradicted any of the statements. There were also frequent repetitions that she had taken bamboos filled with sago flour from the pool called Telibe'em there; and that the pool was one where a spirit was. The senior man of those who use the Gabagi day house, Maluna, imitated the gesture of her stretching down her arm to take the bamboos, then jerking his arm back suddenly over his shoulder to enact the moment of the *malet's* jumping into her. He said the *malet* had jumped from her hand into her neck and then coursed down to her pubis and buttocks. Others contradicted the view that it went to her neck, and said that the spirit entered her arm as she put it in the water, followed up her arm and then went straight down to her pubis and buttocks. At the same time as some were discussing the moment of the *malet* jumping into her, others in loud voices, almost shouting (because of the interrupting multiple cross-fire of talk in animated discussion), were telling each other that she had been struck in the pubis and the buttocks – the emphasis in this being the site of her illness, her pains. They said she was struck first in the pubis and the illness went through to her buttocks. These discussions were repeated as new people arrived.

All this while Saoga remained inside her house. The men discussed the cause of her illness, relying on what others told them as they arrived and joining in with their views. No one went to see her or to ask her about her movements or the pains. Only a few related women visitors went inside the hut where she lay. These were: two of her brothers' wives from Bi'ip; her husband's widowed sister from Wimalu; a lineage 'brother's' wife from Pakuag, and a classificatory daughter married at Animbil. The men meanwhile went on talking. They explained in answer to my questions that the pool at Telibe'em belonged to the Wuninangiwut men who hold the myth of Marusi and the land around the pool. Marusi and Panu'et were the same, just two names for the spirit. No one had specifically referred to her *bengbeng* or the spirits said before to have possessed her. I asked about them. They then answered that the spirits of the lineage were angry with her for coming too soon close to the new planted yams and taro, they struck her and the *malet* Panu'et/Marusi jumped into her because of their preceding attack. The other point brought forward was the similarity of Saoga's illness to one Maluna, the senior man of that day-house, had had about 15 years before. The *malet* Panu'et/Wolpawei had shut the path by which he urinated and defaecated, he had great pain in his pubis and buttocks. They recounted in detail his treatment by Panu'et and how after many days he passed a urine of pus, filling *limbum* containers with it, and got better. How one of the men who had treated him afterwards fell ill by the spirit and died.[1] During and interspersed in the discussions of her illness, the older men told the younger ones, especially from Watalu and the Wuninangiwut youth from Animbil, that they must go off to prepare the image of Panu'et at Walyibat, with ritual plants to be collected there. They shouted out sporadic lists of the woods and herbs needed but none of the younger men appeared to pay attention or show any doubt or hesitation over their ability to make the figure.

[1] At another time this dead man's brother, who was present during the comparison of Saoga's and Maluna's illnesses, told me about his brother's death, but said nothing of Panu'et or Maluna's illness. He had explained it by sorcery from quite another source.

It was by then about 9.30 a.m. and most of the younger men went off to Walyibat to prepare the image, accompanied by Saoga's husband and her three brothers. The older men settled down to lazy chat and making arrows, or weaving arm bands. The wives of the Watalu men went off to get food. Saoga meanwhile had been sitting inside her house. She now came outside walking round the house followed by all eyes and groaning as she walked, supported by a stick, smeared in dirt and ashes which, with her *grile* (*tinea imbricata*), made her look quite grey coloured. She walked to a small declivity beside her house where she lay down. Some of the women at first went closer and looked at her in her sickness. She remained lying in this hollow throughout the day until in the afternoon they brought Panu'et to her. During the day some of the related women I have mentioned went and sat with her, and rubbed her from time to time with nettles. Although men passed by on the path just above the hollow where she lay, and a few paused briefly to gaze at her, none that I noticed went down to speak to her or look more closely.

At about 3.30 p.m. the men returned with the image of Panu'et which was decorated, bespelled and the short ritual performed in which the image was touched over her body, the lineage ancestors and the spirit invoked and exhorted to leave her, the image struck into the ground and 'killed', the spirit sent away, and a morsel of bespelled soup made of certain herbs given to her. The rest of this soup was given to the others present, mainly women and children. After this Saoga was washed. Rain fell. Saoga went into her hut. When the rain had stopped she went off with her brothers' wives back to Bi'ip to stay there. The people of Watalu explained this as a precaution to avoid further danger from the lineage spirits which were concentrated round Watalu.

The next day her husband and some Watalu wives went to Bi'ip and reported that she had passed some blood vaginally in the evening after the ritual and felt better and was eating. After two days she returned to Watalu. But again she had similar pains on 21 January and in the night she went to Bi'ip. The next morning only people from Bi'ip, the other women closely related to her, her husband and two other Watalu men gathered at Bi'ip. This episode of pain was put down to Panu'et again because she had been preparing sago at a different place, Namelim. The next day her husband alone fetched the herbs for making Panu'et and carried out a less complex ritual of Panu'et in which the herbs are only crushed, bespelled and placed over red hot stones. Water is poured over them so that scented steam billows over the patient. On that day she had no pain. But the next day a return of pain led to a further large gathering at which it was decided that the illness continued because while she worked at the sago, she had brushed against a dangerous great fern (called *nembe'et*) that grew in the marshy sago place and must have had a spirit resting in it. Therefore on 24 January her husband with two of her brothers went and cut out the whole fern, cut it in pieces and threw it in a stream. In the course of the next two days she felt better and got up and about although she continued to stay at Bi'ip with her elder brother's wife. On 30 January she passed some more blood *per vaginam* but without pain. She sent someone to ask me for some pills but no further ritual treatment was thought necessary. She remained at Bi'ip until 17 February, partly to be sure of being well, but the stay was prolonged because her eldest brother cut down a sago palm for her to process into sago flour.

She returned to Watalu for two weeks, but again feeling ill decided to go to her brothers as a precaution against the dangers of the spirits at Watalu. At Watalu it was supposed she had the same pain and I was assured by some of the Watalu women she had again passed blood. Saoga said in fact she had passed no blood but had merely felt premonitory aches in her chest and back and therefore fled to Bi'ip. After a week she came back to Watalu. But again from 15 April to 3 May, Saoga went to stay at Bi'ip. The reason the Watalu people gave was that her brother's widowed sister of Wimalu was preparing sago at Namelin, the bush where Saoga had been struck in late January and therefore avoided; the lineage spirits had followed the widowed sister back to the village and again harmed Saoga. However Saoga, when asked why she had gone to Bi'ip, said only because her brother Dawei had cut another palm for her to process. She said that she was well and had no pains and that it was not fears concerning her husband's widowed sister's work that lay behind her move.

In my opinion the real reason for her last move to Bi'ip was that Dawei her brother had had a furious dispute with his wife and his wife had run back to Watalu with their smallest child, vowing never to return, but leaving him with their two older children. The Watalu Wuninangiwut men, including Saoga's husband, were classificatory fathers to Dawei's wife and were responsible for her as her own father was dead. They were most concerned to patch up the quarrel between husband and wife and persuade the wife to return. As Saoga's marriage represented, though not exactly an exchange, a balance to Dawei's marriage, Saoga should in loyalty to her brother have returned to him until the matter was smoothed over. She was barren. He and his children needed someone to cook for them. If she had gone ostensibly to equal and reciprocate his wife's action, the quarrel instead of being purely between the husband Dawei and his wife might possibly have become a dispute rather between two injured husbands, each supporting sister against husband, and therefore potentially harder to resolve. As people maintained that Saoga had gone to avoid illness, her move required no overt linking to the quarrel between husband and wife. Saoga herself just laughed about the quarrel and placed the blame neither on the husband nor the wife. The efforts of Watalu to persuade the wife to return were successful although Saoga had by then come back to Watalu. Saoga had no subsequent pains after this.

(2) The second case is that of Malden, a Saikel man who lived at Bi'ip. I have mentioned the diagnoses brought forward for his illness on p. 245. He was a widower aged about 60, frail and withered in appearance. He was looked after by his younger daughter Baito, aged about 18 years old and ready for marriage.

About a month before the onset of his illness, his daughter appeared on a list sent to Rauit of those for whom no tax had been paid. As he with certain others still would, or rather could, not pay the tax, a policeman was sent to collect it in company with the Local Government Councillor, Weibi from Mandubil, responsible for Rauit too. Malden did not understand Pidgin English. In the explanations about the tax and the policeman partly conducted in Pidgin, Malden evidently misunderstood Weibi's well-intentioned offer to pay the tax for him and to lay a claim thereby on Baito as a wife for his, Weibi's, unmarried younger brother. Malden, furious, took his bow and tried to draw it threatening to shoot Weibi; Wani, another irascible senior Saikel man of Bi'ip, also tried to draw his bow but both were quickly restrained by other Bi'ip men there. The policeman went off to report the events whose subsequent developments are not further directly relevant.

After about a month, Malden fell ill. He retired to his house on 5 July 1969. I received no request to treat him. On 12 July, it was decided that he must be treated by the ritual for Panu'et in which an image is made, on the grounds that he had eaten mushrooms collected by Baito, his daughter, from beside a specified place for preparing sago. This was done on the 13th. At the gathering for this, it came to light that he had eaten about two weeks before his illness began, some of a snake killed on land belonging to his matrilateral kin, thus breaking the prohibition on eating any creature that lives in a hole, if killed on matrilaterally owned land. On 14 July a ritual to avert harm by the snake was performed: an image of the snake was made from a certain creeper (*lambet dint*), bespelled in its mouth by a Bi'ip man who knew the ritual, then wound round Malden's body, its neck broken, and its back was repeatedly twisted and bent until the snake image was limp and broken.

Malden had become seriously ill and removed to sleep in the porch of his daughter Baito's house. He had lobar pneumonia and was refusing food and drink. On 16 July I was asked to treat him. As I gave him an injection, people and children crawled into the porch to watch. Malden began to make little movements and snuffles of agitation, his respiration became jerky. His elder married daughter noting this, said loudly 'He doesn't want these women close by. If they stay close he is afraid he will stay heavy and sick.' His son repeated that and called out loudly for the women and children to go further away. They made no attempt to move. Malden did not say anything.

At noon that day, Weibi the Councillor, returned from a Council meeting at Lumi. He stopped at my house. A number of Rauit men were gathered there. Wani, who with Malden had also threatened him, came up all smiles to hear his news. Weibi in a teasing amiable way said to Wani, 'So you were going to shoot me.' Wani laughing denied it: 'No, it was only Malden angry over his daughter. How could I shoot you? I "come up"[1] from you.' 'Ah if you shot me, that would be all right. My blood

[1] Wani's mother was born in Weibi's lineage and Weibi is therefore one of his matrilateral kin.

would have washed your home, the spirits of my dead would have struck you down,' Weibi replied. 'Yes, how could I have shot you. I come up from you, your blood, your ancestors would have struck me down.' The bantering exchange went on in this vein for a short while, and then conversation turned to Malden and how sick he was and what had been done so far to treat him. Weibi said he would go to Bi'ip with them to see Malden. When he got there, he went into the house where Malden was, and spat water over him as he called out to the spirits of his dead that if they were angry and afflicting Malden because of the threat he had made to shoot him then they must leave him. After eating at Bi'ip Weibi returned to Mandubil. From the time I heard of Malden's illness, I had waited to hear speculations either of sorcery or of ancestral attack linked with Weibi to account for Malden's illness, yet this was the first occasion that I heard it brought forward. It was done in an oblique indirect manner.

There was some improvement in his condition in the succeeding days but Malden still refused most food. Then I trod on an arrow point and was unable to go to see him for a few days. During these days neither his son nor daughters came to get medicine or some food I had been giving him although I sent messages through other Bi'ip people for them to come and in fact sent the things. On 24 July I found him lying dehydrated and apathetic, most of the penicillin tablets I had sent uneaten. Bespelled poles of bamboo had been set up as a fence against spirits around his daughter's house where he lay. His children said that he would not eat and therefore he would probably die. However they got him to drink a mixture of sugar and water I prepared.

On the next day he was moved from Baito's house to the house where Wani's sons slept because they thought his wife's dead spirit might also be at work in his illness, and Baito's house stood where hers had been. His Watalu clan relatives gathered in sympathy with the men of Bi'ip and then went over other possible sources for his continued illness. They remembered that about a month before Wani had cut down a caryota palm for grubs of which Malden had eaten some. The stump of the palm still stood and they suggested the roots and stem of the palm were crushing Malden down. Some of Wani's sons went to dig it up, cut out the roots and throw them in a river. Wani spat and invoked an ancestor who was said to have owned the palm. In the three days that followed, Malden continued to worsen and his children expected him to die and made few efforts to persuade him to eat or drink. On 28 July he died. The *garamuts* announced his death and many Mandubil people came to mourn including Weibi and his relatives. The circumstances of his death were related, the grubs and the palm explained. There were no accusations or signs of suspicion of Weibi. In general, the prevalent attitude seemed to be that Malden was ready to die and old and his death provoked no marked distress, no divination to find out sorcery. Privately a senior man of Watalu, closely linked to Malden (for Malden had once lived at Watalu), told me that he did not know the cause of this death, that it might have been either from the grubs and the palm, or from the snake, or from destructive magic performed by Mandubil on bananas at Saikel bush over which there had been a bitter dispute between Mandubil and the Rauit Saikel men over a year and a half before.

(3) The third case illustrates a first factual explanation which was later altered. Sunikel was a 12-year-old girl who had for years had occasional epileptic fits in which her face went blank, she jerked and fell unconscious, sometimes being incontinent at the same time.

On 27 August 1968, early in the morning, she was sent to fetch water, but did not return. Her brothers and sisters and her father went to look for her. Her father went to the water pool at Lugeban and he found her head downward in the pool. He pulled her out by the legs. She was dead. At 8.45 a.m. a sudden burst of crying from Animbil. People rushed there. In front of her mother's house her body was laid out and her father squatted by it. Women wept and wailed. Her father said what he had seen and done. He said Sunikel must have had a fit and fallen into the pool. Others said it was wrong to have sent her alone, he knew she had fits, he had plenty of other children who could have been sent.

People from all the hamlets gathered. Her father, after squatting crying, or rather sniffing, for an hour got up and began clearing the ground to make a grave. The body was taken into her mother's house to prepare it for burial. Sunikel's father's younger brother went to the water hole and measured its depth with a bamboo pole which he notched; it was about three and a half feet deep.

On his return he stood it against a much younger child than Sunikel to compare the depth and the child's height.

Some men sitting near me began to discuss *sanguma* sorcery (*langasutap*) and to agree with each other that it must have been *langasutap* for her to fall and drown in such shallow water. They considered by what likely paths the men with *langasutap* could have come. This was now about two hours after the body had first been laid out in the village. The theme of sorcery was taken up. By the afternoon it was decided to go and fetch a clan relative of Sunikel's father from the village of Brugap who was able to perform an Au method of divination on the *garamut* using a bamboo pole which would be entered by the spirit of the dead girl and beat out the answers to questions on the *garamut*. Her father left in the afternoon to fetch his relative at Brugap. Many people fasted and slept the night at Animbil in sympathy with the bereaved. The man from Brugap could not come the next day which was spent by the village sitting in sympathy at Animbil. There was further discussion of *minmin*, the other form of *sanguma*, over which new fears had then but recently been started (see p. 206). On 29 August, the men from Brugap came. They placed the pole suspended from the ridge pole inside the men's house, its upper end by the main post of the *gamaiyit* (men's house), its lower end protruding through the wall until it nearly touched a *garamut*. At 7.30 p.m. after night had fallen, most of the village assembled. There was no light except from a crescent moon. Torch flares were doused. The Brugap man squatted with Sunikel's father squatting immediately behind him with his arms passed on either side of the Brugap man. Both held out their outstretched upturned hands just under the pole. Sunikel's father began to call on her to enter the bamboo and reveal whether she had only fallen or if *langasutap* had struck her or *minmin*. He cajoled and entreated her to answer, telling her who was there with him listening, asking her the questions repeatedly. Others in the assembled crowd also suggested questions later for him to ask. After a long while the bamboo pole began to move, tapping on the *garamut*. The listening crowd called out encouragement to her and commented that as she was so young she would not know how to beat the calls properly. They called on certain of her dead relatives to help her beat out her answers. The fast rhythm and vigour of the beats were judged to show her positive answers. At intervals certain men were invited to come and feel the pole move so they should feel how her spirit moved it and that there was no trickery.

The answers indicated that she had fallen, not just from a fall but because *minmin* struck her. Some of the questions were later repeated and then gave the answer *langasutap*. By questions about where the sorcery had come from, they found the men with *langasutap* were from Winalum or Nembugil. They began going through names of individuals to discover who had done it. They asked where the *langasutap* struck her, whether her faeces or her urine had been taken. To each of these questions they obtained some positive replies. Then they asked about possible causes behind her killing, bringing up reasons for people within Rauit to seek such revenge. They asked about a Wimalu group who had not received the final mortuary payment due to them as matrilateral relatives for the death of Maiyan, whose land Sunikel's father had inherited; and about a former quarrel between the same Wimalu group and Maiyan concerning some sago which again her father had inherited. There was no positive response to these questions which were probably in part prompted by the fact that she had drowned at the pool, Lugeban, which was formerly also part of Maiyan's land. They returned to re-questioning about the *langasutap* and the men who had worked it but the bamboo fell silent. The session had lasted about four and a half hours. They tried to get her spirit to re-enter the pole, freed now and held cradled in the arms of the man from Brugap and her male relatives, so that it might lead them to the spot where the *langasutap* men had stood hidden to strike her; but her spirit would not enter it, so they abandoned the attempt.

The next morning the general view was that she had died by *langasutap* struck on the back of the neck and both sides of the jaw, that this was accomplished by two named men from Winalum, and one from Nembugil – but there was no answer for a reason why they should have done it except to exercise their power of *langasutap*. No further action was taken that I was told of. Some of those who had watched the divination told me privately afterwards that they thought the truth had not been learnt about Sunikel's death, and said a Gnau, and not an Au, method of divination should have been used.

On 13 September I again asked Sunikel's father why he thought she died. In the meantime there had been much discussion of *minmin* in connection with a death at Winalum. He said Sunikel had died by *minmin*, that the divination had shown it, and that Winalum was where the men had come from – he said this without any show of anger or vengefulness, he seemed just to be telling me the facts.

(4) Napesi, a woman of Animbil, roughly 40 years old. On 1 September 1969, Napesi fell about 10 feet from a *tulip* tree while she was collecting leaves. She fell heavily on her back, bruising it and struck the right side of her face which was grazed and swollen. There were no signs of fractured bones. The tree was in the gardens. Her husband and another Animbil man made a stretcher of saplings and leaves, and she was carried to Animbil where small cuts were made along the bruised swelling on her back to let the blood out. She lay on the stretcher on her right side, not tearful or crying out but highly agitated. There was a general commotion with people rushing to see, all talking about her and staring at her. With stuttering high-pitched talk she described what had happened. As I examined her, she developed a rapid shivering shaking in her legs and especially in her jaw muscles. Her husband and many others explained the accident. The tree she had fallen from had been burnt round the trunk during the firing of the garden and was dry: it had snapped at that point. This was the cause of her fall. The exact circumstances were retailed to all the newcomers. An Animbil man of her clan pointed out to me that his ancestor and namesake had planted the tree. An old woman of Watalu, who had been born at Animbil, after seeing her said vaguely it must have been a *malet* (spirit) that made the tree snap and perhaps that was because of the Panu'et ritual for the building of the men's house at Wimalu (which was being performed during this period). I heard another woman say to her companion, as she went away, that Napesi must have collected too many leaves from the one tree, if she had only taken fewer it would not have happened.

The immediate emphasis was on the straightforward description of the fall and the state of the tree. With the observation that no bones seemed broken, the general anxiety about her quite rapidly evaporated. But Napesi who still had considerable pain, remained for the next three days inside her house, avoided food and remained miserable in manner, telling me she was afraid she would be ill for a long time and that a spirit might still strike her down if she were to eat normally. On 4 September she tried sitting outside and on 6 September, finding she could stand, she declared she felt better and within a few more days she was back to normal life.

The four case histories above contain many points that might be explained or analysed at greater length. However my purpose in presenting them was to provide actual illustrations of the processes of diagnosing and managing illness. The first case, Saoga's, shows the general form of discussion, explanation and decision over treatment where the illness leads to a gathering and general concern. The emphases in discussion on the physical features of her illness and on the details of the mode of attack and the comparison with an earlier case, were unusually clear. The explanatory theme remained consistent throughout the illness, the various treatments for Panu'et occurring mainly after she showed some exacerbation or return of pain. The case also illustrates the behaviour of someone ill, the precautionary changes of residence, and the obligations and interest of a married woman's brothers (or nearest natal agnatic kin) in taking a part in her care. The general tempo of her illness, with its remissions and exacerbations, was accompanied by a declining concern for it, probably reflecting other people's perceptions that each episode would improve quite soon and was not serious. Little was done to treat her for the later episodes. In contrast the second case, Malden's, which also lasted over a long period, was obviously serious and worsened until it became clear that he would die. In his case, the explanations for his illness were added to and altered, and a variety of treatments were attempted. The indirect reference to a recent quarrel, an appropriate treatment before he died, the vague suspicions of sorcery soon after his death, illustrate the kind of case which in retrospect much later may be cited as one of death by destructive magic or sorcery from another village. But in fact no divination and no generally accepted explanation occurred then: they did not perform a divination in part probably because his death seemed acceptable on grounds of old age and frailty. The case of Sunikel shows almost the reverse process, for at first her death had an obvious direct and adequate explanation by what was known of her epilepsy, but within three hours this was superseded by the suspicion of sorcery and eventually confirmed by divination. Although a few people were sceptical about the details revealed by the divination, I think everyone believed that her death was due to sorcery and this probably reflects both that she was a bright, vigorous girl despite her occasional fits, too young and strong to die, and that her death came without warning, without preliminary illness; it was unacceptable purely as a tragic coincidence. Whereas in Napesi's case, the fall, the detail of the observations about the tree, remained at a factual observed level because it was quite soon apparent that she had not received serious injury, although the first public consternation and her own agitation might soon have led, I think, if the consequences had been otherwise, to a more elaborate explanation. Her case also illustrates how people speculate quickly, casually and privately about why an illness occurred: most such speculations must have escaped my hearing, and of course many such are never told out loud.

THE METHOD OF GNAU EXPLANATION AND ITS ANALYSIS

When an accident happens, say, to someone in England, he may well consider the time, the place and what he did in order to decide whether it was an accident, a chance coincidence of natural events. He may decide that a certain likelihood of risk or damage attaches particularly to one or other component of the circumstances; or he may decide that included in the events is some suspicious oddity that makes it probable that it was not chance but contrived by someone; or if he is superstitious or religious, suppose it produced by destiny, bad luck or the will of God. To sort out the possibilities and select an explanation he must begin by looking at the timing and circumstances surrounding the event. His conclusion may, if it goes beyond factual description of the accident, light on certain components of the situation as specially significant for understanding how and why the accident occurred. The cognitive processes involved are analogous to those commonly used by the Gnau in diagnosing illness. When they name the kind of illness, they name a cause. This is their diagnosis, and in order to show how the different diagnoses were reached in the cases I recorded, I intend to analyse the significant components involved in them. Just as in a car accident, the explanation might be focussed on the activity, car driving, which is somewhat hazardous, and the place it occurred, a dangerous cross-roads, and the time, night, so in Saoga's illness, for example, one explanation was focussed on the place, a garden, and her action, walking through it at a time when it was newly planted. In Saoga's case, the place and the time, and the planter were further significant for identifying who should treat her as the lineage spirits involved in watching over the garden were no doubt invoked to strike down trespassers by the planter just after he had planted it and therefore he had to be identified for her treatment. The timing was significant because it is only thought dangerous to pass through a garden in the few days just after planting, or just after certain other garden activities. Thus the diagnosis rests on the intersection of three components in the circumstances. The explanation is a deduction from straightforward observation. In looking at the different diagnoses they made, I shall specify only such significant components in the diagnosis. By assembling all the various recorded instances of explanation by some one cause, I have tried to characterize the different patterns of criteria involved in making that kind of diagnosis. If they had used clinical signs and symptoms to make their diagnoses, such assemblies of component features would in effect have amounted to the characterization of the syndromes or symptom complexes which that diagnosis applied to. As they do not do this, but instead make the diagnosis by reference to circumstances, timing, and occasionally by reference to revelation or special signs, what I analyse are rather the syndromes of circumstance which lead to a particular diagnosis.

I have taken all the explanations recorded so that for some cases of illness there are many different ones coming from people standing in various relationships to the patient. In almost any illness it is possible to find people who will say that it has merely happened and they know of no cause for it, just as it also is possible by persistent questioning to get someone to speculate on a possible cause. As I deal with the different diagnoses I will make some comments about the sources of the recorded explanations and their relation to treatment, but I have included each recorded diagnosis since each represents someone's thinking about an illness and a diagnosis.

As the intersection of more than one significant component element in a set of circumstances is a common feature in many diagnoses, I have summarized the recorded patterns of each type of diagnosis by means of Venn diagrams,[1] in which each significant element (for example, food or time or place or action) is represented by a circle, and where two or more circles overlap, a diagnosis within the area of overlap is one which required the two or more elements to be taken together for the diagnosis to be made. Thus the diagnosis of Saoga mentioned earlier is one that must come in the area of overlap of the three circles for time, place and action respectively (the intersection of Time, Place and Action: $T \cap P \cap A$ expressed in logical notation). The number of diagnoses based on the component element(s) involved is given within each segment or overlapping segment of the circles. The circle labelled 'sole' refers to diagnosis unaccompanied by description of circumstance.

NOTE ON THE DIAGRAMS TO FOLLOW SUMMARIZING DIAGNOSIS

In the syndrome summaries, the severity and duration class symbols are the same as have been used previously. These are: *medical severity* class A = serious illness, B = moderately severe illness, C = trivial or mild illness, D = ill-defined severity; *incapacity class* I = not restricted to village, II = restricted to village, behaviour appropriate to symptoms, III = behaviour demonstrative and markedly inappropriate for signs of disease, IV = recumbency forced on the patient by the severity of illness, V = illness in infants; *duration class* – 1. = one day, 2. = one day to one week, 3. = one to two weeks, 4. = two to four weeks, 5. = more than one month. The *age categories* are: A1 = 0–4 years, A2 = 5–15 years, A3 = 16–45 years, A4 = over 45 years. The patient or the person most closely related to him (or her) is cited as the source of diagnosis if the same explanation was obtained from more than one person. A family member refers to someone in the domestic grouping to which the patient belongs, i.e. the group of people primarily dependent on the food cooked

[1] A detailed account of the methods of analysis using logical notation and Venn diagrams, as I have employed them in this chapter, may be found in Feinstein (1967).

by a woman (see pp. 69–70) or to someone who is or has been a member of the same nuclear family, e.g. father and married son, brother and married sister. The circles for an explanation involving food or place or action etc. are labelled.

THE DIAGNOSIS: PANU'ET

Panu'et is the commonest spirit to which illness is ascribed. If someone is asked to name, for example, one cause of illness, Panu'et is the most likely one to spring to mind. The frequency with which I heard Panu'et named in relation to illness in my early inquiries, combined with the fact that some men were said to be expert in the diagnostic technique of 'smelling out' (*natemitepa nagegera* – he smells it he finds it out) the cause of illness by a technique associated with the name of Panu'et, made me suppose at first that illness and its management was chiefly an aspect of a cult of Panu'et. But this is not so. The techniques of Panu'et for smelling out an illness are not frequently used, nor necessarily used in serious illness.

Panu'et is more commonly given as the cause of illness in females (31 instances of explanation) than males (11 instances). It is also used for children's illness, and for that of babies (class V) which otherwise are ascribed commonly only to the spirits of the dead. It is a diagnosis given during an illness rather than after death or retrospectively. For pre-eminently Panu'et is a treatable cause of illness, even though it is said in theory, as it is said of every cause of illness except breaking a taboo, that Panu'et untreated will destroy the patient. Illnesses of all kinds of severity are represented and the mild C class of illness and shorter lasting illness, if they are explained, tend to be ascribed to it. In making the diagnosis, the method is usually deductive from circumstance. Where, as in three instances, the diagnosis was associated with dreams, these revealed particular named individual spirits of the dead who contributed to form a more elaborate explanation of why the illness had occurred. Divination by 'smelling out' lent support to three diagnoses, two of which were for infantile illness. Two of the diagnoses were given with the intention of duping me as I explain in the analysis of the diagnosis of sorcery, and perhaps Panu'et as the most obvious cause of illness was the reason why it was chosen. It is also a diagnosis often made by the patient or his immediate family and acceptable to them.

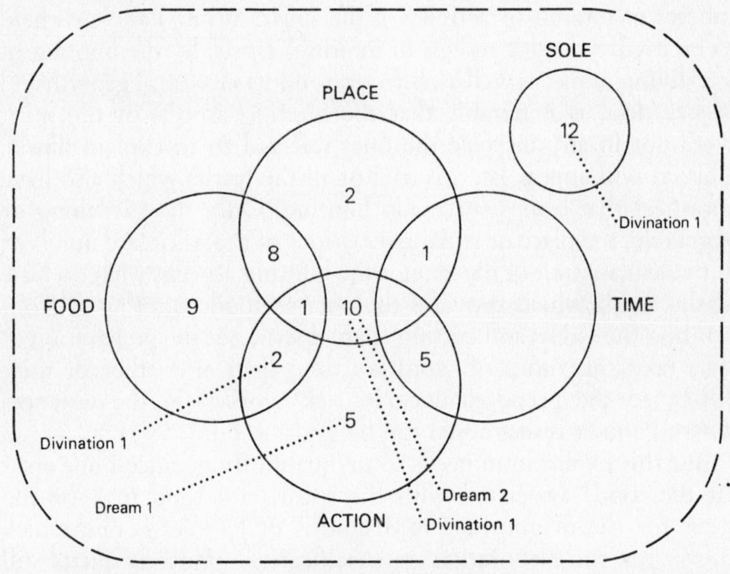

Fig. 31. The diagnosis: Panu'et

Total recorded instances of diagnosis = 55
Total cases of illness in which diagnosis made = 42
Number of instances in which diagnosis unassociated with appropriate treatment = 17
Number of instances of retrospective diagnosis (i.e. after recovery, or after death) = 3

Case characteristics

Sex and age

	A1	A2	A3	A4
Males	1	0	2	8
Females	5	4	11	11

Types Med.	Sevty	Incap.		Duratn	
A	11	I	7	1.	2
B	12	II	9	2.	22
C	8	III	13	3.	9
D	11	IV	9	4.	5
		V	4	5.	4

Source of recorded diagnosis

Patient	Member of Pt's fam.	Other
22	27	6

Diagnosis involved

Divination 3 instances
Dream 3 instances

In the account of Panu'et I have described the main features and spheres of interest or activity of the spirit. While Panu'et is held to be involved with success in hunting, especially the hunting of tree-living game, as well as with sago and its successful growth and preparation, it is notable that the hunting aspects of the spirit were not in any instance the ones referred to to explain illness. This, as will appear later, is true of all the spirits which also have an aspect that brings success in hunting. Only the gardening or vegetable, the place or ritual associations of the spirit, are involved in the explanation of illness; not the hunting aspects. Men do little of the work which provides their staple food, sago, apart from planting the palms and cutting them down, but the preparation of sago takes up more of women's time than any other of their duties, so the preponderance of sick women in the instances where Panu'et is diagnosed can be understood.

But this explanation needs some qualification, since both sexes eat the foods associated with the spirit, and food may be the focus for the diagnosis. The diagnosis of Panu'et is one which allows for the elaboration or specification of other spirits still contained within that diagnosis. In Chapter 5 I discussed the way in which there is an overlap or a lack of sharp distinction between the different categories of spirit – the named great spirits, spirits of the undifferentiated lineage dead or ancestral spirits, and the spirits of specified individual dead people. Ancestral spirits may be considered to activate or to enter into and be involved in the named great spirits and what they do. Thus a diagnosis of Panu'et may be elaborated by specifying the lineage spirits watching over the sago at a grove of palms, or watching by the pool from which the patient took prepared sago flour; or the individual spirit of the man who planted the palm may be said to be cross with how much she took at one time, or with her wastefulness in working on a second palm when she had not completed work on the first; and in treatment these spirits are invoked and appealed to as the patient is bespat and the spells blown onto her. In this respect wives who take their place only progressively in the group into which they marry[1] are thus at risk more than the men from spirits prepared to regard them as strangers or interlopers. In the invocations, it is common to hear the men call out words to the

[1] In formal terms, they are not detached from the lineage of their birth fully until after death with the final mortuary payment.

effect 'Do you not know Saoga (or whoever it may be). Saoga is one of us, ours. Do you not see who it is? Turn your eyes from her. Saoga, it is her land. What other gardens can she go to? It is her sago, our sago, our only sago. Let her be, leave her alone.'

Twelve of the diagnoses of Panu'et were unaccompanied by particular specification of when, where or what was done to make the spirit cause illness. And in all these cases the sickness was that of a woman. Of the other cases, the chief foods which formed a significant element in the Panu'et diagnosis were sago (10 instances), the mushrooms that grow on the rotting piles of discarded sago pith (5), pandanus fruit (3 instances). The activities leading to the diagnosis were taking prepared flour soaking in bamboos at a pool (4), chipping sago (1), and cutting the giant fern (*nembe'et*) which grows by marshy sago places and is dangerous itself but was here associated with Panu'et or some ancestral spirit which lodged on it using it for a bed. Men attributed their illness to cutting the sago palm in four cases. Another common element to explanation is the garden grove site (7 instances) since this localizes the danger and may indicate a place to be avoided by the patient in the immediate future, the site from which ritual plants must be collected for treatment, or the spirits to be appealed to. But the most common single focus is a pool (13 instances). Although some pools are especially associated with a *malet* spirit named by the name of the pool (as the pool Telibe'em was said to have a *malet* associated with it in Saoga's case) when pools are an element in explanation, the diagnosis is most often made in terms of Panu'et. The pools are also identified because mud from the particular pool is required sometimes to prepare the ritual soup (*wa'agep*) and make the Panu'et image for treatment. This is described in the account of Panu'et. Small children are said to be afflicted by Panu'et sometimes because they are supposed to lack the sense or control not to defaecate or urinate in pools, and in two instances a child's illness was attributed to this. Of the five cases involving the elements 'activity' and 'timing' ($A \cap T \cap \bar{P}$), in four the diagnosis was made because the Panu'et ritual for the building of a new men's house was in progress. The way in which some major ritual activity acts as focus for the explanation of illness occurring during that time will be clearly seen later in relation to the Malyi diagnoses.

Given the place of sago in daily life, it is perhaps easy for them to find a reason to suspect Panu'et in an illness. But possibly an additional, though latent, factor behind the diagnosis is that there are various treatments for it, from a simple therapeutic spitting with an appeal to lineage spirits, to the more elaborate and impressive treatments briefly described in the account of Panu'et.

THE DIAGNOSIS: TAMBIN

Few cases were attributed to Tambin, despite the important place of Tambin in regard to hunting, the initiation of young men, and the growth of yams, taro and bananas. Tambin is in theory associated with the village and with madness (p. 213), and these elements contributed to the diagnosis of two cases. Once in an infant with cerebral malaria who became suddenly irritable and tense, then limp and vacant. It was thought she had come in contact with the decorative leaves of a spider lily (*dangasun*) planted in the village which her father had picked and placed on his house thatch[1] from which the leaves had slipped on to her. In the other case, a man already seriously ill from Malyi, became delirious and then the clinical sign of madness was taken to indicate Tambin. This diagnosis was explained by reference to some tomatoes I had given him to eat which had been grown on the site of a *gamaiyit* (men's house) relatively recently demolished and belonging to the clan holding the ritual of Tambin *garut* or first. In two other cases, the diagnosis was related to a performance on one night of the complete ritual Tambin song which was sung to end the celebration for the birth of a couple's first child. In these two cases the recent performance was part of a diagnosis linked to an action – taking bananas and taking yams and taro respectively. The cause in another case was revealed in *bengbeng* possession of the victim who had eaten a *yammami*.

Tambin may strike if certain taboos are broken; the ones mentioned to me involved in theory eating cassowary and certain leaves at the same time. In practice I recorded one case of Tambin associated with the mixture of two activities that should have been kept separate and not performed on the same day, the two

[1] Thatching from houses in the village is used in preparing ritual images for Tambin treatment, rather as epiphytic plants that grow on sago palms and mud from pools are used in Panu'et treatments.

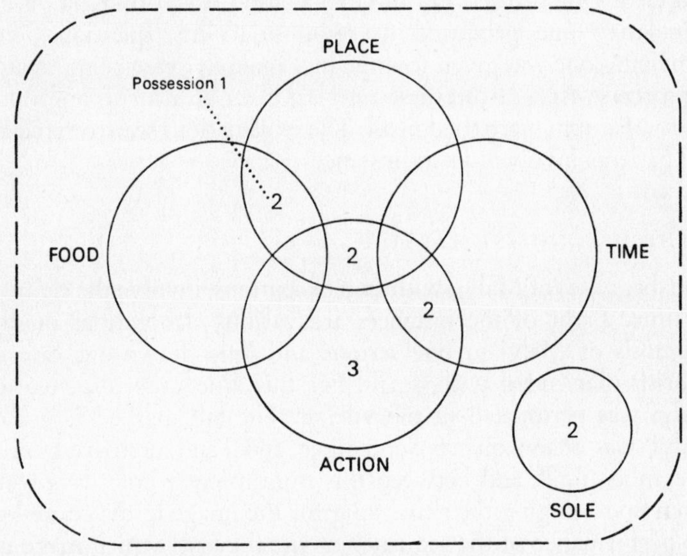

Fig. 32. The diagnosis: Tambin

Total recorded instances of diagnosis = 11
Total cases of illness in which diagnosis made = 8
Instances of diagnosis unassociated with treatment = 2
Retrospective diagnosis after death or recovery = 0

Case characteristics

Sex and age

	A1	A2	A3	A4
Males	0	0	2	2
Females	1	0	3	0

Types	Med. Sevty	Incap.		Duratn	
A	2	I	1	1.	0
B	1	II	1	2.	5
C	1	III	3	3.	1
D	4	IV	2	4.	1
		V	1	5.	1

Source of recorded diagnosis

Patient	Member of Pt's fam.	Other
6	5	0

Diagnosis involved

Possession 1 instance

mixed actions were thatching a bush house and digging up yams and taro. One further Tambin explanation was, I think, a purely speculative one produced in response to my questions. The remaining one was given to dupe me, again in a case being treated for sorcery. Apart from these two last cases, treatments appropriate for Tambin were tried in all. The explanations were offered by the patients involved in six instances.

THE DIAGNOSIS: MALYI

The diagnoses of Malyi, with two exceptions, involve the element of time. Eight of the instances are various elaborations on the diagnosis of Malyi in one serious and long-drawn-out case of arthritis that ended with death. For this illness the full ritual of Malyi was performed in the village. The tall masked figure of Malyi was made on 11 September 1968 and destroyed on 3 December 1968, and between this time many whole days were given up to singing the ritual song for the image to dance, and to the performance of the sequence of ritual events which make up its full rites. For this time, the spirit was present, localized and concentrated in the village.

In December 1967, I travelled looking for a village to stay in, and passed through the Au-speaking village of Wititai on the second day after its inauguration of the Malyi ritual (called Meni in Au). The next day I came for the first time to Rauit, Wititai being half a day's walk away. On 23 June 1968, the ritual at Wititai was ended and the images[1] of Meni destroyed. I had gone to witness this, the Wititai *garamuts* having announced it for the previous few days, with a small party of Rauit men who had kin there. On this day, when the spirit was sent off from Wititai, a man at Rauit fell heavily from a tree when the branch he stood on broke. There was no doubt of the diagnosis. People came out half way to Wititai on our return path to fetch us back. The man had severely bruised his back, and though there was no clinical evidence of a fractured pelvis, he could not pass urine or faeces. Eventually I had to catheterize him to relieve his urinary retention. On the night of his fall many went to sleep and fast with his family at his hamlet, among these his brother-in-law. Two days

[1] Two images are danced in the Au performance though Rauit dances only one.

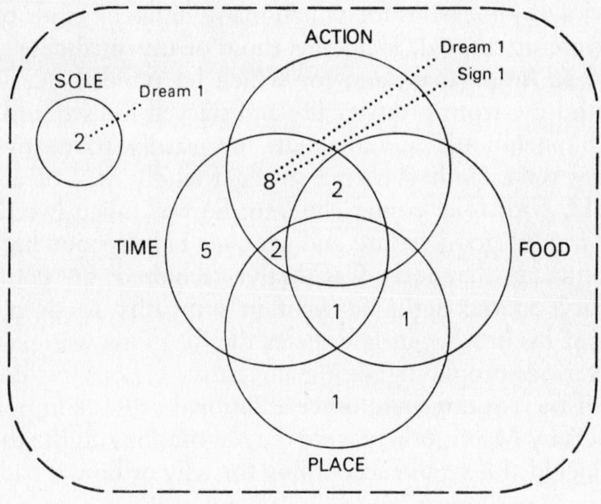

Fig. 33. The diagnosis: Malyi

Total recorded instances of diagnosis	= 22
Total cases of illness in which diagnosis made	= 13
Instances of diagnosis unassociated with treatment	= 13
Retrospective diagnosis after death or recovery	= 1

Case characteristics

Sex and age

	A1	A2	A3	A4
Males	0	0	5	4
Females	1	1	1	1

Types	Med.	Sevty		Incap.		Duratn	
	A	5		I	3	1.	3
	B	4		II	5	2.	5
	C	1		III	0	3.	2
	D	3		IV	4	4.	1
				V	1	5.	2

Source of recorded diagnosis

Patient	Member of Pt's fam.	Other
9	8	5

Diagnosis involved

Sign 1 instance
Dream 2 instances

later this brother-in-law, Dauwaras, seemed to twist his knee as he came back up a hill from garden work. This was the beginning of a series of joint pains for which many different kinds of treatment were attempted, including those of my medicine and the hospital at Anguganak, and for which he avoided many foods and withdrew from ordinary life and starved himself and passed through pneumonia and madness, eventually to death on 18 February 1969. He had been a strong friendly man of about 40 years old, with four young children; he was much loved in the village for his good nature and vigour. Throughout his illness, the dominant diagnosis was Malyi, acquired by contact or proximity on the night he went in sympathy to sleep in the hamlet of his brother-in-law. Later the diagnosis was elaborated on by various people suggesting alternative reasons for his illness. Some of the reasons were other additional causes compounding the illness by Malyi; others were the elaborations on the theme of Malyi included here and accounting for why or how it had struck him.

Soon after he had slipped, he withdrew to his wife's house and he was sitting in the half dark inside, when a cricket jumped from the roof on to his knee; his knee began again to throb with pain. The cricket had jumped just after Wanukei, a young woman, came down the hill from another hamlet, Wimalu, to Watalu where he lay. The cricket, he deduced from the pain, was a sign or vehicle for the spirit of the dead Tupan who had died of Malyi at Wimalu many years before and must have followed Wanukei to Watalu to strike him with renewed pain. He called for his wife and his brother's daughter to catch the cricket and kill it but they could not find it. This is a good example of the selective attention given to ordinary events during an illness. It was in fact two days after the cricket's jump that Wanukei finally returned to Wimalu rejected as wife after two months spent timidly seeking acceptance by Dauwaras's eldest brother's son. But no one said outright that her rejection and her return had anything to do with the illness: indeed they denied it. A divination by the 'smelling out' technique of Panu'et also later found Tupan.

Dauwaras, in the course of his long and agonizing illness, told me many times that he had had confirmatory dreams in which a great black pig occurred and sometimes tried to savage him: this is the conventional dream manifestation of Malyi, and the spirit

Malyi in cryptic speech is referred to as the Pig (*Belu'et*). Dauwaras's elder brother had also been struck by Malyi about twelve years before and then had nearly died. During the performance of Malyi for Dauwaras, he too had a return of dreams of a black pig. When this happened while he had a cold, he left the village and slept at a garden house, interpreting the dream and the cold as warnings. One other man also put down his trivial aches to the presence of Malyi during the performance of its ritual in the village. In these cases no treatment specifically for Malyi was performed, the diagnosis thereby seeming rather an explanation than a guide to treatment, although avoidance of the hamlet where Malyi was had a prophylactic if not therapeutic aim. About five months after Dauwaras had died, another man in the course of many speculations as to the cause of his serious illness (heart failure), attributed his condition to his having gone to sing for Malyi. And his very aged mother, after he had died, also took this line of explanation.

The instance I recorded of Malyi diagnosed before Wititai sent the spirit off, was in an explanation to me of someone's infected swollen hand by the man who had just treated it. The owner of the hand had gone earlier that day, I knew, to have it treated by this man because he supposed the infection due to destructive magic protecting an areca palm from theft. He had received the areca nut from the man he asked to treat it, who must have bespelled the palm, and this was the man who told me the explanation by Malyi. Either he was hiding from me the real reason for his treatment or this case is an example, of which there are others, where a treatment is performed despite the two participants having differing, undisclosed and conflicting views on its rationale.

THE DIAGNOSIS OF OTHER SPIRITS – MALET

This explanation was given more often for illness in men (14 instances) than in women (4 instances): it was noted especially in the older adult men (10 cases) and was associated with aches and pains of an ill-defined nature supposed to come from the *mama* spirit of *wadagep* (yams and taro). Thirteen of the 22 instances have to do with yams and taro, and the gardening activities associated with them. These, in contrast to the work of sago preparation, are primarily male duties. Indeed women are prohibited from planting the tubers and covering over the young *yammami*, both of which are performed with ritual spoken of as dangerous especially to women. The work of yam growing in other ways offers certain parallels and certain contrasts with the work involved in preparing sago. The wives have a small significant ritual role in preparing the yams and taro magically just before they are planted; the men have the small but important role of planting and cutting down the sago palm. The line of yams and taro, and the spells men use in planting them, are owned and transmitted within the lineage and clan.[1] The lineage ancestral spirits watch over them. A diagnosis of illness through association with *wadagep* could be attributed either to Tambin or Malyi, or to the watching lineage spirits, or to the *mama* spirit of the yams; just as sago work may lead to a diagnosis of Panu'et, or ancestral spirits or the spirit of a pool. But illness in men from their own *wadagep* or their gardening activities is attributed more often directly to the *mama* spirit rather than to their own ancestral spirits who are seen as protective. While for women the reference is to Panu'et, or to the ancestral spirits intolerant of the wives, rather than directly to the *malet* of a pool (the three cases of this *malet* of a pool diagnosis involved one woman, one small girl and one man). The other point of parallel between sago and *wadagep* is that while a woman must do so much work on sago chiefly to benefit her husband and his family and his agnatic relatives who often share his food, and come to visit him, the men regard their hard work at growing yams as chiefly for the benefit of their affines and their matrilateral relatives, since the most important annual exchange obligation is the presentation of the yams and taro they have grown to these relatives. But where the *wadagep* of someone outside the lineage form the focus of a diagnosis then the diagnosis is more likely to be made in terms of the ancestral spirits of the planter and owner of those *wadagep*. In the invocations to their ancestors at the time of planting *wadagep*, the men who plant them usually appeal for ancestral spirit aid to make what they will plant grow well since (and this they call out at the time) they have given all their good *wadagep*

[1] One man attributed his illness to his ancestral spirits because he told me his spells for planting yams and taro and allowed me to assist him when he planted a garden.

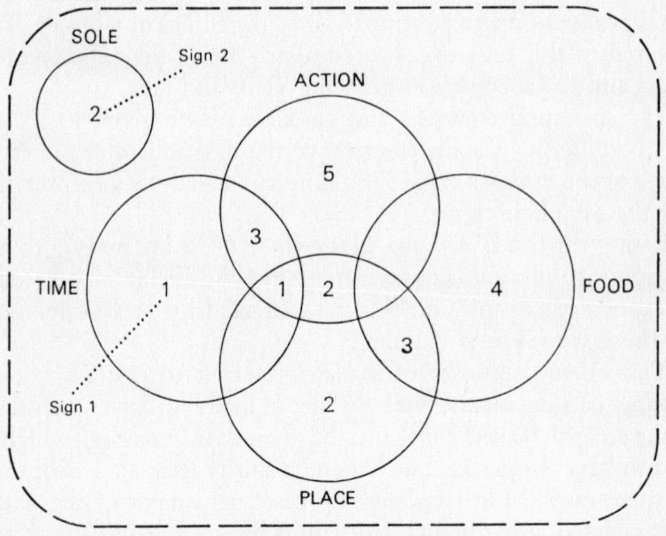

Fig. 34. The diagnosis: Spirit (Malet)

Total recorded instances of diagnosis = 23
Total cases of illness in which diagnosis made = 22
Instances of diagnosis unassociated with treatment = 7
Retrospective diagnosis after death or recovery = 0

Case characteristics

Sex and age

	A1	A2	A3	A4
Males	1	1	4	10
Females	0	2	2	2

Types

Med.	Sevty	Incap.		Duratn	
A	4	I	3	1.	3
B	5	II	6	2.	14
C	4	III	8	3.	1
D	9	IV	4	4.	1
		V	1	5.	3

Source of recorded diagnosis

Patient	Member of Pt's fan.	Other
12	9	2

T

Diagnosis involved

Sign 3 instances

to their affines and their matrilateral relatives, and kept back only the little puny ones for themselves, and these they must use for the reproduction and continuation of their lines of *wadagep*. They referred to this sometimes to convince me of the efficacy of the ritual and the ancestors in growing yams and taro.

The structural contrasts and parallels I have given to account for the differing sex distribution of the diagnosis of Panu'et and *mama* of the *wadagep* are, I should note, an analytic interpretation, not their explicit views.

Eating the food, *wadagep*, alone ($F \cap \bar{A} \cap \bar{P}$ 4 instances) provides a diagnosis and a guide to treatment since the spicule 'arrows' of the *mama* of *wadagep* may quickly be extracted by a technique learnt by those who 'know Panu'et'.[1]

The other diagnoses of a *malet* referred to contact with or cutting certain plants, viz. the great inedible 'taro' plants, the snake creeper (*lambet bulti*) and the great fern (*nembe'et*), which are said to have dangerous but unnamed spirits associated with them. In these cases, as in two *wadagep* cases, treatment of the patient was effected at a distance from him by cutting out, destroying and throwing the pieces of the plant in a stream or river. One other diagnosis was pure speculation dependent on the observation that a child was stunted and frail and must therefore have passed under a spirit python. Two other speculations concerned a man bitten by the Papuan death adder. The snake it was said, must have been a *malet* for his mother too had died by snakebite, and it was also noted that he was bitten on the morning after a 'comet' (*dyulin*) had been seen. I did not see it – it may have been a space capsule, but I was told about *dyulin*, the myth of Dyulin, and the danger from *dyulin* immediately then the night before the man was bitten – to the anthropologist a coincidence excellent strange but true. *Dyulin* is the word for stars with long tails that move yet are not the ordinary brief shooting stars (*nungabuti*).

In all these cases, except for those with the signs of stunted

[1] The ability to 'extract' such tiny spicule arrow heads is part of their expertise. The 2 cases in the summaries of the food and action elements to diagnosis on pp. 312 and 319 where, under the heading Panu'et, I have included an instance of reference to *wadagep* and to digging them up, do not fit with the theoretical range of the spirit Panu'et's interests. These two cases which both occurred fairly early in my stay are probably put wrongly under Panu'et because I misunderstood the reference to the healer as a man who 'knew Panu'et', that is the expertise, to mean that Panu'et was the cause.

growth, the snake and the *dyulin*, the diagnosis was based on deduction from the very recent actions or circumstances of the patient. None was offered retrospectively after death or recovery.

THE DIAGNOSIS: COLLECTIVITY OF THE LINEAGE DEAD

With this diagnosis, we enter a field in which considerations of current social relations are sometimes explicitly held relevant to the diagnosis and this reflects the supposed concern of ancestral spirits with the welfare and the quarrels and the good behaviour of their descendants. The illnesses referred in some way to ancestral spirits covered a wide range of severity, though the more medically severe illnesses predominated. The illnesses of children as well as adults were included and the sexes were fairly equally represented.

Of the foods significant in the diagnosis, *wadagep* (7 instances) received from affines, sisters' children or cross cousins were commonest. But place, either garden land (17 instances) or village (9 instances), was the most important element in explanation because the association of spirits with particular places provided the ground for indicating which or whose spirits were involved, the places of risk and this was also relevant to treatment. In ten instances, one focus of the explanation involved a quarrel and in all these instances I have included the timing of the quarrel, for this was necessarily related as part of the explanation. The interesting point about the timing of the quarrels is that 5 out of the 12 instances involved disputes that had occurred more than a month before, and it is rare for other elements contributing to a diagnosis to have occurred long before an illness except where this is the diagnosis, or where it involves named individual spirits, or sorcery.

The relationship of the sick person to the afflicting lineage or clan spirits differs according to the sex of the patient. Married women were afflicted by their husband's lineage spirits in 6 out of 10 instances, the other 4 instances involved first the unspecified spirits of some people killed by the woman's husband's group, second a woman's own natal lineage spirits and the *wadagep* she had received from her brother, third the lineage spirits of some men whom her husband's hamlet had fought with in a dispute

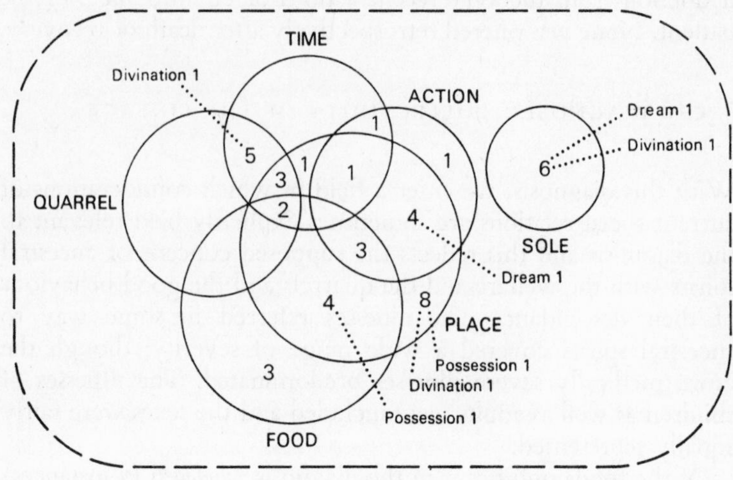

Fig. 35. The diagnosis: collectivity of lineage spirits

Total recorded instances of diagnosis = 42
Total cases of illness in which diagnosis made = 30
Instances of diagnosis unassociated with treatment = 15
Retrospective diagnosis after death or recovery = 2

Case characteristics

Sex and age	A1	A2	A3	A4
Males	4	2	3	8
Females	0	3	7	3

Types Med.	Sevty	Incap.		Duratn	
A	11	I	4	1.	2
B	10	II	7	2.	8
C	5	III	6	3.	10
D	4	IV	8	4.	5
		V	5	5.	5

Source of recorded diagnosis

Patient	Member of Pt's fam.	Other
24	13	5

Diagnosis involved

Divination	3 instances
Dream	2 instances
Possession	2 instances

over land, and fourth, spirits at a hamlet where the woman's daughter was married, and which she unwisely visited before she had recovered from her illness.

When women marry into a group, apart from the formal aspects of their incorporation into it discussed in Chapter 1, they take some time to find their place in it and to feel that they are among its members: they build up only gradually the complex ties of accepted familiarity. Most wives in the earliest stages of their marriage tend to be self-effacing, biddable, dutiful and uncomplaining. After they have established themselves by bearing children they play a more spontaneous assertive part in its affairs, at first confining this to their relationships with the other women there. In the early stages of married life, for either her own illness or for that of her infant child, the young mother is likely to go back (and to take her child with her if she has one) to the security and care of the family group into which she was born. Later on in marriage, wives only do this for an illness perceived as serious. The movement away from the husband's hamlet is sometimes additionally explained as a way to avoid the dangerous attention of the husband's lineage spirits. In four of the cases of an infant's illness given the diagnosis of affliction by its father's lineage spirits, the infants were first children. The diagnosis was made by the mother or her natal family in three instances and in these cases the illness in the child was explained partly as malevolence on the spirits' part towards the mother for some minor infraction of care or duty.

But the diagnosis in men involved chiefly the spirits of lineages in other villages (5 of 7 such instances were associated with disputes over land or trespass), two instances each were attributed to affinal and to matrilateral lineage spirits. The two affinal cases were speculations by a husband who, I think, resented his brother-in-law's great influence over his wife and children. The diagnosis of matrilateral lineage spirits was revealed by the patient's dream of his mother's brother cutting down a tree,[1] for the tree growing up from the land is a conventional simile for the matrilateral relationship of 'coming up' from some group. Two illnesses in children were in retrospect also ascribed to the spirits of a mother's brother, dissatisfied by the payment he had received for his

[1] This act is in fact part of a method of magical attack by a mother's brother.

sister's daughter's puberty ceremony. The aspect of bad or incorrect behaviour leading to attack by lineage spirits cropped up also twice in relation to breaking taboos, and once in the case of an elderly widow who explained the cause of her own bronchitis by her husband's lineage spirits' displeasure provoked because her two daughters-in-law fought over which of them should work on a particular sago palm.

As I mentioned in regard to Malden's case, the diagnosis of affliction by lineage spirits is one which is made during illness and offers the possibility of treatment by spitting and invocation to the ancestors presumed responsible. In such diagnosis of illness caused by spirits belonging to members of the village the treatment is readily and willingly performed, for if refused, intended harm or appeals to the ancestral spirits to cause the illness might be discerned in the refusal. Thus in Dauwaras's long illness by Malyi, on three occasions there were general invocations by many assembled men from the village lest anyone's ancestors might, unintended, be afflicting him. Where the spirits of other villages are involved the diagnosis is likely to be replaced, if the illness leads to death or looks as though it will, by the diagnosis of sorcery. Ancestral spirits may work harm because of insult or injury to their descendants either, first, without their descendants' wish or knowledge, or second, by their descendants' expressed wishes furthered by ritual appeals to them; and thirdly, a man may practise destructive magic or sorcery. The diagnostic lines between these three diagnoses are subtle and the direction easy to shift.

THE DIAGNOSIS: A NAMED SPIRIT OF A DEAD PERSON

From the observer's point of view this diagnosis was often related to anxiety occurring after a recent death or when death was expected soon. It was validated by revelation (through *bengbeng* possession in 5 instances, through dreams in 7 instances, by divination in 2 instances) or by the occurrence of some physical sign (such as the cricket and the snake). In a sense the occurrence of the supposed illness was itself a sign in those cases which happened soon after a death in the family, so that the parents brought their children to me after a sibling had died, saying they had seen blood in the remaining child's stool, or the child had a pain, and I could find nothing to bear out the account they gave

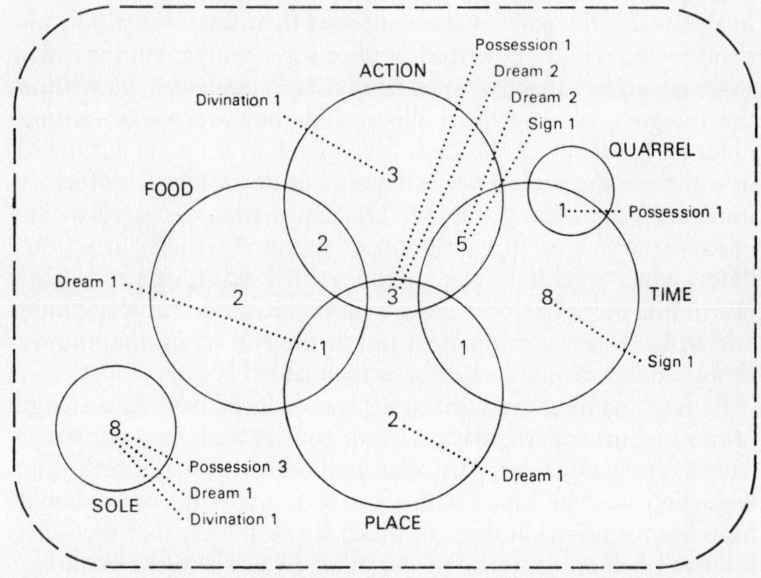

Fig. 36. The diagnosis: named spirit of a dead person

Total recorded instances of diagnosis	= 36
Total cases of illness in which diagnosis made	= 24
Instances of diagnosis unassociated with treatment	= 17
Retrospective diagnosis after death or recovery	= 2

Case characteristics

Sex and age	A1	A2	A3	A4
Males	3	1	2	5
Females	2	1	5	5

Types Med.	Sevty	Incap.		Duratn	
A	6	I	4	1.	4
B	5	II	4	2.	10
C	4	III	7	3.	4
D	9	IV	7	4.	4
		V	2	5.	2

Source of recorded diagnosis

Patient	Member of Pt's fam.	Other
14	15	7

Diagnosis involved

Divination	2 instances
Dream	7 instances
Possession	5 instances
Sign	2 instances

(4 instances). Similarly the parents themselves complained of pains (2 instances) and in one case of vomiting just after the death. In these cases the parents also expressed their fears directly to me that the dead child's new spirit wished for a companion for it was so young and so attached to its family. Such cases were put within the category of ill-defined illness and they were short-lasting illnesses. In all, 11 of the cases followed after a recent death and in 9 of these the patient was a member of the dead spirit's former immediate domestic grouping. The explanation appeared to the observer almost as an expression of the grief of loss. In serious illness when an elderly patient approached death, or after his or her death, the spirit of a dead wife or husband was sometimes said to have struck the patient just at the end of an illness, even though other diagnoses had been maintained before.

In the remaining cases, diagnosis was deduced from knowledge of movements at particular places, or contact with trees known to have been planted by particular individuals (5 instances). The deduction was combined with some reason why the spirit should have been annoyed in three of these; it was merely that the spirit followed behind someone in the other two. These explanations, as with some of the dream or possession revelations, served to elaborate with detail the reason for an illness and its circumstances. Dauwaras's illness also received an additional explanation through a man's possession on the night of an earthquake, when he spoke as the spirit of a man long dead from his hamlet asserting he had died by the sorcery of Dauwaras's eldest brother and other men of Dauwaras's hamlet. Therefore his spirit struck Dauwaras in revenge. This revelation, indirectly transmitted to Dauwaras's brother, was interpreted as an oblique demand on the part of the other hamlet for compensation money and indignantly rejected. The accusation of sorcery was an old one, long since proved false by ordeal.

In 8 instances the diagnosis was produced unaccompanied by a statement of circumstance and followed either from relevation (5 instances), or from speculation. Seventeen of these diagnoses led to no specific related treatment partly because the anxiety was set at rest by the soon apparent lack of illness, or by my reassurance. But they may well have invoked the spirit to do no further harm in a brief spitting ceremony which did not come to my notice. This was done in other cases.

THE DIAGNOSIS: DESTRUCTIVE MAGIC OR SORCERY

This diagnosis was not frequently made. It was applied to serious illness, usually after death or at the end of an illness in which many other treatments had been tried without success, or else it was brought forward by the sick woman herself through *bengbeng* possession (3 instances) in illnesses of an ill-defined nature and accompanied by the demonstrative conspicuous behaviour of illness. In other cases the sudden onset and the disastrous nature of the illness were associated with the diagnosis of sorcery, as distinct from destructive magic. The cases in the segments A, $F \cap \bar{T} \cap \bar{Q}$, $F \cap P$ were all supposed due to inadvertent contact with protective or destructive magic; the knowledge of circumstance made it possible to identify the appropriate person to treat the patient. In contrast the cases in the segments $P \cap \bar{A}$, T, and Q were all associated with death and its retrospective explanation, or with the fear of imminent death. The predominant focus on the element of place stems from the need either to identify where the contact with destructive magic occurred, or to find the village of the people responsible for it. Time is relevant in two ways, either to define the moment of being struck and so by extension the place, mode of attack or circumstance; or else time is part of an explanation of motive arising out of a previous quarrel.

The Gnau do not lack beliefs about sorcery and destructive magic, but the way they apply them to explain illness shows some of the force in favour of village harmony or solidarity. They approve of the use of destructive magic to protect property. If it is supposed that someone has come in contact with it and so fallen sick, the assumption is that this has been inadvertent and no malice lies between the co-villagers concerned. There is open discussion of the possibility and remedy by counter action, as in the case of Dauwaras, where on one day all the men in the village knowing a certain form of destructive magic were called on to treat him lest he might have come into contact with it unwittingly. But the fact of death proclaims intended malice and hatred. The crucial issues in a diagnosis of sorcery after death are the intention to kill and who was responsible. An accusation of such sorcery or destructive magic within the village would openly disrupt relations within it. So such suspicions must, unless there are very

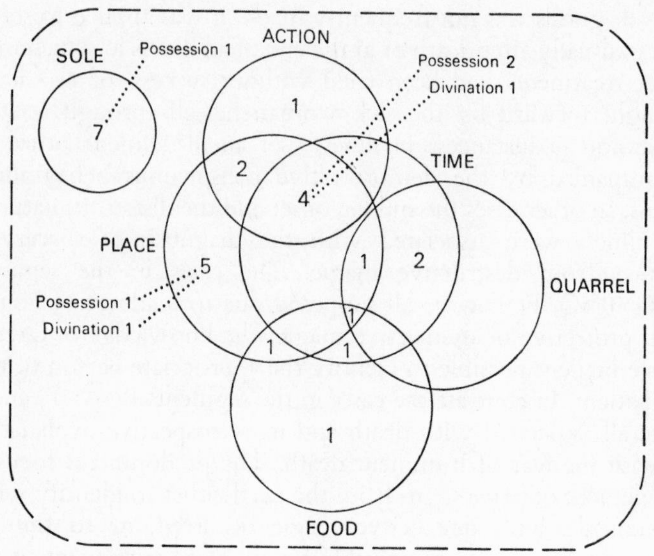

Fig. 37. The diagnosis: destructive magic or sorcery

Total recorded instances of diagnosis = 26
Total cases of illness in which diagnosis made = 17
Instances of diagnosis unassociated with treatment = 10
Retrospective diagnosis after death or recovery = 9

Case characteristics

Sex and age

	A1	A2	A3	A4
Males	0	1	1	6
Females	0	3	4	2

Types Med.	Sevty	Incap.		Duratn	
A	7	I	0	1.	2
B	3	II	2	2.	6
C	1	III	8	3.	1
D	6	IV	7	4.	4
		V	0	5.	4

Source of recorded diagnosis

Patient	Member of Pt's fam.	Other
8	9	9

Diagnosis involved

Possession 4 instances
Divination 2 instances

pressing grounds to bring them forward, remain private speculation or be referred to the malevolence of spirits. Instead accusations of sorcery are turned outwards to other villages. Formerly accusations of sorcery between armed and hostile villages rarely provoked denials, there were no attempts to show innocence; the modes of divination acted to confirm suspicion and strengthen a determination to seek vengeance. In present conditions, rumour of such accusations led to the accused hurrying to face his accusers, demanding that he try some ordeal. Presumably more often now the results of divination, in theory incontrovertible, are called into question.

In only two cases were public divinations after death performed: for Sunikel as I have described, and for Dauwaras by a Gnau method (*lari'in wulyiwug* – they shoot the eyebrows) in which his eyebrows and axillary hair were shaved off, set fire to and shot with special arrows high into a coconut palm where the night wind took the embers and they drifted. Watchers were posted on the roof of the men's house where he used to sleep. The embers drifted in the night sky over to mark the village of Yankok and suddenly sparked, thus revealing the village of the sorcerers. I could not see this. Overtly, at least, both divinations were not followed by attempts at revenge or talk of vengeance sorcery. In the case of Dauwaras a secret attempt was made to kill by sorcery anyone who might have worked sorcery against him and yet been so bold faced as to come to mourn him. I know this because I was privately asked to supply the newspaper to be offered round to all those who came to mourn (with some tobacco laid on Dauwaras's chest on the night he died and then bespelled). After the divination, a ritual (*lege'ai gablit*) was performed to aid his spirit when it went to search out his sorcerers and revenge itself on them. But for obvious reasons, duplicity and disguise attend the practice of sorcery.

No diagnosis of sorcery by *langasutap* was made apart from Sunikel's case, although this sorcery was often talked of. The sorcery of *minmin* displaced concern with *langasutap* for many of the months I stayed there. A treatment appeared for it (as was not the case for *langasutap*), but in keeping with their theories of magic, the man who could treat *minmin* could also strike down by *minmin*. In three cases, a diagnosis of *minmin* led to treatment by the method of 'extracting' the bone arrow heads of *minmin*. To accomplish this treatment, the people at Rauit called in agnatic kinsmen from the villages which traditionally they considered knew *langasutap*. The distribution and spread of knowledge of *minmin* was supposedly similar to that of *langasutap*. In each case where I witnessed the treatment I was told at the time that it was treatment for another cause (Panu'et in two instances, and Tambin in a third): but some time afterwards it was admitted that I had been duped in each case, and I was shown the arrow heads then taken out. One reason for duping me may have been the wish to disguise from me that the outsider knew about *minmin*. At least one of the practitioners took pains to assure me that what he had just performed was only a beneficial and traditional therapy (*gutpela marasin bilong mipela, bilong kanaka, bilong bipo iet*). But also behind this deception, there may have been the need for disguise, for not speaking plainly about things at the critical time. This is a recurring feature of various situations – for example, avoiding the use of a patient's name; or the spirit's name when Malyi was first brought into the village; the euphemisms or avoidance names used for the materials with which the images of a spirit are made, or the cryptic names for the bait used in traps at the time they are prepared and put down; not speaking out the truth about what game has been shot when men are still hunting at distant bush; shooting first, for example, a dummy arrow at the divination for Dauwaras, the second arrow being the true one with hair from his eyebrows.

THE DIAGNOSIS: BREAKING A TABOO

This was the least frequent of their diagnoses and this is notable considering the complexity and variety of forbidden acts and foods. Of the 15 cases, 8 were given to account for illness in older men; in 9 instances it was a diagnosis provided by someone outside the immediate family of the patient, since such a diagnosis may well carry a taint. The recurrent illnesses of two old men were explained by their having broken the rules against eating game shot by their sons or younger brothers. Another man was said to have eaten a forbidden lizard which he had shot himself, and eaten it even though he knew a certain form of destructive magic (*nunt wola*): thus the diagnosis implied three serious violations of taboo. It was highly discreditable. The man so

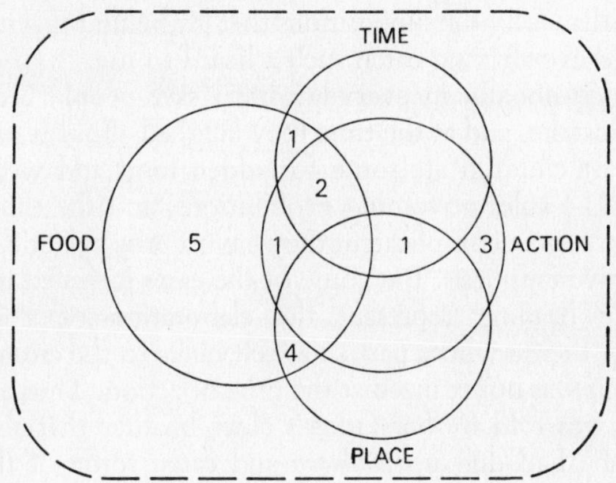

Fig. 38. The diagnosis: breaking a prohibition or taboo

Total recorded instances of diagnosis	= 17
Total cases of illness in which diagnosis made	= 15
Instances of diagnosis unassociated with treatment	= 8
Retrospective diagnosis after death or recovery	= 2

Case characteristics

Sex and age

	A1	A2	A3	A4
Males	2	1	0	9
Females	0	0	2	1

Types Med.	Sevty	Incap.	Duratn
A	4	I 2	1. 2
B	5	II 4	2. 6
C	5	III 3	3. 2
D	1	IV 5	4. 3
		V 1	5. 2

Sources of recorded diagnosis

Patient	Member of Pt's fam.	Other
6	2	9

Diagnosis involved

No divination etc.

slandered was ostensibly treated for the dangerous recoil of his magical knowledge upon himself, but did not himself, so far as I know, realize fully the suppositions that lay behind this treatment. He denied ever having eaten such a lizard to me.

Very occasionally in everyday life I saw people break some rule by mistake, and at the time they laughed about it when they realized; or children ate some forbidden food and were briefly scolded. The rules governing prohibitions, and the things to be avoided are most complicated; they have a prophylactic, guiding, preventative emphasis. But some of the cases included under this diagnostic heading represent the elaboration of a generally restricting theme whose particular relevance to the circumstances in question was not realized at the time of action. Thus an adolescent girl was told by her father's elder brother that she was ill because she had dug up *wadagep* and eaten some of them that same night, two actions which she ought to have separated by a longer space of time; the man who thatched his house and dug up yams on the same day; the little boy who ate some game shot too near home when it would have been all right if it had been killed further from the village. All these were instances of a taboo theme elaborated on. The explanations drew on features common to more formal restrictions, yet the danger in the action was not clearly predictable. Such explanations were sometimes combined with a diagnosis of another spirit intervening to strike someone made vulnerable first by his wrong action, as with Tambin in case of the man who thatched his house and dug up his yams. In theory it is possible to counteract very few taboo infractions but as other causes are held to intervene in association with the taboo these other causes may be treated. The broken prohibitions were cited rarely in active illness, probably I think because nothing much can be done about them. They explain the state of those who are ruined or permanently damaged by illness, the chronically ill like the old men with bronchitis. Food is the most common focus of the diagnosis. A broken taboo is almost the only diagnosis, apart from one case of sorcery, in which animal foods provide the substance (5 instances, to which 4 further instances may be added where eating game unspecified but shot by a junior man or son was supposedly the cause). Two cases of eating the betel pepper grown on matrilateral land (F∩P∩Ā) are included; aching jaws or teeth are almost inevitably linked with this particular diagnosis. Treatment by any matrilateral relative is simple and straightforward: the matrilateral kinsman spits on the painful jaw and appeals to his ancestral dead.

THE CONTENT OF THE 'EXPLANATIONS'

In the following section I shall look into the elements which contributed overall to the various Gnau diagnoses I recorded with a view to seeing what was involved in Gnau 'explanation'. It may be possible to find out something about the relative weight of concern put on the different elements that went into their 'explanations'. 'Explanation' here is limited to a special sense – the sense of causes which produce their effects as spirit agents do which, the Gnau say, intend their harm; they speak of them, at least, as agents aware of those whom they cause to be ill; or the illness is produced by human action, through sorcery or destructive magic, or through the effect of the breach of taboo. These are the diagnoses of the Gnau. But there are three points to note first.

(a) The 'explanations' are about some only of all the illnesses I recorded. Out of a total of 274 cases of illness 117 cases were 'explained'. So 43 per cent were 'explained' and 57 per cent were not. I have examined (pp. 235–44) how age and sex, the severity and length of the illness, and the incapacity it produced, affected whether I recorded an 'explanation' for it or not.

(b) If the numbers of cases of illness given each different kind of Gnau diagnosis are summed, the total number of cases involved is greater than 117: the total is 171. The reason for this is that some cases were given a diagnosis by more than one kind of cause, for example, by both Panu'et and a named spirit of the dead. Such multiple diagnoses may represent the thinking of different people about the same patient, or they may represent the same person's changing views expressed at different times, or an elaboration which specifies in greater detail the precise mode by which one kind of cause was linked with another. Twenty-eight cases of illness had multiple diagnoses. The distribution of these cases among the 117 cases that were 'explained' shows that multiple 'explanations' by different *kinds* of diagnoses were significantly less frequent in illness associated with the mild type II incapacity. Multiple diagnoses tended to be more common with severe and incapacitating illness; with illness that lasted a month or more, or ended in death; and with illness in which there was an inappropriate showing of ill behaviour. No significant difference according to the age or sex of the patient could be found among those with multiple diagnoses. The distribution of these 28 cases can be found in the Appendix, Table 44.

(c) The total number of all *instances* of diagnosis is 232. This total is greater than the ones just given. It still refers to the same 117 'explained' cases of illness, but the number is larger because sometimes people made the same *kind* of diagnosis but gave different reasons for making it. As I was interested in the ways people arrived at a diagnosis, I recorded the different ways of reaching the same *kind* of diagnosis for one patient as separate *instances* of diagnosis, for they each revealed aspects of the knowledge and understanding necessary for the diagnosis. On the other hand, when the same diagnosis was reached for the same reasons, even though by different people, I recorded it as only one instance of the diagnosis and ascribed it to the person most closely related to the patient or, if he had given it, to the patient himself.

Of the 117 'explained' cases 42 cases (36 per cent) were ones with multiple instances of diagnosis, either because the kind of diagnosis differed, or because the reasons for the same one kind of diagnosis differed. The distribution of cases with multiple instances of diagnosis again shows the tendency for these to be associated with long, more severe and incapacitating illness, and with illness in which there is an inappropriate show of illness.

Plate 9. *Panu'et: treatment* (*i*). The sick woman stands leaning on a stick. A *lyimungai* banana leaf is held over her while the bespelled image of Panu'et, whose base is covered with nettle leaves, is touched repeatedly against her body. Her face and clenched jaw muscles indicate her distress. The men standing behind her sing spell verses from the ritual of Panu'et. One of them holds the special soup (*wa'agep*) of which a morsel will be given her. The blurred hand close to her back flicks her with a sprig of nettle leaves.

A brief description of this kind of treatment can be found in the section on the spirit Panu'et (pp. 176–80). Plates 5, 6a, 6b show how the image is made.

A coconut palm leaf tied as a taboo marker on a palm is visible in both this plate and Plate 10. Such proprietary markers prohibit others from taking food – in this case coconuts – and the leaf marker may be bespelled with destructive magic against a thief.

The class II type of incapacity is associated with significantly fewer multiple instances of diagnosis (chi-square = 7·61, d.f. = 1, 1 per cent level of significance) among the cases that were 'explained'. There is also a significant difference between males and females overall in the number of multiple instances of diagnosis among the 'explained' cases of illness: females provided more cases with multiple instances than males (chi-square = 4·7, d.f. = 1, 5 per cent level of significance). This difference was significant for girls compared to boys (chi-square = 4·39, d.f. = 1, 5 per cent level of significance) but not for women compared to men. I think the reason for it was that girls happened to outnumber boys in the classes of A and IV type 'explained' illness, and these were the severe illnesses in which multiple instances of diagnosis were more common. The distribution of the 42 cases of multiple instances of diagnosis may be found in the Appendix, Table 45.

The first total (a) of 117 cases 'explained' out of the 274 cases of illness provides an answer to the question 'for how many of the illnesses studied did I record at least one Gnau diagnosis?' The second total (b) of 171 cases of different *kinds* of Gnau diagnosis provides the basis from which I shall look at the question 'If they diagnosed a person's illness, which *kind* or *kinds* of diagnosis did they choose?' The third total (c) of 232 *instances* of diagnosis provides the basis from which I shall look at what went into the reasons they offered for their diagnosis. The totals (a), (b) and (c), rest on information that is progressively more and more subject to the limitations of my evidence that I discussed earlier (pp. 230–5), since (a), (b) and (c) depend progressively more on the richness of recorded detail, on my understanding of the culture and the language, on familiarity and ease in talking to the people concerned, on my persistence and interest in finding out what

Plate 10. *Panu'et: treatment* (*ii*). The image of Panu'et has been 'killed'. Shredded plants from the inside of the image are scattered at her feet where they fell down over her when the banana leaf was torn along its midrib: it too lies at her feet. Her classificatory brother strikes her with a bespelled nettle leaf to startle out her sickness. She cowers under the forceful blows. His lower lip is compressed to give strength to the blow. Her husband holds the bowl of *wa'agep* soup of which she has just eaten a little. He has called to his little grand-daughter to come and take the remaining soup for it to be distributed to other people present.

people thought about someone's illness. I would suggest that only the trends of their concerns in diagnosis will appear from the examination of their diagnoses and the reasons behind them, not sure answers.

CASES AND KINDS OF DIAGNOSIS (b)

If, in the first approach to the 171 cases of *kinds* of diagnosis (b), everything is neglected except the kind of diagnosis we see only the observed commonness of the kinds of cause.

Table 29 shows that only 19 per cent of 'explained' illness is primarily put down to people's actions, and 81 per cent is explicitly ascribed to spirit agents. Spirits are clearly seen to be more common than breach of taboo, destructive magic and sorcery, as causes of illness. Indeed the great spirits and the *malet* spirits account for 50 per cent of all kinds of diagnoses, and they are spoken of as universal, more general, spirits rather than as ones closely linked with the affairs of particular social groups (despite the myths and rituals which link some to particular clans). The other spirits, on the other hand, are linked with specific groups of people: the spirits of the lineage dead as a collectivity are concerned with the interests and affairs of particular lineage groups (they account for 17·5 per cent of the diagnoses), and named spirits of individual dead are associated with people mainly at the level of the domestic grouping (they account for 14 per cent of the diagnoses). To explore the reasons for this distribution, we will need to go into both the kinds of patient diagnosed and the reasons for the diagnosis. At this point, the distribution only indicates general questions to be investigated, such as, why spirit rather than human action, why general spirits more than spirits specially linked with social groups.

When they consider a person who is ill and the diagnosis that is likely, their eventual decision is influenced by a combination of knowledge about the patient and his recent circumstances and activities, the nature of his illness, and their assumptions about the commonness or likelihood of particular causes acting to produce illness. The details about patients' circumstances will appear when we look at the reasons for diagnosis. But at this stage we can look at the distribution and the order of frequency of kinds of diagnosis to find out whether different age and sex categories show similar patterns or not. If we were to neglect how the circumstances and activities of people affect diagnosis, and we were to assume that the agents which cause illness paid no attention to the age or sex of persons, we should expect to find that the frequency and order of commonness of the different diagnoses was the same however we chose to divide the categories of patient

Table 29. Distribution of cases and kinds of diagnosis

Kind of diagnosis	*Number of cases diagnosed*			*Percentage of 171 cases*		
SPIRIT ACTION						
Great Spirits						
Panu'et	42	85	139	24·5%	49·7%	81·2%
Tambin	8			4·7%		
Malyi	13			7·6%		
Other *malet*	22			12·9%		
Spirits of lineage dead as a collectivity	30	54		17·5%	31·5%	
Named spirits of individual dead	24			14·0%		
HUMAN ACTION						
Magic and sorcery	17	32		9·9%		18·7%
Breach of taboo	15			8·8%		
Total	171			99·9%		

by age or sex. But this is not what we find; the order and number of diagnoses vary with sex and age. In Table 30 the number of cases ascribed to each particular kind of cause is shown for different categories of age and sex. As there are different numbers of cases involved, I have also put the percentage of all cases in the category of age or sex ascribed to that particular cause.

If the percentages are examined, the most striking point is the difference between males and females in regard to the diagnosis of both Panu'et and *malet*. The percentage contribution of diagnosis by destructive magic or sorcery to each age and sex category is very similar. Less striking differences are those between children and adults in illness caused by lineage spirits as a collectivity (children relatively more commonly); the difference between

Table 30. Distribution of kinds of diagnosis

Kind of cause	*Number and percentage of cases*													
	All cases		*Children under 15*		*Adults*		*All females*		*Adult women*		*All males*		*Adult men*	
	No.	*%*	*No.*	*%*	*No.*	*%*	*No.*	*%*	*No.*	*%*	*No.*	*%*	*No.*	*%*
Panu'et	42	24·5%	10	25·0%	32	24·4%	31	37·3%	22	36·7%	11	12·5%	10	14·0%
Lineage spirits	30	17·5%	9	22·5%	21	16·0%	13	15·6%	10	16·7%	17	19·3%	11	15·5%
Named dead spirits	24	14·0%	7	17·5%	17	13·0%	13	15·6%	10	16·7%	11	12·5%	7	9·9%
Malet	22	12·9%	4	10·0%	18	13·7%	6	7·2%	4	6·6%	16	18·2%	14	19·7%
Magic and sorcery	17	9·9%	4	10·0%	13	9·9%	9	10·8%	6	10·0%	8	9·1%	7	9·9%
Breach of taboo	15	8·8%	3	7·5%	12	9·1%	3	3·6%	3	5·0%	12	13·6%	9	12·7%
Malyi	13	7·6%	2	5·0%	11	8·4%	4	4·8%	2	3·3%	9	10·2%	9	12·7%
Tambin	8	4·7%	1	2·5%	7	5·3%	4	4·8%	3	5·0%	4	4·5%	4	5·6%
Total	171	99·9%	40	100·0%	131	99·8%	83	99·7%	60	100·0%	88	99·9%	71	100·0%

children and women compared with men in illness caused by the named spirits of dead individuals (men less commonly): men were more commonly afflicted by Malyi with illness than women; and males had an illness diagnosed as the result of a breach of taboo more commonly than females.

A second way to look at this pattern of salience in diagnosis is to rank the orders of commonness for the different age and sex categories.

The ranked orders in Table 31 are almost the same for different categories of age and sex, except for those of males and men. They have a noticeably different pattern from the overall one. In the case of males and men the distribution of diagnoses is spread more evenly over a greater variety of diagnoses than for other categories. Diagnoses by lineage spirits as a collectivity, and by *malet*, head the order in both male categories, breach of taboo comes relatively high up in the list, and Panu'et is not the commonest diagnosis as in all other categories. A diagnosis ascribed to named spirits of individual dead people sinks to a lower place in the case of men than in other categories. In the case of all females and women, the way that Panu'et stands out as the most common diagnosis is the chief point to note, as well as the low position of breach of taboo as a cause for their illnesses. In the cases of children, all females and women, 65–70 per cent of all the diagnoses belong in the first three kinds of diagnosis (i.e. Panu'et, lineage spirits as a collectivity, named spirits of individual dead people).

From these consistencies and differences of order and commonness, the main points to emerge, then, are that women and children, and females in general, have very similar patterns of diagnosis and these are different from those of men. Women and children are most often affected by Panu'et, by lineage spirits, and the spirits of individual dead people which strike members of the domestic grouping to which they once belonged. The diagnoses of men's illnesses are more widely and evenly spread, various *malet* are relatively more common, Panu'et relatively less so, lineage spirits have roughly the same commonness as in other categories, but spirits of named dead individuals a smaller role, and taboo a greater one. Malyi also affected men more than women or children.

These trends appear from the patterns and percentages but the

Table 31. The order of commonness of different kinds of diagnosis

Diagnosis	*All cases* N = 171	*All children* N = 40	*All adults* N = 131	*All females* N = 83	*Women* N = 60	*All males* N = 88	*Men* N = 71
Panu'et	FIRST 24·5%	FIRST 25·0%	FIRST 24·4%	FIRST 37·3%	FIRST 36·7%	FOURTH = 12·5%	THIRD 14·0%
Lineage spirits	SECOND 17·5%	SECOND 22·5%	SECOND 16·0%	SECOND = 15·6%	SECOND = 16·7%	FIRST 19·3%	SECOND 15·5%
Individual dead	THIRD 14·0%	THIRD 17·5%	FOURTH 13·0%	SECOND = 15·6%	SECOND = 16·7%	FOURTH = 12·5%	SIXTH = 9·9%
Malet	FOURTH 12·9%	FOURTH = 10·0%	THIRD 13·7%	FIFTH 7·2%	FIFTH 6·0%	SECOND 18·2%	FIRST 19·7%
Magic and sorcery	FIFTH 9·9%	FOURTH = 10·0%	FIFTH 9·9%	FOURTH 10·8%	FOURTH 10·0%	SEVENTH 9·1%	SIXTH = 9·9%
Taboo	SIXTH 8·8%	SIXTH 7·5%	SIXTH 9·1%	EIGHTH 3·6%	SIXTH = 5·0%	THIRD 13·6%	FOURTH = 12·7%
Malyi	SEVENTH 7·6%	SEVENTH 5·0%	SEVENTH 8·4%	SIXTH = 4·8%	EIGHTH 3·0%	SIXTH 10·2%	FOURTH = 12·7%
Tambin	EIGHTH 4·7%	EIGHTH 2·5%	EIGHTH 5·3%	SIXTH = 4·8%	SIXTH = 5·0%	EIGHTH 4·5%	EIGHTH 5·6%

numbers of cases studied was not large. Tests of the significance of these differences in 'explanation' showed that the diagnosis of Panu'et was significantly more common for females compared with males (chi-square = 8·66, d.f. = 1, 0·25 per cent level of significance), and for women compared with men (chi-square = 5·42, d.f. = 1, 2·5 per cent level); and also that males were more commonly diagnosed as ill from breach of taboo than females (chi-square = 4·52, d.f. = 1, 5 per cent level of significance); but no other differences were found significant in the distribution of diagnosis by age or sex. It may be noted that none of the diagnoses is exclusively restricted to the single category of patient.

The distribution of diagnoses according to the kind of illness when classified by severity, duration and incapacity shows no obvious segregation of diagnosis by kind of illness. All kinds of diagnosis are scattered among the different classes of illness. The numbers of cases do not show clear patterns of distinctive diagnosis, although there is a tendency for the diagnosis of *malet* to occur in class D and class III illness rather than in the classes which I identified with severe organic disease. The distribution of kinds of diagnosis by class of illness may be found in the Appendix, Table 46. The scatter of diagnosis among classes of illness is consistent with the earlier finding of their lack of concern with the symptoms and signs of illness as a means to diagnose its cause.

INSTANCES AND REASONS FOR DIAGNOSIS

In classifying the reasons they gave for diagnoses, I distinguished in broad terms between those which had to do with place, actions, time, food and quarrels, and also diagnoses given without accompanying circumstantial reasons, i.e. the diagnoses marked 'sole'. In many cases elements in these broad categories were combined to provide the reasons for an explanation. If we take all 'explained' illness and neglect everything except these categories, we find, by adding all the instances in which they appeared together, a first general estimate of their relative importance in diagnosis. There were 232 instances of diagnosis of which many involved more than one element combined. The relative importance of the broad categories was as follows (the percentages given are the percentages of all 232 instances which involved that type of reason):

PLACE>	ACTIONS>	TIME>	FOOD>	DIAGNOSES SOLE>	QUARRELS
91 instances	90 inst.	72 inst.	67 inst.	39 inst.	15 inst.
39·2%	38·8%	31·0%	28·9%	16·8%	6·5%

It is clear from this that quarrels do not play a big part in the explicit reasons people give for their diagnoses.

It might be supposed that some of these types of reasons would be conspicuously associated with a certain age or sex category of

Table 32. Types of reason involved in the diagnosis of different categories of sick person

Percentage of the 232 instances of diagnosis provided by category		*Place N = 91 = 100%*	*Action N = 90 = 100%*	*Time N = 72 = 100%*	*Food N = 67 = 100%*	*Diagnosis 'sole' N = 39 = 100%*	*Quarrel N = 15 = 100%*
Adults	79·7%	87·9%	81·1%	77·8%	83·6%	66·7%	86·7%
Children	20·3%	12·1%	18·9%	22·2%	16·4%	33·3%	13·3%
Males	50·9%	50·5%	48·9%	58·3%	49·2%	64·1%	73·3%
Females	49·1%	49·5%	51·1%	41·7%	50·7%	35·1%	26·7%
Men	44·4%	46·1%	46·7%	50·0%	46·3%	43·6%	66·7%
Women	35·3%	41·8%	34·4%	27·8%	37·3%	23·1%	20·0%

patient. If this were so, we would expect that the percentage contribution of that age or sex category of patient to the total 232 instances might be rather different from the percentage contribution they made to the total for the type of reason in question. In fact, as Table 32 shows, this was not the case. Although, for example, there are disparities in the percentage contribution of child cases to the 'place' type of reason, and the diagnosis 'sole', also of women's cases to 'time' reasons and 'quarrels', none of them reach significance at the 5 per cent level when tested by the chi-square test.

The order of commonness for different types of reason is similar in the various categories of patient (Table 47 in the Appendix is provided to show this). The main point to note is that I have not found any significant link between a broad type of reason and a certain age or sex category of patient.

But in contrast, when particular kinds of diagnosis (Panu'et, Tambin, etc.) are examined and we look at the part occupied by different types of reasons in diagnosing them, we see differences

Table 33. The order of commonness of different types of reason in various kinds of diagnosis

	First	*Second*	*Third*	*Fourth*	*Fifth*	*Sixth*	*Seventh*	*Eighth*
Place	Lin. spir>	Panu'et>	Mag. & sorc>	Malet>	Ind. dead>	Taboo	Malyi>	Tambin
91 inst.	26	22	14	8	7	5	5	4
Action	Panu'et>	Ind. dead>	Malyi>	Malet>	Lin. spir>	Tambin	Mag. & sorc	Taboo
90 inst.	23	13	12	11	10	7	7	7
Time	Malyi>	Ind. dead>	Lin. spir>	Mag. & sorc>	Panu'et>	Malet>	Taboo>	Tambin
72 inst.	18	15	13	9	6	5	4	2
Food	Panu'et>	Taboo>	Lin. spir>	Malet>	Ind. dead>	Mag. & sorc.	Malyi>	Tambin
67 inst.	20	13	12	7	5	4	4	2
Sole	Panu'et>	Ind. dead>	Mag. & sorc>	Lin. spir>	Malet	Malyi	Tambin	—
39 inst.	12	8	7	6	2	2	2	
Quarrel	Lin. spir>	Mag. & sorc>	Ind. dead	—	—	—	—	—
15 inst.	10	4	1					

not similarities. We have seen how the age and sex of the patient has a limited bearing on the kind of diagnosis. We are now concerned with reasons for their diagnoses. Reasons, then, would seem to be more likely to be linked with the kind of diagnosis than with the kind of patient. If age and sex had determined specific patterns of exposure to the various kinds of cause they recognize

Table 34. Percentage contribution of various kinds of diagnosis to different types of 'explanatory' reason

	% of all instances *N = 232*	*% of Place* *N = 91*	*% of Action* *N = 90*	*% of Time* *N = 72*	*% of Food* *N = 67*	*% of Sole* *N = 39*	*% of Quarrel* *N = 15*
Panu'et	23·6	24·2	25·6	8·3	29·8	30·8	—
Lineage spirits	18·0	28·6	11·1	18·5	17·9	15·4	66·7
Indiv. dead	15·5	7·7	14·4	20·8	7·5	20·5	6·7
Magic and sorcery	11·5	15·4	7·8	12·5	6·0	17·9	26·7
Malet	10·3	8·8	12·2	6·9	10·4	5·1	—
Malyi	9·4	5·5	13·3	25·0	6·0	5·1	—
Taboo	7·3	5·5	7·8	5·6	19·4	—	—
Tambin	4·7	4·4	7·8	2·8	3·0	5·1	—

for illness, then we might have found these different patterns of exposure shown in the reasons they gave for their diagnoses, provided that types of reason were not so broadly classed as to obscure them. We do not find them so different by age and sex group. But we do in relation to *kinds* of cause. The number of instances of different types of reason supplied by each *kind* of diagnosis is set out in order.

The orders vary markedly. Only three kinds of cause involve 'quarrels' as a reason for the diagnosis. We see that Malyi and named spirits of individual dead lead the list for instances of diagnosis involving 'time', that breach of taboo is second in the list for 'food', lineage spirits as a collectivity are first in the list for 'place', and Panu'et low in the list for 'time'. Each kind of diagnosis provides a certain percentage of the 232 instances. For each type of reason we can find what percentage of instances of that reason were contributed by each different kind of cause. Table 34 shows where the percentages keep in proportion and are therefore similar and where they do not.

I wished to find whether a specified type of reason was significantly associated with a particular kind of diagnosis. For this purpose, I compared the frequency of each type of reason among diagnoses of the given kind with the frequency of that type of reason among all diagnoses taken together. The significant findings are shown in Table 35 (d.f. in each test = 1).

Table 35. Associations between types of reason and kinds of diagnosis

	Chi-square	*Level of significance*
'Time': Panu'et less than expected	5·80	2·5%
'Time': Malyi more than expected	8·31	0·5%
'Food': Breach of taboo more than expected	6·49	2·5%
'Quarrels': Lineage spirits more than expected	9·71	0·5%
Not significant		
'Place': Lineage spirits more than expected	2·71	10·0%
'Place': Spirits of individual dead more than expected	2·74	10·0%

The distributions of diagnoses of Panu'et, magic and sorcery, *malet* as diagnoses 'sole' were not significantly different from expected.

In order to understand these differences which are shown at the level of a crude set of distinctions into types of reason, we must look into what is explicitly involved in them.

FOOD AND DIAGNOSIS

Why should food be a matter for concern in diagnosis? The obvious things about food are that everyone must eat; that food enters the body; that it is liked and valued, different foods differently; and that there are various rules about who may eat what, when and how. The kinds of food which are part of the reasons offered for diagnosis are overwhelmingly vegetable foods. Of the 67 instances involving food, non-vegetable foods were specified only in 7 cases. In 4 other instances the food was not specified although it was perhaps hunted game that they had in mind since these were cases which involved eating the food of someone junior, and the rule of prohibition stands out as one related to eating game shot by someone of one's own lineage but junior. They talk a great deal about hunting. They speak of game and animal foods as the most tasty (Pidgin, *swit*, Gnau, *sinati*, succulent and salty, *nempisa*, best, very good). Meat is food for feasts and special occasions, yet it is inconspicuous in diagnosis. Their staple foods are vegetable. They put a lot of work into producing them and they depend on them. They depend on sago more than any other single kind of food and they eat it all through the year. Women do most of the work to produce it. The mushrooms they eat grow on the piles of discarded rotting sago pith: the mushrooms just appear there. Sago and mushrooms accounted for 28·3 per cent of the food reasons for diagnosis (sago 13 instances, mushrooms 6). The root tubers (yam, *mami*, taro) are eaten in season and the work to produce them involves men more than producing sago does, and involves more ritual. Tubers were referred to in 25·4 per cent (17 instances) of the diagnoses involving food. Sago, mushrooms, and tubers stand out as the important foods in diagnosis. Their production involves hard work. Pandanus fruit (3 instances), breadfruit (*ginati*, 1 instance, *genanget*, 1 instance) bananas (2 instances), unspecified garden vegetables (3 instances) were also brought into diagnoses, but apart from planting them and taking the crop, they do not involve much work, and they are not so often or so regularly eaten.

The *teltug* leaves (of the tree *Gnemon gnetum*) were not given in reasons for diagnosis. The exception is notable as they are eaten almost as regularly as sago. Nor was *pitpit* (*Saccharum edule*) cited, which is also eaten throughout the year. None of the leaves (*nalyigup*, *benang*, the *Ficus* or *niyipe* leaves or fruit, ferns) nor beans, nuts, coconuts, sugar cane, or fruits (*tila'at*, mango). It would seem as though both the work involved in providing the food and a conspicuous association with spirits make them refer most to sago and tubers. Other vegetable foods, including the ones which I have mentioned because I recorded no instance involving them, could be part of an explanation but I would expect that accompanying factors such as coincidence, the place or person they came from, would also be part of the explanation. An example of what I have in mind is a diagnosis involving tomatoes which was made because the tomatoes were grown on or just beside the site of a men's house (*gamaiyit*) which had been demolished about a year before, and the site had therefore strong links with both spirits and ritual. Other introduced foods were not mentioned, except for a pawpaw in one case. The sweet potato, also introduced, which is grown and eaten by many people, was in no instance the kind of tuber referred to in the tuber-related diagnoses.

Chewing betel is not the same as eating food. But I have included here the 5 instances of diagnosis linked with the areca nut, and the 3 instances linked with the betel pepper, because they are chewed. The enjoyment of betel chewing and the desire for it, the rules about chewing, ritual spitting with betel, links of areca and betel pepper with place and spirits, prohibitions on their use, the ideas about sorcery which can be done with areca, betel pepper, and lime, contribute to make the things required to chew betel a focus of attention.

Drinking water was not given as a reason for a sickness.

Both males and females eat largely similar food – the differences in rules of prohibition and permission are matters of detail and relate chiefly to kinds of animal food, named varieties of bananas, etc. Both men and women had illness explained by reference to sago (males 6 instances, females 12 instances): mushrooms (males 2 instances, females 4 instances): and tubers (males 5 instances, females 12 instances). The meat foods affected males more than females (males 5 instances, females 2 instances) and all the explanations which referred to areca and betel pepper concerned men's illnesses.

Food goes into the body. The link of food eaten with somebody's illness seems understandable. If illness can be the result of entry into the body of something harmful, then food may be seen as a vehicle or means of entry. If the food itself harms, we should think of it as poisoned or infected. But these are not the main reasons for Gnau reference to food. Instead what prompts them to it is the idea that spirits watch over foods. Eating the food may then single out a person for their attention. The spirit may harm or strike him because of his greed or negligence. But there were very few instances which gave explicit grounds for understanding why a spirit chose to strike the patient. Most 'explanations' did not state or imply that the ill person had done something wrong or rash to provoke his illness. A spirit may strike and it is not predictable. This appears in the rather vague way that many reasons given for a diagnosis go no further than identifying some food eaten not long before, and implying that a spirit may therefore be involved. In effect such reasons make no positive assertion that the sick person concerned has done something stupid, irresponsible, naughty or immoral. They suggest only that spirits are concerned about food. So the relative emphasis on different kinds of food in diagnosis implies a relative emphasis in the Gnau ideas about spirit concerns with different vegetable food rather than with social or personal reasons for any attack. Far more often the food involved in the diagnosis is food grown or provided by the patient, or by people in his domestic grouping or in his lineage, rather than the food of other people. The food was that of other social groups in 11 instances only. So one is made ill by food belonging rightfully to one's self and the spirits that watch over it rather than by food and spirits coming from others. I discussed before differences between men's and women's work in producing sago and tubers. I made the point then of the attention of spirits to wives who gain acceptance as members of the domestic grouping and lineage (see pp. 277–80). Five instances of diagnosis involved men who received food or betel pepper or areca nut from their matrilateral relatives, and of these 3 were ones in which a taboo was said to have been broken.

The entry of the food into the body of the person concerned singles him out and makes food a reason for ascribing a diagnosis to the particular person, and for naming the food. But in 3 cases of babies' illness, food eaten by the mother was part of the reason for her child's illness, and in one man's case, he and other people said his illness was made worse because people who had eaten foods dangerous to him came close to him and so affected him. These 4 cases are of interest because they show the idea that the spirit attends to those who eat the food of concern to it, following them and their movements and contacts. These cases would conflict with a view that the spirit gains entry into the body by ingestion, the food acting as a vehicle or substance infected with the spirit. People say they abstain from certain foods when they are ill because to eat them would annoy the spirit (or spirits) or make it attend to them; they do not say that by eating they would be more infected or more poisoned. But these do not seem to be carefully thought out views. Sorcery and destructive magic performed on food, comes close to the notion of poisoning: if it is done on some food and then someone eats it, he will be affected. On the other hand, sorcery and destructive magic can also be effectively performed, in their view, on the remains of some food which someone has eaten and was innocuous when he ate it. The link and emphasis on the food substance itself (the part eaten and the part uneaten) in harmful sorcery is close in pattern to that implicit in a method of treatment for spirit-caused illness in which the person who has eaten part of some food falls ill and, to treat him, the remaining part, which may still be in the garden, is dug up, cut in pieces and thrown away into a river or a stream or cold water to make him better. The harm linked with the part which is in his body is altered by what is done to the part not in his body. They do not attempt to rid a sick person of the food involved in the diagnosis by trying to make him vomit (or by purging, rid him of it) as they would if he were thought to have drunk fish poison. With the bites of snakes or centipedes that are thought poisonous, they try to cut out the site where the poison is. The way they remedy illness related to foods does not fit with a view of them as something close to an ingested poison.

The time span between eating something and its relevance to a diagnosis is short. They do not refer back to something eaten more than three or four days before the onset of the illness to explain it. I have only noted time as an explicit element in explanations also involving food in 10 instances. These were ones where the time element was explicit because of its relation to ritual performance or a quarrel (6 instances), or to breaking a prohibition on eating the food and doing something else on the same day (2 instances), or to eating a particular food during illness already present (2 instances).

If certain foods, or food eaten in some special circumstances, were seen as conspicuously dangerous, we might expect to find that the span of attention to it went further back to single it out. But this is not so. The food is nearly all ordinary daily food, not food for example eaten at feasts or received from exchanges. Ordinary food of the sort eaten daily, occasionally happens to lead to illness. The implication is that spirits choose to attack occasionally, but their motives are not made clear in each instance. They are not so intelligible or predictable. The actions which were associated with the diagnoses involving food show an element of expectation when the diagnosis was one in which the food was eaten during the performance of ritual, or when the food was thrown away wastefully, or too much taken, or when someone's actions were clearly responsible because they broke a taboo (13 instances). It also seemed to me that the trivial aches or ailments were 'explained' as ones caused by the *mama* spirit of tubers only because they had just eaten the new *wadagep* for that year and thought it likely they might suffer from its watching *mama* spirit, and so they paid attention to trivial aches which otherwise they would have neglected.

Most of the diagnoses involving food either specified only the food (24 instances), or both food and the place from which it had come (24 instances). Together they account for 71·6 per cent of the explanations involving food. Nearly all the places were either garden land, the sago grove site, or the pools near to which sago had been prepared. The instances of explanation by reference to food alone tended to be rather vague ones, e.g., an explanation to account for the death of an old person when asked for one. Five were the suppositions of people outside particular men's families discreditably accusing them of the breach of taboo, 4 were the attributions of trivial aches to tubers eaten. But the explanations by both food and place contributed more specific and positive identifications of the circumstances of the illness. They were ones made more clearly with a view to what should be done to treat the patient, or avoid future danger. Some were more precise elaborations made in a complex set of explanations. Dreams revealed the precise explanation in 3 cases, and possession

Plate 11a–d. *Discussion at a gathering in the day-house at Watalu.*

These photographs give some impression of what a gathering is like when someone is ill and the men there discuss what might be the cause of the illness. In the first photograph, the man standing under the eaves of the house is making some assertion and speaking loudly. He stresses his point by holding his arms in the posture of someone drawing a bow, the point will be marked by his right hand coming down to thwack his buttock. But note that the sitting men do not seem to be taking notice of him. In the second photograph the man with his raised hand makes a gesture in which he waggles his forefinger and hand forward at someone. The gesture means 'You are joking or teasing, or telling a fib; it's not true'. In fact he was teasing a child in front of him. In the lower photographs, the men are just chatting to each other, smoking and relaxing. The photographs are intended to convey something of the unfocussed, casual crossfire of talk, chat and relaxation at such gatherings.

by spirits in 2; 2 of the dream instances happened to the son of the patients, in the others the revelations were made through the patients themselves.

Food, then, in diagnosis tends to reflect a pervasive view of the special concern of spirits with food. It is ordinary food that serves to provide an acceptable, though often vague, explanation not much associated with clear social reasons for sickness, nor much with specific motives for the spirits to attack the particular individuals. In the diagnosis of breach of taboo, food plays a conspicuous role, and animal food is referred to which otherwise is not an important element in the diagnosis of illness. Most food diagnoses have to do with common staple vegetable foods. Sorcery and destructive magic provided only 4 instances of diagnosis involving food. The spirit responsibilities for different foods are allotted in diagnosis in a way consistent with Gnau views when stated in general. One of the commonest questions about illness, a cliché of the Gnau, is 'But what has he eaten to be ill like that?' (*Ba nanu meni wa lin wolen?*). In fact food eaten came into 28·9 per cent of their explanations for illness. That was all.

ACTIONS AND DIAGNOSIS

The category of explanation which I have labelled 'action' is one that might include a very wide range of things people do. Almost anything except what I counted as to do with place, eating food, time or quarrels was put into it. Yet it will be seen that the Gnau turn to a restricted range of actions when they explain why an illness happened. It is hard to know how to classify all the various things they do (or have done to them) which played no part in the explanation of illness. Almost nothing was recorded of activities to do with hunting; almost nothing to do with sex, marriage, reproduction, child-rearing, cooking, house building, sleep, washing, travel, visiting, public discussions and decisions, plantation work, councils, missionaries,

Plate 12a. *At the burial of Malden.* The women daubed with clay in mourning come from the village of Mandubil (see pp. 257–60).

Plate 12b. *A place of Panu'et.* In the gardens at a grove of sago palms, children by a pool.

Table 36. Food in diagnosis: summary

'Explanation' involved	*Panu'et*	*Tambin*	*Malyi*	*Malet*	*Lineage spirit*	*Individual dead*	*Magic and sorcery*	*Taboo*	*Total*
Food only	9	—	—	4	3	2	1	5	24
Food and place	8	2	1	3	4	1	1	4	24
Food and action	2	—	—	—	—	2	—	1	5
Food and time	—	—	—	—	—	—	1	1	2
Food, time and place	—	—	1	—	—	—	—	—	1
Food, time and action	—	—	2	—	—	—	—	2	4
Food, place and action	1	—	—	—	3	—	—	—	4
Quarrel, time, food and place	—	—	—	—	2	—	1	—	3
Total	20	2	4	7	12	5	4	13	67
Sago	9	—	—	1	—	3	—	—	13
Mushroom	5	—	—	—	—	1	—	—	6
Pandanus	3	—	—	—	—	—	—	—	3
Areca	2	—	1	—	1	—	1	—	5
Betel pepper	—	—	—	1	—	—	—	2	3
Yam, taro	1	1	1	5	7	—	—	2	17
Banana	—	—	—	—	1	—	1	—	2
Meat	—	—	—	—	1	—	1	5	7
Other	—	1	2	—	2	1	1	4	11
Total	20	2	4	7	12	5	4	13	67

the Administration, white people; nothing to do with crossing rivers, movements at night, getting lost, theft, adultery, menstruation, the weather, earthquakes, frights, disappointed love, sudden awakenings, snakes, dogs, cassowaries; nothing to do with touching valuables, making armbands, arrows, fishing, clearing paths, pig rearing, or wearing clothes. And so the list might go on and on.

But of all the 90 instances involving 'actions', 50 (55·5 per cent) had to do with some aspect of gardening or subsistence activities, and 13 (14·4 per cent) to do with the performance of major rituals. These are the chief kinds of activities which they brought forward in the 'explanation' of illness, and we should try to understand why they turned to them as things which offered a reason for illness, implying a recognition of risk, exposure, or vulnerability.

In broad terms the things to do with gardening can be put under the three heads of planting, cutting, and taking: A. planting tubers; and covering over the base of the growing *mami* vine (10 instances); B. cutting down trees or plants or chipping the sago palm (20 instances); C. taking a food crop (20 instances) whether taking prepared sago flour from the pool in which it was left to soak, or digging tubers up, or taking fruits or leaves from a tree. All the diagnoses which involved gardening activities were ones ascribed to spirits except for 4 instances in which the actions were considered to involve the breach of taboo. Planting *wadagep* (tubers), covering over and mounding up the base of the growing *mami* vine, are both set seasonal garden activities done in concentrated periods of intensive work by men. The work is accompanied by the observance of special behavioural restrictions and rules, and by appeals to spirits. It is work done with the knowledge that spirits are concentrated where it is done, present and watchful, activated and aware. It is also hard work and important to the people's livelihood. The cutting activities are, with 3 exceptions, all to do with the work of sago production. Eleven of the 20 instances involve cutting down the large fern (*nembe'et*) or the snake creeper (*lambet bulti*) so as to clear the sago palm or the space where it was to be pounded. The fern and the creeper are both singled out for fear because they say they may be associated with their own watching *malet* spirit, or with spirits of the dead, or Panu'et, for which they are as a house or resting place would be for a man. In cutting things down they see themselves as cutting down things which belong to certain spirits, or in which those spirits have a protective, jealous interest. The same sense of a possessive, jealous interest, of things that belong to certain spirits, goes with crops ready for picking or harvesting, and prepared sago. When cutting is involved the imputation is that spirits are annoyed or angered at the injury or destruction of their things; when things are taken, the imputation is of their anger or spite at the loss of what they hold dear, protect, benefit, and hoard. In general terms, the ideas involved in the risks of gardening and subsistence activities are ones of spirit presence, localization or concentration, attachment and interest, awareness and possessiveness. But these ideas are part of the complex ambivalent views they have about the power of spirits which also has its other face – that of benefit, securing crop growth and abundance, aiding people's efforts to produce their food. The power of spirits is essential to successful gardening activities. The benefits must be sought and so the risks must be run. They are not wholly predictable and avoidable risks, even though people carefully observe proper prescribed forms of behaviour in gardening. Things to do with the production of sago (23 instances) slightly outweigh those to do with *wadagep* (19 instances) in the number of instances of explanation I recorded. I have stressed the division of labour between men and women in work to produce tubers and sago. But it would be wrong to suppose that this difference is clearly mirrored in the sex of those whose sickness was 'explained' by reference to *wadagep* or sago production. The distributions by sex are almost equal: the sago activities were involved in explanation for males' illnesses in 10 instances, for females' in 13; and *wadagep* gardening for males' illnesses in 11 instances, and for females' in 8. The men plant and cover up *wadagep*: the balance was 7 males' to 3 females' illnesses supposedly connected with planting. The women take the prepared sago from pools: the balance was 1 male's to 5 females' illnesses linked with this. However in cutting down and clearing the sago palm, men take part in sago production, and women are present at the planting of *wadagep* and have particular jobs to do during it, and also they dig the tubers up when they are harvested. The relatively equal distribution of these 'explanations' according to the sex of the patient goes against an expectation that the relative amount of time and effort spent in production would be correlated with the kind of explanations given for illness in some direct and specific fashion. Rather it would seem that both sexes run the risks which attach to time, place and the concentration of the spirits on these activities. Both sexes benefit from the results of the labour of each. In all except 6 of these instances, it was the action of the patient himself or herself which was linked with the illness. Those few exceptions which link the action of another person to the patient's illness act as 'explanations' because of assumptions about the attention of spirits and a conspicuous social tie between the two people concerned. For instance a mother chipped sago, left her work unfinished and came back to her child, and the child fell ill struck by the spirit which had followed her mother; a convalescent wife received the visit, late one afternoon, of her sister-in-law just back from working on a sago palm, the wife fell ill again; an elderly man was ill because his daughter-in-law pounded and chipped a sago palm that he had planted many years before.

The interval between most of these activities and the onset of illness is relatively short, in most cases not more than three or four days, but sometimes it may be two weeks. The timing was not explicitly singled out for comment and for most such cases I did not note it as an element in the explanation, except when the illness seemed to begin during the action or immediately after it. Five of the gardening instances were associated with the precise revelations of dreams. An example of one of these will bring out more fully how these actions are understood as 'explanations' for illness. Two very old sisters, both widows, had pneumonia. About two weeks previously they had gone to collect mushrooms at a sago working site by a pool where there were some ferns (*nembe'et*) which they had cut. They lighted a fire there to cook some food and the fire caught on some of the cut fern. The son of one of the widows had a dream during their illness in which his dead father and his father's classificatory elder brother, also dead, appeared to him and they said they were cross with the women, especially with the iller one, because they had burnt the fern and the fern was their house in which they had left their stringbags hanging up and their arrows. They had left them in the house and then returned to find them burned. They said that they together were looking after the sago site in question and planting things there, and that the site did not belong to the iller of the two widows. The man who had this dream went and told it to the son of his own father's dead classificatory elder brother and they went to the widows, told the dream to them, and warned them not to go to that site in the future. They also spat over them calling on their fathers to be placated and to end afflicting the women.

In 13 instances the explanation was explicitly linked to the performance of major rituals for great spirits. I commented on such 'explanations' in the section on the diagnosis of Malyi, for 7 of them were diagnoses of Malyi. In major rites, spirits are thought to be concentrated in the village, present and attentive to people. When the rites are going on, people have the spirit concerned much in mind and foresee a possibility that someone may be struck by it. There are times of special risk such as the moment of ending the rites and sending the spirit off. In most of the cases, the illnesses were explained by nothing more than the fact of illness during a performance. The 'explanations' stem chiefly from coincidence and expectation. The high significance of rites performed is apparent from the span of time and distance over which they are sometimes suggested to work. In 2 instances, the ending of a ritual in a village half a day's walk away was said to be the cause of illness at Rauit – the village was at the edge of the range of villages with which Rauit had social ties. In 4 instances, the explanation referred back to a performance held three or four weeks before to account for an illness beginning after that long an interval. The rites for Malyi and the rites for the building of a new men's house were the only two large scale major rituals that happened during my stay – the men's house rites account for 4 instances of 'explanation' through presence at the ritual, and Malyi for 7 others.

At one point there had been talk of getting the Tambin rites going when the batch of men, then expected, got back from the plantations. At the time of this talk, the full song of Tambin was sung through once on a night of celebrations for a couple's first child. Two instances of illness were diagnosed as from Tambin because of this night of singing and the illnesses began two or three weeks later. In the explanations referring to major rites the presence and performance was enough. There was no identification of the particular action or the special way in which the patient was singled out, except for one instance in which an elderly woman had the role of dancing before Malyi to lure the spirit out for the first time onto the dancing space, and she had some pain afterwards. There were a few instances in which the fact of performance was linked with a specific action, for instance, taking bananas, or digging up yams, to imply that that was the moment and reason for being struck. It is a feature of public ritual in the village that everyone must come to the special stages in its progress, or they must come at least within the village at these times. People must not be so casual and indifferent that some go about their gardens doing ordinary work while major events are taking place in the village. The activities of people are co-ordinated by warnings and by *garamut* announcements. It is a way of preventing the casual confusion of activities. The underlying idea of the risk or danger involved in such confusion is rather like their idea of the risk or danger that lies in the confusion of two sorts of activity which should be kept separate. Such confusion may be seen to constitute a breach of taboo. At the final mortuary rites in which the spirit of a dead man is released and sent off, the people of the village should be within the village. So one man put down his own illness to fetching some bananas from a garden very close to his hamlet on the day of someone's final mortuary rites.

The explicit element of explanation often associated with ritual performance is 'time' – 12 of the 24 instances of explanations linking time and action are ones to do with major rites. With gardening activities 'place' is the explicit element commonly associated in explanation.

I have put the remaining instances (as well as that of the man just mentioned who fetched bananas on the day of the funeral) under the miscellaneous heading of 'other'. There are 27 instances. Three of them rest on the idea that the illness jumped from one person to another because they came into proximity. Seven more associate people's movements with attack by spirits – again the idea is of localization, attention and proximity. Three of these explanations include a notion like that of contact with another sick person, except that the identified person was dead, having died of his or her illness a long time before. Someone from the place where he or she had died came to visit another and, in the explanation, it was discerned that the visitor came with the dead's spirit accompanying them, bringing a power to transfer the illness it had died of to another living person. The 4 other instances of people's movements involved first, a convalescent woman who visited the hamlet into which her daughter had married and she was said to have been struck by the lineage spirits there which noticed her weak condition; second, a new-born baby who died because the mother-in-law of the baby's mother came back after cutting bamboo, accompanied by the lineage spirits which watched over that bamboo and struck the vulnerable child when she came close to it; third, the case involving the movement of people who had eaten foods dangerous to a man who lay already sick; and fourth, Saoga's movement through a newly planted garden (see p. 252).

Saoga's action was done in ignorance. If she had known, she would not have done it. Ignorance of a wrong action was also the feature recognized in retrospect as the explanation for the illnesses of two little girls who were said to have defaecated or urinated into pools, and thereby provoked attack by spirits. Thoughtlessness, stupidity, or rashness appear in a very few explanations, such as the ones which link illness with a man eating tubers which had been rootled and part eaten by wild pigs, the woman whose child fell ill because she began to work on another sago palm when she had not first completed the work on a previous one, the woman whose child fell ill because she threw away unfinished food, the instances considered as breaches of taboo because two actions were confused which should have been kept separate, the man accused of eating the lizard he had himself shot, and the death of a child because his parents had not the sexual restraint to space the birth of their children a proper interval apart.

Diagnoses of destructive magic and sorcery provide 7 instances under this miscellaneous head. The notable point about these instances is that they go on further than identifying the action by which the necessary contact was made between the vehicle of sorcery or magic and the victim. None of them contains implications about motives, or antipathy between the human agent and the victim. Indeed these 'explanations' for a diagnosis of sorcery are about the means by which it was done and tell nothing of intentions or the reasons why it should have been done. The identity and personality of the sorcerer is quite obscure and undisclosed in them. But in 3 instances the diagnosis was of inadvertent contact with destructive magic put to protect property against theft, and in these instances it was made clear

Table 37. Actions in diagnosis: summary

'Explanation' involved	Panu'et	Tambin	Malyi	Malet	Lineage spirit	Individual dead	Magic and sorcery	Taboo	Total
Action only	5	3	—	5	1	3	1	3	21
Action and place	10	2	—	2	4	3	2	—	23
Action and time	5	2	8	3	1	5	—	—	24
Action, place and time	—	—	2	1	1	—	4	1	9
Action and food	2	—	—	—	—	2	—	1	5
Action, time and food	—	—	2	—	—	—	—	2	4
Action, food and place	1	—	—	—	3	—	—	—	4
Total	23	7	12	11	10	13	7	7	90
Plant									
yam, taro	—	—	—	2	3	—	—	2	7
cover *mami*	—	—	—	3	—	—	—	—	3
Cut down									
fern	3	—	—	1	—	2	—	—	6
snake creeper	—	—	1	2	—	2	—	—	5
sago palm	3	—	—	—	—	—	—	—	3
sago work	2	—	—	—	—	1	—	—	3
other tree	—	—	—	—	3	—	—	—	3
Take out									
yam, taro	1	3	—	2	1	—	—	2	9
sago from pool	3	—	—	1	—	2	—	—	6
other	3	—	—	—	—	2	—	—	5
Present at ritual	4	2	7	—	—	—	—	—	13
Contact or proximity	1	1	4	—	3	2	7	—	18
Other	3	1	—	—	—	2	—	3	9
Total	23	7	12	11	10	13	7	7	90

by the explanation whose magic was involved: the actions involved were touching or stepping over or under bespelled *tila'at* tree wands (*nembigug*), stepping past a bespelled post marked as a sign to close a path as private, climbing a tree just beside an areca palm and touching the bespelled leaf protecting the areca nuts from theft. In the 4 instances about sorcery, the explanations identified how and also where the victim stepped over a hank of bespelled grass (2 instances), or left urine at a spot beside a pool where the sorcerers took it, or went for treatment to the hospital at Yankok and there exposed himself to the attention of strangers who must have made sorcery against him. The 'explanations' answer questions about how, where, and when, not why, it happened.

QUARRELS AND DIAGNOSIS

Quarrels do not enter into many explanations for illness. They were involved because they presented a reason for the illness happening. In only 3 of these instances was the explanation brought forward by the patient, and in 2 of these 3, the quarrel itself was not spontaneously brought into the explanation, but I asked about it because I already knew about it. It is quite possible that there were other diagnoses with quarrels covertly behind them which I did not know about. But it is still fair to say that it must be a rare feature. In all the other instances the quarrel was referred to spontaneously and these explanations were given by people outside the domestic grouping of the sick person in all except for 2 instances. Half of the 10 instances provided by people outside the patient's domestic grouping came from members of his hamlet (and in 3 they were given by members of the patient's clan); the other half came from people of another hamlet.

As to the nature of the quarrels – first, those between people of different villages. Four of the instances related to one dispute over some land closer to Mandubil than to Rauit. In the first month of my stay, large parties from both villages met on the land for a hot-tempered discussion about its division and use. A fight almost broke out but my presence was used as a reason for stifling it. At one point during the discussion, Malden ran to stab at someone with a spear but he was stopped. The main protagonists on the Rauit side were clan, though not lineage, relatives of Malden.

They used the land with Malden too. On the Mandubil side were the sons of a woman killed on the land by the father (and others) of a Rauit man belonging to the clan involved who did not seek to use the land himself. He took a major part in arranging the compromise decision that resulted from the discussion. Four days later he fell ill and his illness was attributed to the lineage spirits of the woman whose blood his father had spilled on the land. Five months later, the grandson of the main Rauit protagonist was briefly ill and the diagnosis was of Mandubil lineage spirits. Three months later the main Rauit protagonist himself was ill, and the diagnosis was sorcery. Eighteen months later Malden was ill and the diagnosis was also sorcery. In each case the reason was overtly related to the dispute by people outside the clan of the sick people. I have described Malden's final illness and his other dispute with the Mandubil Local Government Councillor on pp. 257–60, the diagnoses involved the Councillor's lineage spirits while Malden was ill, and then possible sorcery after he had died.

Lastly a quarrel between men of one clan but different villages: a young Rauit man went hunting with his Laeko clan relatives. He was ill on the hunt which went on for a week. He returned to Rauit with a share of the game killed that was regarded as unfairly small. He was still ill. In fact he had pleuritic pain and a loud pleural friction rub. His Rauit lineage relatives were angry with his Laeko relative who took him on the hunt, and gave him so small a share to bring back. But their diagnosis was that the Laeko lineage spirits had struck the young man for no clearly stated reason as he hunted in that bush.

The quarrels between people belonging to the same village were between members of different clans in 6 instances, and between members of the same one in 2 instances. A ceremony was held jointly for the puberty of a girl and her father's elder brother's son's first child. Money was distributed by the fathers concerned to both the girl's matrilateral lineage and to the first born child's matrilateral lineage. The two matrilateral lineages belonged to branches of one very large lineage living in different hamlets. Both the girl and the child fell ill within three months of the ceremony though at different times. During their illnesses various other explanations were given but almost a year later, I was told by the father of the mother of the first-born child, in a chance turn of conversation on a walk, that both the illnesses had been the result of attack by the lineage spirits of the mother's brother of the girl concerned, because he had been dissatisfied with the amount of money he received. He said that the mother's brother was unjustified in his dissatisfaction. He did not quite accuse him in plain words of having made the lineage spirits attack. Between the man I talked to and the mother's brother, there was no open dispute that I knew of but there were no close relationships of loyalty and shared interest for the branches of the lineage had lived apart for many generations and they identified themselves with the interests of their different hamlets. The quarrel in another instance was over the use of land between men who claimed, on the one hand, a matrilateral link, and on the other, a clan link, to some land primarily associated with a lineage that had become defunct. The quarrel led to a fight with sticks and blows. When the wife of one of the clan men who had fought, seemed ill about two months later, it was thought she was afflicted by the lineage spirits of the men who had claimed a matrilateral right to use the land. Her husband held this view. The next instance came up in the divination of Sunikel's death (pp. 260–3), which was already decided as one due to sorcery. The question was put that the agents were those of men who should have received a mortuary payment from her father's lineage who now used the land of a dead man, last of his lineage, but the payment had not been made. The answer to this question provided by the divination was no.

One embittered sick man supposed his own illness came from attack by the spirits of his wife's brother's lineage through food they had given him. This was a private view he told me which I thought was linked with a long past history of quarrels he had had with them, his own sense of failure, and his resentment at the influence they had over his wife and children.

When Dauwaras was ill, there was a small earthquake one night. A man became possessed and revealed that the spirit of a dead man of his clan was the cause of Dauwaras's illness. His explanation was linked with an old accusation of sorcery as the cause of the death. It had been made and disproved years before (see p. 286).

The remaining 2 instances which involve intra-clan dispute are first, a dispute about a tract of gardening land in which there was a shouted argument between two men. When one of them, five months later, was ill, he attributed his illness to gardening on that land and the watching lineage spirits. I asked him about the quarrel which he did not bring up spontaneously. The second instance was a fight with sticks between the young wives of two brothers. The wives disagreed about who should work on a particular sago palm. Their mother-in-law fell ill four days later,

Table 38. Quarrels in diagnosis: summary

'Explanation' involved	*Lineage spirits*	*Individual dead*	*Magic and sorcery*	*Total*
Quarrel and time	5	1	2	8
Quarrel, time and place	3	—	1	4
Quarrel, time, place and food	2	—	1	3
Total	10	1	4	15
Quarrels with:				
physical fight	3	—	—	3
public shouting	3	1	3	7
private resentment	4	—	1	5
Total	10	1	4	15

and she herself said she was ill because the lineage spirits of her husband's lineage were displeased at the fight between her two daughters-in-law.

I have been able to outline all the instances of explanations involving disputes because there were so few. Apart from drawing attention to the long time intervals involved, and the issues in the quarrels which were mostly to do with land or relations with affines and matrilateral kin, there are too few cases to show clear patterns. I should also mention that during my stay at least 10 people were injured in some way, or ill directly after fights, but their state was not explained other than by reference to the physical violence they had received.

PLACE AND DIAGNOSIS

In accounting for the relevance of food and actions to diagnosis, I have discussed some aspects of the localization of spirit presence and power. My impression of these views is one of fields of forces which may be more or less powerful at different times, more or less concentrated. They may affect people who move into them, or may follow them in their movements, and also may be made to vary by some human actions. There are some relatively more fixed points of reference for these powers; first would be the pools linked with their spirits and Panu'et, a few strange rock formations, then the link of ferns and the snake creeper with spirit powers; less fixed the links of lineage spirits as collectivities with tracts of garden land and particular hamlets; the links of dead individuals with trees they had planted and land which they had gardened and, if they were killed, then the place where they fell which was usually marked by a planted croton; least fixed, the great spirits at once capable of being almost anywhere, linked generally with certain foods and crops, and capable of great concentration at particular places through ritual. The Gnau move in an environment that is, as it were, variously magnetized by the concentration of spirit powers.

In many of the diagnoses involving gardening activities and foods, the place was an explicit element mentioned in the explanation, making it more precise and containing information that might be relevant to treatment and future care, or avoidance of further illness. The explicit mention is presumably a consequence of what they consider important in the diagnosis, for in some of these cases, for instance, those to do with food, they might not have bothered to mention the place it came from. In other explanations involving food, they did not bother even though, no doubt, if asked specifically, they could have said. Perhaps the point about it is that in most cases the place did not seem to them either so obvious or so irrelevant as to be left out. In the case of major rituals the place which they referred to was usually obvious and therefore unmentioned.

Place came into 91 (39·2 per cent) of 232 instances of explanation. Of these, 91 instances, 23·1 per cent involved places of settlement (hamlet or village), 52·7 per cent garden land or bush, 17·6 per cent pools, and 6·6 per cent variously included paths, a particular tree or a coastal plantation (once only), the hospital at Yankok (once). Nearly all the pool instances were linked with a diagnosis of Panu'et. Gardening land was associated with explanations of the diagnosis of lineage spirits in 18·6 per cent of all the 'place' instances, and the same diagnosis was linked with the village or hamlet in 9·9 per cent of all the instances. Only 12 instances (13·2 per cent) referred to places not within the bounds of Rauit and the land its people regarded as theirs: these other places were the villages encircling them or their land, except for the coast plantation and the hospital (Mandubil in 5 instances, Nembugil in 2, De'aiwusel, Laeko, and Winalum one instance each, the coast and the hospital).

If a simple division is made of all the place instances into those instances in which the place specified is the normal hamlet or garden land or bush which the sick person lives at or uses, and those in which it is not, one finds that 67 instances involve places which, in a rough sense, belong to him or her, and only 24 involve places belonging to other people. In the case of married women, I have of course counted their normal hamlet and garden land as that of their husband. Of the 24 instances of other people's places, 19 were to explain the illnesses of males, 5 the illnesses of females. The instances of males ill because of the lineage spirits of other places (9 instances) just outweighs the number of those ill from their own lineage spirits at their own places (8 instances). With women, attack by their husbands' lineage spirits is more easily understandable (see pp. 281–3). In the case of females, 7 instances involved their husband's lineage spirits, while only 2 involved other people's.

In cases in which lineage spirits were thought dangerous to the sick person, he or she moved to stay usually at another hamlet, but sometimes only to another house in the same hamlet. On this evidence, the harmful influence within the village would seem localized, since moves to other hamlets did not often involve more than two or three hundred yards' distancing, and in some cases much less. When fences were set up to isolate and protect the patient from the harmful influence of people passing by, they were rarely more than 10 or 20 paces distant from where he lay. Avoidance of a place because of illness did not often last more than a month or so after the sick person recovered. The appeal to spirits to recognize, tolerate and not harm the patient was clear in a number of treatments. This concern is most understandable given that the places involved so often were those that the sick person lived in and worked at normally. The powers which cause most of their illnesses belong to familiar and necessary places and things.

Table 39. Place in diagnosis: summary

'Explanation' involved	*Panu'et*	*Tambin*	*Malyi*	*Malet*	*Lineage spirit*	*Individual dead*	*Magic and sorcery*	*Taboo*	*Total*
Place only	2	—	1	2	8	2	5	—	20
Place and food	8	2	1	3	4	1	1	4	24
Place and action	10	2	—	2	4	3	2	—	23
Place, action and time	—	—	2	1	1	—	4	1	9
Place, action and food	1	—	—	—	3	—	—	—	4
Place, quarrel and time	—	—	—	—	3	—	1	—	4
Place and time	1	—	—	—	1	1	—	—	3
Place, quarrel, time and food	—	—	—	—	2	—	1	—	3
Place, time and food	—	—	1	—	—	—	—	—	1
Total	22	4	5	8	26	7	14	5	91
Village	2	2	1	1	9	2	4	—	21
Garden or bush	7	2	3	3	17	5	6	5	48
Water pool	13	—	—	3	—	—	—	—	16
Other	—	—	1	1	—	—	4	—	6
Total	22	4	5	8	26	7	14	5	91

TIME AND DIAGNOSIS

Place is one of the co-ordinates of presence and so is time. There is probably a greater element of bias in my recording of time than place because I probably gave it more attention when I noticed coincidence or a long interval. I tended to neglect to put an equal mention of timing on their part down as an element of the explanation when the explanatory theme was merely some recent gardening activity or food eaten. When I was told about a diagnosis involving major ritual or a quarrel, I have usually noted the timing as an element of the explanation in a way I did not bother to with food and many instances of gardening activities. This is the reason for the association of Malyi with the element of time in explanation. Nearly all the diagnoses of Malyi were connected with the performance of its major rites in the village.

Coincidence or the very close association in time of two events, one of which is the illness or its onset, makes the timing seem in some instances the most important reason for making the explanation. The explanations in which time and action, or time, action and place, are involved include most of the coincidence cases. They are ones to do with major rites or else to do with signs such as revelatory dreams, the cricket jumping on to a painful leg as a girl came down from her hamlet to the one where the sick man lay (see pp. 276–7), the *dyulin* or comet, or else they are to do with trivial aches that were noticed immediately after planting or digging up *wadagep*. The interest of timing in relation to diagnoses of illnesses sent by the spirits of named dead individuals lies in the interval between their deaths and recourse to them as explaining someone else's illness. With some quite recent deaths, even the suspicion of an illness in someone of their immediate family was linked to the recent death and the supposed loneliness of the parted spirit, reflecting expectation and grief in the way I discussed earlier (see p. 286). The intervals here were not longer than about a month except for one case which happened about seven months later. The long intervals of years between the death of an individual and his or her role in causing an illness were connected with special signs like the snakebite and a previous death by snakebite; with dreams or possessions; and with links to the place where a person was killed, or a tree that had been planted by him, or the house he used to sleep in. In the short

Table 40. Time in diagnosis: summary

'Explanation' involved	*Panu'et*	*Tambin*	*Malyi*	*Malet*	*Lineage spirit*	*Individual dead*	*Magic and sorcery*	*Taboo*	*Total*
Time only	—	—	5	1	—	8	—	—	14
Time and action	5	2	8	3	1	5	—	—	24
Time, action and place	—	—	2	1	1	—	4	1	9
Quarrel and time	—	—	—	—	5	1	2	—	8
Time, food and action	—	—	2	—	—	—	—	2	4
Time, quarrel and place	—	—	—	—	3	—	1	—	4
Time and place	1	—	—	—	1	1	—	—	3
Time, quarrel, food and place	—	—	—	—	2	—	1	—	3
Time and food	—	—	—	—	—	—	1	1	2
Time, place and food	—	—	1	—	—	—	—	—	1
Total	6	2	18	5	13	15	9	4	72
Timing									
coincident	5	—	9	4	3	4	4	4	33
in week	—	—	4	1	2	4	1	—	12
in month	—	2	3	—	3	3	1	—	12
in year	—	—	1	—	3	2	1	—	7
over year	1	—	1	—	2	2	2	—	8
Total	6	2	18	5	13	15	9	4	72

spans, we observe an aspect of the persistence of grief and the sense of loss; in the long-term ones, more varied aspects of the persistence of memories associated with people, and especially with the manner of their deaths, and with the places to which their spirits are still attached, and the people who matter to them. Otherwise the longer spans of time between events and their relevance to an illness involves quarrels, which I have already commented on, or else the occasional references to former illnesses identified as caused by some particular spirit and said to have left the patient vulnerable. These were remembered at times when some major rites were in progress.

In general, the ordinary events which bear on illness have to have taken place recently (within a week or so of the onset of the illness) and their commonness in the explanations of illness is a reflection of a prevailing view of the risks involved in them. When events like deaths and quarrels and rites are referred to which happened a long time before the illness, we see a measure of their persisting significance. Trivial things may be made significant because of coincident timing. Activities like major rites may carry such a load of expectation that when illness happens during their performance it is almost inevitably put down to the attendant concentration of the spirit concerned.

DIAGNOSIS 'SOLE'

When I learnt a diagnosis but was not given circumstantial evidence to support it, I counted it as a diagnosis 'sole'. No doubt some of these instances belong to this category because I failed to find out the evidence. Relative to other instances of diagnosis, the proportion of diagnosis 'sole' is higher in diagnoses of magic and sorcery (26·9 per cent of the instances so diagnosed), illness from individual spirits of the dead (22·2 per cent), and from Panu'et (21·8 per cent), than in the other kinds of diagnosis. The instances of magic and sorcery were ones in which the diagnosis was attached to an illness of sudden onset, or unexpected collapse, or it came in the first reaction to a death as the raising of a possible explanation. The 8 instances which involve spirits of named dead people were nearly all revelations through dreams or spirit possessions, or divination, which identified the spirit. The revelations were made directly to, or through, the sick persons in

4 of these instances. All the 12 instances of Panu'et diagnosis 'sole' refer to illness in women and girls. In most of these, the diagnosis represented little more than a reasonable speculation about what may commonly be expected to cause their illness. Two instances were supported by the 'smelling out' kind of divination. The

Table 41. Diagnosis 'sole': summary

	Number of instances	*% of diagnosis 'sole': N = 39*	*% among instances of the particular kind of diagnosis*
Panu'et	12	30·8%	12/55 = 21·8%
Individual dead spirit	8	20·5%	8/36 = 22·2%
Magic and sorcery	7	17·9%	7/26 = 26·9%
Lineage spirits	6	15·4%	6/42 = 14·3%
Tambin	2	5·1%	2/11 = 18·2%
Malyi	2	5·1%	2/22 = 9·1%
Malet	2	5·1%	2/23 = 8·7%
Taboo	—	—	—
Total	39	99·9%	

others fail to show any distinguishing features as to the kind of illness involved or the kind of person who made the diagnosis. Two instances were those in which the diagnosis was given to dupe me. The diagnoses 'sole' of lineage spirits (6 instances) were rather similar to the Panu'et ones except that they included 4 males' illnesses (notably those of baby boys) and 2 females'.

I do not think much can be learnt from these instances of diagnosis 'sole' except the connection of revelation with the diagnoses of named spirits of individual dead, and the link of suddenness and death with the idea that it could be due to sorcery.

Conclusion

The observations might go on and on. Already the accumulation of findings, their scatter and detail, makes the need pressing not just for summary but for some integration which will show what has been learnt, what we know as a whole, of the recognition and explanation of illness among the Gnau. In attempting it now, I am aware of having concentrated on the recognition and diagnosis of illness, and, in this study, I have not chosen to analyse their treatment of illness with equal care. Indeed there are only tangential comments on it here. For a comprehensive view of illness in Gnau life, a full consideration of treatment would be required.

The first two chapters provided a summary of the main features of the social structure and mode of life of the Gnau people. These two chapters were based on more detailed observations and the account was selective. I set down some items of observation, and made generalized assertions with a view to providing a conspectus which might serve as background for the chief subject of my later attention – illness. I then presented a record of the illness observed over a period of time in a defined population. This record sought to distinguish the amount of illness and its severity as seen by a medical observer. Its aim was to be objective but this aim could not unambiguously and wholly be achieved because of ways in which measures of disease must take the response of the sick person into account. The response to illness depends in part on what the sick person notices about the changes in himself and their significance to him.

The fourth chapter on the behaviour of the sick person began from the observer's standpoint and turned from it to consider the subject's response. The interpretation here was concerned with inferences about the meaning of illness in general which could be drawn from observation of Gnau conduct in illness, and also with some aspects of intention and motive allied to the behaviour which they told me about. With the move to the chapters on the causes of illness and causality in illness, the account became a report of what I learnt about Gnau knowledge and understanding of these subjects. The task was to convey their views as accurately as possible, and the chief difficulty was that of translating them correctly, and describing them with just balance. Having presented the knowledge they have of the causes of illness, I then went back to the illnesses recorded to study how they applied this knowledge to them.

The discussion of illness in general came in between an observer's account of the social organization and a statement of their ideas about the causes of illness. The causes to which they paid special attention seem to be mostly spirits or magic. If we are to say what from an anthropological point of view we have learnt about illness among the Gnau the issues fall into two main areas: those to do with the connections we may discern between their social arrangements, religious beliefs and their behaviour in illness, and those to do with understanding their view of illness as though we were one of them.

What counts as physical illness quite probably attains a fair degree of constancy in different societies. 'Life, long life, ability to procreate, physical capacity, strength, little fatiguability, absence of pain, a lasting state in which the body, apart from pleasurable feelings of its existence, is disregarded as much as possible' (Jaspers 1963, p. 780) are all so obviously desired by everyone that we should not be surprised at the general degree of constancy. The Gnau do not differentiate illness into many varieties of clinical disorder as we do. The main terms of their clinical divisions are (1) those which distinguish between present illness and a completed, altered state; and (2) their distinction between illness in a part and illness of the whole person. This second distinction is the crucial one by which they identify serious illness. The relations and interplay of parts of the body and the whole are glossed over in a decision that the person is ill as a whole. In terms of the verb *neyigeg* the person is held to be either sick or not. They are not so concerned to localize the seat of trouble in a certain anatomical organ or a certain physiological process. The sufferer is either made ill as a whole by some cause, or he is not. The diagnostic emphasis is then on the kind of cause and not the clinical manner or mechanism of illness, the disordering of particular parts which may exercise more or less far-reaching effects on other organs or functions.

The decision about whether someone is ill as a whole is largely left to the individual concerned, unless a child. This contrasts strikingly with the way in which the final decision is held to rest with medical experts in our culture.

Withdrawal and isolation from normal social life mark the behaviour of someone who has taken this decision about sickness. Now the question arises as to the general view of the Gnau about the nature of what is happening in sickness. Is illness something to be expected as a 'natural' event, an intrinsic part of living? Or does it result from an intervention by some cause disordering the 'natural' state of man? The Gnau public view would seem to be weighted towards the optimistic view of life. Their view is that people are in essence healthy, and this is their normal state, from which they are struck down by sickness. The boundary between health and illness of the whole person is made more sharp by the self-decision either sick or not, with sickness shown in behaviour and the notion attached of being struck down by a cause. The person is made a passive victim, impaired in capacity to fulfil his normal roles, withdrawn and cut off from ordinary social life by the intervention of this cause. But for that, he would have been, and should be, well. This view is slightly modified by the more pessimistic understanding of human life which is seen to have a course waxing to full strength and tried experience, and waning then with increasing age into feebleness and vulnerability.

The view of a victim struck down by illness provokes some search to make sense of this kind of event, a search to find why or how he was struck down. This may be interpreted partly in moral terms. Illness harms someone. It prevents him from doing what he would have wished to do, or it denies him the chance to take part in social life as he had expected or hoped to. The reasons for illness may be linked with (1) what is inherent or innate in the human constitution; (2) with things external to people on which they must depend, such as objects, resources and creatures in their environment, the weather; (3) with the knowledge needed to deal safely and wisely with these things and with other people. People make plans, they order and discipline their lives, and the knowledge of how to do things is there to guide their actions. But things go wrong. Illness is one way in which things go wrong. Having the freedom to act, choose, and make plans, people may be held responsible for what goes wrong to the extent that they should know or could have predicted the risks and outcomes of their activities. If things in the environment are known to be intrinsically dangerous to health, the man who flouts some danger may be thought ignorant or foolhardy. Or else he may be thought to have braved the danger for other reasons which outweighed the risk. Here there may be room for fine judgement and difference of opinions about his good sense. But if things in the environment are thought to contain or let loose dangers which people cannot take fully into account before they act, then they cannot be held responsible for suffering which may result. The risks in external things then may come close to appearing as natural risks for they are just there, intrinsic and unpredictable.

If it is illness that they cause, the danger can be recognized only afterwards when it is shown up by the illness. In such a view, the haphazard power in external things to harm is seen to strike some people and neither they nor other people can be blamed for it. The illness is not a punishment but rather an accident of bad luck or chance. It may grieve others to see someone suffer, and it may seem unjust to them. In many cases, the Gnau public or general view of someone's illness resembles most this one of accident and natural misfortune. But to call it natural misfortune is slightly misleading because it would not imply to most readers that, according to Gnau understanding, the external things cause illness usually on purpose and are thought to be aware of their victims. The issue of predictability complicates the field because it is a relative, not an absolute, consideration, a matter of degree. There is a smaller or larger measure of predictability in respect to many things and circumstances, but certainty is not approached. So in the general view of illness, blame or contempt is rarely focussed on the sick person. He is pitied for if only he had known then he might have avoided it, but there may also be some who feel, although less certainly, that he should have known of a risk, or might have guessed at it. These views are retrospective to the illness.

The general attitude to the external causes of illnesses is rather hard to characterize in terms of blame. The notion of an intent or purpose to cause illness, or awareness of the victim, implies some personification of these causes. But they are not blamed in the same way as people are when they are thought to have caused someone's illness. The reason for this is that the causes in external things (in objects and situations) despite their personification as spirit agents, are not persons as people are. They are persons only in fragmented, highly abstracted, respects. Moral judgements are primarily made about the good and bad to be discerned in the ends, means, and intentions of people. Between similarly accountable human moral agents, blame and responsibility can be apportioned. But the Gnau do not know how to judge or understand the ends, means, and intentions of spirit agents as well as they can those of other people. So the interpretation of blame and responsibility is not the same. The wind may harm something or someone; it has the power to do so. If people know nothing of its ends, means, or intentions, or if they consider that it has none, the wind may be blamed as a natural power but its effects are meaningless in moral terms; it is not judged accountable as a human moral agent would be. The distance between moral evaluation by the Gnau of illness thought to be caused by human agents and that thought to be caused by spirit agents reflects how far away their personification of spirits is from a simple anthropomorphic view. Even though they may speak of spirits intending to cause illness, or of spirits being aware of their victims, they do not present such diagnoses as they do those attributed to human agents which carry a heavy moral load. The attitude to illness caused by spirit agents resembles more often and more closely our attitude to the natural forces which cause illness rather than our attitude to those people and situations which we judge in moral terms. The Gnau do not have a sure and clear understanding of the intentions or purposes of spirit agents.

Pity and distress, a sense of injustice, moral evaluation, good sense or stupidity measured against reasonable expectations and a reasonable knowledge of rules and norms, are combined in complex interplay when a particular case of illness is sized up. If the details of particular cases are neglected so as to arrive at an estimate of the general public attitude to illness then it is the view of a person struck down by something close to natural misfortune that first predominates among the Gnau.

As a victim, unfortunate and incapacitated, the sick person by withdrawal and the show of sickness puts on others the obligation and responsibility to seek to get him well again. The distress occasioned in others by someone's sickness, and their recognition of responsibility towards him, also bears witness to their affection for him and their sense of his worth. The fact of illness draws marked attention to the affected person as a particular individual, bringing consideration of his social worth and conduct into play and singling him out. The pattern of isolation and withdrawal in sickness sets the individual apart conspicuously.

In the section above I have had in mind the public or general view of sickness. The sick individual himself must view it with concern for the particular detail of his own case and situation: generalization is less appropriate. His self-decision about sickness is determined by his detailed understanding of the possibilities which might explain what he has noticed in himself, his fears and doubts about his future, the degree and kind of his suffering or incapacity. His individual case, its emotional significance, the isolation of himself as the sufferer, the questions of particular detail, reasons and injustice, may be presumed to dominate over detached interest in it as a general kind of event. In like but less immediate ways, the close relatives of the sick person are most concerned with the particulars of the case and also do not view it with detachment. Illness may present an intellectual problem over knowing why it should happen and what sort of thing it is for the public in general, but for the sick person in particular, the more general intellectual problems are bound up and submerged in the emotional and personal significance of his own case.

One feature to stress about illness is how in a small community like a Gnau village, it focusses public attention on an individual.

In certain respects there are parallels to the events of illness in rituals, particularly in *rites de passage*. Passage through a crisis and special attention are common to them both. Special and selective attention is given to ordinary things and they may gain greater or changed significance in the light of the illness. Religious ideas and items of belief or knowledge are drawn on to understand it. But the relation of illness to such knowledge and belief is contingent on the illness having happened. There are, on the one hand, rules or established ideas which relate certain actions or events to a possibility of illness. These serve as guides for safe conduct, as well as asserting a view about the risk and significance of certain actions and events. Ritual and *rites de passage* serve in part to establish and assert the value and significance of various particular objects, actions or states. The rites are carried out according to set patterns and are highly ordered. They are done in a planned, prospective way. On the other hand, illness is most powerful in giving significance to events retrospectively. Illness upsets the ordinary pattern of life and thereby provokes a search to understand its cause and significance. Because it comes into everyday life unexpected and unplanned, it may impose, at least in the view of the observer who does not share Gnau ideas or thinks them false, a strain on ordered or systematic aspects of their knowledge and belief if they are to be used to explain it. The illness comes at a tangent to the system of belief but an explanation has to be worked out which will meet its contingencies. The fact of the illness may cast a new or different light on what had gone before. It reveals things. Knowledge and belief has sometimes to be accommodated to the facts of illness. The observer who does not think illness results from the causes they refer to may then look with interest at how they accommodate their knowledge to explain it, and he may hope to see in their choices and methods some reflection of the relative significance which they attach to these beliefs.

The scale of Gnau society is small, both in numbers of people, and the range of their movements. In activities and expertise, and in style of life, there is no marked variation between its different members. The positioning of village houses makes the spatial organization of social groups appear stable and clear, and fits with the main features of daily frequent social contact. The village is nucleated and divided into hamlets. Men remain based on one hamlet for all their lives. Women move to the hamlets of their husbands. Until recently the men slept in a single common hamlet's men's house, but there are now sometimes two or three men's houses in a hamlet; each woman and her small children sleep in a separate house. The women's houses are rebuilt from time to time and they may be placed in slightly different arrangements, but always within the hamlet ground. In daily contact, hamlet relations are close and habitual. Its members go to work at gardens and there the separation of component families is evident for they may go off to different areas of bush. They return to eat and sleep in the hamlet. Organized hunting by men is done mainly in hamlet groups. The annual celebration of the first yams of the gardening year is a hamlet event. Large-scale rites are organized in effect by one hamlet and the rest of the village comes to take part. The village as a whole is also a clear bounded unit, and relations between its members are habitual, but less close and frequent than those within hamlets. Most marriages take place within the village. All people, except some women because of marriage, live out their lives in one village. For most common purposes, people take hamlet or village as the basis of social grouping when they think or act in co-operative alignment for disputes or defence, or co-operation in major ritual, in hunting and in claims to land. Spatial proximity and the closeness of daily social relations go together almost parallel.

The conjugal family is clearest as a unit in the production of food, and in most gardening activities. It is differentiated also by its perennial exchange obligations towards matrilateral and affinal kin, these involve garden food exchange. The family has its own separate garden house. Conjugal families linked by common patrilineal descent co-operate in some of the heavier gardening activities and associate at tracts of garden land. Their different garden houses are often close together. They also tend to share a day-house in the hamlet and a particular part of the hamlet ground. The wives of such groups of families sharing common descent often work together in sago production. The wives help each other in looking after children. The groups of families co-operate closely in large-scale transactions to do with marriage, stages of the individual life-cycle, and death.

Common patrilineal descent also links dispersed sets of families who share lineage or clan. These links may be between families in different hamlets of the same village and between families in different villages, even between people in villages where different languages are spoken. Ties of common descent are spread more widely than alliance through marriage. Such ties of shared descent within one village may lead to association at gardens and in hunting, because of common claims to land. They also entail assistance in the major marriage and death transactions, and they imply certain kinds of shared ritual knowledge and the duty to assist in some ritual activities. Ties of descent between villages are the bases of possible claims to assistance in fighting and dispute; rights of refuge and provision of land to use in other villages if needed; duties to come to mourn for the death of members of the group; to come for major rites: and generally to maintain the link by occasional visits.

But daily relations are overwhelmingly restricted to ones

within the village. Hamlets form the chief arena of close daily contact. Matrilateral and affinal relationships produce a dense network of ties between families of different hamlets, and to a less important degree with certain families of the nearest neighbouring villages. The relations involve perennial exchange obligations, duties at the *rites de passage* of members of the families; help in crisis, and visiting. Patrilineal descent provides a network of links between families dispersed, in some cases, in different hamlets of a single village, but more importantly in different villages. These recognized ties are dispersed more widely than ties of marriage. They provide the widest potential range of safety, welcome and assistance. Imposed peace and administrative change has of course altered the range of safe travel. It has led to men going to plantation work, and it has created new political and administrative alignments of villages through the system of local government. But the scale and range of ordinary social relations has not yet altered much, except in respect of the new range of travel by men going to plantation work, their long absences, and the frequency with which other nearby villages are visited because they are now safe to go to.

Gnau social organization is stable in the sense that people do not move from one village to another, do not change their hamlet of residence, do not continually shift the groups with which they co-operate. They live out their lives associating with roughly the same people and see a great deal of them. They have to accommodate to each other. But there is a big difference between the sexes because women go to live in their husband's hamlet at marriage. They may have to change villages. Marriage is a point which allows some choice at which new links may be established between families and to a lesser degree between hamlets and villages. The relations created by marriages involve the conjugal and extended families most intensively, and once established by the birth of children, some obligations are set up between families which should last for the next two generations. Again stability can be noted in the peculiarly persistent and exact nature of Gnau attention to genealogy and the traditions of clan links and dispersal but these ties are not used for many practical purposes in daily life. Most families would go for short stays at other villages only about two or three times a year. The new habit of peace allows people to stay at distant bush camps to hunt, sometimes for a few weeks, and then people may stay at the camps of clan, affinal, or matrilateral relatives belonging to their own villages but not of their own hamlet. Such stays provide some variation for the most familiar hamlet round of daily life.

As to categories of social person, the important differences are those to do with sex, age, marital and reproductive status. The distribution of most job activities is segregated according to sex. For women these activities do not change much with age; only the burden changes and is heavier when a woman's family is growing. For men, the activities of garden work do not change much after marriage but experience and age bring greater ritual responsibilities; in some hunting activities men's responsibilities change with proved experience and achievement. There is a measure of competitive differentiation between men in the graded acquisition of hunting magic and the marks won to show achievement. Formerly achievement in fighting and killing was also significant. In most rituals men of age and experience (but not women) take responsibility for their organization and different roles are taken on by those who stand in appropriate kinship position to fill them. In most other respects more specific than general type of subsistence activity or job, the rights and duties to act in relation to other people and their requirements are set by kinship relationship. These relations provide the important categories for determining the distribution of roles in co-operative social, political and religious activities. There is no alternative enduring structure of offices to be achieved through special expertise or knowledge, either in religious or political life, except for the positions introduced by the Administration which were called *luluai*, *tultul*, *siutboi* and, though officially discontinued, they still remain as titles used by the Gnau to refer to the men who last occupied them. There are also the present offices of local government called *kaunsil* and *komiti*.

Some aspects of these general features of social organization are reflected by behaviour in illness. The particular pattern of the stereotyped show of illness by social withdrawal acts as an effective call on other people's sense of responsibility in a community which is small in numbers, where people see a lot of each other, and news spreads quickly. I think the higher frequency and intensity of hamlet relations was shown up by the preponderance of cases I learnt about from the hamlet in which I lived, although of course it might be argued that this reflects more on my conduct with them, rather than on their own natural conduct among themselves. Dependence on the village community is marked and the lack of mobile intervillage experts in healing reflects the boundedness and self-sufficiency of the community. The lack of occupational specialization is a feature of their medicine as it is in their general organization. Older experienced men tend to play a more important role in diagnosis and in organizing treatment as they do in other ritual activities, but kinship relationships are also important in these spheres.

Certain differences between men and women were found in men's readiness to take their own trivial illnesses seriously and in the younger women's demonstrative show of illness to justify themselves in not fulfilling heavy domestic duties. The mobility of women in illness who return to their natal hamlets, and certain different patterns of explanation for their illness reflect the particular activities of women, the change of residence required of a wife, and her gradual slow involvement and acceptance in her new hamlet of residence. In general their diagnoses show few differences distinguishing age and sex markedly. Explanation mostly involves familiar things which come from within the range of home territory and the emphasis in general is not on disruptions of social relationships. It tends to avoid imputations of ill-will between villagers.

We face now the question of identifying what type of religious system the Gnau have, and then the place of illness in it. My first concern is to note the spheres of ordinary Gnau life in which religion enters. Here I am looking for what parallels there are between everyday or common ordinary concerns and the concerns shown by their religious life. The bias of this look is given by the suggestion that religion may be approached as a collection of ideas and practices which are socially determined, or present social realities in another guise. Yet it may be argued that one of the effects of religion is to establish relative priorities and values among people's different concerns. Or reversing back to the first stand, it may be held that social priorities dictate religious forms. To take the one side or the other is to argue for a causal connection and its direction: to take neither is to look only for correlation. It is obvious that food is of concern for all people, that for the Gnau a great part of their time is spent in growing, finding or producing it, that the work of men and women in producing the different kinds of food they eat is not identical and in this respect they must depend upon each other. It is true that their main food is sago and that women do most work to produce it, but they could not live by sago alone. Given their physical environment, yams and taro might be alternative to sago as the staple, yet their place is secondary, and marked by the way they garden so that there is a co-ordinated annual cycle to Gnau life, clear in the gardening year, which does not seem so strictly imposed on them by climate and rainfall. They use yams and taro for special purposes in social life as stuff for gatherings and feasts, and stuff to be given in special token of the relations set up by marriage and childbirth. There is a variety of other vegetable foods, some of which are put within the province of great spirits, but none so clearly as sago belongs to Panu'et, yams, taro and *wadagep* to both their *mama* spirit and Tambin and Malyi. And yet some other vegetable foods like the leaves and fruit of *teltati* tree and *pitpit*, have no special spirit linked with them. The concern of particular great spirits with particular kinds of vegetable food makes a division of spirit labour. To such great spirits the Gnau would seem to impute a general watching brief over specific kinds of vegetable wherever these kinds of food are found, and not a parochial concern only for what some restricted social group of people grow. The spirits which watch over the parochial concerns of particular social groups are those of the lineage as a collectivity. These are associated with tracts of land, as well as with hamlets and men's houses. A claim to land and a right to use it to grow things on is also required for food to be produced in peace. Lineage spirits are said to act on great spirits, to be a way of approach and appeal to them, to activate them. Both general kinds of food and particular tracts of land are necessary: both great spirits and particular lineage spirits are concerned with food.

There is some specialization among the great spirits and an allocation of differentiated responsibilities and attributes to them. These spheres of responsibility and relevance to mundane activities and food are not bound by local accident and history only to certain social groups. But some social groups hold priority in the knowledge and performance of the major rites of great spirits. Different lineages of the same clan may be distributed in various villages, each at its place holding and sharing that ritual priority. Since people are all alike in the kinds of food they produce, and since only some have a priority of ritual access in the major rites, the miscellany of major rites of the great spirits that the various people at a given village may perform comprise a common wealth of major ritual exercised occasionally and for the common good of all the village members who come together to take part and assist those who put on the rites which they hold first and before other people.

There is no local god or spirit of the village as a whole, single and unshared by others, peculiar to it as social and political unit. But the village is a federation of clans and lineages. Those clans and lineages with special rites for great spirits perform them in company with the whole village. And the benefits are not restricted and exclusive. In certain instances, the great spirits recognized by particular clans, and some in foreign villages, are identified despite their different names with one of the great spirits, as though whatever name the spirit has elsewhere, it is recognizable according to the division of its interests. There is a tendency to universalize the great spirits.

In comparison to vegetable foods, different animal foods are not clearly associated with the interest of one or another spirit. No one kind of animal belongs so exclusively to a great spirit as sago does to Panu'et. Performance of the major rites of all of them are said to have some virtue for success in hunting. The emphasis is, however, not so much on the particular kind of animal food as on the kind of activity by which it is procured.

It might be argued that the things which people talk a lot about and boast about provide clues to what they value and admire; we should therefore look for religious themes that may correspond to them. I will take my impressions for rough guides. It should be noted that on many occasions the men were assertive and boastful, but Gnau women were very rarely so, or rarely so in my presence. The men boasted of their land and its great extent; that they were first there and the true owners by virtue of their ancestry; that they had much food; that they hunted well and with success. Talk about hunts was drawn out, animated and assertive: it was perhaps the most congenial subject at gatherings of men. Though peace had been imposed more than twenty years before, they still talked enthusiastically over the details of former fights, of what each man had done, of how they were strong then, and feared as a fierce village.

They also talked, but less loudly, of their numbers, their progeny, their physique and health, their adherence to tradition, the magnificence of their rites if they should put them on. Subjects such as the arrangement of marriages, disputes both within and between villages, domestic disputes, illnesses and sorcery, men going off to plantation work, taxes and their lack of money, their disadvantages of distance and neglect in opportunity to obtain the goods that could be acquired by having white men among them, were also recurrent (but less evident) themes of discussion. They did not talk much about rearing pigs, or about leading men and their merits, character, qualities, or following. There was no focus on big men.

No people look upon the world and see its objects and events objectively, solely as matters of existing fact. They all give some sort of selective meaning to the world bound up with emotional responses. They pay it attention and are pleased or fearful about some things, indifferent to others. In these responses they assign value, interest, and meaning to mundane things, but selectively and according to particular perspectives and prejudices. There is a difference between the mere sensing of all that is around, and the perceiving of it, and seeing its significance. The goals and common sense activities of ordinary life provide many important perspectives on things and events, but religious knowledge and items of belief also have effects on the priorities and relativities among these common sense interests. Knowledge of skills and social rules largely order people's activities in some spheres of life and they follow proper procedures, either for fear of failure in what they would wish to accomplish, or for fear of punishment or contempt at the hands of their fellow men. Then what does religion add further and how far does it pervade and alter ordinary activities and their significance: what are its claims on human attention and performance?

For the Gnau, there are prescriptions and prohibitions on specific acts, the field of their taboos, in which the dangers of non-obedience are intrinsic. To generalize, this field for the Gnau is one in which the rules are set by the status of the person in age, sex and achievement. Taboos apply to individual persons according to these criteria and not according to membership of specific social groups such as clan, lineage, village or hamlet ones. For both sexes some of these rules relate to physical growth, development and maturity, and some to interpersonal relations of kinship. The aspect of achievement, first couched in terms of physical development, later becomes differentiated between the sexes so that the rules alter according to reproductive achievement and status particularly for women, and alter for men particularly according to achievement in hunting, and, as it used to be, by achievement in killing. In the case of men, the typical emphasis ascribed to the danger in disobedience of taboo is failure in hunting or incapacity to hunt. In the case of women it is either illness or harm to her or her family, or harm to her husband's ability to hunt. These are taboos linked chiefly with general conduct, the body and its functions, and eating kinds of food. More specifically in the context of particular gardening activities, there are rules or taboos in which the harm of disobedience falls chiefly on the crops and secondarily carries a risk of illness to the actors. The diagnosis of breach of taboo has a significantly different distribution among men and women.

From the point of view of Gnau men, many of the taboos concerned with development and achievement have to do with strength, health and the ability to hunt well. The ability to hunt and kill can still be seen to be so closely linked that I suppose in the past this stress was more clearly woven up with fighting and security as well as with hunting. To stand out as a man of achievement required success in hunting and killing. Hunting still remains as the field of competitive aspiration and boasting. Meat food is specially valued. It is used in major exchanges, particularly at the points of development and changes in the family, at marriage, first birth, puberty and death, when affinal and matrilateral relations are established or reaffirmed. It is used for feasts and celebration but not ordinary daily eating. It is no staple. The value set on hunting achievement, desire and care for it, are put into many requirements and fixed rules of taboo. They affect the personal conduct of men, and some aspects of the conduct of women are also fixed by rules in which disobedience is said to harm not themselves but their men's capabilities. The glamour of achievement is for men not women. In the field of taboo there are many signs of that segregation of the sexes seen also in the pattern of daily life, in sleeping arrangements, jobs, housing, social intercourse and at meals. The men hold the public eye. They lead, the women follow.

The *rites de passage* of the life cycle and the rites of progressive initiation into esoteric hunting knowledge are determined by the particular development or achievements of individuals, rather than organized according to an independently fixed calendar or cyclical order. The rites are not the major rites of a great spirit, though elements within the rites throw out lines of association to bits and pieces of major rites and beliefs belonging to great spirits. But the *rites de passage* are specific to their purpose, not centrally associated with one spirit.

They are specific to their purpose in the same way as the major rites called Lyigut, though grander, were fully specific to the achievement of killing an enemy, and were celebrated by the whole village at the hamlet of the killer, or killers, as necessary first to the occasion and its moment for the man, not first because a spirit or the spirits of his lineage claimed this attention, even though lineage spirits and others spirits were invoked in the rites of Lyigut as they are in *rites de passage* and hunting rites.

The major rites of Tambin are an exception to what is written above in the sense that they are the central rites of a great spirit and are also performed for the chief reason, the Gnau at Rauit said, that men had to go into seclusion and pass through the rites to become fully adult and have their benefit. Passage through the rites was required as the most proper way to gain the distinction of wearing adult male head-dress. The rites had to be performed periodically so that batches of young men could be initiated in them, but they were the major rites of the spirit Tambin. These rites, though not yet extinct, have fallen into desuetude.

By coming back now to gardening activities after the foregoing remarks on hunting, it is easier to see the difference in religious focus. In gardening, the rules of performance which have behind them reference to religious knowledge or items of belief, are orientated, not chiefly to the persons who do the gardening, nor to the spirits involved (i.e., great spirits or lineage spirits), but to the activity in hand and its outcome – that things will go well with the crop or food. People perform these set acts as necessary to the job of growing or producing the food and perform them more or less individually at the garden sites where they work. The performances or activities are not like major rites in which the whole community or some smaller congregation focusses its attention on a performance expected, exacted, or required of them by a spirit which claims this worship from them. The activities of gardening are fixed chiefly to the mundane and material job of producing food, although some bits of what must be done are explicitly directed at spirits, or may be explained by their exigencies. Certain actions and objects involved may be associated with what is done or used in major rites, and also with risks to persons. The focus on practice and the gardening job is such that religious ideas and knowledge about the unseen beings or powers which are behind, and responsible for, natural things enter into the conduct of everyday gardening and pervade it but in a way that is less religious than magical. Success in these activities may be secured if the job is done rightly in a regular ordered way according to proper techniques. But attention to the spirits associated with aspects of these ordered activities is not marked as such, except in special circumstances and usually then it is retrospective. The sense of security comes from the satisfactory and proper performance of tried and tested techniques rather than from something like the reassurance to be obtained in the experience of worship of a great spirit or a god.

The major rites of great spirits are different in the way that attention is given to the spirit which claims the performance. By performance the spirit is concentrated and localized among them. They do the rites for the spirit. But of course there are other reasons apart from this for doing them. For example, the main rites of Panu'et are done when a new *gamaiyit*, men's house, is built. This must be rebuilt from time to time. In these rites a particular hamlet is the stage, the house is built for its men and their lineage spirits, to fire their hunting ash. The rites of Tambin used to be done periodically to put the young men through them, and make them men. The rites of Malyi, which serves in some other villages as Tambin does at Rauit, were performed at Rauit because they were required to treat someone sick. They were done at this instance. But in all these major rites, there are many associations with benefits and circumstances associated with their performance and linked to other activities, situations, and contexts outside the time and place of performing the rites. The magnificence of the rites, the size of congregation, and the orientation to the spirits, give a quality of worship to them but only to a relative degree which is shot through with assertive and coercive invocation, desire for specific favours to be granted in return for the attentions given.

Each time that major rites are held, some particular hamlet is the centre of their staging. They are held at the hamlet of the group which instigates and organizes their performance. There are those who put them on and those who assist them. From different points of view the groups primarily concerned are more or less finely distinguished: to people of other villages, it is the given village group which puts them on: within the village, it is the particular hamlet; within the hamlet, the particular lineage or clan. As a congregation, the whole village is involved by the requirements of assistance. The people's activities and attention are regulated and co-ordinated by involvement in the rites. Visitors from other villages may come for a day or two to them because they have some clan or other kinship tie with the chief organizers of the rites. But they are not so closely involved as all the home villagers. The stage for the rites and the group of organisers shifts around the village. Because rites must take place at a definite hamlet and be instigated and organized by a particular group, so for a given performance there is a place and group singled out as the local leaders of the rites each time that they are done. They put them on. But a distinction between ritual officiants and congregation is not clearly emphasized. Rather it is a matter of participation in which some take a relatively greater part and others a lesser part. In major rites the older and more experienced men tend to organize the performance, but those who have instigated it, lead and decide its timing, not dictatorially, but easily and guided by discussion, volunteered advice, opinion and proffered readiness to co-operate. According as some men are acknowledged to have good grasp of how to do the rites or have by ancestry a special link with them, so they may be listened to when advice on the performance is given; or they may help to organize it, even though the rites are not primarily put on by them at their own hamlet. But they would not be seen by others to have led them in the sense that the men of the hamlet where the rites are done are said to. The organization is not that of a priesthood in a cult – a priesthood with special expertise in doctrinal, liturgical and ritual matters. Men, generally, in part for reasons attached to birth, kinship and ancestry, in part for reasons linked with achievement and experience, come to the fore in ritual in various ways that shift according to the choice of time, place and occasion.

The spirits identified by the Gnau comprise a miscellany of almost accidental entities. In a single village, the ones to be found are accidental in that they result from the associations and dispersals in the past of different social groups who knew about them. The different spirits in each village are not ordered systematically in one hierarchy, nor are the people. There is no original, supreme or local god, no spirit of the village as a whole. Each lineage has its lineage spirits and these are associated with places as well as with the groups. The lineage or the clan may also claim a special relationship to certain great spirits. There is to some degree an ordering into more general and more particular spirits – the more general or universal are the great spirits, the more particular the lineage spirits, but the separations between them are not distinct and unambiguous, either in speech and the words to designate them, or in ways of approach to them, or in the identifications of their interests and responsibilities. There is no priesthood specially concerned with doctrinal and ritual nicety, with religious system and ordering. Their spirit beings form a frankly pluralistic aggregate of higher and lower things and principles rather than a unitary system. Their universe is composed of many original principles, accidental and irrelevant for some spheres of life, of central concern in others, or on other occasions, or for other people. In practice, much of their religion relates to everyday concerns, to commonsense and mundane activities. It is a religion of this world, pervading a great variety of contexts. Its domain is not contracted to a demarcated and occasional sphere of social life but it is part of common life. Except for the sporadic major rites when they are put on, religious knowledge and items of belief enter daily life as natural observances rather than as something demanding the intense attention and conviction which might be expected of observances associated with the supernatural or the sacred. The observances are for the most part highly determinate and related to specific persons, relationships, or activities in hand, or to specific situations, and they have the magical character of clear context and purpose rather than the larger more diffuse emotional, moral, or intellectual character of aims set by sacred duty towards spirit beings.

It would be hard to see in these observations causal connections that clearly run from the form of their society to the form of their religion, except in some more general ways. For example, the importance of sago and vegetable foods as staples, and the spirit commonwealth, but then why are some vegetable foods left out? An absence of hierarchy either among spirits or among men is common to both: but the village is clearly bounded and a political unit, its people and their social organization stable, not mobile, in many respects, yet there is no local god, no rite for the village as a whole, and little emphasis on the fixed associations of spirits to places. A selective eye and casuistry would be needed to persuade the detail of their religious beliefs and practices to fit a mould putatively set by their social organization as a whole. There are ways in which their religion serves to set value on social life, or to put relative emphasis and priority on different acts and situations, as, for example, by the major rites of great spirits which require co-ordinated action by the village and are thought to bring certain benefits to all the village participants, and their spirits form a commonwealth; or as hunting is differentiated from gardening activities in the values given them. If it is suggested that the causal connection is from social forms to religious ideas, then in some fields of Gnau life we can point to plausible correspondences, and we have a sense of understanding why the beliefs are so, but this only after the parallel has been found. I cannot set out an account of their society and then go through it feature by feature to say what we should expect of their religion and show we find it. The suggestion of correspondence and connection would hold only for selected items, and even then might hold only with zeal for the interpretation. To maintain the view, if it can only be done by selection and interpretation, would also require an explanation with reasons for the neglect of other features and a statement of the principles of the interpretation. I shall not try to maintain it.

As to control and good order in social life, religion and items of belief support many rules of conduct by prescribing definite observances and by indicating or suggesting risks consequent on disobedience. They apply to many different contexts and activities, sometimes to pose a threat, sometimes to justify a line of conduct or a claim of right. The rules, the rights and duties of main importance, are quite clear and generally known. Because the range and variety of situations are similar and limited for all people in the community, there are rules or guides for most of what is common and familiar in their life, for most eventualities. The scale of the community is small, hardly any social dealings take place with anonymous others, each is usually well known to the other. There was, before the imposition of peace, little chance of acceptance anywhere but at one's home village. The community in a village had to accommodate to each other. Upbringing and knowledge of the rules, readiness to abide by them, especially in areas where disobedience would infringe on the rights of others, provided and still ensures a large measure of village harmony. Neglect of duty towards others would or might provoke a reciprocal suspension of support or assistance. More hurtful wrong done to others has to be resolved, either through toleration by reason of weakness, or by redress. Redress of serious wrong depends most on self-assertion and on an earnest willingness to fight for rights and to revenge wrongs. Within the village both protagonists expect and need support from their kin and neighbours. Thus disputes may be divisive and acutely disruptive in the village, because the point of physical fighting is easily reached in open dispute about flagrant wrong. The habitual trouble-maker puts a heavy burden on his kin, and on others more widely, and there may be strong reasons for them to persuade him to change or make him correct his conduct. Dependence on support from others provides a strong incentive for straight dealing and observance of the basic rules of conduct towards others. It used not to be easy to flee from trouble to another village. There is also knowledge of the prospect of attack by others' lineage spirits, and the possibility of black magic used against one, if one does wrong to someone else. Insofar as personal idiosyncrasy does not obstruct or harm the rights of others, the Gnau seemed to allow a latitude in behaviour and to tolerate individual variation. There was little evidence of any organized punishment by which to repress behaviour that might be described as a crime against the interests of society as a whole. When individuals or social groups had wrong done them, then they sought to right it if they felt they were strong enough to do so; if not they had to tolerate it or resort to secret redress through magic or sorcery. There is room for individual initiative and some flexibility of response towards such wrong depending most on the strength of support that can be recruited among kin. Collective authority dependent on all people thinking the same about the rules of right and wrong is not enough to ensure observance in the detail of each situation; flexibility of response and variation is to be seen in the social consequences of wrong action. Part of this flexibility derives from the estimate of individual merit, worth and achievement in an egalitarian small society. Within the social unit of the village different people are too well known as individuals for them to be treated as faceless social persons whose individual qualities are overridden and submerged by their identification with whatever particular social position they occupy.

Illness comes into life unexpected and unplanned. Because Gnau religious beliefs and items of knowledge are pluralistic and not ordered into a flawless unitary system, the world of their conceptions allows many possibilities of harm from one or other of the aggregated principles held to be at work in it. The explanation of illness does not have to be accommodated to one single line and sole original source for this evil in human life. There are many ways in which people might be maladjusted with (and so harmed by) things, powers or principles in their environment, which are relatively unordered and accidental on a natural plane. I have indicated above that there are few situations apart from major rites in which people's attention is concentrated on spirits and belief rather than on practical activities. But illness, once it has happened, does require a careful consideration of such knowledge and beliefs to understand, if it be serious illness, why it has happened, and what treatment should be done. The sick person and those close to him must come to a decision about what they really think and believe and it is this that gives to illness a special place as revealer of unseen powers and forces that are part of everyday life but not normally given special attention. It is a question of the use of knowledge and the answers may reflect an estimation of its truth and relevance. They show up conviction and belief. Illness generates part of this knowledge. It constitutes for the Gnau an acute and distressing form of contact and experience of things to do with their religion. It prompts people to perform rites of treatment directed at spirits, sometimes major rites. In the variety of their diagnoses, concentration was found on spirits in relation to food and gardening activities, on one's own work and places and familiar things, rather than on things of strangers, or on quarrels and disharmony in social relationships. If major rites awaken ideas and sentiments, attach the present to the past, the individual to the collectivity, so also does illness. Its peculiar character, however, is given in the Gnau situation by the retrospective emphasis and the individuation, or singling out and separation, of the patient.

As a mode of medicine, it lacks the systematic ordering and institutionalization that would fit it to be called a medical system. Made as it is of a great variety of kinds of knowledge to penetrate why things should be as they are, questions of proof and disproof remain uncertain. The reference to evidence in diagnosis, and interpretations of it, follow general rules of logic in terms of space, time, category, person and cause. But in detail the variety of bits and pieces of possible evidence, the selective attention given now to one facet of the situation, then another, permit multiple explanations for the same illness along different lines of reasoning. The pressure in present illness is to know what to do about it, and the desire to bring about the healing of the sick person leads them to try the remedy if there are grounds for thinking it might work. Consistency, logical closure, uniformity and singleness of explanation are not prized in the face of serious illness and the overriding need to make decisions about treatment. The pressure to rationalize the decision would be greater if the range of possible explanation were confined to a more strictly limited and ordered scheme of knowledge, or to a single theme of explanation, or if it fell only to special experts in healing to give an expert diagnosis, for then the rightness or wrongness of their verdict would involve the justice of their professional claim to special knowledge and their authority. As many treatments may be made in one illness, as the prognosis, and the speed of action of a treatment, are unspecified and uncertain, the conditions of proof or disproof for some particular explanation and remedy are not set out or clear. The eventual view of what really caused an illness or what made it better is a matter of assertion or of personal conviction rather than one of public import and consensus. The Gnau would belong to the Empirical rather than the Rationalist School in medicine.

The data assembled in the previous chapter showed the conditions for which explanations were provided. The severity of illness received some recognition, and there was no evidence that illness in women was disregarded. Although I have examined at length diagnoses and the elements that went to their making, it must be recalled that over half the illnesses were not explained. Much of this was illness of a trivial sort where the cause of the illness or the source of pain or irritation was visible and directly understandable, or it did not last long or seem to worsen enough to provoke that concern which would lead them to bring forward a diagnosis. At the beginning of many illnesses there is a period of waiting, perhaps accompanied by withdrawal and precautionary food avoidance, to see whether it is just a brief sickness, something 'without cause' (*gipi'i'*), that will disappear by itself, requiring no explanation or special treatment. The withdrawal of the patient has itself a therapeutic aspect: at least it is seen as a protective measure. But sometimes even in transient or trivial illness, there may be reasons for anxiety and for discerning some cause and taking steps to treat it.

They deal with experience, as all people do, selectively. Their first attention is given to recent circumstances and they review these in the light of what they know of risk and danger, the predictability and likelihood of illness. The rules and prohibitions for right conduct, the statements of belief about the activities and interests of spirits contain much for guidance in what must be done, controlled, or avoided if the basic need of freedom from illness is to be achieved and the ideal of health to be approached. Their way in the diagnosis of illness is rather similar to the approach we use to discover the cause or causes of an accident. In this book I have chosen to deal with the recognition of illness and the explanation of its causes. I have sought to present the whole range of features involved in their interpretations of illness, and have first used external medical criteria to decide the scope of my inquiry. Thus I have neither selected only cases of interest or concern to them, nor only a particular collection of cases in which explanation and treatment were coherently and systematically related. Instead I have tried to define the total extent of bodily misfortune and then to show how far and in what ways they understood it. This emphasis on the recognition and explanations of illness in their society has precluded an account of treatment in Gnau society. My choice of emphasis was influenced by the wish to show the place of illness in their view of the world.

In discussing the behaviour of the sick person, I raised the question of comparison and the use of a category such as 'medicine' in anthropology. It is clear that not all societies agree about the conditions to be counted as illness. They hold various views about the causes involved. I asked whether there were any clear external grounds to differentiate the sector of human misfortune we call disease or illness, and argued that there were certain biological criteria for doing so. If these were acceptable then we would have a basis for comparing the social or cultural factors affecting its occurrence, recognition and treatment. If on the other hand, it were argued that social criteria necessarily played a large part in deciding what was to be called disease, then the decision would vary from group to group; the demarcation of disease would shift and we would be worse placed to analyse the interrelations between disease and culture. In passing I would point out that the biological standpoint advocated here applies equally in our own culture, and puts the onus on medicine to show what there is that is harmful to survival or reproduction about some of the human conditions which we define as appropriate for medical care. It may equally oblige us to reconsider and to recognize that sometimes what we call illness is only what we are brought up to disapprove of. It is also true that with the development of medical knowledge, we have been led to realize that the causes of some kinds of condition or behaviour are biological, and not sin, immorality or wickedness; and our treatment of such conditions has sometimes thereby changed to become more reasonable, effective and humane. To look at another society and see how it delimits the field of illness and how it treats it may bring us to a clearer recognition of how far social forces or convention determine responses to disease and affect its outcome.

But apart from this comparative issue, I also considered whether there was anything about disease which might lead us to expect a universal recognition of illness as distinctive in some way from other misfortunes. It has been argued that in some societies illness is not distinguished from other forms of misfortune. The fact, often recorded, that the causes of illness are the same as those for other kinds of misfortune does not convince me that illness is not distinguished. Among English people, there are some ready to speak of bad luck causing illness; the fact that bad luck may show itself in illness or a lost bet does not imply failure to distinguish the kinds of misfortune any more than the fact that fire may burn a house or someone's skin implies the forms of misfortune are not distinguished. Why should the same not be true of a spirit which causes crop failure and human infertility? My point of departure was the recognition of sickness in a person. The reason is simple. For it is what has happened to him or her that must be helped, healed or explained. If people did not fall sick – as they do in every society – there would be no need to find explanations or causes for such misfortunes or to treat them. Illness is a distinctive form of misfortune by its outstanding characteristic, that some individual is directly harmed. That individual, a self, is the subject, or for others the human object, of the harm, having a private direct experience of it which cannot be equally or identically shared by anyone else. Thus illness is a misfortune sensed by the sick person in ways which other misfortunes, like his house burning down, are not. And since some diseases destroy or maim the individual, having the power to alter or abolish a living identified member of that society, it seems to me unlikely that any society would fail to distinguish at least part of the whole field of disease from other misfortunes.

The discussion of whether illness can be distinguished from other kinds of misfortune is in part obscured by an ambiguity, when one speaks of illness, arising out of its dual reference both to causal entities and to the conditions of people. Illness would not be known without the change in condition of a person first occurring. The essential criteria of the biological view of disease – functional changes that harm the capacity of an individual to survive and reproduce – are matters of life and death and essential to the continuation of any society. In the Gnau word for critical sickness (*neyigeg*) we find recognition of this relationship to death, and I think the great emphasis on the treatment of infertility and barrenness that is found, for example, in the indigenous medicine of various West African peoples – the stress on this as a major component of medicine – becomes in part more readily understandable with the realization of what is involved in the biological view of disease.

The condition recognized, then follows the question of its explanation and the question of how illness is placed in a given cosmology. If illness is in varying degree a matter of life and death, the causes believed to produce illness might be expected to reveal much about the nature of the culture through their interrelations with other aspects of the society and culture. I have provided a general account of the various beliefs by which illness is explained in Gnau thought. The explanation of illness did not fall within a single or a sharply demarcated frame but ramified into many aspects of their culture. The occurrence of actual illness poses a problem of selecting explanation, and choosing treatment; the outcome also reflects back upon the discerned causes of the illness. The great spirits to which the Gnau ascribe some illnesses are, in one sense of the word, natural; they are present and a part of the Gnau world, though neither directly visible nor wholly predictable. In this, the view of spirits as causes of sickness does not differ so greatly from our view of certain bacteria or viruses, which are present in our environment and may sometimes, though not predictably, cause illness.

The Gnau rules of correct behaviour, the warnings about rash action in regard to these spirits give some, but not certain, protection against the illness caused by them. As the detailed analyses of their diagnoses showed, they selected only certain aspects of the spirits' interests to explain illness. These were ones primarily associated with vegetable foods, garden work, subsistence and, less often, with the performance of major ritual. Work to produce the food essential to subsistence is hard, the labour repetitive and unexciting; it is not the object of social competition with prestigious rewards, since the Gnau have not made food exchanges a focus of social competition. Food exchanges are rather matters of obligation to affinal and matrilateral relatives and chiefly confined within the village, serving to confirm continuing social bonds. On the other hand, success in hunting is the main criterion of admired male achievement, now that fighting is forbidden. The formal marks of advance, the right to carry a hunting bag (*lagil bawug*) to wear the hornbill on one's back, permission to eat certain foods, come only with proved success. Although the same spirits have influence over success in this sphere as well as over success in subsistence activities, the spirits' interests and responsibilities for hunting were not brought forward to account for illness. Gardening activities and vegetable foods, the matter of daily subsistence and survival, provided the commonest grounds for explaining illness; and the risks from spirits held to be involved in this area of their lives received frequent confirmation by illness, while the risks involved in the dramatic, highly valued and prestigious field of hunting did not. Hunting comes within the sphere of social competition between men, and the positive beneficent aspect of the spirit, its potential for bringing success, seems to outweigh the negative aspect of its powers.

Where illness is referred to the great spirits present in nature, the occurrence of illness acts as a reminder of their power and active presence. If they bring repeated benefits in good harvests, they also often cause sickness and pain. People have only a partial ability to control and direct their power. The illness is a price paid for these benefits. It represents a risk involved in living and subsisting, belonging to the sphere of nature as they conceive it, rather than to that of competitive or quarrelsome social relations, or to moral aspects of behaviour. It may be because in general a great spirit is not held to be concerned with competitive social relationships between people that hunting, which is closely related to social prestige and competition, rarely forms the basis of the diagnosis of illness caused by the great spirits.

Since in general adults are responsible for the work which ensures subsistence, and senior adult men especially for the performance of the ritual aspects of planting and gardening, they see themselves as more frequently exposed to its hazards, and their illnesses in consequence more often receive these explanations. The collectivity of spirits of the lineage dead, who may participate in what the great spirits do, or activate them, also serve as mediators between the great spirits and men and are always appealed to in treatment. The lineage dead have a pivotal position in regard to other spirits and their descendants. I have tried to elucidate the lack of sharp boundaries between spirit categories in Gnau thought. The central importance of the collectivity of lineage dead comes out in their activating and intermediary relations to great spirits, their power to harm or to bring benefit, and their watching concern for the welfare of their descendants. The Gnau emphasis on genealogical knowledge validating identity, claims to certain rights, linkage to a collection of ancestors and the related myth – *malet* – spirit, might seem consistent with this pivotal position of the ancestral dead, although the very anonymity of the lineage dead, the reference to them as a collectivity rather than by their genealogically remembered names, makes this a less convincing argument.

The collectivity of lineage dead are usually held to act in support and aid for their descendants. The position of women who marry into a group and become progressively incorporated into it, has been discussed in relation to the risks they are thought to run from illness caused by these spirits. As the collective lineage dead act on behalf of their descendants so they may harm others within the village. But the emphasis in favour of preserving reasonably smooth relations within the village appears in the way they relegate such harm ostensibly to the will of the lineage dead, unsolicited by their descendants. The diagnostic lines between the will of ancestors, an appeal to them to harm, unintended harm from destructive magic, and outright sorcery are thin. The diagnosis may shift as an illness is perceived to be severe, life-threatening and finally ends in death. The injustice of premature death, the grief and disruption it causes to the bereaved family moves diagnosis or at least suspicion towards sorcery. In sorcery the motives are human malice, revenge, rivalry, evil; the revealed intention was to kill. The diagnosis is taken out of the sphere of spirit – caused illness. It marks an intense feeling of the iniquity of causing such a death. Responsibility for sorcery is almost inevitably thrust outside the village.

Gnau interpretations which involve disturbed social relations are uncommon. In general the explanation of the causes of illness lies in the sphere of spirits and nature. Illness becomes a reminder of the powers present in nature; it brings heightened awareness of contact with them. The powers of which they have knowledge are shown to be real; belief is confirmed. The unpredictability and distress of illness is a frequent cause for such reflections, and it is the most frequent cause for people to gather and perform ritual. There are no other misfortunes so common, or in some instances so distressing. The unpredictable balance of failures and successes in hunting is put down rather to the ill-will of others, and to their ancestral spirits, possibly because hunting is competitive.

I have tried to survey the place of illness in a cosmology. My approach has laid perhaps tedious emphasis on the total body of recorded illness at one place. My reason for this was chiefly one of method. For the observer cannot be sure of his biases. The result of the approach was to make me realize the extent to which they accepted illness and left it unexplained. Despite the spirits involved, illness often seemed a matter of 'airs, waters and places', of subsistence and survival, a natural risk of living. The approach through the total body of illness corrected such tendency as I might have had to draw a picture more distorted by what seemed curious to me or mystical, a matter of sorcery and the seemingly illogical. The Gnau in facing a severe burden from illness seem rather to neglect or tolerate it, preferring to hide, withdraw, to wait first to see what will happen; then to try out explanation and treatment in a way that is pragmatic and testing. They showed little concern for the consistency, or the truth or the certainty of diagnosis. The bounded small village society preserves a semblance, at the least, of harmony, in part by manipulating diagnosis so that disruptive accusation is rarely made between its members.

As to the whole field of illness and its explanation: there are so many issues involved and no simple dominant themes. By selecting some only of their explanations and showing the consistency and order within certain of these schemes and the related modes of treatment, I might perhaps have provided a clearer picture on some aspects of the Gnau management of illness. But to have done so would have been to misrepresent the uneven, eclectic, many stranded nature of their understanding of illness.

APPENDIX

Supplementary Medical Data

The deaths which occurred during my stay and the non-acute illness and defects noted in the village I studied in detail are set out below. This information is followed by a table showing the month of incidence of the illnesses in the overall record on which many of my analyses are based. The hamlet numbers of the illnesses in this record are then given.

MORTALITY

During 20 months of study, there were 17 deaths, but I treated some people who might otherwise also have died. During this time there were 29 births of which three were said to be stillbirths. The crude mortality rate was 30 per 1000 in 1968 and 24 in 1969.

Of the 17 deaths:

Neonatal deaths. Causes uncertain. 4

Infant deaths under 1 year old. At least one and probably all 3 were caused by malaria. 3

Toddler deaths (1–5 years). No diagnosed cause: alleged to have been well, and then coughed or spat blood, then died. External inspection of the body showed no cause. 1

Child deaths. One by drowning after an epileptic fit; 1 by *enteritis necroticans*; 1 by congestive heart failure probably caused by acute rheumatic fever. 3

Adult deaths. Lobar pneumonia 1; congestive heart failure 1; gross oedema – patient not examined 1; bronchopneumonia with cachexia due to starvation 1; uncertain cause 2 – the deaths of frail old women, one said to have collapsed and died in the night after diarrhoea, the other found dead in her sleep after eating supper. 6

CONGENITAL ANOMALIES OR DEFECTS

Red coloured hair and pale skin colour – in 2 full sibling sisters of a sibling group of 8 children.

Absent upper second incisors – in 2 full siblings, one third brother normal.

Mild divergent strabismus in 2 full siblings, one other sister normal.

Epilepsy: 1 girl with focal epilepsy accompanied by loss of consciousness, onset in childhood – she is the girl who died by drowning. In the last 40 years there have been 5 people who had repeated fits in which they fell unconscious. In all, the attacks began in childhood and all have died. Three of them reached puberty. All have died from the consequences of severe burns they had from falling in fires, except the girl who drowned.

Congenital heart disease – clinically, ventricular septal defect, a small lesion causing no discernible limitation of activity. One case.

STATIC DEFECTS OR MUTILATIONS

Unilateral blindness. Two cases caused by burns; 1 case resulting from puncture of the cornea by a thorn in a childish fight.

Loss of digits (4 people have lost a toe by injury and/or suppuration). One man had part of his finger bitten off by a lizard.

Limb contractures – caused by sores (2 of the lower limb, 1 of the upper) – caused by burns (1 of the lower limb).

Limb weakness of one leg, possibly caused by poliomyelitis – 1 case.

Depressed bridge to nose (presumed due to yaws) – 4 cases.

SLOWLY PROGRESSIVE OR RECURRENT CONDITIONS

Motor neurone disease – 1 case with the clinical features of amyotrophic lateral sclerosis but said to have been slowly progressive over ten years.

Leprosy – 1 case under treatment.

Recurrent small sores at the site of contracted scar tissue of a burn – 3 cases.

Third degree piles – 1 case noted, but I made no systematic inquiries or examinations for this condition.

Man, aged about 45 years, often limited to the village by recurrent chest infection.

Asthma – recurrent episodes of tight-chested wheezing about once to twice a year – 1 woman.

DEGENERATIVE DISEASE

Cataract (presumed to be senile cataract) – 3 cases.

Deafness (presumed due to old age) – 2 cases.

Old people limited by loss of agility, stiffness and/or shortness of breath – 5 people.

ENDEMIC CONDITIONS FORMING THE COMMON BACKGROUND OF ILLNESS

Skin cuts, infections and sores; infestations with scabies or head lice; fungal infections.

Malnutrition.

Infections: malaria; hookworm.

THE MONTHLY INCIDENCE OF THE ILLNESSES IN THE OVERALL RECORD

The incidence of cases spread over the months between January 1968 and November 1969 is shown in Figure 39. It is based on the 274 cases used in previous tables: a dotted line shows the peak marking the real incidence of influenza in October 1968. The two months in which I was absent from the village for more than a week are starred.

The number of cases is too small to allow for any clearly significant findings on the monthly pattern of illness. Chest infections occurred in association with colds in February and April 1968 and in October 1968 during the epidemic of influenza: 23/43 respiratory tract infections occurred during these three months and there were the many other cases of October 1968.

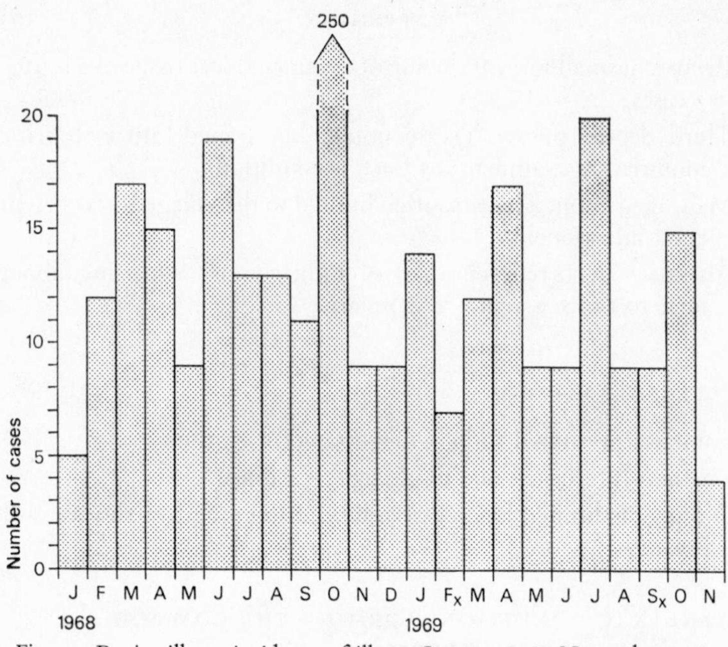

Fig. 39. Rauit village: incidence of illness, January 1968–November 1969

Table 42. Hamlet distribution of illness

	Animbil	*Watalu*	*Pakuag and Dagetasa*	*Wimalu*	*Bi'ip*	*Total*
Average number of people exposed to risk	66	67	68	70	84	355
Medical severity						
A. serious	6	8	5	6	10	35
B. moderate	7	24	13	13	10	67
C. mild	23	44	20	14	17	118
D. ill-defined	7	22	6	8	11	54
Incapacity						
I. active	20	32	13	8	20	93
II. village	8	36	13	16	9	82
III. inappropriate behaviour	7	14	7	2	6	36
IV. forced recumbency	6	6	7	6	4	29
V. ill babies	2	10	4	9	9	34
Duration						
1. one day	6	18	6	7	6	43
2. day to one week	27	50	24	22	23	146
3. week to two weeks	7	17	12	9	8	53
4. two weeks to one month	3	8	1	1	8	21
5. over one month	0	5	1	2	3	11

Table 43. Hamlet distribution of illness by age, sex, and 'explanation'

	Animbil	*Watalu*	*Pakuag and Dagetasa*	*Wimalu*	*Bi'ip*
Males					
	No. of ills/No. of those exposed to risk				
Age					
0–4 years	2/4	9/4	2/6	7/6	7/5
5–15 years	2/9	4/9	1/6	1/12	2/14
16–45 years	7/10	23/10	6/11	4/6	12/16
over 45 years	8/4	22/6	14/7	10/8	7/6
	No. of 'explained' ills/No. of ills				
Medical severity					
A. serious	0/2	4/5	3/3	2/2	4/7
B. moderate	2/2	7/12	3/5	2/6	1/3
C. mild	4/13	4/32	7/11	4/7	2/12
D. ill-defined	2/2	3/9	3/4	5/7	3/6
Females					
	No. of ills/No. of those exposed to risk				
Age					
0–4 years	0/6	6/6	3/4	8/2	2/5
5–15 years	6/11	5/10	2/12	3/15	5/14
16–45 years	9/15	17/15	12/14	7/15	12/20
over 45 years	9/6	12/7	4/8	1/6	1/4
	No. of 'explained' ills/No. of ills				
Medical severity					
A. serious	4/4	3/3	1/2	3/4	1/3
B. moderate	4/5	8/12	2/8	1/7	1/7
C. mild	3/10	2/12	1/9	1/7	0/5
D. ill-defined	2/5	9/13	1/2	1/1	4/5

Table 44. Distribution of 28 cases of illness 'explained' by more than one kind of diagnosis (Each figure is given as the proportion of all 'explained' cases in the given category.)

	Medical severity		*Incapacity*		*Duration*	
	A	10/25	I	3/21	1.	1/16
	B	8/31	II	3/35	2.	12/62
	C	2/28	III	10/28	3.	4/23
	D	8/33	IV	10/21	4.	5/10
			V	2/12	5.	6/6
Total		28/117		28/117		28/117

	Age category A1	A2	A3	A4	Total
Male	0/10	1/5	1/14	9/36	11/65
Female	2/7	3/10	7/19	5/16	17/52
Total	2/17	4/15	8/33	14/52	28/117

Table 45. Distribution of 42 cases of illness for which more than one instance of 'explanation' was obtained (Each figure is given as the proportion of all 'explained' cases in the given category.)

	Medical severity		*Incapacity*		*Duration*	
	A	16/25	I	10/21	1.	1/16
	B	11/31	II	2/35	2.	24/62
	C	4/28	III	11/28	3.	7/23
	D	11/33	IV	15/21	4.	4/10
			V	4/12	5.	6/6
Total		42/117		42/117		42/117

	Age category A1	A2	A3	A4	Total
Male	0/10	1/5	4/14	10/36	15/65
Female	5/7	4/10	10/19	8/16	27/52
Total	5/17	5/15	14/33	18/52	42/117

Table 46. Distribution of kinds of diagnosis according to the categories of illness

Category	*Diagnosis* *Panu'et*	*Tambin*	*Malyi*	*Malet*	*Lineage spirit*	*Named spirit of individual dead*	*Taboo*	*Magic and sorcery*	*Total*
Medical severity									
A	11	2	5	4	11	6	4	7	50
B	12	1	4	5	10	5	5	3	45
C	8	1	1	4	5	4	5	1	29
D	11	4	3	9	4	9	1	6	47
Total	42	8	13	22	30	24	15	17	171
Incapacity									
I	7	1	3	3	4	4	2	0	24
II	9	1	5	6	7	4	4	2	38
III	13	3	0	8	6	7	3	8	48
IV	9	2	4	4	8	7	5	7	46
V	4	1	1	1	5	2	1	0	15
Total	42	8	13	22	30	24	15	17	171
Duration									
1.	2	0	3	3	2	4	2	2	18
2.	22	5	5	14	8	10	6	6	76
3.	9	1	2	1	10	4	2	1	30
4.	5	1	1	1	5	4	3	4	24
5.	4	1	2	3	5	2	2	4	23
Total	42	8	13	22	30	24	15	17	171

Table 47. Distribution of different types of reason given in instances of 'explanation' distinguished according to the age and sex of the sick persons (The figures given are the numbers of instances.)

Order of commonness	*Sick Persons*						
	All	*Adults*	*Men*	*Women*	*Males*	*Females*	*Children*
First	Place 91	Place 80	Place 42	Place 38	Place 46	Action 46	Action 17
Second	Action 90	Action 73	Action 42	Action 31	Action 44	Place 45	Time 16
Third	Time 72	Time 56	Time 36	Food 25	Time 42	Food 34	'Sole' 13
Fourth	Food 67	Food 56	Food 31	Time 20	Food 33	Time 30	Place 11
Fifth	'Sole' 39	'Sole' 26	'Sole' 17	'Sole' 9	'Sole' 25	'Sole' 14	Food 11
Sixth	Quarrel 15	Quarrel 13	Quarrel 10	Quarrel 3	Quarrel 11	Quarrel 4	Quarrel 2

LIST OF WORKS CITED

ACKERKNECHT, E., 1946. 'Natural diseases and rational treatment in primitive medicine', *Bull. Hist. Med.*, **19**: 467–97.

BATESON, G., 1936. *Naven*, Cambridge.

BULMER, R. N. H., 1968. 'Worms that croak and other mysteries of Karam natural history', *Mankind*, **6**: 621–39.

CARR, E. H., 1961. *What is History?*, London.

COHEN, H., 1961. 'The evolution of the concept of disease', reprinted in *Concepts of Medicine* (B. Lush, ed.), Oxford.

COHEN, M. R. and NAGEL, E., 1934. *Introduction to Logic and Scientific Method*, London.

EVANS-PRITCHARD, E. E., 1937. *Witchcraft, Oracles and Magic among the Azande*, Oxford.

——, 1954. 'A problem of Nuer religious thought', *Sociologus*, **4** (1): 23–41.

——, 1965. *Theories of Primitive Religion*, Oxford.

FEINSTEIN, A. R., 1967. *Clinical Judgement*, Baltimore.

FORTUNE, R., 1932. *Sorcerers of Dobu*, London.

——, 1942. The Arapesh Language of New Guinea, *Publ. Amer. Ethnol. Soc.*, vol. 19.

FOUNTAIN, O. C. (undated). *Wulukum*. Land, livelihood and change in a New Guinea village, M.A. thesis, Victoria University, Wellington, New Zealand (roneographed).

FRAKE, C. O., 1961. 'The diagnosis of disease among the Subanun of Mindanao', *Am. Anthrop.*, **63**: 113–32.

GELL, A. F., 1971. 'Penis sheathing and ritual status in a west Sepik village', *Man* (*N.S.*), **6**: 165–81.

HALMOS, P., 1957. *Towards a measure of man*, London.

HORTON, R., 1967. 'African traditional thought and Western science', *Africa*, **37**: 50–71, 155–87.

JASPERS, K., 1963. *General Psychopathology*: transl. by J. Hoenig and M. W. Hamilton, Manchester (1st ed. in German, 1913).

LAWRENCE, P., 1964. *Road Belong Cargo*, Manchester.

LAYCOCK, D. C., 1968. 'Languages of the Lumi Subdistrict (West Sepik District), New Guinea', *Oceanic Linguistics*, **VII**: 36–66.

LEWIS, A. J., 1953. 'Health as a social concept', *Brit. J. Sociol.*, **4**: 109–24.

LEWIS, I. M., 1971. *Ecstatic Religion*, Middlesex.

MARSDEN, P. D., 1964. 'The Sukuta project: longitudinal study of health in Gambian children from birth to 18 months', *Trans. Roy. Soc. Trop. Med. Hyg.*, **58**: 455.

MARSHALL, A. J., 1937. 'Northern New Guinea, 1936', *Geographical J.*, **89**: 489–506.

MARWICK, M. G., 1965. *Sorcery in its Social Setting*, Manchester.

——, 1967. 'The study of witchcraft', in *The Craft of Social Anthropology* (A. L. Epstein, ed.), London.

MEAD, M., 1940. The Mountain Arapesh Part I. An importing culture. *Anthrop. Papers Amer. Mus. Nat. Hist.*, **36**: Part 3.

——, 1949. The Mountain Arapesh Part V. *Anthrop. Papers Amer. Mus. Nat. Hist.*, **41**: Part 3.

NADEL, S. F., 1954. *Nupe Religion*, London.

OESTERREICH, T. K., 1930. *Possession, Demoniacal and Other, among Primitive Races, in Antiquity, the Middle Ages and Modern Times*, London (translation of German original, 1921).

PETERS, W., 1960. 'Studies on the epidemiology of malaria in New Guinea', *Trans. Roy. Soc. Trop. Med. Hyg.*, **54**: 242–60.

POLGAR, S., 1968. Art. 'Health' in the *Internat. Encycl. Social Sciences*, New York.

READ, K. E., 1954. 'Cultures of the central highlands, New Guinea', *Sthwest. J. Anthrop.*, **10**: 1–43.

SCHOFIELD, F. D., 1962. *Trans. Roy. Soc. Trop. Med. Hyg.*, **56**: 60.

SCHOFIELD, F. D. and JEFFREY, D., 1963. 'Tinea imbricata', *Trans. Roy. Soc. Trop. Med. Hyg.*, **57**: 214.

SCHOFIELD, F. D., PARKINSON, A. D. and KELLY, A., 1964. 'Changes in haemoglobin values and hepatosplenomegaly produced by control of holoendemic malaria', *Brit. Med. J.*, **i**: 587.

SINGER, C., 1926. 'The historical relations of religion and science', in *Science, Religion and Reality* (J. Needham, ed.), London.

STANNER, W. E. H., 1956. 'The dreaming', in *Australian Signpost* (T. A. G. Hungerford, ed.), Melbourne.

STEINER, F., 1967. *Taboo*, Middlesex.

STRATHERN, A., 1970. 'The female and male spirit cults in Mount Hagen', *Man (N.S.)*, **5**: 571.

STURT, R. J. (undated). 'The disease pattern in the Central Sepik' (roneographed).

STURT, R. J. and GLASGOW, H. N. (undated). 'Lower respiratory tract infection in a rural Sepik population' (Paper presented to the Annual Meeting of the Papua New Guinea Medical Society, 1969) (roneographed).

STURT, R. J. and STANHOPE, J. M., 1968. 'Mortality and population patterns at Anguganak, West Sepik District', *Papua and New Guinea Med. J.*, **11**: 111–17.

SYDENHAM, T., 1676. 'Medical observations concerning the history and cure of acute diseases' (3rd ed. 1676), in the *Works of Thomas Sydenham* by R. G. Latham, vol. 1, The Sydenham Society, 1848.

TURNER, V. W., 1963. *Lunda medicine and the treatment of disease*, Rhodes-Livingstone Paper no. 15.

——, 1968. *The drums of affliction: a study of religious processes among the Ndembu of Zambia*, Oxford.

WOOTTON, B., 1959. *Social science and social pathology*, London.

The Registrar General's Statistical Review for England and Wales for the Year 1949, Supplement of General Morbidity, H.M.S.O., 1953.

Index